Progressive Trends in Electronic Resource Management in Libraries

Nihar K. Patra
National Institute of Food Technology Entrepreneurship & Management, India

Bharat Kumar
Management Development Institute, India

Ashis K. Pani
XLRI, Jamshedpur, India

A volume in the Advances in Library and
Information Science (ALIS) Book Series

An Imprint of IGI Global

Managing Director:	Lindsay Johnston
Production Manager:	Jennifer Yoder
Publishing Systems Analyst:	Adrienne Freeland
Development Editor:	Christine Smith
Acquisitions Editor:	Kayla Wolfe
Typesetter:	Lisandro Gonzalez
Cover Design:	Jason Mull

Published in the United States of America by
Information Science Reference (an imprint of IGI Global)
701 E. Chocolate Avenue
Hershey PA 17033
Tel: 717-533-8845
Fax: 717-533-8661
E-mail: cust@igi-global.com
Web site: http://www.igi-global.com

Library of Congress Cataloging-in-Publication Data

Progressive trends in electronic resource management in libraries / Nihar K. Patra, Bharat Kumar, and Ashis K. Pani, editors.
    pages cm
  Summary: "This book provides relevant theoretical and practical details from an international perspective on the current e-resources landscape, offering a detailed discussion of the specific aspects of e-resources management"-- Provided by publisher.
  Includes bibliographical references and index.
  ISBN 978-1-4666-4761-9 (hardcover) -- ISBN 978-1-4666-4762-6 (ebook) -- ISBN 978-1-4666-4763-3 (print & perpetual access) 1. Libraries--Special collections--Electronic information resources. 2. Electronic information resources--Management. 3. Digital libraries--Collection development. I. Patra, Nihar K., 1973- editor of compilation. II. Kumar, Bharat, 1975- editor of compilation. III. Pani, Ashis Kumar, editor of compilation.
  Z692.C65P76 2014
  025.2'84--dc23
                              2013027880

This book is published in the IGI Global book series Advances in Library and Information Science (ALIS) (ISSN: 2326-4136; eISSN: 2326-4144)

British Cataloguing in Publication Data
A Cataloguing in Publication record for this book is available from the British Library.

For electronic access to this publication, please contact: eresources@igi-global.com.

Advances in Library and Information Science (ALIS) Book Series

ISSN: 2326-4136
EISSN: 2326-4144

MISSION

The **Advances in Library and Information Science (ALIS) Book Series** is comprised of high quality, research-oriented publications on the continuing developments and trends affecting the public, school, and academic fields, as well as specialized libraries and librarians globally. These discussions on professional and organizational considerations in library and information resource development and management assist in showcasing the latest methodologies and tools in the field.

The **ALIS Book Series** aims to expand the body of library science literature by covering a wide range of topics affecting the profession and field at large. The series also seeks to provide readers with an essential resource for uncovering the latest research in library and information science management, development, and technologies.

COVERAGE

- Academic libraries in the digital age
- Blogging in libraries
- Cataloging and classification
- Collection development
- Community outreach
- Digital literacy
- Ethical practices in libraries
- Green libraries
- Librarian education
- Mobile library services
- Remote access technologies
- University libraries in developing countries

IGI Global is currently accepting manuscripts for publication within this series. To submit a proposal for a volume in this series, please contact our Acquisition Editors at Acquisitions@igi-global.com or visit: http://www.igi-global.com/publish/.

Titles in this Series

For a list of additional titles in this series, please visit: www.igi-global.com

Technology and Professional Identity of Librarians The Making of the Cybrarian
Deborah Hicks (University of Alberta, Canada)
Information Science Reference • copyright 2014 • 300pp • H/C (ISBN: 9781466647350) • US $175.00 (our price)

Progressive Trends in Electronic Resource Management in Libraries
Nihar K. Patra (National Institute of Food Technology Entrepreneurship & Management, India) Bharat Kumar
(Management Development Institute, India) and Ashis K. Pani (XLRI, Jamshedpur, India)
Information Science Reference • copyright 2014 • 224pp • H/C (ISBN: 9781466647619) • US $175.00 (our price)

Cloud Computing and Virtualization Technologies in Libraries
Sangeeta N. Dhamdhere (Modern College of Arts, Science and Commerce, India)
Information Science Reference • copyright 2014 • 385pp • H/C (ISBN: 9781466646315) • US $175.00 (our price)

Revolutionizing the Development of Library and Information Professionals Planning for the Future
Samantha Schmehl Hines (Missoula College of the University of Montana, USA)
Information Science Reference • copyright 2014 • 312pp • H/C (ISBN: 9781466646759) • US $175.00 (our price)

Information Access and Library User Needs in Developing Countries
Mohammed Nasser AI-Suqri (Sultan Qaboos University, Oman) Linda L. Lillard (Clarion University, USA) and
Naifa Eid AI-Saleem (Sultan Qaboos University, Oman)
Information Science Reference • copyright 2014 • 286pp • H/C (ISBN: 9781466643536) • US $175.00 (our price)

Collaborative Models for Librarian and Teacher Partnerships
Kathryn Kennedy (International Association for K-12 Online Learning, USA) and Lucy Santos Green (Georgia
Southern University, USA)
Information Science Reference • copyright 2014 • 282pp • H/C (ISBN: 9781466643611) • US $175.00 (our price)

Advancing Library Education Technological Innovation and Instructional Design
Ari Sigal (Catawba Valley Community College, USA)
Information Science Reference • copyright 2013 • 339pp • H/C (ISBN: 9781466636880) • US $175.00 (our price)

Library Reference Services and Information Literacy Models for Academic Institutions
Rosanne M. Cordell (Northern Illinois University, USA)
Information Science Reference • copyright 2013 • 355pp • H/C (ISBN: 9781466642416) • US $175.00 (our price)

www.igi-global.com

701 E. Chocolate Ave., Hershey, PA 17033
Order online at www.igi-global.com or call 717-533-8845 x100
To place a standing order for titles released in this series, contact: cust@igi-global.com
Mon-Fri 8:00 am - 5:00 pm (est) or fax 24 hours a day 717-533-8661

Table of Contents

Detailed Table of Contents

Chapter 1

Hungwa Shidi, Ministry of Information and Orientation, Nigeria
Solomon Uganneya, University of Agriculture, Nigeria

Chapter 1 addresses the concept of e-resources and the scope and challenges of e-resources management in libraries. E-resources began with MARC (Machine Readable Catalogue) developed in the mid 1960s and has progressed to e-journals, e-books, Websites, and File Transfer Protocol (FTP). Infrastructure gaps and other sundry issues like funding, access model, archiving, preservation, ownership versus access, and lack of continuity in publication are some of the challenges highlighted in the management of e-resources in libraries.

Chapter 2

Jennifer Wright, Western Kentucky University, USA

Chapter 2 talks about electronic resources from a collection development perspective and explains issues collection development staff may need to address when electronic resources are incorporated into the existing collection. These issues include costs and benefits of electronic resources and faculty/staff reactions to the incorporation of new materials. This chapter also strongly advocates the addition of an electronic resource manager or multiple electronic resource staff members and their close cooperation with the collection development staff.

Chapter 3 discusses excellence and looks beyond the dominant line of e-resources research where transitions cycles in information management, knowledge management, competences management, and performance management are the multi-contextual value creators for individuals and organizations. This is done by an extensive review of European policies (Single Information Market, Agenda for Culture) in two steps: first, excellence triggers are analyzed, discussing digital agenda and consumer culture; next, an integrated model of e-resources excellence management is presented. It locates the argument for the importance of convergence in excellence diversity where e-resources are uniquely and contextually interpreted, requiring understanding, and assesses customer consumption processes as an experiential, social, and cultural phenomenon. A variety of informational behaviors, skills, and activities is the measure of the complexity of personal values possibilities and of excellence frameworks development, maturity, and sustainability.

Chapter 4 discusses Patron Driven Acquisitions (PDA) for an effective acquisition model in building "just-in-time" monograph collections to support the information and curricular needs of a variety of users in different settings. Implementation of the PDA model for electronic and print books for the users of Arizona State University (ASU) Libraries has been exemplified in this chapter. The chaptes also explores the history of the use of PDA in a variety of library settings, application of PDA to the purchase of e-books at ASU from the perspective of an Electronic Resources Librarian and a Subject Librarian and Administrator of a branch library, and provides a sustainable model, which may be applied in different types of library settings.

Chapter 5 discusses in detail electronic journals (e-journals), their advantages and disadvantages, and need for subscription. In selection of e-journals, identification of e-journals, their evaluation and purpose for subscription are important considerations for selection of more relevant resource for its patrons. The authors also discuss cost benefit analysis of e-journals and elaborate cost involved in subscription of print and electronic journals and provide their cost benefit analysis.

Chapter 6 covers some aspects of copyright, whether it is document delivery, electronic reserves, online learning tools and course management systems (e.g. Blackboard), or online modules which allow one to share one's references and full-text attachments with others (e.g. RefShare). It also discusses copyright and licensing negotiations with content providers.

Chapter 7 discusses Electronic Resource Management Systems (ERMSs) – open source and proprietary products for managing e-resources. The main purpose of these ERMSs is to manage the workflow of e-resources, access, centralizing data, and improve administrative interfaces. This chapter compares and analyzes the 16 ERMSs and their functionality, standards and compatibility, features, modules, etc. with usefulness and weakness for Librarians and End-Users. These 16 ERMSs are Innovative Interface's Innovative ERM, TDNet ERM Solutions, Ex Libris's Verde ERM, OCLC's Web-Share License Manager, SemperTool's SMDB, University of Notre Dame's CORAL, MIT's VERA, SerialsSolutions's 360 Resource Manager, HARRASSOWITZ's HERMIS, The Johns Hopkins University's HERMIES, Colorado Alliance's Gold Rush, WT Cox's Journal Finder, EBSCO's EBSCONET ERM Essentials, Simon Fraser University Library's CUFTS, SIRSI Corp's E-Resource Center, Priory Solution's Research Monitor. This study concludes with usefulness and weakness of ERMS for Librarians and End-Users.

Chapter 8 identifies the ways to avoid plagiarism and mentions the use of anti-plagiarism software. It explores how far a scholarly work can be treated under the periphery of "fair use." The various derivatives of creative commons are also explained to accustom authors regarding availability of copyright issues in the digital era. The essences of projects like SHERPA/RoMEO and COPE are also discussed.

Chapter 9 discusses the background of open access resources and its initiatives, software, open archives browsers and harvesters, and open access registries. It elucidates the most important international and national projects like the European Library, Europeana, the World Digital Library, Gutenberg Project, Google Books Project, Hathitrust Digital Library, Digital Public Library of America, International Children's Digital Library, the Library of Congress Digital Library, Gallica of the French National Library, National Digital Library of China, etc. The idea behind this chapter is that the world's knowledge should be accessible as a public good to every citizen of the planet.

Chapter 10 contributes to the discussion of electronic resources. This chapter shares the experiences and challenges that the Library and Learning Commons, Monash University Sunway Campus, Malaysia, faced in progressing electronic resources. It discusses two major actions undertaken, namely (1) the implementation of an e-books acquisitions policy and (2) the implementation of search, a Web resource discovery service undertaken in collaboration with Monash University Library Australia. The initiative to realize the action plans and the progress made are also discussed, and outcomes and the learning experiences are shared.

Chapter 11

Jean Inness, South Ayrshire Council, UK

Chapter 11 outlines the successful management style that has pro-actively facilitated innovative changes to a range of library services. This changes discussed are those facing all contemporary libraries starting with an overview of service provision, staffing, the management team, and management style, and the chapter considers the factors required for the effective implementation of innovation in a range of services. The topics covered include creating a library "blog," the benefits of a library bookshop, e-book lending, e-book publishing, creating a library mobile app, and e-magazine lending. The chapter argues that fellow librarians can embrace change and facilitate innovation in ways that are efficient, cost-effective, and cutting-edge, whilst reinforcing the importance of libraries at the centre of our society. Two key factors that are discussed in this chapter on the success of implementing ERM innovation in South Ayrshire Library are effective leadership of a motivated team of professional librarians, combined with library staffs who feel valued. It outlines how ERM projects were successfully managed, developed, and implemented by South Ayrshire Council Library Service.

Chapter 12

Parveen Babbar, Indira Gandhi National Open University, India

Chapter 12 discusses emerging innovative technologies and services for managing e-resources and examines how Indira Gandhi National Open University (IGNOU) Library is increasingly benefited by its new and future services. It discusses the National Open Distance Learners' Library and Information Network (NODLINET), a project of IGNOU Library created for distance learning libraries for sharing collections, e-resources, and services on a common platform. The chapter also discusses how IGNOU Library is moving towards innovative Library Services by providing its users with updated contents and constantly strengthening service capability in the network information environment. It explains in detail the component of Remote Access to e-resources, which is a quick, easy, and convenient service to gain off-campus access to all IGNOU Library subscribed databases and other online resources. The chapter also enumerates the copyright restrictions and licensing restrictions through Remote Access Service and discusses in detail various other initiatives taken by IGNOU Library like cloud computing, course reserves, discovery, and AtoZ services.

Foreword

Without doubt, the management of electronic resources has become one of the key issues academic libraries face in their strategic development. Most academic libraries have seen an almost complete transition of their journal collections from print to electronic formats transpire in the last two decades. Yet, despite this longstanding trend, academic libraries continue to struggle to identify the best ways to manage these collections. Key considerations include how to acquire, process, and describe these collections in the most efficient ways and how to provide optimal access to the students and faculty of the university. Within these core areas, a myriad of details arise that must be addressed as libraries devise their strategies for electronic resource management.

Those outside the library field might assume that the move to electronic resources has simplified the work of libraries. Quite the opposite has proven the case as libraries have begun to shift more of their attention away from handling only print materials. Libraries face much more complexity to manage and provide access to electronic content than were ever required by print collections. It should also be noted that even though the proportions are higher, few libraries deal exclusively with electronic materials. Most academic libraries manage collections composed of digital materials, electronic resources, and physical items. It is an ongoing challenge to allocate efforts between the demands of the print and electronic components of a library collection.

This new volume, *Progressive Trends in Electronic Resource Management in Libraries,* co-edited by Nihar K. Patra, Bharat Kumar, and Ashis K. Pani brings together a dozen chapters by separate authors, each addressing some aspect of the theme of managing electronic resources from a different perspective. I am impressed with the broad international representation, with authors from India, the United Kingdom, Malaysia, India, Serbia, South Africa, Portugal, Nigeria, and the United States. Each chapter in the volume approaches a specific area of interest given from the perspective of practical experience.

All aspects of library organizations have been reshaped through involvement in electronic resources. Technical services units must acquire and describe these collections, reference librarians provide direct end-user support, Web services teams develop or implement tools that facilitate access to remote users, bibliographers, and subject specialists, and collection development personnel make decisions on which new resources will be acquired and which will be cancelled in any given year. Collection development naturally plays a role as selectors shape the collection in each area, working to create the proper balance between print and electronic materials. In the division of labor throughout the library, does it make sense to distribute responsibilities for electronic resources among all personnel, or should libraries have dedicated personnel for managing electronic resources?

The initial phase of the transition to electronic resources revolutionized the realm of serials and periodicals. The publication of scholarly articles has largely moved out of the print world to electronic publication, bringing fundamental change to libraries and researchers. The activity currently focuses on e-books. How do e-books fit within workflows and automation systems that were designed for print? New models of acquisition have emerged that turn the traditional strategies upside down, making materials available "just in time" rather than anticipating interest through the traditional "just in case" selection and acquisition process. Demand driven acquisitions currently stands as a model for selection and purchase of electronic materials that has gathered significant interest, but that comes with workflow issues that significantly impact both collection development and technical services operations.

For most libraries, the move to access to scholarly content through subscriptions to electronic resources has largely moved to completion. Yet, it is important to consider that in some international regions and in specific disciplines, print continues to endure as the primary avenue of publication. As libraries begin to invest in electronic resources, an economic analysis of costs versus benefits can help reinforce the value of its subscriptions. For those thoroughly involved in electronic collections, ongoing analysis is needed to make decisions among competing content packages. Increasingly, analytic tools support data-driven decision making to optimize how library budgets are spent on collection materials. Libraries may want to engage in different types of cost benefit analyses related to electronic journal subscriptions to gain objective data on the impact of their investments in electronic resources relative to their use by students and faculty.

Electronic resources require attention to a variety of legal issues. Librarians often find themselves needing to gain expertise copyright law as they deal with the acquisition and dissemination of electronic documents. The licenses involved in subscriptions to electronic content packages often have complex terms that must be negotiated with their providers and executed as contracts. Key points might include permanent ownership of materials that persists even if the library discontinues its active subscription, whether items can be shared with non-subscribers through interlibrary loan or document delivery programs, whether there are any restrictions on documents when placed on reserve for use by students enrolled in a class. Any advice and knowledge that librarians can gain in addressing such legal details will return practical benefits.

A variety of software applications have been developed over the years to assist libraries in the management of electronic resources. The options range from freely available open source applications to full featured commercial electronic resource management systems. Quite a variety of standalone and integrated products have been created over the years that automate electronic resource management, each with their relative advantages and disadvantages. Many standalone electronic resource management systems find use in many libraries today, but many track electronic resources less systematically using spreadsheets or databases set up by individual administrators. An alternative approach that has arisen in recent years involves library services platforms that incorporate the capabilities for both print and electronic resources. Libraries now find themselves in a new phase of automation where electronic resource management is beginning to be incorporated into comprehensive platforms rather than managed through separate tools.

Libraries have growing interest in the freely available electronic resources available through open access publishers and other channels. Open access publishing, though a part of the academic enterprise for many years, has made substantial gains in recent years, largely due to mandates from the agencies that fund research. It is essential for libraries to find ways to take advantage of these resources, especially those that complement areas of interest for their library in support of teaching and research. In addition to the material acquired through paid subscriptions, identifying additional open access materials and systematically including those resources within the scope of the local discovery service is a challenge but can significantly expand the body of content the library offers to its users.

Readers interested in exploring the realm of electronic resource management will find a wealth of experience and expertise reflected in the contributed chapters of this volume. The authors of the individual chapters have focused on topics and problems representative of the challenges that libraries face in these times where electronic resources increasingly dominate their collections. As with any printed work, some of the specific details will apply to the snapshot in time in which they were written. However, the concepts and issues will endure for as long as libraries continue their journey away from one defined by content delivered primarily in print into a new reality where electronic resources and digital content dominates.

Marshall Breeding
Independent Consultant, USA

Marshall Breeding *works as an independent consultant, author, and speaker focused on library technologies. He has authored the annual "Automation Marketplace" feature for Library Journal since 2002, has authored or edited seven books and hundreds of articles and book chapters. He frequently gives keynote presentations and workshops at conferences throughout the world and is the founder and publisher of Library Technology Guides.*

Preface

Electronic resources (e-resources) have made a great impact on library and users. They are available in a variety of e-journals, e-books, full-text/aggregated databases, digitized and born-digital documents, digital images, streaming video sound, and audio books. Operational and organizational issues of these resources pose a huge challenge to information managers. There is an urgent need to discuss these issues and find optimum solutions for managing these digital resources.

There is a need to have a "one-stop solution" for their evaluation, selection, acquisition, renewal/cancellation, license agreement, open access and institutional archives, access rights, usage statistics, single access point, copyright, implementation, and administration. Electronic Resource Management System (ERMS) exist but their proliferation has also become another issue for libraries to select the right one.

Progressive Trends in Electronic Resources Management in Libraries is an attempt to identify the various issues in the management of e-resources. Authors from different countries provide an international perspective to the subject. The book provides relevant theoretical and practical details and empirical research findings in this area. It also discusses the current e-resources landscape with a detailed discussion of specific aspects of e-resources management. The chapters are devoted to the theoretical details, history, selection, acquisition, fair use, and management of e-resources.

The book will be of use to a beginner in knowing about e-resources and a librarian in understanding the issues in e-resource management. Students will find it a useful source to grasp the issues associated with e-resources. Researchers will be able to identify areas for research in the subject.

This book consists of twelve chapters dealing with the complete life cycle of e-resource, cost benefit analysis, digital copyright, open e-resources, and innovative services by e-resources including E-Resources Management Systems (ERMS). The following paragraphs present the structure of the chapters.

Chapter 1, "Electronic Resources: History, Scope, and Challenges – An Overview," addresses the concept of e-resources and the scope and challenges of e-resources management in libraries. E-resources began with MARC (Machine Readable Catalogue) developed in the mid 1960s and has progressed to e-journals, e-books, Websites, and File Transfer Protocol (FTP). Infrastructure gaps and other sundry issues like funding, access model, archiving, preservation, ownership versus access, and lack of continuity in publication are some of the challenges highlighted in the management of e-resources in libraries.

Chapter 2, "Considerations of a Digital Age: The Hows and Whys of Electronic Resource Management from a Collection Development Perspective," talks about electronic resources from a collection development perspective and explains issues collection development staff may need to address when electronic resources are incorporated into the existing collection. These issues include costs and benefits of electronic resources and faculty/staff reactions to the incorporation of new materials. This chapter also strongly advocates the addition of an electronic resource manager or multiple electronic resource staff members and their close cooperation with the collection development staff.

Chapter 3, "Convergence towards Excellence Diversity: Mapping the Field of E-Resources Emerging Dynamics," discusses excellence and looks beyond the dominant line of e-resources research where transitions cycles in information management, knowledge management, competences management, and performance management are the multi-contextual value creators for individuals and organizations. This is done by an extensive review of European policies (Single Information Market, Agenda for Culture) in two steps: first, excellence triggers are analyzed, discussing digital agenda and consumer culture; next, an integrated model of e-resources excellence management is presented. It locates the argument for the importance of convergence in excellence diversity where e-resources are uniquely and contextually interpreted, requiring understanding, and assesses customer consumption processes as an experiential, social, and cultural phenomenon. A variety of informational behaviors, skills, and activities is the measure of the complexity of personal values possibilities and of excellence frameworks development, maturity, and sustainability.

Chapter 4, "Patron-Driven Acquisitions: A Progressive Model for the Selection of Electronic Resources," discusses Patron Driven Acquisitions (PDA) for an effective acquisition model in building "just-in-time" monograph collections to support the information and curricular needs of a variety of users in different settings. Implementation of the PDA model for electronic and print books for the users of Arizona State University (ASU) Libraries has been exemplified in this chapter. The chaptes also explores the history of the use of PDA in a variety of library settings, application of PDA to the purchase of e-books at ASU from the perspective of an Electronic Resources Librarian and a Subject Librarian and Administrator of a branch library, and provides a sustainable model, which may be applied in different types of library settings.

Chapter 5, "Going Online: Subscription of Electronic Journals and its Cost Benefit Analysis," discusses in detail electronic journals (e-journals), their advantages and disadvantages, and need for subscription. In selection of e-journals, identification of e-journals, their evaluation and purpose for subscription are important considerations for selection of more relevant resource for its patrons. The authors also discuss cost benefit analysis of e-journals and elaborate cost involved in subscription of print and electronic journals and provide their cost benefit analysis.

Chapter 6, "Copyright and Licensing Essentials for Librarians and Copyright Owners in the Digital Age," covers some aspects of copyright, whether it is document delivery, electronic reserves, online learning tools and course management systems (e.g. *Blackboard*), or online modules which allow one to share one's references and full-text attachments with others (e.g. *RefShare*). It also discusses copyright and licensing negotiations with content providers.

Chapter 7, "Comparative Analysis of Electronic Resource Management Systems (ERMS): A Web Study," discusses Electronic Resource Management Systems (ERMSs) – open source and proprietary products for managing e-resources. The main purpose of these ERMSs is to manage the workflow of e-resources, access, centralizing data, and improve administrative interfaces. This chapter compares and analyzes the 16 ERMSs and their functionality, standards and compatibility, features, modules, etc. with usefulness and weakness for Librarians and End-Users. These 16 ERMSs are Innovative Interface's Innovative ERM, TDNet ERM Solutions, Ex Libris's Verde ERM, OCLC's Web-Share License Manager, SemperTool's SMDB, University of Notre Dame's CORAL, MIT's VERA, SerialsSolutions's 360 Resource Manager, HARRASSOWITZ's HERMIS, The Johns Hopkins University's HERMIES, Colorado Alliance's Gold Rush, WT Cox's Journal Finder, EBSCO's EBSCONET ERM Essentials, Simon Fraser University Library's CUFTS, SIRSI Corp's E-Resource Center, Priory Solution's Research Monitor. This study concludes with usefulness and weakness of ERMS for Librarians and End-Users.

Chapter 8, "Knowing Protection of Intellectual Contents in Digital Era," identifies the ways to avoid plagiarism and mentions the use of anti-plagiarism software. It explores how far a scholarly work can be treated under the periphery of "fair use." The various derivatives of creative commons are also explained to accustom authors regarding availability of copyright issues in the digital era. The essences of projects like SHERPA/RoMEO and COPE are also discussed.

Chapter 9, "Open E-Resources in Libraries," discusses the background of open access resources and its initiatives, software, open archives browsers and harvesters, and open access registries. It elucidates the most important international and national projects like the European Library, Europeana, the World Digital Library, Gutenberg Project, Google Books Project, Hathitrust Digital Library, Digital Public Library of America, International Children's Digital Library, the Library of Congress Digital Library, Gallica of the French National Library, National Digital Library of China, etc. The idea behind this chapter is that the world's knowledge should be accessible as a public good to every citizen of the planet.

Chapter 10, "Riding the Waves of Change for Electronic Resources at the Library and Learning Commons, Monash University Sunway Campus: From Vision to Reality," contributes to the discussion of electronic resources. This chapter shares the experiences and challenges that the Library and Learning Commons, Monash University Sunway Campus, Malaysia, faced in progressing electronic resources. It discusses two major actions undertaken, namely (1) the implementation of an e-books acquisitions policy and (2) the implementation of search, a Web resource discovery service undertaken in collaboration with Monash University Library Australia. The initiative to realize the action plans and the progress made are also discussed, and outcomes and the learning experiences are shared.

Chapter 11, "Embracing Change: How South Ayrshire Council Library Service Became a World Leader in Electronic Resources Management," outlines the successful management style that has pro-actively facilitated innovative changes to a range of library services. This changes discussed are those facing all contemporary libraries starting with an overview of service provision, staffing, the management team, and management style, and the chapter considers the factors required for the effective implementation of innovation in a range of services. The topics covered include creating a library "blog," the benefits of a library bookshop, e-book lending, e-book publishing, creating a library mobile app, and e-magazine lending. The chapter argues that fellow librarians can embrace change and facilitate innovation in ways that are efficient, cost-effective, and cutting-edge, whilst reinforcing the importance of libraries at the centre of our society. Two key factors that are discussed in this chapter on the success of implementing ERM innovation in South Ayrshire Library are effective leadership of a motivated team of professional librarians, combined with library staffs who feel valued. It outlines how ERM projects were successfully managed, developed, and implemented by South Ayrshire Council Library Service.

Chapter 12, "Towards Innovative Library Services: A Case Study of Indira Gandhi National Open University, India," discusses emerging innovative technologies and services for managing e-resources and examines how Indira Gandhi National Open University (IGNOU) Library is increasingly benefited by its new and future services. It discusses the National Open Distance Learners' Library and Information Network (NODLINET), a project of IGNOU Library created for distance learning libraries for sharing collections, e-resources, and services on a common platform. The chapter also discusses how IGNOU Library is moving towards innovative Library Services by providing its users with updated contents and constantly strengthening service capability in the network information environment. It explains in detail the component of Remote Access to e-resources, which is a quick, easy, and convenient service to gain off-campus access to all IGNOU Library subscribed databases and other online resources. The chapter also enumerates the copyright restrictions and licensing restrictions through Remote Access Service and discusses in detail various other initiatives taken by IGNOU Library like cloud computing, course reserves, discovery, and AtoZ services.

Nihar K. Patra
National Institute of Food Technology Entrepreneurship & Management, India

Bharat Kumar
Management Development Institute, India

Ashis K. Pani
XLRI, Jamsedpur, India

Acknowledgment

Gratitude can be felt deep inside the heart and is beyond description. Thanks are poor expression of debt, of the gratitude one feels, yet there is no better way to express it. Throughout the one year it took to complete this book, the book demanded constant attention and support from other professionals. Therefore, we would like to express our gratitude to the people who made it possible.

It is a privilege of the editors to express our heart-felt gratitude for the assistance and support in the compilation of this book. We are grateful to the members of our Editorial Advisory Board. Thanks also go to our dedicated team of reviewers for their expertise and time in polishing the manuscript.

It is our profound privilege to express gratitude from the core of hearts to Professor Jaideep Sharma for his unconditional and precious guidance, constant encouragement, and whole-hearted assistance throughout the process of completing this book.

Our cordial thanks to IGI Global for providing us the opportunity to publish the book. We especially express our thanks to Christine Smith, Development Editor, and team members for this project, for their invaluable assistance, guidance, and patience throughout this entire process.

We are thankful to all those who have helped us directly and indirectly during the course of the project, whose names could not be mentioned here but will always in our hearts.

Nihar K. Patra
National Institute of Food Technology Entrepreneurship & Management, India

Bharat Kumar
Management Development Institute, India

Ashis K. Pani
XLRI, Jamsedpur, India

Chapter 1
Electronic Resources:
History, Scope, and Challenges: An Overview

Hungwa Shidi
Ministry of Information and Orientation, Nigeria

Solomon Uganneya
University of Agriculture, Nigeria

ABSTRACT

The chapter addresses some issues with e-resources management in libraries, including the concept of e-resources, scope, and challenges of e-resource management in libraries. It defines e-resources as sources of information that are available and accessible electronically through the use of computers. Using such terms like e-journals, e-books, Websites, File Transfer Protocol (FTP), etc., the chapter defines the scope of e-resources and traces the origin of e-resources in the library environment back to the introduction of the Machine Readable Catalogue (MARC) in the mid-1960s. Infrastructure gaps and other sundry issues like funding, access model, archiving, preservation, ownership versus access, and lack of continuity in publication are some of the challenges highlighted in the management of e-resources in libraries. The chapter finally presents a brief overview of e-resources in the library environment today and maintains that e-resources are a welcome development in the library.

INTRODUCTION

The term electronic resource is an umbrella term that encompasses such expressions like digital resources and digital collection. While some authorities use the terms interchangeably, others see them as a subset of one another yet others see them as similar with no marked differences between them. In library parlance, Harter (1997) submitted that, terms like electronic library, virtual library, library without walls and bionic library are simply umbrella terms that are coined to refer to digitized libraries.

Also, Reitz (2004) defined digital collection as "materials converted to machine readable format" or "produced in electronic forms" (p.216). In a virtual library and library without walls, the collection is said to exist, not in physical forms

DOI: 10.4018/978-1-4666-4761-9.ch001

like paper and microform but electronically in digital format and accessible via computer networks. Martin (1994) looked at digital library as "information housed electronically, delivered electronically and delivered without regards to location and time" (in Idiegbeyan-Ose & Ukpoghome, 2009, p. 79). Agreeing with this submission, Clifford Lynch stated that, a digital library is an "electronic information access that offers the user a coherent view of an organized, selected and managed body of information" (in Sharifabadi, 2006, p. 40). This therefore gives us an impetus to treat the two concepts of digital and electronic information with an aura of similarity and a consideration of the terms as umbrella terms with a similar connotation.

Remarkable electronic resources of current use in the information world include but not limited to Electronic Journals, Electronic Books, Reference sources in electronic format etc. Their debut in the information society has brought a great boost in the information sector. They have the advantage of speed, transferability, ease of use, capacity to save space, ease of search etc. It is expected that, this chapter will provide an understanding of what electronic resources are, their origin, scope and challenges in provision and management of such resources. This will then lead the reader into a full and better grasp of the content of the book.

BACKGROUND

Concept of Electronic Resources

An electronic resource, according to Allword English Dictionary (2012), is information which can be stored in the form of electronic signals and made available usually, but not necessarily on a computer.

According to AACR2, they are "materials consisting of data and/or computer program(s) encoded for reading and manipulation by a computer by the use of a peripheral device directly connected

to the computer or remotely via a network such as the Internet" (as cited by Reitz, 2005, p. 244). They are electronic sources that are made available electronically and can also be accesses as such (electronically) through such facilities like online computer catalogs, the Internet and World Wide Web, digital libraries and archives, government portals and websites, CD-ROM databases, online academic databases such as Medline Online, or commercial databases such as LEXIS and NEXIS all of which are computer networked facilities (Ekwelem, Okafor & Ukwoma (2009). International Records Management Trust (2009, p, 5) define an electronic record as they call it as any:

... component of information created electronically that forms part of an electronic record and that is usually stored separately within the digital file making up the electronic record as a whole. Every electronic record consists of at least one digital object, component or element, such as the bits of data that come together to create a word processed document. And some electronic records, such as photographs, video clips or web pages, may contain many different objects or elements.

Making resources available electronically can be through the use of digital devices like computers to input data in the form of typing and saving, snapping with digital devices like computer webcams, digital cameras, hand phones, etc. It can also be done through the retrospective conversion of already existing traditional print sources or versions through the process of digitization into machine readable forms. This demands the use of scanners to scan photographs, printed texts, manuscripts etc and digital cameras to snap artwork, scenes of events, three dimensional objects, realia etc (Eke, 2011). Accessing them on the other hand can be done through the use of the computer and other accompanying devices like projectors etc.

Libraries are usually identified and sometimes labeled according to the type of holdings they have. Thus mention is made of toy libraries, children's libraries, law libraries, medical libraries and so on. With the advent of electronic materials in libraries, attempts have been made to tag libraries with a special name, which house materials in electronic formats. Various terms have over the years been coined and used synonymously with electronic libraries. They are digitised library, virtual library, library without walls, and bionic library, (Harter, 1997).

Developments through the Ages of Libraries and Library Resources

Traditionally, a library is a building or room in which books used for reading or study are kept or a collection of such. They are said to be as old as the written word dating back to 5,000 years ago when political, social and economic developments had enabled cultures to record and collect knowledge (Hasley, 2009). Historical records, economic records, records of security and military strength were of importance to kings. They were therefore generated and kept in kings' palaces. Some early and medieval libraries were centered around monasteries, the monks serving as scribes and being responsible for kings' records. Some of these libraries, recognized as organized collections of written knowledge according to Braine (n.d.) were at Alexandria in Ptolemaic Egypt and Pergamum in Hellenic Turkey. The establishment of schools of philosophy witnessed the rebirth of another form of libraries. Prominent among them, according to the Encyclopedia Britannica, (2009) was the famous collection of the Peripatetic school, founded by Aristotle. In the later Middle Ages the stranglehold that monasteries had on knowledge in Europe was loosened, as universities were founded in cities like Bologna and Paris, with college libraries to follow (Braine, n.d.). New developments continued to emerge in the areas of private collections, Islamic collections as well as national libraries.

As the development of libraries span through ages and historical times, information materials used by the different libraries continued to change. This change was from stones to clay tablets to cuneiforms and parchments to books etc. Now we have electronic and digital resources.

Origin of Electronic Resources

As early as 1964, Ranganathan's five rules of librarianship gave a pointer to the existence of library resources that will be used extensively rather than kept idle (every reader his book); every reader who wants to read will have access to reading materials (every reader his or her book); no book will be useless for it will find itself useful to a particular person or group of persons (every book its reader); search strategies will be made easier globally so that it will take little time for readers to find what they are looking for (save the time of the reader) and the library, through its effective services delivery to the patron will grow at an alarming rate (the library is a growing organization). Years later, in 1980, Lancaster postulated a paperless society where he assumed that, "all communication could be handled via non-traditional means using information technology" (Harrod's librarian's glossary, 2005). This was even a better indicator to the future existence of electronic resources.

The foundation for electronic resources was laid through the work of Vannevar Bush who conceived a memex machine in 1945 based on microform technology which can store information and cause it to be seen in different locations by different people at the same time. The concept continued to evolve with different advances in information technology (Brown, n.d. and Cleveland, 1998). Lesk (1997) predicted that, by 2015 (70 years after Vannevar Bush) "we will have the equivalent of a major research library on each desk. And it will have searching capabilities beyond those Bush imagined" (p. 270) (in Brown, n.d.). Allard (2000) asserted that, Ted Nelson coined the term hypertext that described the linkage of bits of knowledge in the way that people think (in Aina, Mutala and Tiamiyu, 2008).

The introduction of Machine Readable Catalogue (MARC) in the mid 1960's marked a remarkable point in the history of electronic resources use in libraries. Hawthorne (2008) postulated that, it was 30 years after this that, the World Wide Web was introduced with its ubiquity in 1990 by Tim Berners-Lee (in Aina, Mutala and Tiamiyu, 2008). The development of the mosaic browser, graphic interface and search engines like yahoo made electronic resources especially on the Internet very accessible to users. Hawthorne further added that, this development made it possible for libraries to offer web-based electronic resources like catalogs, bibliographic and full-text databases, electronic journals as well as electronic books to patrons in remote locations without them having to come to the library.

Scope of Electronic Resources

Electronic resources are made up of the following: electronic journals (e-journal), electronic books (e-book), online databases in varied digital formats, Adobe Acrobat documents (.pdf), WebPages (.htm, .html, .asp etc) and more (Brown, 2005).

Mutula and Ojedokun outlined electronic resources as follows:

- **Databases**
- **Electronic Journals**
- **Electronic Books**
- **Reference Sources in Electronic Format**
- **Selected Websites**
- **Online Public Access Catalogues**
- **E-mail and Discussion Forums**
- **Newsgroups:** Resources offering site-based one-to-many, small group and public interaction.

- **Web Conferencing:** A public interaction in web-based environments whose features may vary from Internet mailing lists, web messaging systems, chat and file, photo, or music sharing.
- **Internet Relay Chat:** Live one-to-one and one-to-many interactions with the assistance of chat client software on a local computer system.
- **IPhone:** Internet telephone and audio-conferencing for one-to-one and one-to-many and Internet radio.
- **Internet Radio:** This allows anyone to host a free international Internet radio station in real time or free two-way phone conversation on the Internet (In Mutula & Ojedokun, 2008, p. 104-105).

In their submission, Sharma (2009), Ibrahim (2004) and Aramide & Bolarinwa (2010) identified e-resources to include journals, data archives, manuscripts, maps, books, magazines, theses, newspapers, e-mail, research reports, and bibliographic databases. Added to this list are library websites, online catalogues, and online reference works. Also, worthy of mention as electronic resources are, A-V resources, instructional audio tapes, instructional video tapes, VCD/DVD, radio, television, multimedia projectors, e-resources-electronic databases, e.g., JSTOR, ERIC, e-documents, Internet/e-mail facility, CD-ROMS, computers, telephone facility (GSM/Landline), VSAT, printers, and digital cameras.

Challenges

The thrust of every library and information service is to provide quality information for quality research and development efforts of an individual and nations. This means that librarians, by necessity, must provide and have access to the most efficient and effective systems available to manage the challenges presented by electronic resources.

Providing for information needs of library users with a critical quality resources question should take a far higher priority than dealing with the complexities of electronic information. Sometimes trying to cope with electronic access and management issues make us nostalgic for the simplicity of print, when the most pressing issues were title and frequency changes. However there are consistent issues which are associated with e-resource management in the libraries.

Librarians are charged with spending their scarce budgetary resources wisely to provide access to high quality, urgently needed content. Collection development decisions are driven by many factors. Price is just one. The challenge of finding the budgetary resources to meet conforming price increases is difficult, but armed with information, librarians can show administrators that price increases for e-resources are far higher than other typical measures such as the consumer price index - price history for both medical and related e-resources. The challenge for librarians who must now track changing pricing models, license terms and hundreds of other data elements has been answered in part by electronic resource management systems (ERMs). Once a library purchases an ERM system, the next step is populations and maintaining the massive amounts of data associated with electronic resources. Without the data, an ERM system is just an expensive online filing cabinet. The trend now is toward automating the transfer of essential data between systems to ease the burden of manual data entry and improve accuracy.

The E-Resources Management Initiative (ERMI) was born with the hope that, rather than many librarians creating solutions for their own institutions, they would work together to define the ideal solution. EBSCO as part of e-resource supply chain works with the librarians, who need to purchase and manage content, and EBSCO works with publishers, who produce that content. In managing E-Resource, in terms of acquisition,

EBSCO has detailed information on the orders customers have placed, allowing it to build an integrated knowledge base that is far comprehensive than any other available and is shared across EBSCO's other services such as A-to-Z listing service and link source link resolver.

The Key Challenging Issues

Fee Based Access

Fee-based access to information can take several forms. Historically, bibliographic databases were the early entrants into the electronic collection management arena. Although the Web initially encouraged free and freely available information, as it is maturing, commercial publishers are actively using it for vending their electronic material. The volume of fee-based access via the Web is only going to continue to increase at an increasingly rapid rate.

E-book providers are Web based vendors of online and for the most part popular books. They are fee-based services charged to the consumer. There are a number of services that provide access to e-books. See, (http://www.ebooks.com/) for an example of eBooks. Adobe provides pointers to e-book vendors (http://www.adobe.com/epaper/ebooks/ebookmall/main.html). E-books are typically provided in pdf format one page at a time.

E-journals and highbred journals (h-journal) provide access either by subscription or associate on membership. These include Science and Nature. The Journal of the American Society for Information Science and Technology is offered to members in either paper or electronic format (or both for an additional fee). Companies like MCB University Press, Woulters Kluwer or Elsevier offer bundles of online journal to libraries and individuals.

It is important to note that, copyright or intellectual property (IP) law and some license agreement exist to protect ownership from exploitation in e-resources transactions. Although these rights are intangible in themselves, they nevertheless exist in law and usually have the same status as any other property right.

More far-reaching and of much greater significance to the fee-based access world are the economic rights that owners enjoy. Owners of copyright enjoy a series of rights which vary sometimes from one country to another but can be summarized as follows:

- Copy the work
- Make the work publicly available
- Reform, show, play or broadcast
- Adopt or translate
- Lend or rent the work

These principles by law awarded the authors/creators with monopoly powers (state power) to create/maintain scarcity of their products. However, the "fair use" principle in copyright law is given to the benefit of the society.

Many authors cannot exploit their works in any commercial sense without the existence of some kind of publishers, whether it is a conventional commercial publishing house, a government agency, a research institution or a website host. In return for making the work widely available, the organization doing this will almost certainly want some rights over the work in return. As all IP is a transferable commodity, this can be done in the form of outright selling, licensing for a specific time-span or purpose or format. Authors can set all kinds of conditions on the sale or lease of their IP rights and usually do so. However, this process immediately makes clear the distinction between the rights the author enjoy and those that owners have and why different people have different rights in the same work.

No Fee Electronic Access

The development of open paradigms and models in the 21st Century added an impetus to no-fee based access. For example, the open source movement – the concept of software development wherein the source code is shared and development is collaborative – reflects a fundamental shift away from proprietary software and systems. These open models are appearing in an interesting array of new applications and venues, such as the open knowledge initiative to share learning technologies and open law programme as collaborative approach to crafting legal agreements. This trend towards open models may present more generalized acceptance of collaborative development and sharing of intellectual goods and services. Lessis (2000) suggests that, the creation of a "commons" wherein the free exchange of ideas and collaboration prevail is fundamental to an open society.

This belief stands in stark contrast to that of commercial and other interests, whose goal is to control the Internet and its contents. One could argue that, the notion of the commons also reflect the departure from models that has characterized library operations in the past. Other operations of openness include Open Archiving Initiative (OAI) which seeks to address concerns within the scholarly community about certain aspects of traditional journal publishing especially the notion of the "gift-economy" where intellectual property is ceded to the "for-profit" sector and then repurchased for community use. The Open Courseware (OCW) which is a direct response to the "for-profit" higher education business is also known as "Digital Diploma Mills". There are literally thousands of course wares available online as Open Course Wares. They are found on http://ocw.mit.edu/index.htm

No fee access to digital materials has therefore become increasingly available through the Internet and, thereby, directly to the end user. Materials can be read online or downloaded in a variety of formats, including pdf, Microsoft reader, and html. From the "collection" point of view, providing identification and access to the free sites brings with it a number of issues. Since these are free material and the level of responsibility of the "publishers" vary considerably, collection developers have the difficult challenge of determining whether digital access provides sufficient continuity in their collection development scheme. Maintaining links to free electronic sites is a major collection maintenance challenge for digital collection. Also, because the material is free, most of it is not copyrighted or older out-of-copyright material. One major source of free material that is rather durable and generally of good provenance is US government material, especially policy and technical documents because US government material cannot be copyrighted.

There is another major thrust into free or alternative models of information provision driven by the changing economics of publishing, the increasingly activist use community, and the enabling information technologies around the Internet. This is particularly true in scientific and technical areas where journal costs are fast outpacing libraries' abilities to continue to afford them for their collections. Scholars and universities on the one hand are challenging the journal publication model as too centric and too expensive. Journal publishers on the other hand respond that their costs require economies of scale and higher prices. Some authors are experimenting with self publication on the Web. And a number of e-journals have been created to add structure to the process. The SPARC (Scholarly Publishing and Academic Resources Coalition) Initiative is one such effort to redefine academic publishing and information dissemination (http://www.arl.org/sparc/home/). It is an organization of universities, research libraries, and organizations "built as a constructive response to market dysfunctions in the scholarly communication system". Launched in 1998, the SPARC mission is to enhance access to peer reviewed literature and to act as an alternative delivery mechanism to commercial online publishers.

Many e-journals and some h-journals (hybrid, or journals published in paper and electronically) offer free access to their articles. These include a number of popular and scholarly journals offered in electronic format without charge or subscription; for example, the venerable Scientific American (htt://www.sciam.com/), as well as the information science journals information research (http://information.net/ir/), D-Lib Magazine (http://www.dlib.org/), FirstMonday (http://www.firstmonday.dk), Ariandne (http://www.ariadne.ac.uk/) and CyberMetrics (http://www.cindoc.csic.es/cybermetrics/). Many newspapers offer free access to all or parts of their editions. These include El Dia, New York Times, Wall Street Journal, Le Monde, Helsingin Sanomat, The Times of India, to name a few.

Ownership vs. Access

The move to electronic information resource management has resulted in a number of debates. "Ownership vs. access" has been one of the more important issues. Budd and Harloe (1994) distinguish between the ownership-based and the access-based organization. In the former, collection emphasis is placed on building "on-the-shelf" collections while the latter's emphasis is placed on access to resources, regardless of where they are "owned". Value is assessed differently. For the traditional model, the value of a collection is its size. For the access-based library, value is defined as the ability to retrieve useful information. The former library collects "just in case" material is needed: the latter provides it "just in time".

Both models contain pitfalls and problems. Keller (1992b), for example, has argued that "(n)ew access instead of ownership paradigm leads ultimately to an environment where 'all is meta information', with no or few ideas on the shelves". The issue of access also brings in a whole new set of questions regarding archiving and preservation, intellectual property including fair use, as well as conditions for purchase which have moved to a complex set of conditions in licensing in the case of digital material. Buckland (1997) suggests that libraries consider ownership for high demand items and access for those in low demand.

Given the spread of digital access, union catalogs, and borrowing, it is no longer so important what an information organization contains (owns); rather, the focus is on the services (access) the organization can provide (Ferguson and Kehoe 1993).

Access Models

Access to digital information comes through several modes of access. Each of these forms can be considered as part of the "ownership versus access debate" and impacts the new ways of managing electronic collections. The following describes four models now employed in the digital environment. These are the interlibrary loan model, the universal borrowing model, the no fee model and the fee-based model. In addition, the World Wide Web, as both a content structure and a delivery mechanism, will be discussed in the context of models of access. The interlibrary loan (ILL) model has been with us for many years. Universal borrowing (UB) is a recent phenomenon first seen in the mid-190s. The fee-based electronic access model dates to the early 1960s with the advent of electronic database services like Dialog. Today, a large volume of "no fee" or "free" services are Web-based and emerged as major resources in the mid-1990s.

Information Loan Model

Interlibrary Loan (ILL) is a process by which one library borrows from other libraries, materials it does not hold in order to meet the information needs of its patrons. Interlibrary Loan is not a new concept nor is it one that emerged out of the digital revolution. ILL is however facilitated by various online services including electronic union catalogs (like OCLC's World Cat) and automatic ILL request services attached to OPACs (Online

Public Access Catalogs) and online databases. The ILL community has developed a continuing interest in using the Web and other means to facilitate the ILL process.

The North American Interlibrary Loan and Document Delivery (NAILDD) Project promotes the development of efficient ILL/DD delivery systems using networked technologies. NAILDD has identified three areas of primary concern: "comprehensive and flexible management software, improvements in ILL billing and payments, and system interoperability via use of standards" (Jackson 1998). OCLC has played a major role in developing system interoperability, facilitating billing and financial transfers (IFM or ILL Fee Management), and development of management software. A number of international initiatives led by the Research Libraries Group (RLG), the Library Corporation (TLC), Ameritech Library Services (ALS), AG Canada, and others have sought to improve system interoperability and information flows, thus enhancing digital access.

OCLC manages an international Interlibrary Loan Service or Global Sharing Group Access Capability (GAC), built upon its union catalog World Cat. It utilizes a standard Web interface and software (http://www2.oclc.org/oclc/pdf/printondemand/ill.pdf).

The Interlibrary Loan system is guided by a set of standards (ISO 10160 and ISO 10161). These standards were developed to insure interoperability among electronic ILL systems and their application protocols. These standards and protocols are managed by the ILL ISO Maintenance Agency. The National Library of Canada serves as host.

Typically, ILL exchanges do not require royalty payments to the copyright holder of exchanged materials. Two principles guide this. The first is fair use. The second is the right of the "container". The owner dispose of the container as she sees fit, including lending it to others. Fair use doctrine limits the number of copies of a work one can make as well as the number of pages that can be copied from larger works. In general, fair use would permit the same work or a single copy of a larger work could create an obligation to make royalty payments to the copyright holder. One may, however, lend the original copy as often as it is requested. These conditions are noted here because the whole system of access through ILL has been called into question when dealing with digital materials. This is part of the larger intellectual property issues associated with such materials.

The Universal borrowing models (UB) allows libraries to treat authorized users from one system to borrow (access collections) from libraries within a consortia. The term "universal" actually refers to providing access to everyone within a defined group, not universal in the sense of totally opened.

In the increasingly digital world, the pre-coordinated groups of organizations in consortia have become increasingly active and pervasive due to the need to get the most favourable conditions under licensing agreements. Cost models for publishers of digital information are in serious flux and the need for groups that build collections to work together in their dealings with publishers and in developing access infrastructures for digital collections has become increasingly important.

Acquisition

Information can be acquired through a variety of means as was discussed in the previous sections. Library historians may recall that the acquisition policy of the first library at Alexandria was very straightforward. By law any manuscript entering Ptolemaic Egypt had to be deposited at the library so that it could be copied and incorporated into the collection. Copyright and fair use practices no longer permit such direct taking of the intellectual and physical property of others. A number of principles and laws have been developed that regulate the use of information.

In a paper-based world, the intellectual property had a physical form and, therefore, only one person could possess or use it at a time. Acquisition was the purchase of a commodity. Certainly, with the

advent of photocopying machines, issues arose on the premise of one copy, one possession. To deal with this, copyright has traditionally been balanced by the fair use doctrine. Fair use regulates the rights and privileges of information users to access and use the intellectual property of others. These fair use rights range from quotation, citation, copying and perhaps in cyber-documentation to hypertext linking of one Web page to another. As technology has advanced, limits have been placed on fair use doctrine.

A principle related to fair use; i.e. the "principle of first sale", means that the purchaser of an "information container" may transfer ownership of the container to whomever and whenever that owner wishes to do so. The principle, however, does not extend to all uses of the "contents" of that container. Copyright serves to protect information proprietary interests of the copyright holder who sometimes may be the original creator of the work, but more often, is the publisher. The combination of these two principles is currently being tested in institutions building e-collections and e-services.

Because of the economic implications for these intellectual property issues in the digital environment, in recent years, information suppliers have begun to move away from the sale of information to the licensing of information. The digital revolution has significantly changed the ways in which information can be packaged. It needs no longer to be offered within "physical packages". It can now be transmitted from producer to publisher to end user. That may well render the principle of first sale moot because information containers need not be used. It also means that limits are placed on the ability of the license to transfer or transmit information to third parties.

To restate, when a book, CD, journal DVD, videotape, or magazine is put in a digital collection, the institution buys the container together with certain rights of access to the content therein. The rights of the users are limited by copyright and other legal constraints. However, the owner of the container retains the right to access the information so long as s/he owns the container and retains the right to transfer ownership and associated rights to someone else. In the online world, even these concepts are challenged by the definitions of containers as well as by other provisions in licensing agreements restricting what uses can be made of the material.

Cataloging

New and changing technologies and retrospective cataloging have forced libraries to examine management systems and planning processes (Stamm 2000). As new hardware and software come available for library systems, there will be an inevitable impact on library services as adaptations are made. Consortia agreements also have a place in the development and application or metadata. Libraries long ago began to move away from doing all their cataloging in house to outsourcing some or all of the function to centralized facilities like OCLC or the Library of Congress. Electronic bibliographic information facilitates thus move to electronic cataloging utilities. OCLC now serves as a center for cataloging for its member libraries. It is the provider of major cataloging systems like PRISM and World Cat. Participating libraries contribute to the Online Union Catalog and share cataloging records. The Program for Cooperative Cataloging (PCC) provides core-level standard cataloging. A core record represents a minimum acceptable number of fields to allow participating libraries to adopt the record without significant editing or addition (US Library of Congress 1999).

It has been well established that Web pages and sites undergo frequent change including disappearance. CORC periodically rechecks the integrity of URLs and of page content for its member libraries.

Universal Borrowing Model

In the United States, two examples of Universal Borrowing (UB) arrangement for digital access are under a common jurisdiction- permit inter-jurisdictional lending. This model allows public libraries to form Public Information Network for Electronic Services (PINES). They offer an electronic union catalogue and interlibrary borrowing services.

The Association of Research Libraries (ARL) manages the "Reciprocal Faculty Borrowing Programme" among its member University libraries. Conducted under the aegis of the Research Library Advisory Committee (RLAC) to Online Catalogue of the Library of congress (OCLC), the intent of this programme is to promote and facilitate scholarly research and communication among faculty members of research universities that are ARL members. Privileges may but do not necessarily include borrowing rights.

Archiving

One of the most significant issues in electronic collection management arising out of the conditions of digital content licenses has to do with the long-term ability to access and preserve the collection. The issues of the specific collection are magnified by the realization that the archival copy in some cases may end up residing only at the publisher and the scholarly record is, therefore, hanging on the viability of those publishers with no assured backup. This is quite a different situation from that of paper material where the physical ownership lasted in perpetuity, even after subscriptions or standing purchase orders expired, and redundancy across the world's library collections almost assures perpetual preservation of scholarly works. Specifically, in the digital environment, rights to licensed materials mean that the material may become unavailable when the license ends. This is based on the fact that the resources of the e–collection are accessed as a service rather than owned as a traditional commodity. Digital materials may not be maintained in numerous copies at diverse sites. The potential for loss or destruction of intellectual property is increased as the number of storage facilities decreases.

Archiving in the electronic environment is a complex undertaking. The task force on digital archiving in 1996 report entitled "Preserving Digital Information" concluded that digital archiving system must be developed if we are to preserve our digital heritage. Digital information archiving processes are analogous to traditional archiving (Arms, 2000).

Conventional archiving distinguishes between conservation (which looks after individual artifacts) and preservation (which retains the content even if the original artifacts decays or is destroyed). The corresponding techniques in digital archiving are refreshing (aims to preserve processed sequence of bits) and migration (which preserves the contents at a semantic level, but not the specific sequence of bits).

Migration, refreshing and replication (copying files) require dedicated resources, personnel and capital. It is well understood that, the speed at which the computer/digital revolution is preceeding renders common formation and process absolute in a matter of years, sometimes months. Great care should be taken in the development of digital materials and plan to archive as we develop digital libraries.

The need for digital archiving has been recognized, but it may be difficult to accomplish. There are a number of competing standards and approaches to digital archiving. Each of these standards fulfills a niche requirement, but none have been recognized to address the range of digital archiving demands. The Gail Hodge (2000b) and Michael Day (2000) bibliographies point us to an array of complex problems. For example, Gutthrie

(2001) has questioned the economic feasibility of archiving little used digital documents. Lawrence, et al (2000) explore risks associated with data migration. Kuny (1998) points to the close association between multimedia materials and the hardware and software needed to access them.

If archiving material is complex, archiving the World Wide Web is a nightmare. If most digital documents like their print counterparts are more or less static, Web documents are extremely dynamic. The Web differs from other digital content. Its content undergoes frequent change, movement and disappearance. Some Web pages and cites change content frequently, others rarely.

Preservation

Though the e-resources are enabling information to be created, manipulated, disseminated and located with ease, preserving access to this information posses a great challenge. Unless, preservation of digital information is actively taken, the information will become inaccessible due to changing technology platform and media instability.

Technical Infrastructure

In a digital information service system, infrastructure such as software, hardware, Internet facilities and other physical equipments are required to provide easier, faster, and comprehensive access to information at the right time. Libraries in a digital age need to enhance and upgrade current technical architecture to accommodate e-resource.

Selection of Information for Electronic Collections

The number, scope and type of information resources in electronic and print format are overwhelming. There are many sources from which information can be drawn. And there continues to be a need to effectively evaluate those resources. Libraries have long functioned as one of the chief mechanisms for information and evaluation of quality and relevant information sources.

If we believe that library is a "process" or "service" rather than a "place", libraries must put added focus on how to manage collections. Electronic collection development must be consistent with the mission and an overall collection development plan. At the same time, collection development plans should take into account the electronic resources now available to libraries (Gessesse 2000). As it become easier or more efficient to move electronic and physical objects from a collection repository to the end user, the logic of maintaining redundant collections declines. Through selective collection policies, scarce resources can be used to broaden collections rather than to duplicate them.

Best-Seller Phenomenon

Economies of scale make mass-distributed information cheap and available, and can lead to an environment where smaller-audience information is more expensive and higher to find. Over time this may well lead to the favoring of electronic delivery of entertainment over delivery of information.

Consolidation of Electronic Information Distributors

As corporate mergers, buy-outs, and consolidations leave us with fewer and fewer independent information providers, how will that change what information people get? Will large conglomerates with interest in many different types of industries begin to treat their information distribution divisions the same way they treat all their other distribution divisions?

Flat Fee vs. Pay-per-Use

The movement towards pay-per-use model is likely to severely affect users' habits, particularly as this begins to penetrate Web-based delivery systems. Pay-per-use model tend to discourage exploration

and encourage a viewer/reader to examine items that others have already deemed popular (favoring best-sellers over more esoteric works). Libraries' 1980s experiences with pay-per-use online indexing and abstracting services led many librarians to embrace newer flat-fee models that arose (such as CD ROMs).

Solutions and Recommendations

Some of the challenges confronting e-resources management as highlighted above require proactive solutions in order to make the e-resources library environment user-friendly. As the cost of acquiring e-resources continues to rise, there is need for libraries to offer some form of e-resources pull. Clearly, OPAC and cloud computing presents interactive systems for information generation, storage and retrieval. Full text databases like net library, OCLC, ArticleFirst etc may represent a good platform to pull e-resources either directly by the end users or through e-library intermediaries.

There is also need for proper deployment of the strategies needed for acquisition process as well as infrastructure need for e-resources management in libraries. In addition, information technology and access management tools need to be defined as well as the economic, legal and administrative policies with regards to the management of e-resources in libraries.

Other challenging issues such as access could be resolved by the hybrid model of collection management. This resource management model requires a combination of print and electronic resources in the library. This option seems better for, it will accommodate the computer disabled users and at the same time provides access to information during power failure which is common in less developing countries' information settings. An attempt to enhance information model will take the form of stable infrastructure, multiple tasking computers and software and a stable supply staff who performs "ease of access" functions. This provides library users and research teams with a very productive "e-resources worked environment."

A universally accepted cataloguing model for e-resources management in libraries should be adopted. This will facilitate easy access to electronic resources from various end-users or libraries and at the same time make cataloguing of e-resources easy and less time consuming by libraries. The present situation where various models of cataloguing exist like OCLC, Program for Cooperative Cataloguing (PCC) etc makes cataloguing of e-resources cumbersome and varied.

FURURE RESEARCH DIRECTIONS

As information becomes more distributed and open models of exchange becomes more common, the library's relationship with content creators, purchasers and consumers will change. There is in these open trends evidence of a shift from publications as products to publications and process. When content can be enhanced or supplemented over time by others, it becomes more dynamic and the version becomes more cumulative. This shift is a challenge to the current copyright law which is based on objects fixed in time and space. Such a shift has significant impact on organizations like the library whose role is to manage publication in both traditional and new forms and to sustain the scholarly records for the future. As this shift continues, there is need to look at the future role(s) of the library as information manager and agent in scholarly communication. Rather than being defined by its collaboration or the services that support them, the library can become a diffuse agent within the scholarly community. Increasingly, the models in which the library retains central control over contents, its access and its longevity may no longer be appropriate or sustainable. Instead, a model for instance where the library's role in this case, provides access to information is being reshaped by distributed forces and openness need be evolved. Here too, there is a need to look at the potential for the library's more active engagement and collaboration, moving beyond simple descriptive access to understand and fulfill community requirements for robust retrieval and for providing assurance of the integrity and authenticity of the content.

Recently, visions of the library of the future have been associated with speculations of the demise of the book and the traditional ways of library processes and service delivery. This speculation was based on emerging technological trends associated with library services. Library services as we know them best are based on the technology of paper, but a shift from paper to technical operations steadily being computerized occasioned what we term automated library. The paper library proved efficient and durable for an extended period. Nevertheless, the problems inherent in the paper library are real and substantial. For example, paper is a localized medium. It is rather inflexible and creates space problem.

Automated library systems became desirable for three reasons. First, much of the library work involves accurate updating of records in the file. The tasks are generally tedious, repetitive, and mechanical in nature and therefore led to computerization. Second, it improves cost effective performance by increasing accuracy and reducing the increased rate in the cost of labour intensive activities. Thirdly, automation permits decentralization of access to records. A user/librarian in a branch library can verify the status of other library collections without necessarily travelling to the library.

However, automation came along with some of the problems inherent in paper library. This is because the collection was still on paper, a localized medium and therefore had a limitation of inflexibility and space needed for paper documents etc. Nevertheless, automation represented a significant improvement in library management operations.

The e-library which describes the situation in which documents are stored in electronic form rather than on paper or other localized media later emerged. The rise of e-library with virtually e-resources has been described as revolutionary rather than evolutionary. It defines the future and emerging trends in the management and operations of library services.

The e-library environment has re-defined and re-shaped the way library operations and services are to be carried out. Since library materials in electronic form lend themselves to remote access and shared use, the local assembling of collection becomes less important. More emphasis is placed on coordinated collection development as well as cooperative and shared access to collection. The trend is to digitize everything (sound, images-still and moving- text and numerical data) for storage and manipulation. Documents of all kinds are becoming more homogenous in their physical medium. Limiting libraries to printed documents or indeed written documents makes less or little sense. If that demarcation dissolves, there is blurring of boundaries. The functions of the library, computer centre and the telecommunication office are converging, overlapping or at least more closely related.

Meanwhile, those to be served are changing their information handling habits. Paper and pen are becoming supplemented by desktop workstations capable of using multiplicity of remote sources. This leads to an entirely different perspective from library-centred world view to one that is user-centered. Catalog, collections, building and library staff are the familiar means for providing library services. Computers, networks and electronic resources are emerging trends with interesting possibilities.

The theme of this book is apt: An overview of the history, scope and challenges of electronic resources in the library is intended to bring an insight into the historical changes in the library and information service provision, bring to the fore what constitutes e-resources, the challenges e-resources present and possible solutions to the challenges.

The expectations of users are likely to change in the electronic library environment and this will impact on both the service quality and overall satisfaction rating. The overall satisfaction is likely to have a significant impact on the future of e-resource management in libraries and their competitiveness. Clearly, future research that would help integrate individual indicators' evaluative e-resources delivery into service quality models is urgently needed. Research that will throw light on the complex relationship between e-resources management, scope and quality service delivery is also needed. Reducing this gap is overdue.

CONCLUSION

Library is an integral part of the society that surrounds it. Its history, scope, and functions are shaped and changed by many of the same forces that shape other types of institutions. Librarians need to recognize the changes that are taking place in the library, particularly the emergency of e-resources in the library collection. Then they need to use this knowledge to actively reshape the library. If librarians do not actively involve in this reshaping, key principles from librarianship may disappear in the electronic library environment.

Librarians must resist any changes that threaten basic principles such as equal access to information and fair use. They must be concerned about key challenge areas such as copyright, access model, technical infrastructure, pay-per-use, preservation, and the ownership of electronic resources.

Certain investment must be made if the library is to emerge as a key player in the changing environment. Participation in new learning communities in new ventures for knowledge management of dissemination or in service to new audience requires investment in technology, infrastructure and expertise in the handling of e-resource tools. Collaborative development tools, services/resources and capabilities are required in the new environment. The open source software initiatives, cooperative reference services and universal based initiative to share resources/services requires expertise and professional hands while many libraries and information science graduate programmes have revamped their curricula. It is imperative to assume that, the needed leadership can come exclusively from newly minsted professionals. Investment in professional development and participation in collaborative opportunities that can help address e-resource development and management are essential.

REFERENCES

Allword Dictionary. (2012). *Electronic resources*. Retrieved November 1, 2012 from www.allwords.com/word-electronic%2B

Ancient Writing Materials. (n.d.). Retrieved November 6, 2012 from http://www.skypoint.com/members/waltzmn/WritingMaterials.html

Aramide, K. A., & Bolarinwa, O. M. (2010). *Availability and use of audiovisual and electronic resources by distance learning students in Nigerian universities: A case study of National Open University of Nigeria (NOUN), Ibadan study centre*. Retrieved November 15, 2012 from http://unllib.unl.edu/LPP/aramide-bolarinwa.htm

Arms, W. (2000). *Digital libraries*. Cambridge, MA: MIT Press..

Braine, J. (n.d.). *A brief history of librarians and image*. Retrieved November 16, 2012 from http://home.earthlink.net/~cyberresearcher/History.htm

Brown, E. M. (2005). *History and definition of digital libraries*. Retrieved November 1, 2012 from http://www.southernct.Edu/~brownm/dl_history.html

Buckland, M. (1997). *Redesigning library series: A manifesto*. Retrieved November 20, 2012 from http://sunsitebeakehay.edu/literature/library/redesigning/html

Budd, J., & Harloe. (1994). Collection development and scholarly communication in the era of electronic access. *Journal of Academic Information Management, 20*(5), 83–87.

Calhoun, K., & Riemer, J. J. (Eds.). (2001). *New tools and possibilities for cooperative electronic resource description*. New York: Haworth..

Cleveland, G. (1998). *Digital libraries: Definitions, issues and challenges*. Retrieved November 6, 2012 from http://www.ifla.shodhganga.inflibnet.ac.in/dxml/bitstream/handle/1944/1395/28.pdf?sequence=1

Day, M. (2000). *Preservation of electronic information: A bibliography*. Retrieved November 20, 2012 from http://www.homes.ukolin.ac.UK/-lismd/preservation.html

Eke, H. N. (2011). Digitizing resources for University of Nigeria repository: Process and challenges. *Webology, 8*(1).

Ekwelem, V. O., Okafor, V. N., & Ukwoma, S. C. (2009). Students' use of electronic information sources at the University of Nigeria, Nsukka. *African Journal of Library. Archives and Information Science, 19*(2), 89–97.

Ferguson, A., & Kehoe, K. (1993). Access vs ownership: What is most cost effective in the sciences. *Journal of Library Administration, 19*(2), 89–99. doi:10.1300/J111v19n02_07.

Gessesse, K. (2008). Collection development and management in the 21st century with special reference to academic libraries: An overview. *Library Management, 21*(7), 365–372. doi:10.1108/01435120010372551.

Guthrie, K. (2001). Archiving in the digital age. *EDUCASE Review, 36*(6).

Halsey, R. S., et al. (2009). Library (institution). In *Microsoft Encarta 2009*. [DVD]. Redmond, WA: Microsoft Corporation.

History of Books. (2012). *Wikipedia*. Retrieved November 6, 2012 from http://en.wikipedia.org/wiki/History_of_books

Hodge, G. (2000a). Best practices in digital archiving: An information life cycle approach. *D-Lib Magazine, 6*(1). doi:10.1045/january2000-hodge.

Hodge, G. (2003b). *Selected bibliography of digital archiving*. Retrieved November 20, 2012 from http://www.alpsp.org/biblio.pdi

Ibrahim, A. E. (2004). Use and user perception of electronic resources in the United Arab Emirates University (UAEU). *Libri, 54*, 21–23. doi:10.1515/LIBR.2004.18.

Idiegbeyan-Ose, J., & Ukpoghome, T. U. (2009). Distance learning in Nigeria and the role of the virtual library. *Gateway Library Journal, 12*(2), 75–85.

International Records Management Trust. (2009). *Preserving electronic records: Training in electronic records management*. London: International Records Management Trust..

Jackson, M. M. (1998). *Maximizing access, minimizing cost*. The Association of Research Libraries North American Technology Programme/NAILDO Project.

Keller, M. (1992a). *Foreign acquisitions in North American research libraries*.

Keller, M. (1992b). Moving towards concrete solution base in fundamental values. *Journal of Academic Information Management, 18*(3), 8–15.

Kuny, T. (1998). The digital dark ages? Challenges in the preservation of electronic information. *International Preservation News, 17*.

Lawrence, G., Jehoe, W., Rieger, O., Walters, W., & Kenny, A. (2000). *Risk management of digital information: A file format investigation council on library and information resources*. Retrieved November 20, 2012 from http:/www/clir.org/publib/reports/pub93/pub93.pdf

Lessig, L. (2000). *Open code and open societies*. Paper presented at Free Software: A Model for Society? Tutzing, Germany.

Library. (2009). *Encyclopædia Britannica 2009 student and home ed*. Chicago: Encyclopedia Britannica.

Mutula, S. M., & Ojedokun, A. A. (2008). Digital libraries. In *Information and knowledge management in the digital age: Concepts, technologies and African perspectives* (pp. 101–121). Ibadan, Nigeria: Third World Information Service..

Prytherch, R. (Ed.). (2005). *Harrod's librarians' glossary and reference book* (10th ed.). London: Ashgate..

Reitz, J. M. (2005). *Dictionary of library and information science*. London: Libraries unlimited..

Sharifabadi, R. S. (2006). How digital libraries can support e-learning. *Iranian Journal of Information Science and Technology, 4*(1), 39–56.

Sharma, C. (2009). Use and impact of e-resources at Guru Gobind Singh Indraprastha University (India): A case study. *Electronic Journal of Academic and Special Librarianship, 10*(1), 3–8.

Stamm, A. (2000). The end of an era builds new team spirit: Team playing at its best. In *Managing cataloguing and the organization of information: Philosophies, practices and challenges at the onset of the 21st century*. Binghamton, NY: Haworth. doi:10.1300/J104v30n02_13.

US Library of Congress. (1999). *Introducing to the programme for cooperative cataloguing BICO core record standard*. Washington, DC: US Library of Congress..

Chapter 2
Considerations of a Digital Age:
The Hows and Whys of Electronic Resource Management from a Collection Development Perspective

Jennifer Wright
Western Kentucky University, USA

ABSTRACT

This chapter talks about electronic resources from a collection development perspective. Working from the assumption that most institutions will need some electronic resources to adequately serve their patron population, this chapter explains what issues collection development staff may need to address when electronic resources are being incorporated into the existing collection. These issues include costs and benefits of electronic resources, how the collection development policy will be affected by the inclusion of electronic resources, and faculty/staff reactions to the incorporation of new materials. This chapter also strongly advocates the addition of an electronic resource manager or multiple electronic resource staff members and their close cooperation with the collection development staff.

INTRODUCTION

Electronic resources are not the next big thing in libraries. They are already the thing, less a luxury and more of a necessity. At the San Francisco public library, for example, patrons made a total of two million electronic searches in one year alone (Malnig, 2008); on the cost side, the Association for College & Research Libraries estimates that e-resources made up 44 percent of purchases for the average academic library, as of 2007, with that number sure to rise (Noh, 2012).With numbers like this, that are ever increasing, it may feel that libraries have no choice: evolve or die. This can create panic among an administration that wants their institution to succeed. However, if a library is considering adding electronic resources to the existing collection, or expanding current electronic resource holdings, there are many things to consider before embarking on what can be a

DOI: 10.4018/978-1-4666-4761-9.ch002

costly endeavour. Not all electronic resources are appropriate for all libraries. For example, the University of Idaho began adding E-books to their library's electronic resource collections in 2000, trying to stay ahead of a perceived user demand for E-books, but a recent review of the collection's usage statistics does not provide any evidence of the demand they expected (Sprague and Hunter, 2009). A rush to judgement in this case caused a very expensive error because they misjudged the desires of their patron population.

That being said, for many institutions, electronic resources are still an important step in the evolution of the library. Surveys and usage statistics from the University of Illinois supported their decision to incorporate E-books into their collection (Shelburne, 2009). The reasons for choosing electronic resources are clear: empowering a mobile patron population, facilitating access to materials, and reducing space concerns. However, the concerns of the institution may not be so clear. There may be questions about the cost of materials, duplication of existing materials (or duplication within the electronic resources), and preparation of the library staff and patrons for the influx of new information. A strong collection development policy, updated for the existence of electronic resources, can answer these questions and relieve some of the anxiety associated with adding electronic resources to an institution's collection.

BACKGROUND

What do librarians mean when discussing electronic resources? Simply put, electronic resources, also sometimes referred to as "e-resources", are those resources that are housed virtually and accessed through electronic means. Virtual movie and music collections could also be considered electronic resources. When electronic resource managers (ERMs) talk about electronic resources, they are typically talking about e-books and da-

tabases. ERMs are the people hired to work on the problems that electronic resources cause for libraries. These materials often have complicated agreements that librarians must keep track of, as well as technical problems that ERMs must solve on a daily basis.

While electronic resources have been around in some format since the 1980s, when the first electronic card catalogues were first introduced, some libraries are still fumbling their way around the use of electronic resources. While the public expectation of electronically available material continues to rise, many libraries are lucky if they can get a portion of their funding diverted to electronic resources. This is especially true of public libraries, which frequently have trouble with funding. There, print sources remain strong, with 72% of the reference budget for the average public library paying for print materials in 2003 (Roncevic, 2004 p.5). While trends in public and academic libraries indicate growth in electronic resources, this survey suggests that the growth is slower in public libraries.

It can be difficult for libraries to incorporate electronic materials into their collection for many reasons, including a lack of money or a lack of expertise. Chandel and Saiki note in their article that librarians have been dealing with print resources "for centuries (p. 149)." There are individuals who have been working with print resources for literally decades themselves. Newer and younger librarians may be more familiar with the use of electronic resources, but it cannot be guaranteed that they would have any expertise in negotiations or technical specifications of resources because of the limitations of entry level jobs. The few librarians in between have mainly had on-the-job-training and will be familiar with only certain types of management software and practices, since so much of it is different from institution to institution.

Current hierarchical systems in libraries can also be challenged by the addition of an ERM, as the position often straddles the work of both technical and public services. This may cause friction in both departments, as well as over-work for the librarian in the ERM position. Advertisements for ERM positions reviewed between 2000 and 2008 found that these positions continue to list job responsibilities that are not related to the management and procurement of electronic resources, such as reference work and cataloging (Murdock, 2010). Logic dictates that many of these responsibilities are part of the ERM workload because of budget restraints and staff shortages, but they are no less a problem for someone working as an ERM. Recommendations made by Digital Library Federation (DLF) contradict these current practices; the DLF has recommended that having only one person in charge of electronic resources might spread an individual too thin, much less having that one person manage electronic resources and perform additional duties such as reference or instruction (Murdock, 2010). If electronic resources are going to be a major addition to an institution, the creation of a separate department is ideal.

This is a struggle that has gone on for decades now. It may continue to go on for decades more, until the next big idea takes over. However, a strong collection development policy and some forward thinking may make the transition to or expansion of electronic resources smoother.

COLLECTION DEVELOPMENT CONCERNS

Costs vs. Benefits

The one question that is on every librarian's mind is the cost of the materials they are providing to their patrons. Unlike physical copies of books, that need only be replaced if damaged and thus are a one-time cost, electronic databases through aggregators such as EBSCOhost are reoccurring costs. Furthermore, these electronic databases are much more costly than their print counterparts because the library is not just paying for access

but also the convenience and ease of use. It is much like the difference in price between items in a grocery store versus those same items in a convenience store. One would not expect to pay the same prices for a loaf of bread in both places, because the convenience store can and will charge more; they know that someone coming into a convenience store needs the bread right now, and does not have the time to go to the grocery store. In exchange for more money, they waste less time.

Because of the nature of electronic resources, the library must be willing and able to budget funds for keeping access to electronic databases year after year. This is where it is important for the subject librarians, the collection development manager, the ERM, and anyone else vital to the acquisition of materials to be aware of what their patron population is and is not using. Space considerations aside, a poor choice of a book can sit on the shelf gathering dust for years before anyone even thinks of weeding it, and the prevailing opinion in libraries, when it comes to print materials, is that more is better. To an extent, that is true because it ensures that the library has materials for every taste and research venture. However, when put in a real-world context, a library with this type of policy can hurt both fiscally and physically. As noted by Chan, increased pressure has been placed on libraries to acquire electronic resources, which are costly, while budgets continue to shrink, resulting in a need for reprioritization of funds (2008). This reprioritization may not be across the board, of course, as different disciplines use electronic resources differently, most notably those disciplines in the humanities (Termens, 2008), but a collection development policy can be developed to ensure fair treatment of this issue.

Duplication of Materials

The second consideration when discussing the possibility of electronic resources is duplication of existing collections. Will the agreements cause substantial overlap with the physical collections?

In the past, duplication has not been as much of a concern in libraries as it possibly should be. There are two parts to the duplication problem however, when it comes to electronic resources.

First, there is the problem of duplicating the print versions that already exist in an institution that is making the switch to electronic resources. While duplication of these materials may begin as a purposeful alternative to ever-growing stacks, purchasing large databases with many journals included can quickly get out of hand. Furthermore, there is the duplication of abstract indexes, which may not be complete duplicates. For example, comparing the abstracts in the Physical Education Index to the included materials for SportDiscus, an analogous collection, leads to 47% overlap, according to the holdings of Western Kentucky University. This is quite the overlap, but the materials not included in the overlap are also important. Therefore, this overlap must continue to exist until agreements are made with other vendors to get digital access to the other half of the collection in PEI.

The other half of the problem is much more difficult to deal with. This problem is overlap in the virtual collections themselves. Many journals are included in aggregates by several different vendors, each with their own coverage dates, embargo rules and permissions. This can lead to the library appearing to pay for the same journal over and over again, which is a waste of precious resources. This is a product of the packages that vendors sell to the libraries.

Staff and Patron Preparation

Once the policies are in place and the cost has been considered, libraries should spare a thought to the individuals who will be using the electronic resources. Is the staff of the library prepared to teach the use of the databases? Are they prepared to let go of the physical copies of the materials? Is the patron population prepared to use the electronic resources now offered by the institution. All of the

questions regarding staff and patrons can be broken down into two categories: feelings and knowledge. Either the staff and/or patrons have feelings for print books or against electronic resources or lack knowledge about electronic resources.

There are the proponents of the physical book who may be in the library staff or their patron population. They may be nervous about the addition of electronic resources because it often means the withdrawal of physical copies from the library's collection. The first argument against a de-accession of library materials is the inability to find a physical copy of the journal article or book when needed. This may actually be an important concern – studies show that, in Australia for example, only about 50% of English-language books are available in a library, down from 70% in the 1990s (O'Connor and Jivolsky, 2009, p.122). The trend toward de-accessioning books and serials is growing, with millions of books de-accessioned over a decade, and hundreds of thousands of serials withdrawn over that same time period (O'Connor and Jivolsky, 2009). The second argument is a preference matter – some people do like physical copies of books and articles rather than digital copies. These people will probably always exist, because physical books for some, if not all, subject areas will continue to exist. Some materials are simply better accessed in print, given the current limitations of electronic devices. Third, print copies of books, and to a lesser extent, journals may need to be retained because of the historical and research value of the actual physical copy itself; there may be inscriptions from authors, evidence of unique binding practices, or writing in the margins. Art libraries especially, find that the quality of colour reproduction in electronic scans may not match the quality of the source material and would need to retain print copies of their holdings for accuracy of analysis.

Librarians' objections to electronic resources may also have to do with the ephemeral nature of the internet. Libraries' own websites change frequently, as they add more Web 2.0 technology, or migrate servers or do any other manner of things. Librarians have seen things disappear off their own web pages, which they would like to believe they have some control over. It is not surprising that some librarians may not want to rely on a virtual collection housed elsewhere and provided at someone else's discretion and based on someone else's expertise. When a library gets a printed volume, it becomes their possession. Electronic resources just do not work the same way. Add to that budgetary concerns, and it can seem like electronic resources are fleeting.

Solutions and Recommendations

It seems a little dire to think of all of the problems associated with incorporating electronic resources into a library collection, but there are solutions to the problems, and better yet, in some instances, ways to avoid the problems altogether. Working through the stated problem list, there are several things that library committees and ERMs can do.

The first problem is, of course, money. When it comes to the cost of the new electronic holdings, there are cost cutting measures that can be taken if a budget is the primary concern of the institution. Consortia are an excellent way to split the cost among many member institutions; however, there is some need for caution here if the institution is not a member of a popular consortium. Patrons who visit many libraries (especially, for example, public libraries in neighbouring towns) through the course of their lives may expect materials from the institution that they may not have without membership to the consortium. A real world example of this is the Kentucky Virtual Library (KYVL) system. Over 30,000,000 searches were performed using the KYVL system in the fiscal year 2011-2012. One hundred and seventeen public libraries are members of the system. However, those numbers do not include all the libraries in Kentucky; Kentucky has 120 counties, and several counties, including Breathitt and Ballard, are not members of the consortium that pays for and maintains KYVL. Anyone moving to either of those counties from another county in Kentucky may be dismayed by the fact that they those public libraries do not have the same access as all of the others. Furthermore, many K-12 libraries are also members of this consortium and therefore even the youngest members of the patron population may have expectations of the library. This is no doubt true in other places where there are popular consortiums. The general public is unlikely to understand without explanation that these materials are not free to the library because their access to them is free and there is no physical copy.

At the simplest level, a consortium need not be any more than a buying club, with practical benefits but no management (Termens, 2008). This definition of consortia has been both a positive and negative thing; in one respect, it is felt that consortia should not be any more than that, because it threatens the autonomy of the member institutions, but in another, the lack of guidance and consensus when it comes to the materials can be detrimental to all of the member institutions involved. A better, more organized consortium has, in theory, the power to change how vendors interact with libraries (Sanville, 1999). More active management by all members of the consortium may also reduce friction among the institutions; it has been noted that institutions in a consortium will not always use all of the materials equally (Termens, 2008). This is to be expected, because even among similar institutions, the faculty and students will have different research interests. It is important to be aware of these differences to make sure each member institution feels like they are receiving a sound return on their investment. This will ensure that the consortium continues to exist to help provide the institutions they serve with stable access to materials, a concern already partially covered in this chapter.

The second cost-cutting measure with regards to electronic resources is to take advantage of open-access journals. This is particularly advantageous in academic libraries, where communication with subject librarians and faculty outside the library can help the ERM decide on the best, most well respected open access journals available for the various majors offered at the institution. The most well-known and easily incorporated open access journals are those offered by the Directory of Open-Access Journals (DOAJ), which was founded with the express purpose of aggregating open-access journals for the use of libraries and researchers. The DOAJ defines open access journals as those, "journals that use a funding model that does not charge readers or their institutions for access," which is a commonly accepted definition (Lund University Libraries, 2012). The DOAJ maintains their collection, adding journals based on quality, access, and coverage. They only aggregate journals. Other than the DOAJ, there are other open-access journals available, run by institutions and organizations. Furthermore, universities are beginning to create repositories of works by their own faculty and students, which hold a wealth of information. Many institutions allow faculty members to upload pre-edit copies of materials that are published in journals, subject to the regulations and approval of those journals. In addition, in 2008, Congress mandated that the NIH direct researchers funded by it to submit their research to an open-access database.

The third cost-cutting measure is the librarian's old stand-by, weeding. Weeding a collection to remove unused materials is of paramount importance to keep any collection relevant and vital, but in the world of high-cost electronic resources, it can save the library thousands of dollars. The best way to weed these materials is to track use and eliminate sources that are not used. On the technical side, OpenURL is one of the main components of early usage tracking and is still widely used today. OpenURL and the addition of a link resolver can give the library reports of journal access by measuring the number of times users go through the link on the library website to the resource.

Though it was somewhat slow to catch on, many database providers and other resources, such as GoogleScholar, are now OpenURL compliant (Stewart, 2011). With OpenURL so widespread, the use of simple tracking may be all the library needs to know what resources to keep and which ones to purge. However, there is still more that can be done to track usage and help the weeding process.

Counting Online Usage of Networked Electronic Resources (COUNTER), an international standard for usage statistics, working in tandem with the Standardized Usage Statistics Harvesting Initiative (SUSHI) protocol, can generate usage statistics and is a welcome addition from both the publishing side and the library side of user access (Stewart, 2011). Like all standardization efforts, including OpenURL before it, it has taken some time for journal providers to become SUSHI and COUNTER compliant, but the trend is growing. It still takes a librarian to aggregate the data from several database providers to get a clear picture of resource usage, but even that is changing as third-party tools become available (Stewart, 2011).

Once usage statistics have been gathered for the various databases in the library's collection, it is important to factor in the inevitable duplication that occurs when libraries subscribe to multiple databases. Because of the limitations of packages available from vendors, it will not be possible to eliminate all overlap of electronic databases, but it is important that duplications be eliminated where they are possible. First, it is just good business practice not to be paying for something more than once, if it can be avoided. Second, it will be less confusing to the patron population if there are not multiple access points to materials. Finally, it will be easier in future aggregation of usage statistic data if there are not multiple access points to materials. The only exception to this rule would in the case of experimental or trial access to materials. In that case, it would be more important to keep the previous accessibility of the items in question, in the event that funding is withdrawn for the new database.

Cost-Benefit Analysis (CBA), primarily used in business, can be used to make expenditure decisions in a library setting, but because of its inherent use with money, librarians sometimes shy away from it. Librarians are not in the money-making business, though some services and their means are provided at charge, such as copiers. Instead, librarians view the benefit in cost-benefit analysis in a different light: they want to know how many times a patron will use the materials they provide; the number of uses replaces money in this scenario, but the idea is the same. Materials are expected to be used a certain amount of times for them to be worth purchasing. This does beg several questions, as posed by Linn (2009):

- How does one quantify use?
- Is all use equal?
- If there is a different level of benefit, how much of a difference is there? (p. 83)

and so on. In this case, it is up to the individual library to make those decisions. It is likely that for most resources, any usage would constitute use for the cost benefit analysis.

There is also cost in maintaining a physical collection. Materials in a physical collection must be bound (especially in the case of journals, which are typically released in a paper cover quarterly and then bound together at the end of the year in a hard cover), repaired after substantial handling, and in some cases, replaced. They could be destroyed in a natural disaster. Even a seemingly small problem, like a roof leak, could mean the destruction of whole shelves worth of material. Libraries routinely devote large portions of their budgets to the task of maintaining the collection. The cost is not just in money, either; when studying the time devoted to managing a collection (including shelving, weeding, repairs and replacements, among other activities) it came to

a difference of 45 hours versus 4,000 hours over a year, with digital, of course, being more time efficient (Gadd, 1998, p. 313).

Finally, any budget considerations should be assessed based on the future needs of the library and its programs, not past spending. In a study by Chan, which utilized a modified zero-based budget (MZBB), faculty members endorsed determining budget allocation by current submissions rather than previous expenditures (2008). The library in that study had also made a policy switch to electronic journal subscription preference, and the MZBB rewarded those departments that had made efforts to switch to electronic journals where possible (Chan, 2008). In Chan's own words,

The MZBB review required faculties to justify their future funding needs beyond the base budget by reviewing changes in curriculum/research, cost projections, organizational and environmental changes, such as, current teaching technology, increasing emphasis on electronic resources and diminishing use of printed journals. (Chan, 2008 p. 51)

This was markedly different from other models in libraries, where much of the budget is based on an assumption that any changes to departments will by necessity result in an increase in budget, if only to cover inflation, when this is not necessarily true.

Duplication of library materials is a problem that every library struggles with. However, in print form, it easy to see when materials are duplicated: they sit on the shelf next to each other with identical call numbers. A search of the library's catalogue lists the multiple items. Furthermore, and possibly most importantly, the librarian can choose to purchase a duplicate or refrain from purchasing a duplicate by itself. Even if the book comes as part of a standing order, it can be returned. The packages that vendors of electronic materials sell to libraries have been formulated with a set number of journals, and it does not matter to the vendor if a serial is already in the library's collection from another vendor. In addition, most electronic resources purchased at the beginning of an electronic resources collection will overlap some part of the current physical collection in the library. It is imperative that there is a reasonable and sustainable policy in place before overlaps occur.

Preparations must be made for complete withdraw or storage of items that are deemed superfluous, and process for this should be written into the collection development policy. With shelf space at a premium and the electronic version available to be accessed by multiple at the same time under most agreements, physical versions of journals are unnecessary. The most likely thing to happen to duplicate items is the withdrawal of the item, but some materials may have other value in their physical form or may be rare copies that the library decides to maintain.

The best, most cost effective practice for retaining print copies of duplicated resources, according to Courant and Nielson, is off-site storage, with that method costing $0.86 per year, versus $4.26 per year to keep a printed volume on the shelf (Courant and Nielsen, 2010). The library must be willing and able to acquire off-site storage. This off-site storage, while outside of the library, does not necessarily have to be out of the library's control. An excellent example of this is the Auxiliary Library Facility (ALF) at Indiana University. The ALF is a building that is used for off-site storage of materials at Indiana University that are not needed on a daily basis but have not been deemed unworthy of keeping. This auxiliary facility exists as a repository of materials removed from the larger collection, but is still circulating, thanks to a robust network of technology and staff that allow materials to move quickly among not only the various libraries at the main campus, but also all of the other campuses in the IU system. This means that the IU libraries have achieved the best of both worlds; because the ALF is only accessed by staff, it can be packed tighter and all the way to its ceiling, and yet all of those materials are available to IU affiliates and no doubt their ILL partners.

Dealing with duplication within the electronic format is a more complicated matter. There will always be some duplication of materials in the electronic format as long as there are various vendors from which to get the materials. In fact, there is sometimes duplication of materials within different databases from the same vendor. For example, there are many journals that are cross-listed under the different EBSCOhost databases, with each record listing its own coverage dates. The best practice for trying to manage this problem is to be aware of what materials the library is already paying for from other vendors and making ever attempt to negotiate with the vendors for less overlap. Some overlap can even be a good thing, because it leaves room for future negotiations with vendors.

Finally, once the materials have been chosen and paid for, the administration must address any and all concerns from the people who will deal with these electronic resources. Addressing the concerns of faculty, staff, and patrons, especially in a large university setting where funding comes in part from donations, can be daunting. No one wants to create an ungrateful patron population that will not support its library. This can put librarians into a hard situation however, when it comes to de-accessioning print materials in favor of electronic resources. These concerns were mentioned earlier in the chapter, but they need not stymie the responsible withdrawal of materials.

Preparing faculty and/or staff is the most important thing an administrator can do for its library when electronic resources are introduced. While the patron population will largely deal with reference and instruction librarians to learn about the electronic resources available in the library, staff will have to learn about the electronic resources from the individuals who know the most about them: the electronic resources manager and the collection development department. It is imperative that reference and instruction librarians are not only told about the materials when they first become accessible, but also kept abreast of any situations that might arise with the electronic resources, including scheduled downtimes and outages. From there, reference and instruction librarians, with the help of the ERM, can create teaching aids for the patron population.

Once they are comfortable with using the new electronic resources, the ERM and collection development staff can confront the issue of librarians and patrons who want to keep the duplicated and unnecessary print versions of materials. The first argument for print proponents, the inability to find a physical copy of journal articles and books when needed has three solutions, all of which should be applied in order to best serve the patron population. The most important part of the process is having strong interlibrary loan connections that can be used in the advent that access to materials is lost. The second part is to never de-accession materials to which there are no other access routes. This protects not only the patrons of the institution making the withdrawal but also all other institutions that may rely on the existence of that material in the library; this will account for much of the disappearance of holdings from libraries altogether. This also includes notifying ILL staff of loss of access, especially regarding temporary outages that may not be reflected in the library catalogue or their independent systems. Finally, if the institution desiring to withdraw a book is the holder of the last known copy of a book or serial, they should make an effort to preserve the material themselves, or, failing that, give the books to an institution capable of and willing to preserve the item. The second problem, the matter of preference, must be taken care of based on the population being served by the institution in question. Art libraries, for example, may prefer to use books despite their price because of the detail in the printed images. Some nuances may simply not show up in a digitized copy. Those books that are deemed worthy to keep in their print form because of the uniqueness of the copy should be preserved by institutions invested in their historical value. They become more than books, prized not only for their

intended informational use but also for what they can tell researchers about the past. Other subject areas may have similar concerns because of the quality of digitization of their materials in the past. Early digitization of materials did not occur at the same quality that newer digitization has, and may have been, in some cases, a digitization of a low-quality scan. An effort should be made to find adequate electronic copies and provide the staff with access to said copies prior to removing material from the collection. Communication with faculty and staff about arrangements for these problems will make the transition to electronic resources smoother.

The easiest way to assure patrons and faculty that materials will continue to be available to them, and thus ease their fears, is to review policies on perpetual access of journals. Unfortunately, libraries have not shown a strong commitment to bargaining for perpetual access rights. A survey done by Carr (2010) showed that while libraries say they are committed to securing perpetual access rights to the materials to which they subscribe, they do not bargain for them, reaffirming the results found by Stemper and Barribeau (2005). This is a mistake. While perpetual access rights can be costly, they will do a lot to soothe the fears of faculty and patrons who are concerned about materials disappearing from the collection. Libraries should ask themselves what they think the future of their library will look like, before they give away those rights. Other concerns about perpetual access rights include the vagueness of wording when they manage to secure any perpetual access rights. Stemper and Barribeau noted some of the vaguer wording, including this excerpt from AIP:

AIP will use reasonable efforts to retain in an archive all electronic information published by the American Institute of Physics. (p.102)

This begs the question what "reasonable efforts" are. Also, sometimes the ability to retain such an archive is out of the original publisher's hands, because journals often change publishers. These new publishers will have their own restrictions which override the original agreements. This problem is often not addressed at all (Stemper and Barribeau, 2005). However, all is not lost. There are some publishers who do address the problem, and are willing to commit some vague language toward maintaining original agreements in the event of a buy-out. Walters suggests some criteria for sustainable access based on the criteria at St. Lawrence University: "provisions for permanent library retention of content," "the university must participate through a library consortium," and the "provider must demonstrate a commitment" to perpetual access (p. 302.) Of these criteria, the provisions for content retention are the most important concept for a library to consider. From there, the library can push for provider commitment and consortium involvement.

Strong existing collection development policies are imperative to success in electronic resources management. Review and update of those policies should be undertaken before agreements are made with vendors, so that faculty and support staff can prepare the physical collection, i.e., withdraw items that will be replaced by the electronic resource or move them to storage. A study by Manrum and Pozzebon (2012), of Middle Tennessee State University, found that, "the average completeness of each [studied] policy was 41 percent (p. 111)." Their criteria included policy standards about currency, authoritative standards, scope and depth, cost, licensing issues, termination rights, and interlibrary loan abilities, with the completeness of policy heavily skewed toward issues that also concern physical collections (Manrum and Pozzebon, 2012). Collection development librarians should take this time to decide what access should be available for the duplicate; storage without easy access capabilities can turn into a bigger headache than it is worth. Withdrawal of materials, however, is not the end of the world and can sometimes lead to other opportunities for the library. For example, the addition of an information commons, which

will lead to better access and use of electronic resources, may require downsizing of a physical reference collection.

The ERM and a collection development/acquisitions representative should review the policies regarding the new electronic resources with the faculty and staff responsible for various areas of the collection. They should also be able to present a clear idea of usage statistics for existing materials and project usage estimates for the new electronic materials, bolstering the cost benefit analysis previously discussed. This individual consideration should not stop at the staff. The patron population should be made aware of the introduction of electronic resources, including what materials are offered, what physical material may be removed, and how best to access the new materials. For institutions merely expanding their electronic resources, this may not be of utmost importance, but even then, it should still be a consideration. No one wants to spend money on a new database that no one knows about.

FUTURE RESEARCH DIRECTIONS

The way to go from here may not always be clear, as more technologies are added to libraries each and every day. It is not even possible to say with certainty that patrons will use the electronic resources given to them by our public and academic library. However, there are some things that can be kept in mind while turning an eye to the future.

The costs and benefits of electronic resources will always fluctuate. While the monetary cost, for example, of databases may continue to go up, the costs of providing access to patrons may start to go down. E-readers are becoming more affordable with each passing day, opening the experience up to patrons who might have thought they could not own such a device. This means that there could be fewer devices for the library to own and maintain. Consortia too, may grow, as well as the number and popularity of open access journals. These ideas need to be studied, modeled, and researched, with the data available for all libraries to access so that they can make an informed decision on including electronic resources in their collection.

CONCLUSION

Because of the cost of electronic resources, it is not a step that should be taken lightly. It may not even be a step in the right direction for many libraries. This chapter asks the questions that every librarian involved in electronic resources management should ask themselves before resources are purchased; while all problems may not be foreseeable, there are many problems that are foreseeable and can be prevented or solved before they become too big.

There will be changes to the patron population. As discussed, the ideal patron may become more or less technologically literate over time. They may also become differently technologically literate – meaning that while they may be adept at various technologies, the technology of electronic databases or e-readers may be foreign to them. It is important that libraries do not assume that their patron population, and their abilities, are staying stable over time. Periodic assessment of patron populations, at all levels, should be conducted, even if it is as simple as anecdotal data provided by reference librarians. Though computers and other electronic devices are more widespread than ever, many devices are designed so that individuals are given information; they do not have to find it. That is where the librarian's role lays: in the finding of specific information among the millions of pieces of data thrown at humans daily.

REFERENCES

Carr, P. L. (2010). The commitment to securing perpetual journal access a survey of academic research libraries. *Library Resources & Technical Services*, *55*(1), 4–16. doi:10.5860/lrts.55n1.4.

Chan, G. R. Y. C. (2008). Aligning collections budget with program priorities: A modified zero-based approach. *Library Collections, Acquisitions & Technical Services*, *32*, 46–52. doi:10.1016/j.lcats.2008.06.001.

Chandel, A. S., & Saikia, M. (2012). Challenges and opportunities of e-resources. *Annals of Library and Information Studies*, *59*, 148–154.

Courant, P. N., & Nielsen, M. B. (2010). On the cost of keeping a book. In *The Idea of Order: Transforming Research Collections for 21st Century Scholarship*. Washington, DC: CLIR Publication..

Gadd, E. (1998). Comparing paper and electronic short loan collections. *Library Management*, *19*(5), 311–317. doi:10.1108/01435129810218492.

Linn, M. Jr. (2009). Cost-benefit analysis: A disparagement of its misuse and misexplanation. *The Bottom Line: Managing Library Finances*, *22*(3), 82–85. doi:10.1108/08880450910999640.

Lund University Libraries. (2011, November 26). *Directory of open access journals: FAQs*. Retrieved November 10, 2012 from http://www.doaj.org/doaj?func=loadTempl&templ=about&uiLanguage=en

Malnig, A. (2008). Libraries march toward a digital future. *Seybold Report: Analyzing Publishing Technologies*, *8*(9), 8.

Mangrum, S., & Pozzebon, M. E. (2012). Use of collection development policies in electronic resource management. *Collection Building, 31*(3), 108–114. doi:10.1108/01604951211243506.

Murdock, D. (2010). Relevance of electronic resource management systems to hiring practices for electronic resources personnel. *Library Collections, Acquisitions & Technical Services, 34*, 25–42. doi:10.1016/j.lcats.2009.11.001.

Noh, Y. (2012). A study measuring the performance of electronic resources in academic libraries. *Aslib Proceedings, 64*(2), 134–153. doi:10.1108/00012531211215169.

O'Connor, S., & Jilovsky, C. (2009). Approaches to the storage of low use and last copy research materials. *Library Collections, Acquisitions & Technical Services, 32*, 121–126. doi:10.1016/j.lcats.2008.08.001.

Pan, D., & Howard, Z. (2009). Reorganizing a technical services division using collaborative evidence based information practice at Auraria library. *Evidence Based Library And Information Practice, 4*(4), 88–94.

Roncevic, M. (2004). Introduction. *Library Journal, 129*(5).

Sanville, T. (1999). Use levels and new models for consortial purchasing f electronic journals. *Library Consortium Management, 1*(3/4), 47–58. doi:10.1108/14662769910305740.

Shelburne, W. A. (2009). E-book usage in an academic library: Attitudes and behaviors. *Library Collections, Acquisitions & Technical Services, 33*, 59–72. doi:10.1016/j.lcats.2009.04.002.

Sprague, N., & Hunter, B. (2009). Assessing e-books: Taking a closer look at e-book statistics. *Library Collections, Acquisitions & Technical Services, 32*, 150–157. doi:10.1016/j.lcats.2008.12.005.

Stemper, J., & Barribeau, S. (2005). Perpetual access to electronic journals: A survey of one academic research library's licenses. *Library Resources & Technical Services, 50*(2), 91–109.

Stewart, C. (2011). Keeping track of it all: the challenge of measuring digital resource usage. *Journal of Academic Librarianship, 37*(2), 174–176. doi:10.1016/j.acalib.2011.01.002.

Termens, M. (2008). Looking below the surface: The use of electronic journals by the members of a library consortium. *Library Collections, Acquisitions & Technical Services, 32*, 76–85. doi:10.1016/j.lcats.2008.05.004.

William, W. H. (2003). Criteria for replacing print journals with online journal resources: The importance of sustainable access. *Library Resources & Technical Services, 48*(4), 300–304.

ADDITIONAL READING

Baudino, F., & Northwest Missouri State, U. (2011). *Brick and click libraries: An academic library symposium (Maryville, Missouri, November 4, 2011)*. Online Submission.

Brumley, R. (2009). *Electronic collection management forms, policies, procedures, and guidelines manual with CD-ROM*. New York: Neal-Schuman Publishers..

Bullis, D. R., & Smith, L. (2008). Looking back, moving forward in the digital age: a review of the collection management and development literature, 2004–8. *Library Resources & Technical Services, 55*(4), 205–220. doi:10.5860/lrts.55n4.205.

Cole, J., & Jones, W. (2012). *E-Serials: Publishers, libraries, users, and standards* (2nd ed.). Hoboken: Taylor and Francis..

Davidson, C., & Kyrillidou, M. (2010). The value of electronic resources: Measuring the impact of networked electronic services (MINES for Libraries®) at the Ontario Council of University Libraries. *Research Library Issues: A Bimonthly Report from ARL, CNI, and SPARC*, 271, 41–47. Retrieved December 15, 2013 from http://www.arl.org/resources/pubs/rli/archive/rli271.shtml.

Fieldhouse, M., & Marshall, A. (2012). *Collection development in the digital age*. London: Facet Publishing..

Fourie, I. (2012). Collection development in the digital age. *The Electronic Library*, *30*(5), 749–750.

Gregory, V. L., & Hanson, A. (2006). *Selecting and managing electronic resources: A how-to-do-it manual for librarians*. New York: Neal-Schuman Publishers..

Hoffmann, F. W., & Wood, R. J. (2005). *Library collection development policies: Academic, public, and special libraries*. Lanham, Md: Scarecrow Press..

Hughes, L. M. (2012). *Evaluating and measuring the value, use and impact of digital collections*. London: Facet Publishing..

Kovacs, D. K., & Robinson, K. L. (2004). *The Kovacs guide to electronic library collection development: Essential core subject collections, selection criteria, and guidelines*. New York: Neal-Schuman Publishers..

Lee, S. D. (2002). *Electronic collection development: a practical guide*. New York: Neal-Schuman Publishers..

Lee, S. H. (2012). *Electronic resources and collection development*. Hoboken: Taylor and Francis..

Lee, S. H. (2012). *Digital information and knowledge management: New opportunities for research libraries*. Hoboken: Taylor and Francis..

Lesk, M. (2012). A personal history of digital libraries. *Library Hi Tech*, *30*(4), 592–603. doi:10.1108/07378831211285077.

Linn, M. (2011). Cost-benefit analysis: Examples. *The Bottom Line: Managing Library Finances*, *24*(1), 68–72. doi:10.1108/08880451111142123.

Lupton, A., & Salmon, M. (2012). MULER: building an electronic resource management (ERM) solution at York University. *Journal of Library Innovation*, *3*(2), 105–122.

Nisonger, T. E. (2003). *Evaluation of library collections, access, and electronic resources: A literature guide and annotated bibliography*. Westport, Conn: Libraries Unlimited..

Novak, D. D., Paulos, A., & St. Clair, G. (2011). Data-driven budget reductions: a case study. *The Bottom Line: Managing Library Finances*, *24*(1), 24–34. doi:10.1108/08880451111142015.

Payne, L. (2007). *Library storage facilities and the future of print collections in North America*. Dublin, Ohio: OCLC..

Price, A. C. (2009). How to make a dollar out of fifteen cents: Tips for electronic collection development. *Collection Building*, *28*(1), 31–34. doi:10.1108/01604950910928493.

Su, D. (2007). *Collection development issues in the online environment*. New York: Haworth Information Press..

White, M., & Sanders, S. (2009). E-resources management: How we positioned our organization to implement an electronic resources management system. *Journal of Electronic Resources Librarianship*, *21*(3-4), 183–191. doi:10.1080/19411260903445883.

Wikoff, K. (2012). *Electronics resources management in the academic library: A professional guide*. Santa Barbara, Calif: Libraries Unlimited..

Zambare, A., Casey, A. M., Fierst, J., Ginsburg, D., O'Dell, J., & Peters, T. (2009). Assuring access: One library's journey from print to electronic only subscriptions. *Serials Review*, *35*(2), 70–74. doi:10.1016/j.serrev.2009.03.002.

KEY TERMS AND DEFINITIONS

Aggregator: A company that organizes and consolidates various journals and/or databases into collections for libraries to purchase.

Collection Development: The act of gathering materials for a library which align with the library's expressed mission.

Consortium: A network of institutions that pool monetary resources to purchase access to materials.

Cost-Benefit Analysis: A comparison of what it takes to purchase and maintain materials versus the usefulness of the resource.

Electronic Resources: Library holdings designed to be accessed in a digital format.

ERM: Staff member whose primary responsibility is to maintain the digital holdings of a library.

Off-Site Storage: A place to keep library materials that are not withdrawn but do not have a place in the library's main building.

Perpetual Access: The right of a library to continue accessing already purchased materials after an agreement with a vendor has expired.

Chapter 3
Convergence towards Excellence Diversity:
Mapping the Field of E-Resources Emerging Dynamics

Paula Ochôa
Nova University of Lisbon, Portugal

Leonor Gaspar Pinto
Nova University of Lisbon, Portugal

ABSTRACT

This chapter extends current discussions about excellence and proposes a look beyond the dominant line of e-resources research where transition cycles in information management, knowledge management, competences management, and performance management are the multi-contextual value creators for individuals and organizations. This is done by an extensive review of European policies (single information market, agenda for culture) in two steps: first, excellence triggers are analyzed, discussing digital agenda and consumer culture. Next, an integrated model of e-resources excellence management is presented. It locates the argument for the importance of convergence in excellence diversity where e-resources values are uniquely and contextually interpreted, requiring understanding, and assesses customer consumption processes as an experiential, social, and cultural phenomenon. A variety of informational behaviors, skills, and activities is the measure of the complexity of personal values possibilities and of excellence framework development, maturity, and sustainability.

INTRODUCTION

E-resources[1] have gained a foothold in library practices worldwide; however, emerging changes in excellence models and in the structure of information use are challenging the traditional methods of achieving strategic organizational benefits. One of the key questions facing e-resources managers is how to combine existing skills and value perceived by users and other stakeholders to greatly increase the impact of these practices on excellence results in the new paradigm of digital transition.

DOI: 10.4018/978-1-4666-4761-9.ch003

Tracing the development of library assessment methods helps researchers to understand better the performance cycles and the evolution of quality management theories and models. Results orientation, customer orientation, leadership, process management, people development and involvement, training, partnerships and corporate social responsibility are convergence concepts that maintain its topicality and relevance. Among the emerging themes, the European Foundation for Quality Management (EFQM, 2003, 2012) has emphasized creativity and innovation, sustainability, organizational agility, risk management and promotion of products and services.

Current models tend to analyze reciprocal effects between technological issues and organizational issues without a clear focus on transitions phases. Based on the concept of Excellence and the analysis of library impacts, this chapter aims to present the mapping of the field of e-resources emerging dynamics that cross the European Agenda for Culture and the Digital Agenda (2010-2020). This contribution is anchored in an Evidence-Based Librarianship research line developed in Portugal since 2007 (Ochôa & Pinto, 2007).

The chapter is organized in two main sections; each of them examines the main challenges faced by the current excellence concept: the convergent/divergent directions and the dynamics of e-resources field. The context of analysis is focused on how e-resources react and contribute to the accelerated changes of a knowledge-based economy in the European Union (EU). Based on institutional European sources and on an e-resources management (ERM) literature review, we focused on documents that critically present the ongoing change. They cover a time span of twelve years (2000-2012) and respond to four specific selection criteria:

1. Studies on the evaluation of e-resources impact in libraries.
2. Critical studies that explore ERM problems or good practices.
3. Current investigations about Excellence.
4. Comparative information (studies that report information to one or more scientific fields).

The chapter suggests the necessity of consolidating a theoretical framework that can support and explore new visions in libraries quality management.

We categorized two e-resources excellence triggers - *Digital Agenda* and *Consumer Culture* - within two dynamics – convergence and diversity and five emergent excellence fields: *Knowledge and skills in quality management, Perception and trust, Information behavior, Quality of life,* and *Society and economy*. E-resources convergence and diversity dynamics are considered in an integrated model where transition points are highlighted: *e-skills, e-consumption, e-value* and *e-excellence.*

As the growth of evidences about the ways consumption practices impact on e-resources use continues to accelerate, it is appropriate to reflect on the directions this movement is taking. A multitude of "excellences" is now possible, creating new models and assumptions regarding e-resources, providing the context for the recommendations and action steps outlined at the end of this chapter.

CONVERGENT/DIVERGENT DIRECTIONS: ROOTS FOR E-RESOURCES EXCELLENCE

The concept of *Excellence* is closely tied to the development of quality management theories and models and to performance evaluation dynamics in organizations. According to EFQM's business model (EFQM, 2012), the main concepts are focused on results orientation principles, leadership, processes management, development and involvement of people, continuous training, partnerships and social responsibility. Organizational maturity and sustainability of results pose new issues related to new Excellence meanings and perspectives Integrated, balanced, multidimensional, comprehensive and holistic models are frameworks used as tools to reach an excellence stage. However, and not surprisingly, many organizations, public and private, fail to develop performance measurement approaches that address all the criteria of standard excellence. It is the interface between measurement, management and leadership that is crucial in ensuring that performance measures drive value creation. For too long, management initiatives have resulted in the organizations meeting the needs of the respective model (ISO 9000; Investors in people; EFQM Excellence Model; Balanced Score card, Servqual) whilst loosing the opportunity to develop skills and adding value through people knowledge.

Discussions about Excellence variety are growing with particular interest in the investigation of several themes: *quality management models and its forms of development and implementation in organizations* (Jones, Kinnell & Usherwood, 2000; Oakland, 2003; Di Domenico, 2004; Cullen, 2005; Truccolo, et al., 2005; Wilson & Town, 2006; Herget & Hierl, 2007; Saarti & Juntunen, 2011, Borbely, 2011); *main tendencies about economic value*[i] (Aabø, 2011; Almauk, 2012); *leadership styles, benchmarking initiatives and good practices* (Staes & Thijs, 2010; Poll, 2007; Laitinen, 2012); *public policies about performance evaluation* (Bouckaert, 2012; Pinto & Ochôa, 2012); *organizational learning* (Senge, 2006, Ochôa & Pinto, 2006); *critical factors of digital success that promote Excellence* (Huijboom & Van der Broek, 2011; Gonçalves, Moreira, Fox & Watson, 2007; Plum, Franklin, Kyrillidou, Roebuck & Davis, 2010); *evidence-based management* (Town, 2011; Tanner & Deegan, 2012; Rankin, 2012); and *results and impacts to consolidate new and convergent contexts of Excellence* (Streatfield & Markless, 2009; Broady-Preston & Lobo, 2011; Poll, 2012; Tenopir, 2012).

Libraries assessment has been mainly about quality rather than value (Town, 2011) and excel-

lence (Ochôa & Pinto, 2012). After the first performance measurement revolution, a second one is needed and will happen soon. New measures linked to institutional objectives are needed and must be communicated (ACRL, 2012): long term holistic and coherent measures that assess societal benefit, educational impact and intangible assets resources, like relational capital, organizational capital and human and intellectual capital (Corrall, 2011), transferable skills, collections, services, research management, research information, meta content (Town, 2011) and user-defined value metrics of electronic resources (Chew, Stemper, Lilyard & Schoenborn, 2012). Knowledge management and competences management are considered important components of organizational strategy and pillars of success and they are a welcome shift in thinking about these issues.

Measures of success are faceted across several categories (Tanner & Deegan, 2012):

- **Users, Audience and Stakeholders:** How ERM benefits them.
- **Innovation and Development:** Evaluating the value of digitization in terms of how it enables the users and providers to do new and innovative actions (new research and teaching methods, web 2.0 type interactions, new modes of collection development and curation)
- **Internal Processes:** Evaluates how the digitization strategy provides value to the way the organization operates.
- **Financial Benefits and Outcomes:** ERM evaluation.

Value map relating library behaviors to end user benefits is one of the proposals that highlight value. In the case of the University of York Plan[2], the strategic objectives are clearly rooted on *Excellence, Internationalization, Inclusivity* and *Sustainability*. Value mapping goes beyond performance measurement and acts as a performance management of Excellence, using and supporting assessments, as well as planning, decision making, communication, facilitation and evaluation. Librarian's commitment to service and professional values are important values in the digitalization market (Jenkins, 2012).

Within the digital environment, Excellence is not seen any more as a distinction, but as a primary condition of positive value to be remembered, used and re-used by people. Diversity of value chains and multiple uses constitute the basic field of Excellence in virtual economy[3], characterized by multiple ways of *convergence* and *hybridity* that highlight complexity, interdependence and transition and are associated with *flux* and *in-betweenness* (Chadwick, 2011) between technological, theoretical, cultural, political and social areas.

In contrast with previous decades, Excellence is now a new and emerging phenomenon, not only with organizational impacts but also with strong emphases on several transition moments. This is an interdisciplinary trend (Management, Sociology, Information Science, Communication, and Marketing) that studies the confluence of different variables refocusing on boundaries. One of those studies is concerned with *convergence culture* (Jenkins, 2006) and information environments thinking hybridization as a process of integration and fragmentation, particularly during periods of unusual transition, contingency and negotiability (Chadwick, 2011). These periods or cycles require a different understanding of how the new cycles work.

Defining the nature of transition moments in this cycles is also important but difficult. Current literature on digital services management suggests that the Excellence continuum must be discussed in other terms. According to Hobohm (2012, pp.8), "we find a concept of quality which indeed stems from the warehouse paradigm and is not rooted in modern customer-oriented quality management".

E-resources Excellence is influenced by social determinants, such as social inequalities that are (re)gaining public interest and drawing the attention of Social Science researchers to its global nature. In that sense, the notion of *global inequalities* would have to be considered when further exploring the new cycles problems, namely by placing them within the context of the inequalities of human development, the relations between national and global inequalities, the new global classes, the objective and subjective inequalities in the world today and the issues of social justice and public policies at world level (Costa, 2012).

The first group of inequalities that needs to be addressed is the digital divide due to its capacity to reduce the potential of the labor force and innovation. In Europe, it is still a problem, presenting gaps between Northern and Southern, Western and Eastern Europe and gaps between population groups (Van Dijk, 2008, 2012), which two types of policies have tried to solve on the last fifteen years. The digital divide appeared as a policy problem for governments during the second half of the 1990s with two emphases: stressing physical access (first phase); and enacting the principles of universal and public access and of universal service and highlighting skills, usage and motivational access (second phase). The long-term strategy i2010 gives a strong emphasis to full participation and provides people with basic digital competence.

In this context, three facets of eInclusion are highlighted: the *access divide* (gap between those with and without access); the *usage divide* (primary digital divide, those who have access but are non-users) and the *divide stemming from quality of use* (*secondary digital divide*, based on differentials in participation rates of those people who have access and are users). The problem is framed by terms like computer, information/multimedia literacy and computer skills or informational capital. According to Van Dijk (2008), usage determinants and gaps can be measured in four ways: *usage time*, *usage applications* (number and diversity), *broadband/narrowband use*; and *active/creative use*. Despite its image of being interactive, the contemporary promises of the Web 2.0 and the rise of participatory media perspectives, most Internet usage is passive and consuming. Active contributions consist of publishing a personal website, creating a weblog, posting a contribution on an online bulletin board, news group or community and exchanging music and video files. A growing pirate culture is being reported in Europe, with several ways of access and use.

Many investigations conclude that all familiar social and cultural differences in society are reflected in computer and Internet use, being reinforced by them. Differences of skills and preferences are becoming more important for society. This aspect implies more focused policy options.

Six policy areas for inclusion are defined: older workers and elderly people; the geographically digital divide; eAccessibility and usability; digital literacy; cultural diversity in relation to inclusion; inclusive eGovernment. In all of them, e-resources can be considered operational, informational or strategical options towards excellence.

The following types of resources frequently figure in the digital divide (Van Dijk, 2012):

- Temporal (having time to use digital media)
- Material (possession and income)
- Mental (technical ability, motivation)
- Social (having a social network to assist in using digital media)
- Cultural (status and linking of being in the world of digital media)

Smiers (2012) identified six classes of divides that might put at risk the realization of democratic debate and confrontation, including in the digital field:

1. **Digital Divide:** It concerns the fact that many people are excluded from the use of digital tools.
2. **Punitive Divide:** It is another form of exclusion; industries are trying to persuade the authorities to punish people and organiza-

tions that violate copyright by cutting off their Internet connections. Nevertheless, the European Parliament has declared that a person's Internet connection may only be cut off following a court ruling.

3. **Democratic Divide:** It prevents people from fully participating in democratic decision-making and all the steps related to it. The democratic divide can also come about when the so-called net neutrality is abandoned.
4. **Information Divide:** Digitization can help facilitate the efforts of whistleblowers to make public many facts and data that were secret.
5. **Society-Related Divide:** It is about past and present tensions, misunderstandings that prevent people from neighboring societies from living together in virtual harmony. Digitization can enable stereotypes to be reduced but, on the other hand, it may become stronger. Racial and political tensions are emerging.
6. **Critical Divide:** It relates to the importance of having feedback from observers who critically describe and evaluate what happens in the Internet. Substantial parts of the population do not benefit from the results of critical studies and, therefore, do not learn how to deal responsibly with their communication methods in Internet.

In order to make these communications more democratic, Smiers (2012) outlined that a couple of paradigm shifts should be implemented: using competition and anti-trust policies to make market domination of cultural conglomerates substantially smaller and ending the system of intellectual property rights. The future of global cultural relations is also an important issue to Leadbeater (2012, pp.31). In his vision, we will have many varieties of digital clouds, commercial, social or public, either open or closed: "Commercial clouds are either enabled or managed and supported by a commercial provider, who might also mine data from the cloud and provide tools for people to contribute. Flickr's clouds of photographs would probably fit into the commercial cloud sector. Google and Amazon are offering commercial cloud services. The World Digital Library, on the other hand, which is being created by government-funded libraries around the world, is prime example of a public cloud. Wikipedia is a social cloud: it has mainly been created through voluntary effort".

The digital cloud will change culture, creativity and the relationships between them, forming the *cloud culture equation, a vast cultural eruption embedded in international cultural relations*: "new stores of digital culture artifacts will become more accessible in more ways to more people that ever. More people will be able to explore these digital stores to find things of value to them. (....) the more people that see a collection of content, from more vantage points, the more likely they are to find value in it, probably value that small team of professional curators may have missed.

Cloud culture should be a rare and delicate mix: more decentralized, plural and collaborative; less hierarchical, proprietary and money, the boundaries between amateur and professional, consumer and producer, grassroots and mainstream are breached, if not erased. Open source software communities and collaborative science, based on shared data sources and open access journals, point the way what will be possible in other areas" (Leadbeater, 2012, pp.34).

To avoid threats of a corporate control of the clouds, it will be necessary to focus on maintaining a diversity of funding for the development of web platforms, so that some will be social and public, as well as on ensuring that people have a anti-monopoly cloud based services, keeping open spaces for experimentation on the web and defending net neutrality.

In this scenario, perhaps libraries will have a new role[4]: to support freedom of cultural expression alongside the curation of cultural artifacts and digital collections. The movement of convergence between libraries, archives and museums will provide new services in the networked information environment and a stronger management of electronic resources as trusted sources, increasing social responsibility and value for citizenship. The paths to this convergence are multiple and depend in part upon the evolution of exploitation and management of information by governments, business organizations, non-profit organizations and people. Excellence is in a period of transition and it is essential to sustain the valuable features of e-resources and the key players that support information core values and diversity of practices.

MAPPING THE FIELD OF E-RESOURCES DYNAMICS

The definition of what e-resources fields are has evolved significantly along with digital movement transitions. ERM presents new challenges to library professionals in terms of administering complex hardware and software, but also new services, collections and competition from other information service providers. Preservation and access, meeting information needs, expansion of services, the blurring of customary boundaries, new possibilities for cooperation between libraries and organizational challenges are the main issues discussed (Jenkins, 2012; Johnson, S., *et al.*, 2012[5]). In this scenario, the potential levels of interaction to access, adapt and create knowledge are ERM strong points. One weak point is the general absence of user-centered methods of evaluation. Conway (2010) proposes to address the problem of funding and demonstrating value for digital preservation initiatives through better Quality Control processes for textual e-resources and Mullen (2010) advocates for measures of digital quality in collection development.

Current developments must be scanned with specific areas of excellence triggers and important turning points being highlighted and discussed. We have developed a new framework by drawing on the European Agenda for Culture and the Digital Agenda (2010-2020). Therefore, we would like to argue that these dynamics can contribute to demonstrate that these dimensions help answering questions such as *What will be the impacts of e-resources in Excellence concepts and consumer culture?* and *What will be the impacts on libraries of new focuses on consumer behavior?*

The triggers for Excellence considered here are consumer culture and the Digital Agenda.

Consumer Culture

Consumer culture emerged in the 1920s in the United States, defining individuals acting as consumers through the acquisition of products (Zwass, 2010). Consumer role in the market is changing[6] in post-modern European societies. Individuals are on a never-ending identity quest to define the meaning of their lives. Communities foster consumer's strength and ability converging to what is termed *Generation C* (Content - or digital) in a "mainstream trend, one that keeps giving, with millions of consumers uploading their creative endeavors online, and tens of millions of others enjoying the fruits of their creativity (…) with (particularly younger) consumers expecting to create anything they want as long as it is digital, and in order to facilitate their customization and personalization of many physical goods, the next frontier will be to digitally design products from scratch before turning them into physical goods" (Cova & Dalli, 2009, pp.5).

According to Zwass (2010), the continual emergence of new business models assembling and incorporating various aspects of co-creation points up its economic importance. Consumers perceive their own empowerment and influence in organizations and this self-perception is evolving and must be studied: "the issue of the distribution of the economic value produced by the co-creators is (…) a weighty one that will require further research and, perhaps, new practices" (Zwass,

2010, pp. 38). All the organizations compete for attention and convenience (Connaway, Dickey & Radford, 2011).

In this context, value, in a customer-dominant logic, is formed in multiple visible and invisible spaces, linked to the life of customer, with multiple dynamic time frames and multiple levels. Value is personal, but it can also be collective and shared. It is the customer that determines what value is. As Voima, Heinonen and Strandik (2010, pp. 133) say "the internal and external contextual layers of the customer cannot explain her thoughts and behavior and changes in it. During the same day the customer may among others take the role of a parent, legal advisor, co-worker and a mentor. The biological states in life are continuously changing (age, status, family structure, etc.) together with the mental state of the customer (education, personal history, roles, etc.) which influences how the customer thinks, feels and acts."

Two types of challenges perspectives are decisive for ERM (*vid.* Table 1):

Within e-resources consumption several research questions should therefore be tackled: *What is the role of e-resources in life context? What influence does this type of consume has on Excellence management? When is Excellence perceived and determined by the customer? What are the interrelations between Excellence and informational behavior, e-skills, e-consumption and e-value?*

The self-service perspective creates other implications: users want to use collections as a whole, mining and organizing the information in novel ways, interacting with collections of artifacts or with data corpus. It will be necessary to provide high-powered workstations with analytical tools for researchers to work with e-resources with access by licenses or agreements and take analysis outputs (Johnston, 2012).

In this perspective, evidence must be obtained through literature reviews, personal contacts and organizational contacts, statistical measures and

Table 1. Provider/customer-dominant challenges

Provider-Dominant Challenges	Customer-Dominant Challenges
How does the customer consume the service? What are the service models? How should the service be designed? How many the service process be developed? How does the customer want to co-create? How is the library collection used? How do people interested seek information? What are stakeholder's perceptions of the library?	How does the customer live life? What routines does the customer have? What delights the customer? What does the customer enjoy and have an interest for?
How/why does the customer make decisions? What influences the customer's choice of service/distribution channel? Why is the customer unsatisfied?	What are the internal and external living contexts of the customer? What is the mobility of the customer? What is the general life situation of the customer?
When and how does the customer want to be served? What is accessible? What local resources can individual libraries make accessible? What place does the library occupy in the information network and in the network of this community?	What is the customer's personal time-frame?
How does the customer behave? What role does the customer have in the service process? Who influences the customer's decision making process? How may the customer be segmented? How has the digital resource delivered a positive change in a defined group of people's live? How can users contribute to collections? How can libraries surface information about existing collection materials relevant to emerging fields? How can automated processes facilitate the development of globally accessible collections?	Who is the customer? What role does the customer have in life? How is the customer's social life structured? What does the customer believe in? What customer life profiles may be identified? What aspects of information seeking (selection, accessibility and use of e-resources) are considered inconvenient and hard to use?

Based on Voima, Heinonen and Strandik (2010, pp. 134); ACRL (2012); Tanner & Deegan, (2012); Corrall & Roberts (2012)

evaluations, but also by listening to users (*narrative approaches*) to personalize data. Another method used in knowledge management, especially effective for capturing tacit knowledge, is storytelling as an organizational story (Dalkir, 2005; Cortez & Colon-Aguirre, 2009). According to Tanner and Deegan (2012, pp.40), "These narratives add clarity to those benefits and provide a sense of the way digitization actually creates and delivers changes".

Digital Agenda

As a common and consistent long-term strategy (2010-2020), Digital Agenda is focused on concrete actions, instruments and principles to consolidate information society in EU. Information, authentic data, validated content and critical

mass are being considered drivers for economic impact, research innovation and social benefits, underpinning competitiveness and a knowledge economy, allowing the rapid sharing of findings through online publication, dealing with multiple technologies, source types, formats, methodologies and appealing to multiple audiences and uses. Evidence can be identified through literature (published reports, policy statements, survey results, statistical measures and evaluations), web searches, personal knowledge and organizational contacts, detecting key areas where user engagement has been particularly useful and the successes and challenges of pro-actively involving users. People and place, global and local are key words for libraries all around the world.

One of the most powerful triggers is open data, affecting the way that organizations value data, posing challenges for information management and protection of confidentiality. As Berners-Lee and Shadbolt (2011) pointed out "data is the new raw material of the 21st century – a resource that gets more plentiful every day", creating new businesses, new opportunities and great resources for all citizens, generating innovation and growth in a time of austerity, distributing new public goods and economic and social resources.

The re-use of Public Sector Information (PSI) began to be studied in 2004 after the European Directive 2003/98/EC of 17 November 2003 was published. The *MEPSIR study* (Dekkers, Polman, Velde & Vries, 2006) defined six main domains for investigation:

1. **Business Information:** Chamber of Commerce information, official business registers, patent and trademark information, public tender databases.
2. **Geographic Information:** Address information, aerial photos, buildings, cadastral information, geodetic networks, geology, hydrographical data, topographic information.
3. **Legal Information:** Decisions of national, foreign and international courts, national legislation and treaties.
4. **Meteorological Information:** Climate data and models, weather forecasts.
5. **Social Data:** Statistics – economic, employment, health, population, public administration, social.
6. **Transport Information:** Information on traffic congestion, work on roads, public transport and vehicle registration.

This study distinguished seven types of conditions:

1. **Availability:** If there is not at least some information available for re-use in a particular sub-domain, there will not be a market.
2. **Accessibility**
3. **Transparency**
4. **Accountability**
5. **Non-discrimination**
6. **Actual demand**
7. **Economic results**

European countries were included in a framework with three typologies:

- **The Closed Shop:** The production of very valuable information is in the core of the public task and the value chain.
- **The Battlefield:** The information is very valuable but the position and involvement of the public sector is disputed, with the argument that the production is not a public task.
- **The Playground:** The government opens up their resources, providing the data against significantly lower costs/free.

In this *"big data"* movement and boundaries of openness, Digital Agenda for Europe intends to promote open data benefits between governments, public services and citizens (EU's *Open Data Strategy*), which in turn feeds into new applications and services, both fixed and mobile within public sector information. PSI is the largest source of information in Europe and it includes digital maps, meteorological, legal, traffic, financial, economic and other data that could be re-used or integrated into new products and services for everyday use, such as car navigation systems, weather forecasts, financial and insurance services.

The access to large quantities of data has recently become a focal point for PSI and a pivotal aspect of open data as increasingly governments have to deal with large and continuously updated data sets that they still need to make available as open data – *big data policies*. Drivers for opening data are highlighted by Huijboom and Van der Broek (2011): the example of pioneer countries in devising strategies, employing tools and getting the benefits from an open data approach; political support at the highest level; open data initiatives at supranational level and supported by civil society; lower costs for technology; legislation and policies; monitorization initiatives; and open data champions.

Taken to the strategic level, open data, freely available and re-usable is an important turning point in digital transition processes, value and skills. Projects funded under the EU's Seventh Framework Programme for research (FP7) or other European initiatives are representative of the new dynamics:

- Project *commercially empowered linked open data ecosystems in research* (CODE) are focused on the digital content and languages side of the big data equation. *Linked Open Data* (LOD) shows enormous potential as the next big evolutionary step of the internet. CODE is developing an ecosystem for commercializing LOD based on a value-creation-chain among traditional (e.g. data provider and consumer) and non-traditional (e.g. data analyst) roles in data marketplaces.
- Project *Linguistically motivated semantic aggregation engines* (Limosine) is looking to leverage language and semantic search technology to improve online experiences, towards semantic aggregation.
- Project LIVE+GOV is developing an "m-government" solution that allows citizens to express their needs to government through mobile sensing technologies already in smart phones, alongside established mobile e-participation formats.
- *Data infrastructures ecosystem for science* (D4Science-II), an interoperable framework for e-infrastructures which is like an ecosystem in which data, computing and software resources belonging to different e-infrastructures can be shared regardless of location, technology, format, language, protocol or workflow. Their ecosystem has supported VRE (Virtual Research

Environment) in fields such as high-energy physics, biodiversity, fisheries and aquaculture resources. It has helped open up new areas of research between them and is being extended to new domains.

Excellence is a fundamental part of digital libraries universe in Europe. A significant role has been played by the Cultural Heritage and Technology Enhanced Learning. Delos Brainstorming Workshop envisaged a Digital Library as a system that enables any citizen to access knowledge. The vision created for digital libraries was based on goals to be person-centric, support user-to-user communication and collaboration.

The DELOS Network of Excellence on Digital Libraries Project (2004-2008) defined essential concepts and relationships and produced the first Digital Library Reference Model that provided a common vocabulary to facilitate communication between researchers, users and designers of digital libraries. In 2011, it was consolidated in the Digital Library Reference Model Conformance Checklist, introducing the audit process. The digital library service is structured in six domains: *content, user, functionality, policy, quality* and *architecture*. From the quality domain point of view a digital library must meet the following criteria (Ross *et al.*, 2011):

- Resources must be characterised by a set of quality parameter(s)
- Any Digital Library can be considered from a quality point of view by a Digital Library actor. The expression of the Actor's assessment is the quality parameter.
- Every quality parameter must represent the assessment of a Digital Library Actor, whether human or machine, on a resource. A quality parameter is always the expression of an assessment made by an Actor on a resource.
- Every quality parameter should be expressed by an Information Object, con-

trolling description, management and use within the Digital Library as a prerequisite for assessment of content and services and quality interoperability.

- Every quality parameter should be evaluated by specific measurements and have a specific value.

In European Countries there is an active dialogue on library policies lobbying towards a *common library policy for Europe* (EBLIDA), following the recommendations of the i2010 initiative and the launch of the European Digital Library, promoting digitization activities and access to knowledge and information. This change is built through a new focus at European level after many years of local policies developments. The *Banguemann report* (1994) was the beginning of new roles for libraries in Europe.

Traditionally, Information Society strategies in Europe were most commonly associated with the Information Market actions plans with several critical stages since 2000 (Lisbon Strategy): the EU intended to become the most innovative economy in the world by the year 2010. More recently, the EU (27 member states since 2007) have embraced the idea of a Digital Agenda as a way to coping with a variety of informational problems, namely digital divide and digital skills gaps. To get Every European Digital in a common and multi-stakeholder platform is a convergent vision that can summarize some of the European initiatives to create a Single Information Market, linked to Excellence management practices in public and private organizations.

Europeana

The importance of open data is under discussion without reaching full agreement. Two European business models were materialized: the Europe's Digital Library aggregator portal – Europeana - and the European data exchange agreement. Launched by the European Commission and

the EU's culture ministers on November 2008, Europeana gives access to over 23 million objects from more than 2300 institutions from 33 countries, in cross-domain (museums, archives, audiovisual archives and libraries). It brings "clarity to the users, helping them to access trusted, authentic cultural objects on their original sites without tedious individual searches, without getting frustrated because of ambiguity, duplication and uncertainty. Without this normalization of metadata and this aggregation of content, users would have to go and search every single cultural institution." (Niggemann, 2012, pp.6).

In the line with Le Deuff (2009), we can identify a new *practical turn in Information Science as a moment of re-documentation,* turning to old concepts but transforming them into new practices and ideas. Digitization in libraries and other memory institutions is considered as a practice to enhance access to collections and as a knowledge organization practice, a *signifying practice,* expected to embody, mediate and document particular discourses and identities within various organizations, *reshaping cultural heritage and transforming libraries and archives identities and roles* as a result of the development of new professional tools (Dahlstrom, Hansson & Kjelman, 2012).

In this scenario, national libraries and research institutions have an important role, choosing between a *mass digitization strategy* and a *critical digitization one.* Mass digitization systematically digitizes whole collections with no particular means of discrimination, with momentum and scale value, but many times the items are decontextualized. Critical digitization implements several links in a manual, intellectual and critical way, concentrating on what is unique and contingent in the documents, developing project-specific practices and tools. As Dahlstrom, Hansson and Kjelman (2012, pp.464) say "critical digitization is in other words a more exclusive strategy (in more sense than one) and thus comes closer to the digitization ideal and strategies of a museum. If mass digitization is immediately being embraced by libraries as a pragmatic ideal in harmony with the library's traditional tasks and ideals, critical digitization might represent a middle ground between libraries and museums. It is furthermore retrospective in the sense that it ties a historical bond to older bibliographical and knowledge organization traditions of libraries, while also looking forward to new possible institutional roles of selecting, choosing, exhibiting, and deliberately re-contextualizing the digitized documents". This transition phase of re-contextualization of documents is characterized by the transformation of metadata as a knowledge organization tool and by the creation of larger and virtual super-collections, in a new environment of practices, promoting new discussions at technical and ideological level, enriching and broaden cultural heritage concept as a whole. Digitized texts and images can be constantly reinterpreted, recontextualised and reconstructed, which is linked to new forms of cultural consuming and information behavior.

Challenges are also related to the impact of globalization and the digital shift in business models, that must be sufficiently flexible regarding unity in diversity opportunities and alert to the new forms of how cultural goods are made, managed, disseminated, accessed, consumed and monetized under the principles of liberty, tolerance and democracy. A priority is making digital literacy, digital skills and technology-supported learning central to the public policy agenda, engaging all stakeholders. Europeans are motivated to think not of "what is"; but "what could be" the opportunities of the digital future.

The massive dataset (Europeana Data Model - EDM) is the descriptive information about Europe's digitized treasures, released under the *Creative Commons CC0 Public Domain Dedication*, meaning that anyone can use the data for any purpose - creative, educational, commercial - with no restrictions. This release, which is by far the largest one-time dedication of cultural data to the public domain using CC0, offers a new boost to the digital economy, providing electronic entrepreneurs with opportunities to create innovative apps and games for tablets and smartphones and to create new web services and portals. The strategic plan includes the tourism sector and researchers as target groups. It represents a strong strategy for convergence of data and users.

Until 2015, Europeana will be sharing the metadata following four strategic areas: 1) aggregate content to build the open, trusted source of European heritage; 2) facilitate knowledge transfer, innovation and advocacy in the cultural heritage sector; 3) distribute their heritage to users wherever they are, whenever they want it, 4) engage users in new ways of participating in their cultural heritage.

European Research Area

European future is linked to research and innovation through the creation and development of the European Research Area by 2014, aiming at Excellence in frontier research across the EU through smart specialisation and deriving maximum value from public money invested in research (best-practice performance), optimal circulation, access to and transfer of scientific knowledge via digital format (European Commission, 2012). Horizon 2020 is the European policy dedicated to create Excellence in the Science Base, with four main elements: *frontier research*, *future and emerging technologies* (FET), *skills and career development* and *research infrastructures*. Science Europe has a vision roadmap to manage the transition phases and include seven points: *open access*; *European grant union*; *ex-post evaluation of funding schemes and research programmes*; *peer review*; *research infrastructures*; and *European research careers*. From 2014 onwards, this programme will combine European research and innovation funding in a single framework in which "transnational synergies and complementarities are fully exploited" (European Commission, 2012a, pp.4)

As priorities, the Commission will establish open access to scientific publications (policy Horizon 2020), will adopt a recommendation on preservation of scientific information in the digital age, proposing a road-map for e-infrastructure development to support e-science and developing assessment initiatives. The EU supported project *Open access infrastructure for research in Europe* (*Openaire*) aims to make everything accessible for everyone, forcing to adapt to changing public expectations and political culture, requiring effective communication: "data must be accessible and readily located, they must be intelligible to those who wish to scrutinize them; data must be assessable so that judgments can be made about their reliability and the competence of those who created them; and they must be usable by others" (Royal Society, 2012, pp.7).

According to the British Royal Society´s report *Science as an open enterprise* (2012, pp.8), these approaches will come from six changes: "a shift away from a research culture where data is viewed as a private preserve; 2) expanding the criteria used to evaluate research to give credit for useful data communication and novel ways of collaborating, 3) the development of common standards for communicating data; 4) mandating intelligent openness for data relevant to published scientific papers; 5) strengthening the cohort of data scientists needed to manage and support the use of digital data (which will also be crucial to the success of private sector data analysis and the government's Open data strategy), and 6) the development and use of new software tools to automate and simplify the creation and exploitation of datasets."

Universities and research institutes should play a major role in supporting an open data culture and developing a data strategy to curate knowledge resources. Research is a competitive field in which one of the keys to success is collaboration based on the ability to efficiently find and use quality data in the immediate and in the long-term future, reinforcing the value of Excellence (Aarhus Declaration of Excellence, 2012).

The Australian example of discussion of policy development (Wolsk & Richardson, 2011) is important by the extensiveness of areas included, the instruments available and the questions raised:

- The definition of research activity, research data and research outputs.
- The university's support for open access publishing and support for Creative Commons licensing.
- Policy on where researchers are required to store research outputs (internal storage and external cloud services; the difference between storing descriptive metadata and a data store location versus actual stored research data).
- What are the terms and conditions of storing data in enterprise repositories?
- What needs to go into strategic, operational and performance plans to implement policy?
- Advocacy – what is the role for key positions in educating or persuading researchers, disseminating, information?
- Networks – what are the key networks impacted?
- Funding – who will be providing resources to implement the various policy objectives?
- Direct action – or organizational units such library delivering new practices to encourage a change in behavior or to provide the resources necessary to lower the cost of adopting new practices.
- Regulatory – a university may consider imposing data management plans for each research grant.

"Excellence research depends upon world-class facilities and research infrastructures (RIs) including ICT-based e-infrastructures (eRIs).

Such RIs attract talent and stimulate innovation and business opportunities. eRIs in particular enable increasingly prevalent data-intensive collaborative research by geographically dispersed teams – eScience" (European Commission, 2012, pp.9). Libraries are included in these research infrastructures. Lossau (2012) defines RIs as a priority for EU (e.g. the 7th Framework Programme - 2007-2013- with 1.715 million Euros or the ESFRI project[7]).

The DG Information & Science funds ICT-based-Infrastructures reaching across disciplines. Some initiatives are relevant for ERM and have many libraries as consortium partners:

- *OpenAIRE* (December 2009-November 2012) is a research e-infrastructure initiative for publications and is considered a success story in Open access, being invited to transfer the European "model" to other countries. Its basic objectives are to provide a support infrastructure for researchers in Open Access, establishing a network of National Open Access Desks (NOADs) with partners in all European member states, in what had engaged multiple stakeholders (research project coordinators, researchers, repository managers, research administrators and policy makers). Key challenges are the weak mandate of the European Commission and the reluctance of researchers to comply, a different level of Open Access maturity in EU member states, and the dynamics of publishers' counter-activities, and repository managers' that slow uptake of the guidelines. (Lossau, 2012).
- *OpenAIREplus* (December 2011-May 2014) as an expansion of OpenAIRE aims to link publications to research data. "This initiative could be defined as an RI initiative that crosses from the publication into the data world" (Lossau, 2012, pp.320).

- *EUDAT* (October 2011-September 2014) – *European Data Infrastructure* aims to contribute to the production of a Collaborative Data Infrastructure, a cross-disciplinary dimension. It is closely linked to the COAR Interoperability Initiative. COAR – the Confederation of Open Access Repositories leads to the interoperability between various components of e-research. There are no libraries involved here.

Lossau (2012) discusses how these developments can impact libraries, concluding that research libraries will benefit only marginally from the funding if they stick to research publications and the digitization of cultural heritage. There is a potential risk that funding for universities and their libraries will be reduced or that funding for national digitization programmes will go down, increasing this risk in times of a financial crisis. He recommends libraries to develop the "Scholarly Communication" Steering Committee into a "Scholarly Communication and Research Infrastructure", addressing Open Access policy and implementation and becoming a key actor in this movement. The focus in Education and Training is also important and it will be necessary to build on the Excellent activities of the "Organization and Human Resources" Steering Committee and expand the portfolio of the "leadership seminar" to broad scale research librarians education and training.

European divergences, problems and gaps are well known: research careers and mobility, brain drain, irregular levels of funding, asymmetric pan-European research infrastructures of strategic interest, different knowledge transfer modalities, access and share scientific information through Open Access, weak international dimension to engage in effective international cooperation, insufficient gender incentives and the need to create conditions to discuss common principles and ethical issues. There is no financial plan at the national or European level to finance RIs in the long term. Four policy options are in discussion: 1) discontinuing existing EU action; 2) no policy change; 3) implementation of a policy framework in the form of soft law; 4) implementation of a policy framework in the form of approximation of legislation.

Cultural Agenda

The impact of globalisation and the digital shift on the cultural sector is recognized in EU as causing the need to develop new business models and the potential for growth in taking advantage of digital technologies. The groups affected by these changes are:

- The users of cultural products (consumers, audience, the general public) who rely on supply of cultural and creative works;
- The developers of creative and cultural works (authors, play writers, translators, publishers, etc), which do not have the capacity to operate on a transnational level and thereby optimise potential economies of scale;
- The providers of access to culture.

The lack and shortage of comparable data on the cultural sector is widely recognised. A new category of support for "policy support groupings" was created for working on exchange, comparison and consolidation of existing quantitative data and evaluation methods, linked to the priorities of the European Agenda for Culture. The options for programmes are convergent and no more by different cultural sub-sectors, since Culture 2000, a programme that adopted an interdisciplinary approach. The evaluation made confirms the benefits of this kind of convergence due to the developments in the cultural sector, but also due to the impact of digitisation, in which boundaries between sectors are becoming more fluid and cross-sector experimentation in common.

Important to maintain cohesion and democracy values in Europe, cultural policies are striking to develop strong evidence based policy grounded in new quality indicators (CulturalWatchEurope[8], 2012), looking beyond the fact that culture is still a marginalized and a jumbled sector, despite being also a changing and transformative sector. One strategy to be monitorized is related to the building of evaluation indicators on public policies of culture and the construction of an index of cultural participation of European citizens. Among the main issues in discussion, we can find the guarantee of cultural access/basic values and the creation of conditions and possibilities to consider culture as change agent/merger of ethical orientations.

The ethical aspects are general in all the areas of Excellence and are another aspect of diversity in convergence (*ethical pluralism*). Floridi (2010, 2011) has been developing the concept of *info sphere* to represent the complex informational environment of production and consumption of information. The digital transition has strong impact on ethical aspects: information as ethical resource; information as ethical product and information as ethical target - the three aspects being represented in the *Model RTP* (*Resource-Product-Target*). The informational ethics needs a global one that can preserve the identity and the cultural diversity (Ess, 2009), towards a new *philosophy of information cultures* (Briggle & Mitcham, 2009).

Another emerging area is the *creative ethos* (Florida, 2002, pp.7):"Where people once found themselves bound together by social institutions and formed their identities in groups, a fundamental characteristic of life today is that we strive to create our own identities. It is the creation and re-creation of the self, often in ways that reflect our creativity that is the key feature of the creative *ethos*."

According to the results of the *CultureWatch Europe Conference 2012* (Laitio & Helsinki, 2012), it is possible to capture these kinds of impacts across Europe in areas of transformation that are relevant: self-confidence, skills, ability to communicate, employability and citizenship.

Another important question is related to the differences in the way European countries perceive Excellence in several areas, namely in emergent sectors like digital products and services. The value and benefits of e-resources for learning, teaching, research and enjoyment and general performance within digital collections in libraries are strong evidences for primary (memory institutions and cultural heritage organizations; custodians of special collections; librarians, managers of digitized resources; universities and academic; publishing, media and business sectors) and secondary stakeholders (national and international citizens, governments, policy makers).

E-RESOURCES DYNAMICS TOWARDS EXCELLENCE: A MODEL OF MULTIPLE CONVERGENCES THROUGH DIVERSITY

These cycles of hybrid transition requires that all new policies, programmes and projects be subject to a comprehensive ERM where customer experience of quality and consumer behavior and contexts are perceived as excellence. Customer value in experience (customer's perception of value over the entire course of the customer experience) is a concept that must receive more attention when studying e-resources dynamics, addressing the full scope of the four stages of customer experience (Arnould, Price, & Zinkhan, 2004): anticipated consumption, purchase experience, consumption experience, remembered consumption and nostalgia. The notion of the *customer journey* is important to evaluate quality of e-resources as user perception may vary as the journey is made, preceding the service and continue after it in a set of interactions and experiences at different levels (rational, emotional, sensorial, physical and ethical). Can e-resources encompass *the total experience?* The rich literature about service quality makes

the point that this response may be multifaceted (Lemke, Clark, & Wilson, 2011): comparing performance on product/service quality dimensions against expectations is one of the answers, being the other one, quality as a value perception, both arising due to multiple contextual factors.

The customer experience quality categories (Payne *et al.*, 2008; Lemke, Clark, & Wilson, 2011) identify 17 experiences related to information, business and entertainment needs, grouped in six areas: *communication encounter*; *service encounter* (product quality, service quality, network quality); *usage encounter* (relationship with other customers; social impact); *experience context* (hedonism, involvement, product complexity, relationality), *value-in-use* (utilitarian, hedonic, relational, cost/sacrifice) and *relationship outcomes* (commitment, purchase, retention, word of mouth). Library users want to access e-resources (bibliographical resources, full-text e-resources and portals/aggregator products) from home, office or anywhere they need information and expect quality in their experiences.

Current developments must be scanned with specific areas of Excellence triggers highlighting important turning points in customer experiences and quality perceptions.

A fundamental contribution of the quality movement was to recognize the dynamics of satisfaction linked to quality of information products, services, user experiences and its effects in life and in a global community of stakeholders. Whenever a library collection is presented as a product or a service, it either explicitly or implicitly employs a service model and a value creation model. The significance of Excellence demonstrates how value is created and delivered to customers. As a consequence, many libraries have responded to market competition primarily by emphasizing the value of products (resources), the value of processes (digitalization, portals, digital libraries, licensing, and legal issues) and the value of the impact on society. These movements can be classified as convergent. However, the aspects of diversity (consumer's usages, perceptions and needs; personalization of information behavior) are less discussed and the relationship between the two dynamics must be managed. Some sub-dynamics for ERM are suggested throughout this chapter and summarized in Figure 1.

The model (a variation on the Venn diagram) illustrates an integrated approach to represent ERM dynamics and inter-relatedness with sub-dynamics. As discussed earlier, consumer culture and the European digital agenda are the triggers of the Excellence convergence movement.

Various aspects of the e-resource life cycle and management (policies, discovery, trial, selection, acquisition, ownership and licensing, access, us-age, data curation and preservation, guidelines and best practices) are linked to information environment variables: information life cycle (*creation, distribution, seeking, utilization*); competences life cycle (*assess, plan, acquire, validate*); knowledge management life cycle (*creation, securing, distribution, retrieval*) and performance management life cycle (*ad hoc, basic, emerging, managed, excellence*).

Figure 1. Model of e-resources excellence management

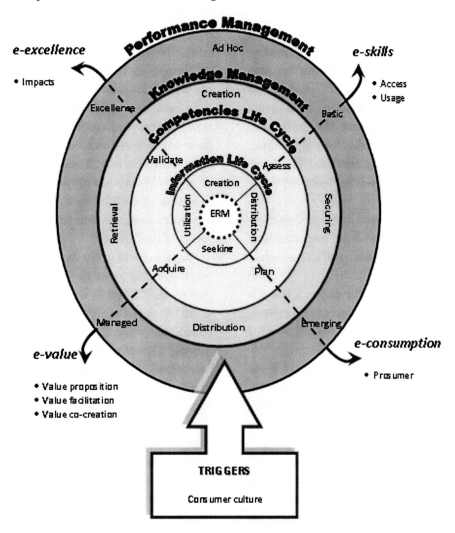

ERM needs to integrate into an existing library collection and the broader institutional environment, other applications and services, including the use of e-resources as linking sources/resources for metasearching. To assist librarians in decision making about collection development, competences and knowledge management practices that provides a global picture of the e-resource world and a comprehensive knowledge base about what is available (packages, interfaces and providers) must exist. Knowledge management uses existing information resources and methods of recalling but emphasizes the value-adding effects of bringing people with different backgrounds and with different levels of expertise together. Performance management related to e-resources expenditures expressed in cost and usage entities is another important aspect in the global market place, assuring long-term access to e-resources and practices of iterative development between users, producers and stakeholders. Access and usage are essential for e-resources investment, being relevant the development of e-skills for e-consumption processes and e-value propositions, facilitation and co-creation services. The result of these dynamics will be e-Excellence explicitly portraying impacts.

The dynamic links created in this process show value transfer processes and the importance of capturing value from a diversity of experiences:

- ERM associated to information life cycle is the first group of evidences to be collected. *Value in use is the first impact in value transfer and diversity.*
- Management of ERM competences life cycle of staff means the difference in a quality service assessment. Intellectual capital is an important factor for success and for value transfer.
- Existing knowledge management evidences report that value transfer is moderate by cumulative information and competences management, in house or in converging organizational partnerships.

- The value of ERM is estimated by multiple approaches – economic benefits or other types of assessments. Performance management is then the guarantee of Excellence sustainability.

The focus then turned to understanding the emergent dynamics: *e-excellence*, *e-skills*, *e-consumption* and *e-value* in a convergence value transfer by diversity.

E-Skills

In order to take advantage of these policies and engage in fortuitous explorations, individuals must develop e-skills to deal with EQF – the European Qualifications Framework (2008), another instrument of convergent actions in education and training fields or the European e-Competence Framework (e-CF). The EQF is a common European reference framework which links countries' qualifications systems together, acting as a translation device to make qualifications more readable and understandable across different countries in Europe. It has two principal aims: to promote citizen's mobility between countries and to facilitate their lifelong learning. It uses learning outcomes as a common reference point in eight levels of proficiency.

In the context of education and employability, it is interesting to see the importance that the notion of an ICT proficient workforce has gained in the EU agenda (McCormack, 2010). The eight competences are: Communication in the mother tongue; Communication in foreign languages; Mathematical competence and basic competences in science and technology; Digital competence; Learning to learn; Social and civic competences; Sense of initiative and entrepreneurship; and cultural awareness and expression (European Commission, 2007). To move from the technical use of ICTs to the development of e-literacies/e-skills is a manifest challenge that has to be faced. This trend reflects a shift in focus from the tool to the content, from computer user to e-competent user. This means that the technology is not as relevant as the knowledge and the information that can be accessed, understood, create and communicated. Relatedly, *The Key Competences for Lifelong Learning*, an European Framework (2007), identifies digital competence as one of the key competences described in the programme Education and Training 2010 (European Commission, 2007, 2008).

The *European eSkills Forum* (2004) proposes a definition of e-skills covering three main categories:

- **ICT Practitioner Skills:** The capabilities required for researching, developing, designing, strategic planning, managing, producing, consulting, marketing, selling, integrating, installing, administering, maintaining, supporting and servicing ICT systems, for the benefit of others.
- **ICT User Skills:** The capabilities required for the effective application of ICT systems and devices by the individual. User skills cover basic digital literacy, the utilization of common software tools in an office environment and the use of specialized tools supporting major business functions within a large number of sectors.
- **E-Business Skills:** Strategic and innovation management skills.

For years, technological infrastructure has been one of the priority strategies of education policies (OECD). The European e-Competence Framework (e-CF) (CEN, 2010) is another common and shared tool to support organizations and training institutions in recruitment, assessment, competence needs analysis, learning programmes, career path design and development. It also aimed to support policy makers to define policies related to e-Skills development in education and in work place. The definitions are in line with the EQF definitions.

The concept of digital skills was introduced by Steyaert (2000) and Van Dijk (1999) as a succession of three types of skills: *operational skills* (the capacities to work with hardware and software); *information skills* (skills to information management cycles that can be formal or substantial) and *strategic* skills (capacities to use computer and network sources as means for particular goals and for the general goal of improving one's position in society). In Europe, the only data studied is about operational skills, crossing three social demographics data: age (considered the most important), educational level and gender. Recently, Van Dijk (2012) refined the concept into six types of digital skills, considering *medium related skills* (operational skills and formal skills) and *content-related skills* (information skills, communication skills, content-creation skills and strategic skills).

According to Van Dijk (2008, pp.299), "measuring computer and internet skills with general surveys poses two fundamental problems: a measurement problem and the problem that only operational skills and not information and strategical digital skills are considered. The first problem is the validity of survey measurement for this purpose: are self-reports valid measurements of actual skills possessed?" Surveys and tests are showing that the divides of skills access are bigger than the divides of physical access and that while physical access gaps are more or less closing in the developed countries, the (relative) skills gaps tend to grow, the gap of information skills in particular.

Concepts as e-awareness; technological literacy, informational literacy, digital literacy and media literacy are components of e-skills, linked to life-long learning, digital citizenship, formal and informal environments, assess, connect and critically use the information in different formats depending on the context, create, adapt and share information and knowledge in multiple formats. Therefore, e-skill is a meta-competence evolving as the new technologies and the labor market evolve.

One of the EU studies due to be carried out in the next year is related to the international dimension of the e-skills strategy (especially the efforts to promote ICT professionalism), assessing the impact of globalization on high-level e-skills requirements (ICT practitioners' skills and e-leadership skills), as well as analyzing major policy initiatives and best practices in the world. E-skills have been a strategical approach and a major effort towards the development of Excellence for Europe.

The creation of a *European researcher development framework* (Metcalfe, 2012) intends to provide a single European language for describing researchers' skills and facilitating mobility, meeting the objectives of the European Charter of Researchers (European Commission, 2005). The charter recognizes several principles: research freedom, ethical principles, professional responsibility, professional attitude, contractual and legal obligations, accountability, good practice in research, dissemination, exploitation of results, public engagement, relation with supervisors, supervision and managerial duties, and continuing professional development.

The identification of emerging skills is enhancing and amplifying the combination of human capital and digital technologies as a solution to the needs on value creation through innovation and e-talent applied to each link in the e-resources value chain. In the case of digitization, there was a general trend towards developing projects to investigate best practices and how to share solutions with other stakeholders in a joint effort to formulate agreements upon standards and recommendations for technical formats and work practices. This opportunity of sharing information creates convergence flows in skills domains.

E-Consumption

Another research line with important contributes to this discussion is on marketing evolution and convergence (Wind & Mahajan, 2002), analysing *production*, *consumption* and *prosumption* forms in the age of the digital *prosumer* (Ritzer & Jurgenson, 2010). *Prosumer* is a concept introduced by Alvin Toffler (1980) in his book *the third wave*, combining co-production of products, meanings and identities. Given the recent explosion of user-generated content online, prosumption involves both production and consumption rather than focusing on either one (production) or the other (consumption). New prosumers are proactive and are different from early adopters by attitudes through information and social media (Xie, Bagozzi & Troye, 2008). They represent one of the pillars of innovation and one of the agents of consumption culture (Langer, 2007).

Conceptual tools that aim to comprehend digital consumer practices are yet to emerge[9], studying new consumer subjectivities, cultures and new markets (Denegri-Knott & Molesworth, 2010) and supporting e-resources fundraising and revenue development plans, audience development and evaluation and impact assessment (Tanner & Deegan, 2012).

The history of the digitalization of consumer culture (*on line shopping wave*, *participatory consumption wave* and *virtual consumption wave*) shows how information society interacts with consumer society (sites, processes, subjects and objects of consumption) in what Lehdonvirta (2012) calls *digitalization of consumption* where the subjects of consumption are the consumers themselves, their practices and beliefs.

Two theoretical perspectives are identified: *consumption as social signification* (structural approach focused on the use of tools for communicating and constructing social bonds and distinctions) and *consumption as a hedonistic project* (hedonistic approach explaining where preferences come from). Technologies (Web2.0; social media, open source software) and design techniques as blogs, RSS feeds, tags, social networking, web networking and mobile communication technologies have permitted individual consumers to self-organise and to have a more active role, participating in the experience, appropriating the goods to new uses and combining and altering the goods to create entirely new experiences, often acquired from peer-to-peer networks without paying for a licence and transforming consumers into producers in *crowdsourcing* mode, collecting friends, like mentions, comments and compare themselves with their peers (Lehdonvirta, 2012).

The value is based on information contents, structuring social relationships and creating virtual communities. Information goods are linked to virtual goods, a new marketing concept, suggesting that consumers use virtual goods to seek fulfilment to needs, to communicate and construct social distinctions, bonds and identity positions.

The roles of virtual goods have been debated around the ways in which use-value and exchange-value function can be implemented in the information market and a reconceptualization of service[10] through a *Service-Dominant Logic* (Vargo & Lush, 2004), relating to profitability, affordability, social belongings, status, conspicuous consumption, identity and individuality (Ng, Vargo & Smith, 2012; Groonroos, 2011). Service is defined as the application of specialised competences (skills and knowledge), through deeds, processes and performances for the benefit of another entity or the entity itself (self-service), with emphasis upon the outcomes realised with customers[11]. Vargo and Lush (2008) make a distinction between *operant* and *operand resources*. *Operant resources* can act on or in concert with other resources to create value. They are the fundamental source of competitive advantage. *Operand resources* require action to provide benefit. Individuals are considered *resource integrators*, with both personal and business motivations convergence[12] (Baron, & Warnaby, 2008).

A prototype classification system of customer-perceived organizational operant resources supports several resources (Warnaby, Baron & Konjier, 2009) and it has implications for Excellence research, namely in the areas highlighted in Table 2.

Experience and especially the concept of quality in *total service experience* (Brown, Gummersson, Edvardsson & Gustavsson, 1991) remain nuclear on studying consumption experiences, perceived value and satisfaction outcomes, evaluation and service performance. We all re-

Table 2. Classification system of customer-perceived organizational operant resources

Customer Operand Resources	Customer Operant Resources	Customer-Articulated Organizational Operant Resources	Customer-Articulated Organizational Operand Resources
Economic Material Objects Physical spaces	Physical • Sensorimotor • Endowment • Energy, emotions • Strength Cultural • Specialize knowledge and skills • Life expectancies and history • Imagination • Social • Family relationships • Brand communities • Consumer tribes • Commercial • Relationships	Representational • Reputation • Goodwill • Comfort/Congeniality Cultural • Ethos • Knowledge • Knowledge management • Know how • Capabilities • Service Quality • Technology Social • Staff friendliness/ helpfulness • Social Atmosphere (C2C networking) • ERM consumer culture	Geographical • Location/Place Building/Space Products (Collections, ERM) E-resources preservation/ curation

Adapted from Warnaby, Baron and Konjier (2009, pp.4)

member the importance of "moments of truth". Nowadays, the notion of *appropriation* has been introduced (Filser, 2002) to clarify the mark of psychological action within the context of experience, which transforms and personalises it. Therefore, *immersion* and *transformation* are privileged outcomes of consuming experience (Cova & Dalli, 2009) and important managers of discovery, access and delivery in information services.

Another perspective is given by Gronroos and Ravald (2011) making distinction between *production* (organization process of providing resources for customer's use) and *value creation* (customer's process of turning resources provided into value in use). The skills are a resource integrator and affect value creation and customer is always a value creator. When providing in put resources into the customer's value creation process, the organization is facilitating customer's value creation. Value cannot be created without the customer.

With the technologically enabled broad movement of individuals into productive activities, it is worthwhile to study the strategies, methods and technologies of co-creation in an integrated manner. Digital goods are nonrival (not consumed in use and available to all who have access) and the collective processes of sharing data, information and knowledge vastly contribute to the growth of activities.

Contemporary changes in the realm of consumption highlight some of the ongoing transitions occurring in consumption of personal digital devices and in the use of digital cultural content. Special attention is being given to three tendencies in self-consumption and how knowledge and practices involved in these uses: 1) active manipulation of commodities by consumers, culturally and materially integrated in several contexts of consumption; 2) engagement in device modification, acquiring competences and knowledge to manipulate data using web tools (Beer & Burrows,

2010); 3) increasing significance in consumer culture of forms of symbolic manipulation and criticism by consumers, mobilizing ideas, values and identities around this practice.

The concept of *prosumption* (Ritzer & Jungerson, 2010, pp.19) intends to clarify this trend: "Web 2.0 is defined by the ability of users to produce content collaboratively, whereas most of what exists on web1.0 is provider-generated. It is on web 2.0 there has been a dramatic explosion in presumption. It can be argued that web 2.0 should be seen as crucial in the development of the 'means of prosumption'; web 2.0 facilitates the implosion of production and consumption".

E-Value

Production, effort coordination and distribution are also facilitators of the continuing development of co-creation (Zwass, 2010). The intellectual space of co-creation involves virtual communities, the commons (open and shared access), collective intelligence (idea generation, aggregation of dispersed information and knowledge) and open innovation. Zwass (2010) has debated the great variety of autonomous co-creation - *knowledge compendia*; *consumer reviews*, *multimedia content*; *mashups, virtual worlds, hardware co-creation* - and, considering the richness of the domain, presented a taxonomic framework of factors in co-creation:

- **Performers:** The world, pre-qualified individuals, community members, skilled contributors.
- **Motivation:** Altruistic desire to contribute; passion for a task, inner need to reciprocate in view of the contribution of others, enjoyment, self-expression, identity-construction, forming personal relationships, community norms, competitive spirit, learning, satisfying one's affiliation needs,

self-esteem and self-efficacy, acquiring social capital and peer recognition, career advancement; own use.

- **Governance:** Individual autonomy, collective norms, software code, facilitators, adhocracy, bureaucracy, market mechanism, hybrid forms.
- **Task Characteristics:** Structural complexity, intellective demands; effort intensity; time frame.
- **Principal Mode of Product Aggregation:** Searchable corpus, hyperlinking, progressive refinement, statistical ratings and rankings, competitions and voting, information markets; bottom-up taxonomy (*folksonomy*); moderators, auditors and facilitators.
- **Economic Beneficiary:** The world, the community; the sponsoring firm; the aggregator; the contributors.

This author highlights that this typology should serve to further differentiate studies and discriminate among them within a well-defined context, but also to keep integrating the findings in more refined systematic studies.

The technological environment supporting the co-creation is being investigated. Information technology enabled services and value co-creation where production and consumption of service can be described as spatiotemporally separated. Keiskala, Hiekkanen, Korhonen, and Aalto (2011) note that with "this digitalization of services processes and actions also means that the locus of the human labor in service processes will change. As human interaction is mostly eliminated from direct "first-line" customer interaction, the locus of labor is moving up in the capability hierarchy: from delivery of service to handling of exceptions, (re)definition/(re)negotiation of value propositions and designing and implementing entire service systems (e.g value facilitation). Human insight, intelligence and knowledge will be the keys factors in designing, implementing and operating these services".

Some technological issues are the next challenge to consumers, such as convenience and reach. Mobile devices will soon become the main way people use social networks; challenges of social on proprietary platforms; mobile sensors will drive innovation and business value and social customer care; mobile apps integrated with social networks; digital business models shift to mobile platform providers; and information flows more potent, yet harder to control in converged social/mobile. Social networks and mobile apps provide higher levels of reach and scale, being more challenging given how quickly and easily information can be spread, copied, and lost. Organizations will have to become even better data managers and experts in Big Data techniques to make the most of mobile and social channels.

According to Ng, Vargo and Smith (2012), there is therefore an urgent need for greater integrative frameworks that are transdisciplinary for the purpose of transferability across sectors. Only in this way, service design can be systemic, structured and socially meaningful to ensure sustainable service Excellence since value creation happens in the context of networks of resources integrators.

E-Excellence

The level of Excellence convergence through diversity must be based on better evidence of ERM impacts. The types of change to be measured are diverse: economic, social, educational, cultural, health, political and environmental, etc. Impact is as any effect on service, event or initiative (individual or group), of short or long duration, positive or negative, resulting in changes in attitudes, behaviors and results. Change is the essence of impact (Markless & Streatfield, 2006).

Based on Global Learning (GL) Impact Planning and Assessment (IPA) Road Map, we took into account five levels of impact - *knowledge and skills in quality management*; *perception and trust*; *information behavior*; *quality of life*; and *society and economy* – as illustrated in Figure 3. The IPA Road Map model was created by Streatfield and Markless (2009) to evaluate programs' performance and impacts, namely the Global Libraries Initiative of the Bill & Melinda gates Foundation (Global Libraries Initiative, 2008). Impact is, therefore, an important issue for libraries, a concept still under discussion.

Selecting the Excellence emerging fields not only requires understanding the evidences available, but also a keen comprehension of librarianship strategies.

Table 3 presents some impacts with reference to ERM Excellence: *Quality management knowledge and competences*; *Information quality*; *Efficiency*; *Information behaviour*; *Information uses*; *Concepts and levels of services focused on experience, time and user attention*; *Social and economic impacts of the creation of a single European Digital Market that supports European culture, Information as a resource, product and ethical target* and *Evaluation of public policies*.

These areas can be applied to policy and project appraisal and evaluation.

SOLUTIONS AND RECOMMENDATIONS

In order to answer effectively to e-resources dynamics and multiple convergences, managers need to provide evidences of ERM growth strategies beyond the library sector, focusing on four main areas:

1. Towards a culture-based creativity and cultural consumption, taking into consideration information culture, cultural employment, cultural offering, cultural participation, technology penetration, regulatory and financial support to creation and the economic contribution of creative industries. The European Creativity Index (ECI), as a statistical framework for illustrating and measuring the interplay of various factors that contributes to the growth of creativity in the EU, measures the performance based on six pillars of creativity: human capital, openness and diversity, technology, institutional environment, social environment and creative inputs. By developing a better understanding of what culture and creativity are, impacts of e-resources will need to be included in the composed list of 32 indicators. One of the objectives of the Programme Creative Europe (2014-2020) will be the promotion of digitalization (30 millions of e-resources in 2015). This strategy for digital transition must be studied in terms of its outcomes on ERM emerging dynamics.

2. The customer experience quality must be integrated in ERM life cycle concepts, reshaping co-creation processes and services channels. Methods by which customer experience quality can be elicited in the new information environment (peer-to-peer quality, network quality, relationship quality and consumer usage processes, measurement of the delivery of the promised embedded value or consumer creation of outcomes and value) need to be highlighted.

3. ERM Excellence Journey in libraries must align with fundamental concepts of Excellence (EFQM, 2012): *Adding Value for customers* by understanding, anticipating and fulfilling needs, expectations and opportunities; *Creating a Sustainable Future* (positive impact by enhancing performance whilst simultaneously advancing the economic, environmental and social conditions within the communities they touch); *Developing Organizational Capability* (by effectively managing change within and beyond the organizational boundaries); *Harnessing Creativity and Innovation* (by generating increased value and levels of performance through continual improvement, systematic innovation and harnessing the creativity of

Table 3. Impacts regarding ERM excellence emerging fields

IPA Road Map Levels of Impact		Excelence Emerging Fields
Changes in knowledge and competences	Quality management knowledge and competences	International standard ISO 10018 (2012) - *Quality management - Guidelines on people involvement and competence* International Standard ISO/DIS 2789 (2012) - *International library statistics* [5th ed. due in 2013] International Standard ISO 11620 (2008) - *Library Performance indicators* ISO/TR 28118 (2009) - *Performance indicators for national libraries* ISO/TR 11219 (2012) - *Qualitative conditions and basic statistics for library buildings* ISO 28500 (2009) – *WARC* [WebARChive] *file format* ISO/DTR 147833 - *Statistics and quality issues for Web archiving* [to be published in 2013] ISO 16439 - *Methods and procedures for assessing the impact of libraries* [to be published in 2013]
		Portuguese standard NP 4512 (2012) - *Training Management Systems* [deliverable of the European Commission funded project Q-Cert-VET]. Norma NP 4457 (2007) - *Management of Research, Development and Innovation (RDI): management system requirements of RDI*
Changes in perceptions and trust	Information quality	Creation of excellence centres
	Efficiency	Focus on content, creation times and availability
		Levels of maturity and information value cycles
		Evaluation of data quality
		Library used concept
Changes in specific behaviours	Information behaviour	Topic under constant review within Information Science
		Focus on information behaviour in professions
		Focus on patterns of specializations
	Information uses	Contexts of customization, integrated service provision
		Multiplicity of activities considered, from search to socialization and game.
Changes in quality of life	Concepts and levels of services focused on experience, time and user attention	Change in information delivery models
		Access centred on users lifestyle
		Mobile and geo-social information environments
Changes in Society and Economy	Social and economic impacts of the creation of a single European Digital Market that supports European culture. Information as a resource, product and ethical target. Evaluation of public policies	Europeana
		Internationalization of collections and access policies
		European information policies Open metadata

Adapted from Ochôa & Pinto (2012)

their stakeholders); *Leading with Vision, Inspiration and Integrity* (shaping the future and make it happen, acting as role models for its values and ethics); *Managing with Agility* (recognized for their ability to identify and respond effectively and efficiently to opportunities and threats); *Succeeding through the Talent of People* (valuing their people and create a culture of empowerment for the achievement of both organizational and personal goals); and *Sustaining Outstanding Results* (meeting both the short and long term needs of all their stakeholders, within the context of their operating environment).

4. Copyright legal issues must be closely followed by librarians and other information professionals, especially in what concerns: access to information in the digital age; consumption within the Digital Single Market; the role of Internet and ICT in job creation and growth; the preservation of media pluralism; the harmonization of copyright exceptions for print disabled people, as well for facilitating cultural heritage preservation and archiving across Europe; the safeguarding of text and data mining data-driven innovation as drivers of growth and scientific advance (exemption of copyright licenses); and the regulation of monopoly rights in the online environment (*Copyright for creativity – a declaration for Europe*).

FUTURE RESEARCH DIRECTIONS

This chapter is an initial attempt to encourage a discussion about e-resources emerging dynamics towards an Excellence paradigm. Additional research is suggested with two different purposes. Firstly, this study is focused on understanding consumer's concept of e-resources consumption and the quality dimension therein. As pointed out earlier, the Excellence emergent fields are closely interrelated with a holistic view of management. Therefore, future research should incorporate in ERM evidences in the findings from services management theory, which could provide valuable new insights for both excellence concepts and service marketing.

A second purpose of future research should be to determine more precisely the role of quality models in hybrid periods, where the rhythm of change is too fast. Because perceptions play a

critical role in consumer choice and information is a product with many stakeholders, it will be interesting to analyze the evolution of the digital divide, non/anti-consumers attitude and price levels among competing electronic resources within consume culture theory. Post-modern society has a tendency towards pluralism, diversity and uncertainty of outcomes, but it is also in a process of change and convergence in various areas. Analysis based on social studies and organizational dynamics can illuminate these transition moments.

Finally, Excellence can be a meta-theory with strong evidences for ERM practices and perspectives, enabling this professional area to move forward in the process of regular mapping of innovation, services domain and customer consumption convergence/diversity dynamics in libraries.

CONCLUSION

In this chapter, a literature-driven perspective that analyzes the ERM convergence dynamics into excellence diversity has been presented. The evolution of Excellence concept in Europe and its usefulness as an organizing tool for managing e-resources impacts in libraries assessment was traced. E-resources as products and co-creation services can build up valuable relationships and quality experiences, reframing Excellence concepts on consumer culture. This approach provides some answers to what will be the impacts on libraries of this focus on consumer behavior.

However, the discussion and observations outlined suggest that emergent Excellence is still in a phase of ongoing development. Its theoretical relationship to information management, competences management, knowledge management and performance management was proposed in a model based on a literature review synthesis. The emergence of new value chains and value transfer diversity is a characteristic of e-consumption, e-skills, e-value and e-excellence, providing a frame of reference for mapping the ERM field and a useful point of departure to other type of discussions, namely on library impacts assessment.

REFERENCES

Aabø, S. (2011). The value of public libraries: A socio-economic analysis. In M. Belloti (Ed.), *Verso un'economia della biblioteca: Finanziamenti, programmazione e valorizzazione in tempo di crisi* (pp. 169–176). Milano, Italy: Bibliografia..

ACRL. (2012). 2012 top ten trends in academic libraries: A review of the trends and issues affecting academic libraries in higher education. *College & Research Libraries, 73*(6), 311–320.

Almauk. (2012). *Economic impact toolkit*. Retrieved November 3, 2012, from http://almauk.org/working-together/our_activity/economic-impacts

Arnould, E. J., Price, L. L., & Zinkhan, G. (2004). *Consumers*. New York: McGraw-Hill..

Arnould, E. J., & Thompson, C. J. (2005). Consumer culture theory (CCT), twenty years of research. *The Journal of Consumer Research, 331*(4), 868–882. doi:10.1086/426626.

Baron, S., & Warnaby, G. (2008). Individual customer's use and integration of resources: Empirical findings and organizational implications in the context of value co-creation. *Otago Forum, 2*, 62-79.

Beer, D., & Burrows, R. (2010). Comsumption, presumption and participatory web cultures. *Journal of Consumer Culture, 10*(1), 3–12. doi:10.1177/1469540509354009.

Berners-Lee, T., & Shadbolt, N. (2011, December 31). There's gold to be mined from all our data. *The Times*. Retrieved 12 December, 2012 from, http://www.thetimes.co.uk/Ho/opinion/colunist/article3272618

Black, I. R., & Cherrier, H. (2010, November-December). Anti-consumption sustainability: Sustainable consumption identity. *Journal of Consumer Behaviour*, 445–453.

Borbely, M. (2011). Factors influencing self-assessment in a changing library environment. *Performance Measurement and Metrics, 12*, 7–22. doi:10.1108/14678041111124261.

Bouckaert, G. (2012, May). Managing performance: International and national trends. *Forum AP*. Retrieved September 27, 2012 from http://www.qualitapa.gov.it/fileadmin/mirror/i-valperf/materiali/2012-05-17_VdP_Slide_Bouckaert.pdf

Briglle, A., & Mitcham, C. (2009). From the philosophy of information to the philosophy of information culture(s). *The Information Society: An International Journal, 25*(3), 169–174. doi:10.1080/01972240902848765.

Broady-Preston, J., & Lobo, A. (2011). Measuring the quality, value and impact of academic libraries: The role of external standards. *Performance Measurement and Metrics, 12*, 122–135. doi:10.1108/14678041111149327.

Brown, S., Gummersson, E., Edvardsson, B., & Gustavsson, B. (1991). *Service quality*. New York: Lexington Books..

CEN. (2010). *Building the e-CF: A combination of sound methodology and expert contribution*. Retrieved November 11, 2012 from www.ecompetences.eu

Chadwick, A. (2011). *The hybrid media system: Politics and power.* New York: Oxford University Press..

Cherrier, H. (2010). Custodian behavior: A material expression of anti-consumerism. *Consumption. Markets and Culture, 8*(3), 259–289. doi:10.1080/10253861003786983.

Chesbrough, H., & Spohrer, J. (2006). A research manifesto for service science. *Communications of the ACM, 49*(7), 35–40. doi:10.1145/1139922.1139945.

Chew, K., Stemper, J., Lilyard, C., & Schoenborn, M. (2012). *User-defined valued metrics for electronic journ*als. Paper presented at the Library Assessment Conference: Building Effective, Sustainable, Practical Assessment. Charlottesville, VA. Retrieved September 9, 2012 from http://libraryassessment.org/bm~doc/Chew_Katherine_2012.pdf

Connaway, L., Dickey, T., & Radford, M. (2011). If it is too inconvenient I'm not going after it: Convenience as a critical factor in information-seeking behaviors. *Library & Information Science Research, 33*, 179–190. doi:10.1016/j.lisr.2010.12.002.

Conway, P. (2010). *Measuring content quality in a preservation repository: HahtiTrust and large-scale book digitization.* Paper presented at the Seventh International Conference on Preservation of digital Objects. Vienna, Austria. Retrieved November 10, 2012 from http://hdl.handle.net/2027.42/85227

Copyright for Creativity – A Declaration for Europe. (2010). Retrieved from http://www.copyright4creativity.eu/Public/Declaration

Corral, S. (2011). *Evaluating intellectual assets: New and Informal measures for the transcendent library.* Retrieved November 24, 2012 from http://www.york.ac.uk/media/abouttheuniversity/supportservices/informationdirectorate/documents/northumbriapresentations/Corrall-York%202011.pdf

Corral, S., & Roberts, A. (2012). *Information resource development and collection in the digital age: Conceptual frameworks and new definitions for the network world.* Paper presented at Libraries in the Digital Age (LIDA). Retrieved December 2, 2012 from http://ozk.unizd.hr/proceedings/index.php/lida2012/article/view/62/33

Cortez, E., & Colon-Aguirre, M. (2009). *What libraries and information professionals can learn from knowledge and project management.* Paper presented at the 17th Bobcatsss Symposium. Porto, Portugal. Retrieved January 31, 2012 from http://trace.tennessee.edu/cgi/viewcontent.cgi?article=1014&context=utk_infosciepubs&sei-redir=1&referer=http%3A%2F%2Fwww.google.com%2Furl%3Fsa%3Dt%26rct%3Dj%26q%3Dwhat%2520libraries%2520and%2520information%2520professionals%2520can%2520learn%2520from%2520knowledge%2520and%2520project%2520management%26source%3Dweb%26cd%3D1%26ved%3D0CDMQFjAA%26url%3Dhttp%253A%252F%252Ftrace.tennessee.edu%252Fcgi%252Fviewcontent.cgi%253Farticle%253D1014%2526context%253Dutk_infosciepubs%26ei%3D6XPXUOSDKtKThgf06YCwBg%26usg%3DAFQjCNFEYWAWmwRx9Bagcl9BkeyeB19Hbg#search=%22what%20libraries%20information%20professionals%20can%20learn%20from%20knowledge%20project%20management%22

Costa, A. F. (2012). Desigualdades sociais. *Sociologia. Problemas e Práticas, 68*, 9–32.

Cova, B., & Dalli, D. (2009). Working consumers: The next step in marketing theory? *Marketing Theory, 9*(3), 315–339. doi:10.1177/1470593109338144.

Cullen, R. (2005). *Operationalising the focus/values/purpose matrix: A tool for libraries to measure their ability to deliver service quality.* Paper presented at the 6th Northumbria Performance Measurement Conference. Northumbria, UK. Retrieved November http://northumbria.ac.uk/sd/academic/ceis/re/isrc/conf/?view=standard

Dahlstrom, M., Hansson, J., & Kjellman, U. (2012). As we may digitize – Institutions and documents reconfigured. *The Library Quarterly, 21*(3/4), 455–474.

Dalkir, K. (2005). *Knowledge management in theory and practice.* Burlington, UK: Elsevier-Butterworth-Heinemann..

Declaration, A. A. R. H. U. S. in Excellence. (2012). *Excellence revisited – The value of excellence.* Retrieved April 19, 2012 from http://www.excellence2012_dk/presentationspapers

Dekkers, M., Polman, F., te Velde, R., & de Vries, M. (2006). *MEPSIR: Measuring European public sector information resources: Final report of study on exploitation of public sector information – Benchmarking of EU framework conditions.* Retrieved December 18, 2012, from http://ec.europa.eu/information_society/policy/psi/docs/pdfs/mepsir/final_report.pdf

Denegri-Knott, J., & Molesworth, M. (2010). Concepts and practices of digital virtual consumption. *Consumption. Markets & Culture, 13*(2), 109–132. doi:10.1080/10253860903562130.

Despres, C., & Chauvel, D. (2000). *Knowledge horizons: The present and the promise of knowledge management. Woburn.* Butterworth-Heinemann..

Di Domenico, G. (2004). Self-assessment, skill, excellence: The EFQM model in the library. *Bollettino AIB, 44*, 429–444.

Dodson, A. (2003). *Citizenship and the environment.* Oxford, UK: Oxford University Press..

EFQM. (2003). *Os conceitos fundamentais da Excelência.* Bruxelas: EFQM.

EFQM. (2012). *EFQM excellence model 2013.* Brussels: EFQM..

Ess, C. (2009). Floridi's philosophy of information and information ethics: Current perspectives, future directions. *The Information Society, 25*, 159–168. doi:10.1080/01972240902848708.

European Commission. (2005). *The European charter for researchers.* Luxembourg: Office for Official Publications of the European Communities..

European Commission. (2007). *Key competences for lifelong learning – European reference framework.* Brussels: Commission of the European Communities..

European Commission. (2008). *The European qualifications framework for lifelong learning (EQF).* Luxembourg: Office for Official Publications of the European Communities..

European Commission. (2012a). *Communication from the commission to the European parliament, the council, the European parliament, the council, the European economic and social committee and the committee of the regions: A reinforced European research area partnership for excellence and growth*. Brussels: EC. Retrieved December 2, 2012, from http://ec.europa.eu/euraxess/pdf/research_policies/era-communication_en.pdf

European Commission. (2012b). *Executive summary of impact assessment accompanying the document recommendation on access to and preservation of scientific information*. Brussels: EC. Retrieved December 2, 2012, from http://ec.europa.eu/research/science-society/document_library/pdf_06/impact-assessement-executive-summary_en.pdf

Filser, M. (2002). Le marketing de production d'expériences: Statut théorique et implications managériales. *Décisions Marketing, 28*(4), 13–22.

Florida, R. (2002). *The rise of the creative class. Nova Iorque*. Basic Books..

Floridi, L. (2010). *Information: A very short introduction*. Oxford, UK: Oxford University Press. doi:10.1093/actrade/9780199551378.001.0001.

Floridi, L. (2011). *The philosophy of information*. Oxford, UK: Oxford University Press. doi:10.1093/acprof:oso/9780199232383.001.0001.

Global Libraries Initiatives. (2008). *IPA road map*. Seattle, WA: Bill & Melinda Gates Foundation..

Gonçalves, M. A., Moreira, B. L., Fox, E. A., & Watson, L. T. (2007). What is a good digital library? A quality model for digital libraries. *Information Processing & Management, 43*(5), 1416–1437. doi:10.1016/j.ipm.2006.11.010.

Gronroos, C., & Ravald, A. (2011). Service as business logic: Implications for value creation and marketing. *Journal of Service Management, 22*(1), 5–22. doi:10.1108/09564231111106893.

Gronross, C. (2011). Value co-creation in service logic: A critical analysis. *Marketing Theory, 11*(3), 279–301. doi:10.1177/1470593111408177.

Gummesson, E. (2004). From one-to-one to many-to-many marketing. In *Service excellence in management: Interdisciplinarity, contribution: Proceedings from the QUIS 9 Symposium* (pp. 16-25). QUIS.

Hansson, J. (2011). *Libraries and identity: The role of institutional self-image and identity in the emergence of new types of libraries*. London: Chandos..

Harrison, R., Newholm, T., & Shaw, D. (Eds.). (2005). *The ethical consumer*. London: Sage..

Herget, J., & Hierl, S. (2007). Excellence in libraries: A systematic and integrated approach. *New Library World, 108*(11/12), 526–544. doi:10.1108/03074800710838263.

Hobohm, H.-C. (2012). *Can digital libraries generate knowledge?* Retrieved December 1, 2012 from http://www.cceh.uni-koeln.de/files/Hobohm_final.pdf

Huijboom, N., & Van den Broek. (2011). Open data: An international comparison of strategies. *European Journal of E-Practice, 12*.

Jenkins, F. W. (2012). Purposes and challenges of digitized collections for the humanities in academic libraries. *Library Student Journal, 7*(6), 1–19.

Jenkins, H. (2006). *Convergence culture: Where old and new media collide*. New York: New York University Press..

Johnson, S., et al. (2012). *Key-issues for e-resource collection development: A guide for libraries*. Retrieved 9 November 2012 from http://www.ifla.org/files/assets/acquisition-collection-development/publications/Key%20Issues%20for%20E-Resource%20Collection%20Development%20-%20AUG%2016%202012_5.pdf

Johnston, L. (2012). *Digital collections as big data*. Retrieved December 1, 2012 from http://www. digitalpreservation.gov/meetings/ndiipp12.html

Jones, K., Kinnell, M., & Usherwood, B. (2000). The development of self-assessment toolkits for the library and information sector. *The Journal of Documentation*, *56*, 119–135. doi:10.1108/ EUM0000000007111.

Keiskala, M., Hiekkanen, K., & Korhonen, J. J. (2011). *The impact of information technology enabled services on value co-creation*. Retrieved November 23, 2012 from http://www.requisit-eremedy.com/docs/value-co-creation.pdf

Kozinets, R. V. (2002). Can consumers escape the market? Emancipatory illuminations from burning man. *The Journal of Consumer Research*, *29*(1), 20–38. doi:10.1086/339919.

Kozinets, R. V., & Handelman, J. M. (2004). Adversaries of consumption: Consumer movements, activism and ideology. *The Journal of Consumer Research*, *31*(3), 691–704. doi:10.1086/425104.

Laitio, T., & Helsinki, D. (2012). *Counting what counts*. Retrieved November 11, 2012 from www. coe.int/t/dg4/.../HelsinkiReport_en.pdf

Langer, R. (2007). Marketing, presumption and innovation in the fetish community. In *Consumer tribes* (pp. 243–259). Oxford, UK: Buttherworth-Heinemman..

Le Deuff, O. (2009). *La culture de l'information en reformation*. Rennes, France: Université de Rennes..

Leadbeater, C. (2012). *Cloud culture: The future of global cultural relations*. London: British Council..

Lee, M. S. W., Fernandez, K. V., & Hyman, M. R. (2009). Anti-consumption: An overview and research agenda. *Journal of Business Research*, *62*(2), 145–147. doi:10.1016/j. jbusres.2008.01.021.

Lehdonvirta, V. (2012). A history of the digitalization of consumer culture: From Amazon through Pirate Bay to Farm Ville. In *Digital Virtual Consumption*. New York: Routledge..

Lemke, F., Clark, M., & Wilson, H. (2011). Customer experience quality: An exploration in business and consumer contexts using repertory grid technique. *Journal of the Academy of Marketing Science*, *39*, 846–869. doi:10.1007/ s11747-010-0219-0.

Lossau, N. (2012). An overview of research infrastructure in Europe – And recommendation to LIBER. *The Library Quarterly*, *21*(3/4), 313–329.

Markless, S., & Streatfield, D. (2006). *Evaluating the impact of your library*. London: Facet Publishing..

McCormack, A. (2010). *The e-skills manifesto: A call to arms*. Luxembourg: Digital Europe..

Metcalfe, J. (2012). *A pan-European professional development framework for researchers*. Strasbourg, Germany: European Science Foundation..

Mullen, L. B. (2010). *Open access and its practical impact on the work of academic librarians: Collection development, public services and the library and information science literature*. Oxford, UK: Chandos Publishing. doi:10.1533/9781780630229.

Ng, I. C. L., Vargo, S. L., & Smith, L. A. (2012). *Reconceptualising service through a service dominant logic*. Retrieved October 31, 2012 from http:// www2.warwick.ac.uk/fac/sci/wmg/research

Niggeman, E. (2012). *The importance of open data to national libraries*. Retrieved March 1, 2012, from http://conference.ifla.org/past/ifla78/181-niggemann-en.pdf

Oakland, J. S. (2003). *Total quality management: Text with cases* (3rd ed.). Oxford, UK: Butterworth-Heinemann..

Ochôa, P., & Pinto, L. G. (2006). *Quality – An on-going practice and reflection in a governmental library (1996–2006)*. Retrieved March 1, 2012, from http://archive.ifla.org/IV/ifla72/papers/078-Ochoa_Pinto-en.pdf

Ochôa, P., & Pinto, L. G. (2007). Estratégias de gestão baseada em evidências: Investigação e prática em serviços de informação. In *Bibliotecas e arquivos: informação para a cidadania, o desenvolvimento e a inovação*. Lisboa: B.A.D.

Ochôa, P., & Pinto, L. G. (2012). Contextos emergentes da excelência. In *Actas*. Lisboa: B.A.D. Retrieved October 30, 2012, from http://www.bad.pt/publicacoes/index.php/congressosbad/article/view/299

OECD. (2002). *Policies to promote sustainable consumption: An overview*. Paris: OECD..

Ottman, J. A. (2003). *Green marketing: Challenges and opportunities for the new marketing age*. Lincolnwood, IL: NTC Business Books..

Payne, A., Storbacka, K., & Frow, P. (2008). Managing the co-creation of value. *Journal of the Academy of Marketing Science, 36*, 83–96. doi:10.1007/s11747-007-0070-0.

Pinto, L. G., & Ochôa, P. (2012). Portuguese library assessment practices and transitions: A meta-evaluation model for the information and knowledge society. Paper presented in QQML. Limerick, Ireland..

Plum, T., Franklin, B. R., Kyrillidou, M., Roebuck, G., & Davis, M. (2010). Measuring the impact of networked electronic resources: Developing an assessment infrastructure for libraries, state, and other types of consortia. *Performance Measurement and Metrics, 11*(2), 184–198. doi:10.1108/14678041011064098.

Poll, R. (2007). Benchmarking with quality indicators: National projects. *Performance Measurement and Metrics, 8*(1), 41–53. doi:10.1108/14678040710748076.

Poll, R. (2012). Can we quantify the library's influence? Creating an ISO standard for impact assessment. *Performance Measurement and Metrics, 13*(2), 121–130. doi:10.1108/14678041211241332.

Poll, R., & Payne, P. (2006). Impact measures for libraries and information services. *Library Hi Tech, 24*(4), 547–562. doi:10.1108/07378830610715419.

Rankin, C. (2012). The potential of generic social outcomes in promoting the positive impact of the public library: Evidence from the national year of reading in Yorkshire. *Evidence Based Library & Information Practice, 7*(1), 7–21.

Ritzer, G., & Jungenson, N. (2010). Production, consumption, presumption: The nature of capitalism in the age of the digital 'prosumer'. *Journal of Consumer Culture, 10*(1), 13–36. doi:10.1177/1469540509354673.

Ross, S., et al. (2011). *Digital library conformance checklist*. Retrieved November 10, 2012, from http://www.dlorg.eu/uploads/Booklets/booklet21x21_checklist_web.pdf

Royal Society. (2012). *Science as an open enterprise*. London: Royal Society. Retrieved September 20, 2012, from http://royalsociety.org/uploadedFiles/Royal_Society_Content/policy/projects/sape/2012-06-20-SAOE.pdf

Saarti, J., & Juntunen, A. (2011). The benefits of a quality management system: The case of the merger of two universities and their libraries. *Library Management, 32*, 183–190. doi:10.1108/01435121111112899.

Saarti, J., & Laitinen, M. (2012). Evaluating the effects of library e-resources and IL tuition on the research outcomes in Finnish top universities and the quality of the statistical data collected. Paper presented in QQML. Limerick, Ireland..

Senge, P. (2006). *The fifth discipline: The art and practice of the learning organization*. London: Random House..

Smiers, J. (2012). *Digitisation and cultural democracy, an (as yet) unfulfilled promise*. Retrieved November 12, 2012 from http://www.coe.int/t/dg4/cultureheritage/cwe/CWE-TP-Smiers-en.pdf

Staes, P., & Thijs, N. (Eds.). (2010). *Growing towards excellence in the European public sector: A decade of European collaboration with CAF*. Maastricht, The Netherlands: EIPA..

Steyaert, J. (2000). *Digitale vaardigheden: Geletterdheid in de informatiesamenleving*. The Hague, The Netherlands: Rathenau Institut..

Streatfield, D., & Markless, S. (2009). What is impact assessment and why is it important? *Performance Measurement and Metrics*, 10(2), 134–141. doi:10.1108/14678040911005473.

Tanner, S., & Deegan, M. (2012). *Inspiring research, inspiring scholarship*. London: JISC..

Teece, D. (2010). Business models, business strategy and innovation. *Long Range Planning*, 43, 172–194. doi:10.1016/j.lrp.2009.07.003.

Tenopir, C. (2012). Beyond usage: Measuring library outcomes and value. *Library Management*, 33(1/2), 5–13. doi:10.1108/01435121211203275.

Toffler, A. (1980). *The third wave*. New York: William Morrow and Company..

Town, S. (2011). Value, impact and the transcendent library: Progress and pressures in performance measurement and evaluation. *The Library Quarterly*, 81(1), 11–125. doi:10.1086/657445.

Truccolo, I., et al. (2005). *EFQM (European foundation for quality management) and libraries: An organisational challenge for improving the provided services*. Retrieved March 1, 2012, from http://www.cro.sanita.fvg.it/reposcro/biblioteca/eahil_2005-truccolo-doc.pdf

Van Dijk, J. A. G. M. (1999). *The network society, social aspects of new media*. London: Sage..

Van Dijk, J. A. G. M. (2008). One Europe, digitally divided. In *Routledge Handbook of Internet Politics* (pp. 288–304). London: Routledge..

Van Dijk, J. A. G. M. (2012). The evolution of the digital divide: The digital divide turns to inequality of skills and usage. In *Digital Enlightenment Yeabook 2012* (pp. 57–75). New York: IOS Press..

Vargo, S., & Lusch, F. (2008). Service-dominant logic: Continuing the evolution. *Journal of the Academy of Marketing Science*, 36(1), 1–10. doi:10.1007/s11747-007-0069-6.

Voima, P., Heinonen, K., & Strandvik, T. (2010). *Exploring customer value formation – A customer dominant logic perspective*. Helsinki: Hanken School of Economics. Retrieved September 2, 2012 from https://helda.helsinki.fi/bitstream/handle/10227/630/552-978-952-232-088-9.pdf?sequence=1

Warnaby, G., Baron, S., & Konijer, P. (2009). *Toward an understanding of customer perspectives on organizational operant resources*. Paper presented at ANZMAC 2009. Retrieved January 31, 2012, from http://www.duplication.net.au/ANZMAC09/papers/ANZMAC2009-058.pdf

Wilson, F., & Town, J. S. (2006). Benchmarking and library quality maturity. *Performance Measurement and Metrics*, 7(2), 75–82. doi:10.1108/14678040610679461.

Wind, Y., & Mahajan, V. (2002). Convergence marketing. *Journal of Interactive Marketing*, 16(2), 64–79. doi:10.1002/dir.10009.

Wolski, M., & Richardson, J. (2011). *A framework for university research data management.* Paper presented at CCA-Educause Australasia Conference. Sydney, Australia. Retrieved January 31, 2012, from http://www98.griffith.edu.au/dspace/bitstream/handle/10072/39672/69936_1.pdf?sequence=1

Xie, C., Bagozzi, R. P., & Troye, S. V. (2008). Trying to presume: toward a theory of consumer as co-creators of value. *Journal of the Academy of Marketing Science, 36*, 109–122. doi:10.1007/s11747-007-0060-2.

Zwass, V. (2010). Co-creation: Toward a taxonomy and an integrated research perspective. *International Journal of Electronic Commerce, 15*(1), 11–48. doi:10.2753/JEC1086-4415150101.

ADDITIONAL READING

Alemu, G., Stevens, B., & Ross, P. (2012). Towards a conceptual Framework for user-driven semantic metadata interoperability in digital libraries. A social constructivist approach. *New Library World, 113*(1/2), 38–54. doi:10.1108/03074801211199031.

Behrens, S. G. et al. (2012). *Competency lifecycle roadmap. Toward performance readiness. Hanscom.* Canergie Mellon University..

Borgman, C. (1996). Social aspects of digital libraries. In E. A. Fox, & G. Marchioninni (Eds.) Procedings of the 1st ACM International conference on digital libraries. Bethesda (pp.170-171).

Borgman, C. (2007). *Scholarship in the digital Age.* Cambridge, MA and London: MIT Press..

Campbell, C. (2005). The craft consumer: culture, craft and consumption in a Postmodern society. *Journal of Consumer Culture, 5*(1), 23–42. doi:10.1177/1469540505049843.

Carducci, V. (2006). Culture jamming: a sociological perspective. *Journal of Consumer Culture, 6*(1), 116–138. doi:10.1177/1469540506062722.

Chambers, S., & Schailer, W. (2010). Bringing research libraries into Europeana. Establishing a library domain aggregator. *The Library Quarterly, 20*(1), 105–116.

Deegan, M., & Sutherland, K. (Eds.). (2009). *Text editing, print and the digital world.* Aldershot: Ashgate..

European Commission. (2007). *Electronic skills for the 21st century: fostering competitiveness, growth and jobs.* Retrieved December 1, 2012 from http://europa.eu/scadplus/leg/en/lvb/l24293.htm.

Featherstone, M. (2007). *Consumer culture and postmodernism* (2nd ed.). London: Sage..

Fisher, K. E., Erdelez, S., & McKechnie, L. (Eds.). (2005). *Theories of information behavior.* Medford: Information Today..

Held, D., & Kaya, A. (2007). *Global inequality.* Cambridge: Polity Press..

High Level Expert Group on scientific Data. (2010). *Riding the wave – How Europe can gain from the rising tide of scientific data. A submission to the European Commission.* Luxembourg: European Commission..

Hoivik, T. (2012). How much is much? A conceptual study of web traffic. *The Library Quarterly, 21*(2), 276–293.

Neely, A. D., Adams, C., & Kennerley, M. (2002). *The performance prism: the scorecard measuring and managing business success.* London: Prentice Hall..

OECD. (2011). *Divided we stand, why inequality keeps rising.* Paris: OECD..

Pryor, G. (Ed.). (2012). *Managing research data.* London: Facet Publishing..

Savolainen, R. (2008). *Everyday information practices: a social phenomenological perspective.* Lanham: Scarecrow Press..

Streatfield, D. (2012). Impact Planning and Assessment (IPA) of the Global Libraries Initiative (GL) of the Bill & Melinda Gates Foundation. *Performance Measurement and Metrics, 13*(1), 5–7. doi:10.1108/14678041211228526.

Vargo, S. L., Maglio, P. P., & Akaba, M. A. (2008). On value and value co-creation: a service systems and service logic perspective. *European Management Journal, 26*, 145–152. doi:10.1016/j.emj.2008.04.003.

Veletsianos, G., & Kimmons, R. (2012). Networked participatory scholarship: emergent techno-cultural pressures toward open and digital scholarship in online networks. *Computers & Education, 58*, 766–774. doi:10.1016/j.compedu.2011.10.001.

KEY TERMS AND DEFINITIONS

Consumer Culture: The study of consumers and consumption and the relationship between people and material/virtual goods in everyday life. Histories and geographies of immaterial consumption and segmentation typologies are requiring greater detail due to the diversity of consumer's behavior, patterns, values and trajectories/fashion. Global inequalities are also sharpening the vision of consumption and the use of resources.

Convergence: A transformative trend as a result of merging of distinct intentions, initiatives, strategies, policies and different fields of study, into a unified whole that creates new pathways. Information society is characterized by convergent dynamics, where various sectors develop simultaneous actions to beneficiate of the favorable holistic participation capacity of people all around the world. It is considered a new paradigm of a new integrated approach, based on interdisciplin-

ary research and different ideas and uses. In EU is important the sustainability of convergence (mainly economic) but also the single market policy. In this context, e-resources are growing in cross-disciplinary uses and can demonstrate the benefits of convergence in librarianship, through Europeana results.

Digital Agenda: The current political issue to achieve a new stage of information society in EU. It's a plan for ten years (2010-2020) with seven pillars: Digital single market; interoperability and standards, trust and security; fast and ultra-fast internet access, research and innovation; enhancing digital literacy, skills and inclusion; ICT- enabled benefits for EU society. The European Council and the European Parliament have called for further strengthening of the European digital leadership and completion of the Digital Single Market by 2015.

Dynamics: It comprises the actions and interactions of various factors (personal, interpersonal, social, and contextual) and their effects on society. Understanding the dynamics affecting e-resources management is relevant at all levels, from the tactical to the strategic in the overall management life cycles (information, competences, knowledge and performance).

E-Resources: Materials that require computer access, whether though a personal computer, mainframe, or handheld mobile device, being valued in informational environments and subject to rapid change due to technological innovations and consuming habits. They are very important in the contemporary knowledge society and, at the macro level, can stimulate innovation and economic growth. This vision of e-resources value is developed by European Agenda Digital.

Excellence: This management concept manifests itself in several areas of information society. In Europe it reflects the debate from both economic and management viewpoint, tied to the development of quality management theories and models and to performance evaluation dynamics in all kind of organizations. In essence, excellence is determined by organizational performance and by imprecise individual factors (perceptions, expectations, experiences and informational behavior), meaning different things to different people. Excellence diversity requires strategical convergence dynamics in order to achieve maturity and sustainability.

Transitions: Moments of fast change with multiple impacts on society, associated with technological, theoretical, cultural, political and social areas transformations. Economic austerity and demands for new forms of the cultural field in Europe characterize two of the main transitions in EU. Culture fundamental role in Europe is linked to the guarantee of open-mindedness, equality, prosperity and participatory democracy: creator of empathy of difference. This transition should give evidence to the development of a set of European cultural indicators to measure societal and economic impact of culture. E-resources are a multi-dimensional evidence to be measure in information culture.

ENDNOTES

1. The concept adopted here follows IFLA's definition (Johnson, S., *et al.*, 2012): it refers to those materials that require computer access, whether though a personal computer, mainframe, or handheld mobile device. They may either be accessed remotely via the Internet or locally. Some of the most frequently encountered types are e-journals, e-books, full-text (aggregated) databases, indexing and abstracting databases, reference databases, numeric and statistical databases, e-images and e-audio/visual resources.

[i] Cost efficiency, cost effectiveness, cost comparison, financial allocation, contingent valuation and value added, return on investment.

2. This Plan is available at: http://www.york. ac.uk/media/communications/internalcommunications/university-plan%202009%20 to%202019.pdf. To the University of York, Excellence means developing high-quality research; encouraging innovation in all categories of staff and students; ensuring that teaching and learning take place in a supportive environment, informed by research, collaborating strategically with other research-led universities, institutes, agencies and funders in the public and private sector; enhancing the quality of the campus and facilities; developing the information infrastructure and the ability of staff, students and others to use it effectively. To develop internationalization, the University will do high quality, ground-breaking research that will have an impact on thinkers, policymakers and business leaders world-wide, creating opportunities for international exchange with high quality institutions, for both students and academic staff.

3. The Internet has created new business models, like Flickr business model, evolving from gaming to on-line photo sharing, harnessing user feedback generated through blogs. According to Teece (2010, pp.178-179), "Flickr's multiple revenue stream business model involves collecting subscription fees, charging advertisers' for contextual advertising, and receiving sponsorship and revenue-sharing fees from partnerships with retail chains and complementary photo service companies. Yahoo bought Flick in March 2005 for tens of millions of dollars". This model is known as *"freemium"*. Another type of model are cloud-based models, which allow customers to buy virtual server capacity for a single transaction, transforming previous 'fixed plus variable' cost models into entirely variable cost models. The selection/

design of business models is related with organizational dynamics and skills to change and adapt the value chain, cost leadership and differentiation in a *many-to-many marketing* (Gummesson, 2004).

4. Library benefits are stated in the *Alexandria Manifesto* (2005): democracy, intellectual freedom, information literacy, information equality, reduction of poverty and cultural diversity. Outcomes of cultural institutions include: knowledge, information literacy, higher academic or professional success, social inclusion, individual well -being (Poll & Payne, 2006).

5. Driving access to content and digital resources for library users is one of IFLA's key initiatives for 2011-2012. IFLA - the International Federation of Library Associations and Institutions - is working collaboratively to build a legal, technical and professional base that enables libraries to play a major role in collecting, preserving, and offering wide access to all types of physical and digital materials: digital legal deposit - with a focus on legislative certainty for deposit and library user access; digital lending - with a focus on library user access to e-resources and inter-organisation/cross-border uses compatible with fair practice; mass digitization - with a focus on IFLA facilitating information exchange for the library sector; digital preservation - with a focus on legal mechanisms for harvesting and preserving born digital information and local content hosted on websites and in social media.

6. According to Cova & Dalli (2009), many terms have been used to capture new consumer roles, but all of them converge to describe more active and constructive consumers as well as their market experiences and relationships with organizations.

7. The *ESFRI Roadmap 2010* presented six areas of activities: Social Sciences and Humanities; Environmental Sciences; Energy; Biological and Medical Sciences; Materials and Analytical Sciences; Physical Sciences and Engineering.

8. The Council of Europe's CultureWatchEurope is a cultural governance observatory offering an evidence-based overview of culture, heritage and media developments http://www.coe.int/tdg4/cultureheritage/CWE/default_en.asp.

9. In recent years, understandings of consumer behavior have come a long way from expectancy-value models to socio psychological models that account for moral, social, symbolic and affective components, showing how cognitive processes have impact, especially in prosumers behaviors and prosumption processes. Ethical consumption is another issue with high impact on sustainable consumption (OECD, 2002; Dodson, 2003; Harrison, Newholm & Shaw, 2005) and anti-consumption identities (Lee, Fernandez & Hyman, 2009) and practices, such as rejecting, reduction, reuse and recycling (Cherrier, 2010; Black & Cherrier, 2010). Consumer resistance (Kozinets, 2002) and consumer empowerment (Kozinets & Handelman, 2004) are oppositional meanings of consumption.

10. Service has been discussed in literature from two points: as a category of offerings (intangibility, heterogeneity, perishability) and as activities to the customer.

11. In this *Service-Dominant Logic* there are 10 premises: 1) Service is the fundamental basis of exchange; 2) Indirect exchange masks the fundamental basis of exchange; 3) Goods are a distribution mechanism for service provision; 4) operant resources are the fundamental source of competitive advantage; 5) all economies are service economies; 6) the customer is always a co-creator of value; 7) The enterprise cannot deliver value, but only offer value propositions; 8) A service-centred view is inherently customer oriented

and relational; 9) All social and economic actors are resource integrators; 10) Value is always uniquely and phenomenologically determined by the beneficiary. In this sense, it could provide the integrative logic required to unite and progress knowledge (Ng, Vargo & Smith, 2012). Other academic discourse on services is Service Science (Chesbrough & Spohrer, 2006), an interdisciplinary study of service systems in economic exchange, configurating value-co-creation of resources connected to other resources with the aim of creating a basis for systematic innovation. These resources can be competences, knowledge, shared information, technology, people and organizations. It has emerged to study this phenomenon in a globally integrated world. In both views, services are about networked value co-creation. Consumer Culture Theory (Arnold & Thompson, 2005)

also offer complementary insights, viewing co-creation value in terms of cultural framework that focuses on how customers perceive, interpret, understand, and interact with market (emphasizing life projects and life narratives). These theories often converge. Create, abandon, utilize, ignore, configure, reconfigure, specialize, integrate, protect, share resources and relationships to co-create benefits with and for each other, both as individuals and collectives, both for the short-term and the long-term are key words in ERM.

12. A model of the resource-based view of consumers was tested at the British Library. A detailed analysis of individual's operant resources (enabled through accessibility to 565 messages posted to British Library user support forum) provided different strategies to support value co-creation.

Chapter 4
Patron–Driven Acquisitions:
A Progressive Model for the Selection of Electronic Resources

Smita Joshipura
Arizona State University, USA

Christopher E. Mehrens
Arizona State University, USA

ABSTRACT

During a time when libraries are facing reductions in budget, personnel, and space, it is not viable to continue the traditional "just-in-case" approach to collection development. In a user-centric library world, Patron Driven Acquisitions (PDA) has been shown to be an effective acquisition model in building "just-in-time" monograph collections to support the information and curricular needs of a variety of users in different settings. Arizona State University (ASU) Libraries have implemented a PDA model for electronic as well as print books for their users. The chapter explores the history of the use of PDA in a variety of library settings, provides a related literature review, discusses the application of PDA to the purchase of e-books at ASU from the perspective of an Electronic Resources Librarian and a Subject Librarian and Administrator of a branch library, and provides a sustainable model, which may be applied in different types of library settings.

INTRODUCTION

While PDA had its origins in the print world, the business model emerged in 1999 and was based on the knowledge that library patrons infrequently or never used many print monographs in libraries. Over time, it has become an effective and efficient model, which assures that materials purchased will be utilized; that precious shelf space will not be overpopulated; and that new learning modalities and evolving user needs will be met. It is gaining momentum and becoming a popular collection tool in academic libraries as it provides librarians an ability to vastly increase access to information to their constituencies. In this model, vendors are providing MAchine-Readable Cataloging (MARC) records for titles that match established library collection profiles. Later on, they are loaded into the library's local catalog, which allows discovery by patrons, who

DOI: 10.4018/978-1-4666-4761-9.ch004

play a central role in potential library purchases. Rather than obtaining materials in anticipation of possible use, PDA allows libraries to make materials available according to the needs of its constituencies.

The PDA model provides enormous opportunities for users and staff. The benefit to users is that they have seamless and immediate access to vast collections. The benefit to Subject Specialists is that their workflows in the area of collection development are streamlined, which allow them to focus on the acquisition of materials that address the special needs of their users. Further, it greatly reduces the need and the expense involved with Interlibrary Loan process for titles not held by the libraries. Finally, in the area of Acquisitions and to some extent cataloging, workflows are completely automated, smooth, transparent, and painless.

ASU is one of the largest public universities in the United States having five campuses. The ASU Libraries have relied heavily upon approval plans to acquire monographs, supplemented by librarian selection. In 2009, the ASU Libraries implemented a PDA model for electronic as well as print monographs for their patrons. Many reasons accounted for this decision including low circulation data, severe budget and staff constraints, and the realization that PDA would assist in providing students and faculty access to huge pool of potential titles. Two Librarians from ASU will discuss nuts and bolts of PDA, and will share the opportunities and challenges they encountered, as well as the sustainability of this model for ASU Libraries, which may be applicable to various types of libraries.

BACKGROUND

Definition

PDA is a method by which libraries acquire books that delays purchase until it is used by a patron. It is also referred as Demand-Driven Acquisitions (DDA) model, which has emerged in 1999, and gaining momentum mainly in academic libraries. It is defined as a just-in-time method for acquiring library materials based on users input, which is in opposition to just-in-case method, which was very common model in libraries for many years. Though PDA is considered as an emerging model, it is not a novel concept. In the early years a similar concept was applied for acquisition of print monographs such as use of suggestion form submitted by users, and use of interlibrary loan requests to satisfy the user needs. But, with the evolution of e-books, and high demand for electronic content from users, e-book PDA model is becoming a popular model among libraries. Moreover, with growth of distance education and online classes, e-books have become an essential collection for libraries as it can cater the need of off-campus users. The purpose of libraries to implement the PDA model is to reduce costs by acquiring only those books, which are requested by users, to align the library's collection with current user requirement, and to increase discovery options for users by providing larger pool of titles. It can be considered as a monographic acquisition system that includes PDA for both electronic and print books, along with a highly selective approval plan that is complemented by librarian selection as needed.

With the shrinkage in library budget, the traditional "just-in-case" purchasing model for majority of libraries is becoming unsustainable. Also, looking at the history, use of the print collection has gone down over time. One frequently cited study revealed that, "20% of the collection receives 80% of the use" (Trueswell, 1969). "This trend is found in most academic libraries across the United States, where it is estimated that many monographs in a typical academic library collection never circulate" (Kent, 1979). "Starting in the late 1970s, the results of several studies showed that users in major academic library collections checked out an astonishingly low percentage of these largely librarian-selected books" (Kent, 1979). "Over the past ten years, the circulation rate for this sort of speculative acquisition of English-language materials has been approximately 60%".(Levine-Clark, Bosch, Anderson, & Nauman, 2009). These studies indicate that the traditional "just-in-case" model of librarian-selected titles does not serve users efficiently in academic institutions. At the same time, skyrocketing Interlibrary Loan (ILL) figures from the Association of Research Libraries member libraries also indicated that local collections do not meet needs adequately

The first and foremost step in implementation of PDA model is selection of a suitable vendor and setting up an efficient profile. It is critical to develop a strong profile for PDA, which may replace approval plans function of an academic library in future. The approval plans is considered as a core collection development activity, and play an important role in acquisitions of library materials. The primary reasons in implementing approval plans are to ensure that all important publications are acquired by the library, and are received automatically, which would result into significant saving of time of librarians and staff in generating and processing orders. The successful approval plan is based on setting up a profile, which is a collaborative task between a vendor and collection development librarians. "If properly planned and maintained, an approval plan can be an efficient and effective tool in building a library collection".(Fenner, 2004) So, setting up a strong profile by considering various parameters such as cost, publishers, year of publications, etc. helps in controlling and delivering the right contents for users.

Once the profile is complete, the vendor's staff will select materials that fit the profile and send the MARC records to load in a local catalog on a regular base to the libraries. Users have access to these records that look the same as any other e-book records. This process allows users to discover contents, and provide seamless access at the point of need. Moreover, it does not require any

commitment for the libraries to purchase books and they only purchase those e-books, which are used by their users. After a certain number of browses or after a certain amount of time viewing each book, the library pays for the title and adds it permanently to the collection. This model was found viable by the libraries due to severe budget crunch. Also, "librarians conducting subsequent use studies on these titles discovered surprisingly high circulation figures for these patron-selected titles when compared with similar traditionally acquired titles, even considering that at least some of the subsequent use was probably by the same patrons, who placed the initial requests". (Anderson et al. 2002; Perdue and Van Fleet 1999) In one study, "selectors' reviews of patron-selected titles agreed that the vast majority of them were appropriate for the collection". (Anderson et al. 2002).

The Global Recession of 2009 and its Impact on the ASU Libraries

January of 2009 was a significant year in the history of the ASU Libraries because the collapse of the American economy became an important factor in the reshaping of this organization's collections, services and staffing. In the face of a $1.6 billion budgetary shortfall in the State of Arizona, the State Legislature required that all three state universities cut $141.5 million from their budgets. With the severe reduction in state funding, ASU initiated dramatic cost-saving measures to address the shortfall while maintaining the excellence of its academic course offerings. In a press release Dr. Michael Crow, ASU President (2009), wrote the following to the members of the university community,

I want to assure all of you that ASU is committed to continue to deliver all our academic programs to our students, to not reducing academic quality and to maintaining all of our student financial aid programs. We will continue working with internal

groups to find additional prudent cost-saving measures that are consistent with our institutional mission…We well understand that our state – and our nation – are struggling to cope with the worst economic conditions since the Great Depression, and that we all need to do our share of budget cutting…No matter the circumstances, ASU will remain committed to the ideals of the New American University – admitting all qualified students, providing them a high-quality education and having a positive impact on the state through education, research, economic development activity and community service. Please rest assured that we are working every possible idea to keep the university advancing through these difficult times.

Consequently, a reduction in force was executed, a series of furloughs were mandated, and all departments were required to cut expenditures. In response, the ASU Libraries formulated long-term and short-term solutions in response in the President's charge to provide our students "a high-quality education" albeit with limited funds.

From 2009 to 2010, the ASU Libraries Reorganization Planning Steering Committee began to develop a long-term strategic plan, which investigated library services and future opportunities, and in 2010 an initial draft of a four-year strategic plan, "informed by ASU's vision of the New American University," was produced. By 2011, an implementation plan was put into place based on the following pillars derived from the strategic plan: Research Support; Learning & Instruction; Services; Collections; and Place & Space.

At the same time, the Libraries enacted organization-wide short-term solutions to the budget crisis. These included judicious cuts in library personnel, the elimination of unfilled staffing lines were eliminated, the encouragement of early retirements, furloughs, and the significant scaling back of expenditures for library collections (electronic and print resources).

With respect to resources and the impact of reduced funding in support of collections, a series of meetings were scheduled involving Collections Steering Council which, at that time, was a body composed of library directors, department heads, and subject librarians charged with shaping the holdings of the ASU Libraries. During these meetings, decisions were made regarding journal subscriptions as well as the re-alignment of collections. With respect to monographs, the only new expenditures were for course reserves and, to a lesser degree, non-reserve faculty requests.

Subject librarians, acting as liaisons to their respective departments, made efforts to inform their constituencies of the changes taking place. Faculty was informed of resource subscriptions (print and electronic) that were discontinued, that only purchases for course reserves were to be made indefinitely, and that document delivery for non-course related resource was viable and effective in light of the situation at hand.

New workflows in the Bibliographic and Metadata Services unit were also established because of a significant reduction in personnel. One solution was to purchase shelf-ready materials or digital collections with downloadable catalog records. An area significantly impacted was music when a decision was made to eliminate the Libraries' sole music cataloger. This decision was made because it was found that the outsourcing of scores and sound recordings to a contract cataloging service was more economical (music books and videos were still cataloged in-house). With the loss of the music cataloger, a greater turn-around time for the cataloging and processing of scores and sound recordings became a reality, however, through faculty education, last-minute orders became more of an exception and not a rule.

Over time, the cuts to the acquisitions budget eased, but the hiring of personnel remained scaled-back with only essential lines being filled. A result of the fiscal diet imposed on collection building has led to a more sensible, lean approach to ordering materials and resources. While materials beyond course reserves are once-more purchased, careful consideration for materials that support the curricular and research needs of the university. Such belt tightening, while painful, helped to pave the way for the decision to formulate and implement a PDA acquisitions model as a more efficient and fiscally responsible means of purchasing materials to support our constituencies. At ASU, the just-in-case model is a past memory, and our users now play a more collaborative role in the shaping of the Libraries' collections.

Selection and Implementation of PDA Model at ASU Libraries

At ASU Libraries, Collections and Scholarly Communications Office investigated various vendors, who were providing integrated PDA for print and e-book service. After evaluating various vendors the decision was made to implement PDA program, also known as E-stream and P-stream PDA offered by Ingram Content Group on MyiLibrary platform. Since the implementation of this model involves coordination with various library departments, staff from Bibliographic and Metadata Services, Collections and Scholarly Communications Office, Access Services, and Informatics and Cyber Infrastructure Services were involved from the very beginning of this project.

Building an effective profile based on various academic programs at ASU to serve curricular and research needs for our patrons was the primary step at our institution for implementing PDA model. It was decided to use the same print approval profile, which was already in place for PDA model. The profile includes all the major areas such as Arts and Humanities, Social Sciences and Sciences. An integrated e-book and print approval profiles includes subject and non-subject parameters such as publishers, formats/genres, audience, imprint date, price, and other relevant criteria, which would generate weekly sets of titles matching our profiles. It was decided to have e-format as our preferred format for PDA as it provides remote and twenty four hours access to patrons, requires no storage space, eliminates loss or theft, and pro-

vides search functionality to our users. To avoid duplication between print and e-formats, it was decided to keep the time lag of 90 days, i.e. print titles are loaded after 90 days of its availability. So, if the publication is available in e-format within this time lag, the e-stream MARC records would overlay on the p-stream records. If no e-format is available after 90 days, we get the print record. Another important step before the implementation was to negotiate with the vendor about the license terms and conditions, which include number of simultaneous users permitted, amount of material that can be downloaded, printed, or saved. Lastly, it was critical to negotiate about total number of patron usage, which would trigger a purchase. It was decided that the purchase of the books will automatically take place after the third substantive use, i.e. excluding views of the table of contents, title page, or index. Once the profile set up was completed, the first load of MARC records was made available by Ingram, which matched with our library's profile, and we retrieved and loaded the files. It was a small pool of titles due to time lag of 90 days to avoid duplication among formats, as well as recent publication year as one of the parameters. We receive about 100-150 e-stream MARC record loads on a weekly basis, and currently we have about 20,500 non-purchased e-stream records in our library catalog, which has low or no usage. Our profile is considered as very narrow and selective, which could be one of the reasons of our PDA model to be successful and sustainable.

A small test of uploading MARC records before the actual implementation was another important step during this process. The process required some pre-implementation work of establishing parameters for the records we receive from Ingram. Our requirements with the vendor were adding a 655 for Electronic books and a 710 for MyiLibrary in all MARC records, and adding our proxy information. Before the load took place, a cataloger analyzed the batch of MARC records, identified problems, and corrected them with Global Update feature of ASU's Innovative Interfaces, Inc. Millennium system. Once the MARC records were loaded and corrected, patrons were able to discover e-books in the catalog. Test records in the public catalog looked identical to other e-book records, except that they lacked an item record. Patrons clicked on a "Connect to" link (an example of MARC record is below) and went directly to the full text of the e-book hosted on MyiLibraryserver, identical to the procedure and display of other e-books owned by ASU. The access was seamless and user did not recognize any difference in the records or access. ASU never made any announcement about this service, and it went live in February, 2010.

At ASU, we also implemented print PDA program known as p-stream PDA in May 2010 as many scholarly books are not available in e-format at the time of publication or later within two to three months. This model allows our users a wider range of titles for selection and also satisfies those users, who prefer print over e-format.

We receive weekly MARC records for p-stream titles, which match our profiles. These records are loaded before e-stream titles load to avoid duplication of titles. Once the records are loaded into the catalog, users can discover the titles and request purchase. This process is not as seamless as e-stream titles for users as well as for library staff. Users may find it confusing and frustrating since they discover a record of a print book in the catalog, but is not owned by the library, and so cannot access immediately. After a user requests a book, a notification is received by acquisition staff through a public folder. The acquisition staff treat as a rush order. Once it is received, the library will catalog and process the book, hold and notify the user. For p-stream titles, we decided not to receive the books pre-processed from our vendor as it would add additional time for processing before shipping. Though e-stream for PDA is more efficient than p-stream PDA for our patrons and staff, due to time lag between publication of print and electronic, we decided to have both programs

Figure 1. MARC Record

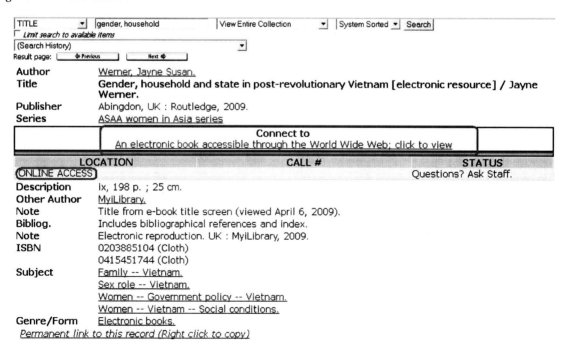

74

running simultaneously. After few months of implementation of print PDA, our print slips approval plan was replaced by this model.

Cataloging

Ingram provides MARC records created from information provided by the various publishers. The process of cataloging is fairly smooth, but requires human intervention. Cataloging receives weekly notification from Ingram about new records available for PDA model. Cataloging staff downloads all of the MARC records from a File Transfer Protocol (FTP) server and loads them into the ASU catalog. These records include many fields, which are not required, and so are either deleted or reviewed for accuracy and consistency. Catalogers update the vendor records before loading by adding 655 note indicating "Electronic books", and 710 field indicating "MyiLibrary" when necessary, so that the library can keep track of these titles. Moreover, all the subject headings are removed except Library of Congress subject headings. These titles are activated in ASU's MyiLibrary account first before we receive the record loads, and patrons access e-books via the ASU catalog or by searching in the MyiLibrary platform. The cataloger also decided that once an e-book was purchased, they would "clean up" the record, making it more uniform with the other records in the catalog. The cataloging staff receives MARC records of the purchased titles, which overlay on 035 fields of old records, and include an order and item record.

Acquisitions

E-stream PDA has brought a paradigm shift in the acquisitions department of ASU Libraries. It has resulted into effective workflow, and saving staff time. It has eliminated manual and physical processing such as packing, unpacking, checking in, binding, labeling, etc. It is also saving the cost and time on the acquisitions process due to instant delivery of an e-book title. Moreover, there is no risk involved such as book being lost, stolen or damaged. The workflow is seamless for the staff from acquisitions to invoice processing. Basically, the staff is not involved from the very beginning when new records are loaded in the catalog. They do not have to create any order record in the library system. Once the full-text content of e-book is accessed three times, it triggers the purchase, and an invoice is received monthly, which includes the cost and usage information. The staff processes the invoice, and sends it to accounting department for payment. The process is very efficient, smooth, painless, and staff appreciate it.

Budget

The total expenditure at ASU from implementation of e-PDA in 2010 until October 2012 is $480,340. In the year 2010, we spent $18,474, which is now gradually increasing. In 2011 we spent $187,757, whereas in 2012 the expenditure was $222,000. For the year 2013, so far we have already spent $52,000. The steady increase in the expenditure could be due to larger pool of titles available for users' discovery as well as more familiarity and ease of access to PDA titles by our students and faculty. The total e-book titles purchased so far are 3,460 volumes, which makes the average cost- per-title to $139. Based on this data, the average monthly purchase is 104 books, as well as the average monthly expenditure is $15,000. We have also noticed that during the peak time of the fall and spring semesters, i.e. from September to December, and February to April, the expenditure increases significantly to about $25,000 per month. Looking at the trend of purchase and expenditure of e-PDA titles, and comparing against the traditional print slips approval plans; this method seems to be reasonable and sustainable model for our budget.

Another interesting data is about subject distribution of these purchased titles. A sample of 1,034 e-PDA titles shows that we have purchased highest books in the field of Social Sciences, including History, which is 44%, followed by STEM (Science, Technology, Engineering, and Mathematics), which is 37%, while the lowest is Humanities & Fine Arts, which is 19%. See the Pie-Chart, Figure 2 e-books by subject

Usage Statistics

The definition of "a use" in MyiLibrary platform is defined as "Successful Section Requests" as per Counting Online Usage of NeTworked Electronic Resources (COUNTER) standards for e-books (Book Report 2). Users can see a preview page with an abstract and table of contents without "a use" being counted. Once they have full-text access of content within the chapters of an e-book, giving them time to review the table of contents, abstract, etc. is counted as "a use". In a unique session, user may navigate and read several books, and the usage counts only as one "user session" for each book viewed. Once the user closes the browser window or logout, the session ends. The sample record of 1,034 e-books purchased by ASU shows the usage below. There are 642 titles showing 100 or less of pages viewed, while about 23 titles with 1,000+ usage.See the Bar graph, Figure 3 e-books by usage.

MyiLibrary delivers invoices and COUNTER compliant usage reports every month through e-mail. It also logs the unique IP addresses of users, although IP addresses are not associated with individual user account names, so patron reading habits are kept confidential. Though collecting and maintaining usage statistics seems to be a smooth process, there are few issues to be resolved.

Benefits

PDA models offer benefits as well as add challenges for libraries. For patrons the benefit of e-PDA is the concept of accessing e-books 24/7. Moreover, the number of books accessible by patrons is surprisingly large, immediate, and seamless.

For libraries, implementation of PDA is tempting as well as terrifying. By applying the profiling techniques developed for approval plans to PDA by librarians, the titles that are not of academic interests can be eliminated. Thus, although PDA is very much driven by patrons, the titles that patrons can select have been filtered by librarians. This model allows librarians to free up their time-consuming process of reviewing and selecting books item-by-item, and using their time more productively. There is guaranteed use of books purchased by the library, and consider as a return on investment for libraries as books are purchased on its use. Moreover, it provides significant use data on titles, subjects, number of uses, which

Figure 2. E-Books by subject

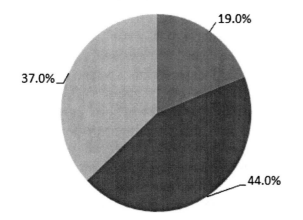

Figure 3. E-Books by usage

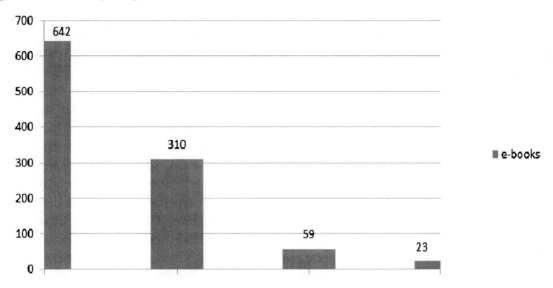

assist the subject librarians in collection decision. The workflow can be considered very smooth as it mainly involves time for processing the weekly load of new MARC records, paying the monthly invoice, and monitoring usage.

Benefits from the Perspective of a Subject Specialist

What follows is an elucidation of the benefits garnered from the implementation of the PDA in the ASU Libraries from the perspective of a Music Librarian. While the narrative is based on a specialized library collection, many of the matters touched upon may be applied to a variety of disciplines supported by all types of libraries.

Historical Precursors

Library budgets and the economy, especially with respect to music collections, have had an important influence in shaping acquisitions models. For example, over thirty years ago Ruth Watanabe, Librarian of the Eastman School of Music's Sibley Music Library, observed:

During the past several years the uncertain economy has affected library budgets, causing such programs as acquisitions and staff development to suffer. Many libraries have had to accept severe cuts in their annual appropriations for scores, books, and recordings. Even those most fortunate libraries whose budgets have not been sliced, or whose budgets have been augmented, the inflationary costs of materials have so far outdistanced any increase in available funds that they have been deprived of a considerable measure of their purchasing power. The decade of the eighties bids fair to becoming a period of selective collection development. (Watanabe, 1981, p. 252)

Nineteen years later, Daniel Zager arrived at the conclusion that "limited fiscal resources" were here to stay and that librarian had to assume the mantle of "arbiter" in the selection of library materials. He writes:

The music librarian as collection developer will use limited resources to shape collections carefully and thoughtfully, with due regard for the needs of the local user group, the potential for regional cooperation, the necessity of identifying collection strengths and building those areas particularly well, new possibilities in electronic and digital information, and vital new directions in music composition, performance, and study. (Zager, 2000, p. 573)

PDA as Modern Want List

Carol June Bradley, in her landmark work, American Music Librarianship: A Biographical and History Survey, identifies the "formative years of American music librarianship" as beginning in 1902 with the appointment of Oscar Sonneck as the "first qualified Chief of the Music Division of the Library of Congress." (Bradley, 1990, p. 2) The method for collection building adopted during his tenure at this important library has left an indelible imprint on music collections throughout the United States, and still looms large in this exciting time of change.

Known as "Systematic Development," Sonneck's goal was to create a music collection at the Library of Congress that would rival those found in the best European libraries, so that American performers and scholars would not have to travel to avail themselves of the best music resources. A major component of Sonneck's collection policies was the creation of "want lists" (desiderata) based on the music librarian's knowledge of his or her collections, which would fill in gaps in the collection with a goal of making them "symmetrical." A further benefit of want lists, as envisioned by Sonneck, is that they would economize the acquisitions process in the form of lessening the "expense of time and money" involved with "clerical labor and correspondence." (Bradley, 1981, pp. 299 -300)

To someone versed in Sonneck's methodology, PDA as implemented at ASU is essentially a modern recasting of want lists. Our subject selectors, knowing their collections, and knowing where their collections have "needs" or are "lacking" with respect to the curriculum in their respective areas, establish a profiles to ensure that new publications are made known to their constituencies, in our case via the Online Public Access Catalog. Our vendor ("dealer") in this venture, being "reliable and energetic" stands poised to make these materials available expeditiously when demanded by our users. The process established by our Bibliographic and Metadata Service department is economical because the "expense of time and money" involved with "clerical labor, correspondence," cataloging and processing has been remedied to a tremendous extent.

The Changing Role of Academic Libraries

Linda Solow Blotner has observed that "[i]n the library world, a game of imagination has been going on for at least fifteen years - predicting the future of libraries in the digital age." (Blotner,, 2007, p. 67) She then lists eleven examples of these predictions, two of which have come to fruition in the ASU Music Library. The first prediction was made by Patricia Cohen and appeared in the New York Times. Cohen writes, "If the library is here to stay, its purpose has radically changed... The campus library has become an intellectual gathering place...moving from being a warehouse to a workshop." (Cohen, 2004, p. 19) The second prediction was made by Sarah Michalak. She observes that, "More than a physical location, the library becomes a medium or ubiquitous utility, a service always ready at hand." (Michalak, 1994, pp. 94-95)

With respect to the first prediction, from 2007 to 2012, the function ASU Music Library has indeed evolved from a warehouse to a workshop and evidence of this transition has been the increased amount of collaborative work, study, and group learning taking place in our facility. This has necessitated new arrangements of furniture, the provision of more group study tables, and the purchase of portable dry erase boards that are used by our users to map ideas and to outline projects among other things. In response to requests, we have added more electrical outlets in proximity to these group study areas because our users make use of laptops, tablets and other portable devices for wireless access to research and library resources during their collaborative work. Beyond our small library, similar uses of library space on a much larger scale are taking place in the Main and Science libraries.

With respect to the second prediction, ASU has steadily increased its online course offerings and the ASU Libraries, in response, have vigorously pursued the acquisition of digital materials to meet the needs of our online learners. In the spring of 2013, the ASU School of Music offered 17 courses online. Beyond this, more of our music faculty are making use of the Blackboard platform to deliver course materials regardless of location (physical or virtual). Because of these new learning environments, whenever possible or practical, items in electronic format are purchased for the music collection. Items in non-electronic formats are only purchased when they are only available in physical formats or in response to a faculty request for a physical item.

Digital surrogates made available via the online catalog bring with them many advantages, first and foremost, the ability for the instructor to link directly to the resource in their course reserves or via their Blackboard course accounts. The benefits are tremendous because instructors no longer have to seek permission to duplicate materials as licensing agreements have been made with the vendor by the ASU Libraries; students have ready access regardless of location; the expense involved with duplication is circumvented; shelf space is freed up for other reserve items and library staff time involved with processing and retrieving reserves is reduced significantly.

Music, Musical Scores and Sound Recordings

While it is true that the discipline of music, in general, does not readily fit into the digital environment, at the present time we are making more gains, more rapidly, than what was once envisioned five years ago. At that time Linda Solow Blotner observed:

...the march towards a digital library has had a slower tempo for music...LPs and CDs are seeing reduced use as more recorded music is made available digitally. Digitization of scores, however, has thus far been limited to archival materials and items in the public domain, and there is currently no organized plan for wholesale digitization of scores by music publishers or the academic community comparable to efforts now underway by various recording companies and vendors... (Blotner, 2007, pp. 73-74)

As early as 2008 the Music Library made efforts to add digital score collections to its list of electronic resources, the first being Alexander Street Press's Classical Scores Library, soon followed by Naxos Sheet Music. Over a three-year period of time, access to this resource steadily increased from 528 times in 2008, to 2,715 times 2009, to 3,808 times in 2010. Although this is a small sample, the viability of digital scores is demonstrated.

In 2012 a meeting was held with representatives of a major music vendor about the possibility of adapting the PDA model for the acquisition of scores. At the close of the meeting, it was concluded that this possibility of implementing scores on demand would be several years off, but that such things are not out of the realms of possibility.

H. Stephen Wright in his chapter on technology in *Music Librarianship at the Turn of the Century* has observed something universal to libraries, but especially to those that are specialized or small, that we are forever combating obsolescence.

(Wright, 2009, p. 32) The first area where this became evident is with our collection of LP sound recordings. In response to freeing up much needed space in the Music Library, we ran a dusty record report on our collection and found that less than 20 percent of the collection had been circulated one time in five year period.

In response to report the sound recordings were placed in offsite storage where our users are still able to request and use them for their studies. At that time, we also indicated that we would relocate any LP to the music library location in response to user requests. Only one faculty member has made such a request, and the number of LP sound recordings returned was infinitesimal. Although audiophiles still preach the superiority of vinyl for playback, the majority of our younger users prefer digital formats for ease of access and use in their studies. This has been especially born out in reviewing the use of our digital sound collections. One of our principal digital sound collections is the Naxos Music Library. Over a three-year period of time, access to this resource steadily increased from 15,706 times in 2008, to 17,521 times in 2009, to 19,336 times in 2010.

One final benefit of the PDA model with respect to music collections is the savings incurred with respect to collection development and maintenance. Endemic to music study is the need to purchase multiple copies of an item, especially scores, for analysis and research. Many musical scores need to be viewed individually because their size is not conducive to sharing. Additionally, music scores are heavily used and subject to loss and damage in the form of damaged bindings, pencil or pen markups (analytical symbols, phrasing, fingering, etc.), page tears, and the general disintegration of less than ideal non-archival paper. Digital surrogates allow multiple users access to the scores for study and, because they are not subject to wear and tear, provides an ideal form of preservation.

Challenges

Though to some extent PDA can be viewed as a library-oriented service, there are few challenges. Some of the drawbacks of PDA model are profile management, discovery, title duplication, cataloging, and licensing issues. Since it allows users more power in selecting than the subject librarians, there is a philosophical shift in collection development practices. PDA model requires a very selective profile, and need to be monitored as well as alter/modify regularly. Otherwise, it may result into an expensive and unbalanced model.

Some of the cataloging issues such as allowing access to wide collection through loading MARC records in the library catalog require a reverse cataloging process. In this method, a large number of records are loaded initially, and later on, records of purchased titles are received and overlaid on the original records. The major concern is for those records, which are not purchased, and when to suppress or remove them from the library system. Furthermore, the imported MARC records do not contain Online Computer Library Center (OCLC) numbers to allow catalogers to easily update holdings in WorldCat once items are purchased. Though records are decent, and additional cataloging is not required, the vendor-supplied records do not always meet traditional or local cataloging standards.

Regarding discovery of these titles, since the e-stream records first loaded are not reflected in WorldCat/OCLC records, and are not indexed in Google, they are not easily discoverable by users through various search engines, and patrons have to rely on the local catalog to discover these e-books.

Many libraries wish to avoid duplicating the same title in print and online formats, but in PDA model it is possible for patrons to trigger purchase of an item already owned in print, as well as for librarians to order a print book, whose electronic counterpart is already available, but not yet purchased. The system rely on International Standard Book Number (ISBN) matching to avoid duplicating print titles in the first MARC batch load, but some duplicate titles failed to match because two records have different format-specific ISBNs. It is also observed that ISBN linking appears to be a problem for many e-book vendors, and encouraged them to include as many ISBNs as possible in their MARC records to facilitate matching and de-duplicating. Also, there are chances of duplication across multiple e-book platforms, which also require careful consideration.

Some of the licensing issues include e-book vendors rarely supporting preservation initiatives, such as Portico, LOCKSS (Lots of Copies Keep Stuff Safe), and CLOCKSS (Controlled LOCKKS), which will support libraries sustainable access to electronic collections. Also, Digital Rights Management (DRM), which is designed to control and limit how and who uses e-book file is challenging. DRM allows e-book vendors to cut off access during the circumstances when a class of students browsing an e-book faster than permitted may trigger an unauthorized access in the system and would result into loss of access. To implement DRM, many e-book vendors require users to view content in proprietary websites that may not be supporting users with disabilities or using mobile devices. Some other conditions such as limit on number of simultaneous users, amount of content that user can access, prohibition of course pack use, interlibrary lending add more challenges, and some vendors are unwilling to remove these clauses. Also, recently it has been noticed that a number of e-book publishers have backed away from the "multi-user" model of e-book access. Some publisher have moved to a "single license" model, where a library must purchase another license usually at the original e-book price in order to provide access to more than one user at a time. In these cases, each license purchased provides access for one additional concurrent user.

Not all publishers have moved to this model, but it is important to remain firm and tough during negotiation process.

Lastly, it is critical to monitor the budget periodically as administering PDA model is very smooth, and may misguide projection of budget. It is important to keep track of invoices, and watch for the use patterns which help in projecting expenditure for the future.

Challenges from the Perspective of a Subject Specialist

Again, as stated earlier under "Benefits..." what follows is an elucidation of the benefits garnered from the implementation of the PDA in the ASU Libraries from the perspective of a Music Librarian. While the narrative is based on a specialized library collection, many of the matters touched upon may be applied to a variety of disciplines supported by all types of libraries.

The Efficacy of the PDA Model at ASU: Caveats for Assessment

Given the relatively short period of time that PDA has been implemented at ASU, data pertaining to the efficacy of the PDA model at ASU is just only being compiled. However, if earlier studies on the usage of e-books are an indicator, the PDA program at ASU will be an efficient and effective means of serving the needs of our constituencies regardless of discipline.

Justin Littman and Lynn Silipigni Connaway (2004) performed an analysis of print and e-book usage at Duke University. Connaway and Littman found that, after their introduction at Duke, e-books received "11 percent more use than comparable print books" and concluded that these results "suggested a "rapid growth in the adoption of e-books." (p.260) At that time, they also found that, "[w]hen analyzed by subject, both e-books and print books were used relatively in proportion to their subject representation in the entire subject set." (p.261) In the Littman Connaway study, subject representation for both e-books and print books was greater for disciplines such as the Social Sciences, Business, Economics and Management, and Literature. Subject representation in the Arts and Education, was significantly less.

As we have seen earlier in this chapter, at the present time and with respect to e-books, subject representation in the ASU Libraries is comparable to that found in the Duke study, with the Social Sciences accounting for 44% of titles held, Science, Technology, Engineering, and Mathematics accounting for 37% of titles held, and the Humanities and Fine Arts accounting for 19% of the held. Consequently, when performing assessment, libraries adopting a PDA model such as implemented ASU, need to keep in mind that subject distribution plays a significant role in the number of times a title is accessed.

Access vs. Use; Use vs. Usage

Michael Levine-Clark published a study of e-book usage by discipline at the University of Denver with special emphasis of users involved in the humanities. He found that the results of the Littman and Connaway study had problems, namely that it did not "take into account usage of print volumes within the library." (Levine-Clark, 2007, p. 7) What this means is that users often consult print titles for their work but do not necessarily feel compelled to check them out, because they take notes of the item in hand, or simply make copies of relevant sections of the sources used. Further, he found that the earlier study did not measure user "awareness" of e-books as a factor contributing to use. Consequently, a survey instrument was prepared with questions measuring user awareness, specifically if they knew that the library provided electronic books, and how they were made aware that this mode of access to information was available. Levine-Clark found that, in general, over 74 percent of those

individuals involved with the humanities were aware that e-books were available. The manner in which these individuals became aware of the e-book format differed according to user type: 50% of undergraduates learning about e-books from faculty and more than 50% of graduate students and faculty discovering electronic books via catalog searching. (Levine-Clark, 2007, p. 8) With discovery, especially in the humanities, being so closely allied with the online catalog, the PDA model as implemented at ASU should serve our users well, especially those involved with humanities research.

Music will never make total use of the PDA model. In part, this has to do with the various formats used for the music study that do not lend themselves to digital surrogates. Many orchestral study scores, given the number of instruments involved, would be impossible to view on most computer screens, tablets, or portable devices. The same is true for many twentieth and twenty-first century scores, which are graphic in nature, or come in oversized or folio imprints (more than 14" tall). Finally given the great variety of music genres, e.g. ensemble music with multiple parts, many digital scores are either too impractical or too expensive to print out for use in rehearsal or performance. However, PDA should not be dismissed out of hand. In such cases, a more hybrid approach may be adopted, where records for print items will be loaded alongside of their electronic counterparts and the seamless experience will still be manifest regardless of format.

Publishers are adopting new sales models (a possible reaction to first sale doctrine) where they are "renting" items to users for a limited amount of time rather than selling them to libraries for unfettered use. Many music publishers are also reluctant to digitize their catalog of scores. This reluctance is understandable because of the time and expense involved and the potential for piracy or the sharing of duplicate copies. That being said, licensed digital music score collections would be a win-win situation provided that the format is conductive to viewing and printing from a workstation. It is hoped that visionary music publishers will ultimately see the cost-savings and profits derived from digital score collections – especially those made available via the PDA model.

Opportunities

Though PDA is not considered as a brand new concept, it is emerging and becoming popular. More and more libraries as well as publishers have started adopting PDA model. Though not many library consortia have adopted this model, it provides significant opportunities for them. It can be considered as a great resource sharing technique, and would save significant amount of budget for participating libraries. Also, this model can be applied for print acquisitions as well as other collections such as journal articles, video and audio files, and reference works.

Recently, we have started the implementation of PDA for Arizona University Library Consortia (AULC), and we are hoping it would prove to be a great resource sharing tool.

CONCLUSION

PDA is gaining momentum, but is still in its infancy stage having many benefits and challenges. Though libraries have assumed that PDA program is unpredictable, strategically implementing and administering can be painless. It is important to understand the chief elements of PDA model, which are budget, purchase trigger, and sound profile. These elements make the workflow predictable and successful. The backbone of PDA program is setting up of profile. Regular monitoring and updating profile as per the need would make this program easily manageable.

Moreover, monitoring budget regularly can prove to be sustainable. It allows libraries to leverage their budget to the most by offering access to large number of books at minimal or no cost. It can save significant amount of budget by purchasing only those books which are used. When the costs of processing and shelving are considered, PDA acquisition models are likely cheaper than traditional print acquisition models. Thus, PDA potentially saves money, aligns a library's collection more closely with the active research of its constituents, and makes it possible to present a much larger number of titles to patrons. It is important to minimize the DRM restrictions for future success of PDA model. Also, making this model more supportive to mobile devices, allowing more downloading and supporting other technologies would be step forward in its success. Though PDA is more popular in academic libraries, this model can be in some way adaptable to other sizes, and types such as public libraries and special libraries.

For ASU Libraries, it is vital to continue to evaluate this model for its sustainability. Though, setting up of profiles requires more detailed work up-front, it is important to review and tweak the profiles periodically in order to ensure a well-balanced collection. Also, it is critical to decide on how to treat PDA titles with zero or one use, which has not yet triggered a purchase, and when to remove them from the catalog.

REFERENCES

Anderson, K. J., Freeman, R. S., Hérubel, J., Mykytiuk, L. J., Nixon, J. M., & Ward, S. M. (2002). Buy, don't borrow: Bibliographers' analysis of academic library collection development through interlibrary loan requests. *Collection Management, 27*(3/4), 1–11. doi:10.1300/J105v27n03_01.

Blotner, L. S. (2007). Music libraries of tomorrow: Virtual or concrete, harmony or discord. In J. P. Cassaro (Ed.), Music libraries, and the academy (pp. 67-79). Middleton, WI: A-R Ed.s, Inc..

Bradley, C. J. (1981). Oscar G.T. Sonneck: Architect of the national music collection. *Journal of Library History (Tallahassee, Fla.), 16*(2), 293–304.

Bradley, C. J. (1990). *American music librarianship: A biographical and historical study.* Westport, CT: Greenwood Press..

Breitbach, W., & Lambert, J. E. (2011, July-August). Patron-driven ebookacquisition. *Info Today*, 17-21.

Cohen, P. (2004, August 1). Spaces for social study. *New York Times*, p. 19.

Crow, M. (2009, January 28). Message from President Michael Crow. *ASU News Online*. Retrieved December 15, 2012 from https://asunews.asu.edu/20090128_furloughprogram

Fenner, A. (2004). *Selecting materials for library collections.* Haworth, UK: Information Press..

Hodges, D., Preston, C., & Hamilton, M. J. (2010). Patron-initiated collection development: Progress of a paradigm shift. *Collection Management, 35*(3-4), 208–221. doi:10.1080/01462679.2010.486968.

Jones, D. (2011). On-demand information delivery: Integration of patron-driven acquisition into a comprehensive information delivery system. *Journal of Library Administration, 51*(7-8), 764–776. doi:10.1080/01930826.2011.601275.

Kent, A. (1979). *Use of library materials: The University of Pittsburgh study.* New York: M. Dekker..

Levine-Clark, M. (2007). Electronic books and the humanities: A survey at the University of Denver. *Collection Building, 26*(1), 7–14. doi:10.1108/01604950710721548.

Levine-Clark, M., Bosch, S., Anderson, K., & Nauman, M. (2009). Rethinking monographic acquisition: Developing a demand-driven purchase model. In *Proceedings of the Charleston Library Conference,* (pp. 549-557). Charleston Library.

Littman, J., & Connaway, L. S. (2004). A circulation analysis of print books and e-books in an academic research library. *Library Resources & Technical Services, 48*(4), 256–262.

Michalak, S. (1994). Planning academic library facilities: The library will have walls. *Journal of Library Administration, 20*(2), 91–113.

Nabe, J., Imre, A. P., & Mann, S. R. (2011). Let the patron drive: Purchase on demand of e-books. *The Serials Librarian, 60*(1-4), 193–197. doi:10.1080/0361526X.2011.556033.

Nixon, J., Freeman, R., & Ward, S. (2010). Patron-driven acquisitions: An introduction and literature review. *Collection Management, 35,* 119–124. doi:10.1080/01462679.2010.486957.

Perdue, J., & Van Fleet, J. (1999). Borrow or buy? Cost-effective delivery of monographs. *Journal of Interlibrary Loan, Document Delivery & Information Supply, 9*(4), 19–28. doi:10.1300/J110v09n04_04.

Reynolds, L. J., Pickett, C., van Duinkerken, W., Smith, J., Jeanne, H., & Tucker, S. (2010). User-driven acquisitions: Allowing patron requests to drive collection development in an academic library. *Collection Management, 35*(3-4), 244–254. doi:10.1080/01462679.2010.486992.

Shen, L., Cassidy, E. D., Elmore, E., Griffin, G., Manolovitz, T., Martinez, M., & Turney, L. M. (2011). Head first into the patron-driven acquisition pool: A comparison of librarian selections versus patron purchases. *Journal of Electronic Resources Librarianship, 23*(3), 203–218. doi:10.1080/1941126X.2011.601224.

Swords, D. A. (Ed.). (2011). *Patron-driven acquisitions: History and best practices*. Berlin: De Gruyter. doi:10.1515/9783110253030.

Trueswell, R. (1969). Some behavioral patterns of library users: The 80/20 rule. *Wilson Library Bulletin*, *43*(5), 458–461.

Watanabe, R. (1981). American music libraries and music librarianship: An overview in the eighties. *Notes*, *38*(2), 239–256. doi:10.2307/939856.

Wright, H. S. (2000). Technology. In R. Griscom, & A. Maple (Eds.), *Music librarianship at the turn of the century* (pp. 29–35). Lanham, MD: Scarecrow Press..

Zager, D. (2000). Collection development and management. *Notes*, *56*, 567–573.

KEY TERMS AND DEFINITIONS

Collection Development: Collection Development is defined as the planned purchase of materials in various formats to match the instructional and research needs of the library within the current fiscal environment and resource sharing opportunities.

Desiderata: *Desiderata* is from the Latin for something that is "desired." The term is synonymous with *Want List*.

Digital Surrogate: A *Digital Surrogate* is a virtual representation of an actual physical item (e.g. book or score) that may be viewed on a computer screen, tablet, or portable device.

Patron Driven Acquisitions (PDA): A purchasing model whereby a library provides a set of books to their patrons, without having to pre-purchase all of them. If a book gets sufficient use, it is then "triggered" for purchase.

Systematic Development: A methodical approach to music acquisitions devised by Oscar Sonneck (1873-1928) to build the collections of the Music Division of the Library of Congress. The approach included the formulation of a collection development policy and the creation of want lists of items to build a comprehensive and unrivaled assemblage of music materials to serve the needs of American musicians and scholars.

Trigger: The amount and type of use required for a PDA book to be triggered for purchase.

Want List: A *Want List* is a list of desired materials not owned by a library that may be consulted for future purchases.

Chapter 5
Going Online:
Subscription of Electronic Journals and its Cost Benefit Analysis

Bharat Kumar
Management Development Institute, India

ABSTRACT

This chapter discussed in detail electronic journals (e-journals), their advantages and disadvantages, and need for subscription. In selection of e-journals, identification of e-journals, their evaluation and purpose for subscription are important considerations for selection of more relevant resources for patrons. The authors also discuss cost benefit analysis of e-journals and elaborate cost involved in subscription of print and electronic journals and provide their cost benefit analysis.

INTRODUCTION

Presently academic libraries are shifting from print to electronic resources because of their ease of accessibility and convenience. Patrons can instantly retrieve numerous full-text articles from a search and they appreciate the convenience of electronic access. Electronic resources consist of variety of resources including electronic journals (e-journals), aggregated databases, electronic books (e-books), encyclopedias, indexing and abstracting databases, etc. In subscription of these resources libraries are making big investments. But selecting a relevant resource for the library is a very difficult issue as over the last few years, there has been a good increase in subscription of e-journals. Often the decision to subscribe e-journal(s) should be made after evaluation of the resource(s) and studying whether it is economical and better choice(s) rather than traditional resource(s) i.e. print. Furthermore, budgets of libraries are decreasing and libraries have to justify their demand for more budgets and subscription of such resource(s). Author had discussed various issues for evaluation of such resources and their cost-benefit analysis (CBA) for these purposes.

DOI: 10.4018/978-1-4666-4761-9.ch005

ELECTRONIC JOURNALS

The introduction of electronic resources can be traced to the 1960s with the development of machine readable files such as ERIC and an early version of the National Library of Medicine online database. In the 1970s OCLC and third party online database vendors, such as Dialog, BRS, and Orbit, became standard sources. The 1980s saw the arrival of personal computers, online public accesses catalogue (OPACs) to replace the card catalogue and databases on CD-ROMs housed on standalone workstations. The early 1990s saw the arrival of local area networks (LAN) to replace standalone workstations. The mid 1990s brought the latest changes are operating system with graphic user interface, Windows, and the Internet. By the late 1990s many OPACs and CD-ROM based databases became available in Web-based systems, and many services became available via remote access to patrons outside the library. The increased reliance on electronic resources was accelerated by decisions to cancel subscriptions to the print formats of sources that became available electronically and the increase of technical to access them.

Any journal available over the Internet can be called 'Electronic Journal' or 'e-journal'. In many cases e-journals are counterparts to familiar print publications, although an increasing number of titles exist only in electronic format. Frequently e-journals appear on the screen exactly as they do in print with similar page design and typeface. These are 'Portable Document Format' (PDF) images of print pages.

Gail Mc Millan defines, "any serial produced, published and distributed via e-networks such as Internet, e-journals may be defined very broadly as any journals, magazines, e-zine, newsletter or type of e-serial publications, which is available over the Internet."

According to Wikepedia (2009) electronic journals, also known as e-journals, and electronic serials, are scholarly journals or intellectual magazines that can be accessed via electronic transmission. In practice, this means that they are usually published on the Web.

According to the Online Dictionary of Library and Information Science by Reitz (2004), e-resources are materials consisting of data and/or computer program(s) encoded for reading and manipulation by a computer or by using a peripheral device directly connected to the computer, such as a CD-ROM drive, or remotely via a network, such as the Internet. The category includes software applications, electronic texts, bibliographic databases, institutional repositories, Web sites, e-books, collections of e-journals, etc. Electronic resources not publicly available free of charge usually require licensing and authentication.

QUESTIONS FOR LIBRARIANS

According to Odlyzko (1995), the development of e-journals is the inevitable outcome of two forces. One is the technology pull, more and more tool are becoming available for scholars to run the publishing business by themselves. The second forces an economic push caused by the exponential growth in scholarly literature. Transit from print to e-journals for librarian poses a number of critical questions, and many authors have commended on the dilemmas associated with e-journals (Boyd, 1997; Brand, 1996; Brown, 1996; Kidd, 1977). In subscription of e-journals, libraries are getting access to the contents saved on publisher's servers. Barnes (1997) has raised whether the e-journals be cost effective than the print journals; what will be the terms and conditions of license agreement; how quickly should I make the transition to e-journals; should library discontinue print subscriptions?; and which e-journals bundle will provide library patrons maximum relevant journals?

Nisonger (1996) points out that "the wider diversity of electronic publication and the rapid changes they are undergoing in the terms of technology, what is available, and the social, economical, and psychological acceptance of electronic journals makes planning by librarians for electronic journals management exceedingly challenging. In fact, a number of people have commented that planning for electronic journals is like shooting at a moving target."

ADVANTAGES OF ELECTRONIC JOURNALS

E-journals have several advantages over print journals. There are several advantages of e-journals over print. Articles are available on Web as soon as they are ready, without having to wait for months for a space in a journal issue. The American Chemical Society puts article on their Web site "as soon as publishable" which can be up to 11 weeks before print. This all means that the information is much earlier than it can be achieved with print. Searchability is one of the major advantages of an electronic format and it is also easier to find articles, the fewer duplicated hits there will be, resulting in less wasted time. Online access allows patrons to search by different approaches like subject, author, title, or keyword(s). Use of Boolean operators facilitates formulation of more precise and complex queries to get maximum relevant hits. For any researcher, availability from a desktop computer means a significant increase in accessibility, particularly for those who do not have easy reach of the library. Electronic format also supporting a large amount of data that can be linked to from the article if the reader wants to look more deeply into the results.

DISADVANTAGES OF ELECTRONIC JOURNALS

The main disadvantages of digital information are the limitations of the computer monitor. This leads to problems with reading, particularly over four or five screens, annotation and portability.

Although the ideal would be to read information from the screen, I think that with printing facilities, this ought not to be a huge constraint on the development of e-journals, because at the moment most people photocopy library copies of journals before taking them away. Once printed, the details of a paper journal remain constant, thus finding them again is easy, and however web sites change their URLs or frequently disappear altogether.

NEED FOR SUBSCRIPTION OF ELECTRONIC JOURNALS

Prof Heting Chu (1999), of Palmer School of Library & Information Science, conducted a survey in 95 academic libraries in US and summarized that users can access e-journals much before the print journals remotely and simultaneously by more than one user with search capabilities and option to save them digitally. There is no chance of mutilation / disfiguring and tearing of pages. It requires no physical processing – receiving, etc -, do not require physical space to store, no missing issue(s), and also reduces staff work like circulation, shelving, and binding, etc. It contains features to link with related items and multimedia information.

SELECTION OF ELECTRONIC JOURNALS

Selection of any bunch of e-journals that will best serve the needs of patrons of an institution today and tomorrow, comprise of three steps - identification of resource, its evaluation and finally selecting the resource.

Identification of Electronic Journals

Identification of e-journals is the biggest challenge for a librarian due to availability of numbers of e-journals. For selecting a most relevant resource librarian can adopt the following steps:

1. Going through literature of the resource;
2. Presentation / demonstration of the resource for faculty members / research scholars from publisher;
3. Trial of the resource;
4. Feedback from faculty members / patrons regarding the resource; and
5. Suggestion from similar institution libraries about the resource.

Presentation of a resource, allows librarians and faculty members to know about the resource, its contents, features, and also provides an opportunity to ask questions about it. Trial for the resource may be requested to use and evaluate it. Trial is free access to a resource for a limited period for use and evaluation of its contents and features.

Evaluation of Electronic Journals

According Merriam-Webster's Collegiate Dictionary "evaluate" means "to determine the significance, worth, or condition of usually by careful appraisal and study". The evaluation of resource is the process of critically analyzing the resource in order to establish its quality or value and decide the credit to give to it. The analysis is done by applying judgment criteria to establish its reliability, authenticity, credibility of the source, the reliability, the validity of the information.

Once the resource is identified, evaluation of the resource is most important and critical step. Evaluation helps librarians to determine authoritativeness of the resource.

Content

For content evaluation, librarians should determine authoritativeness, accuracy, completeness of content such as access to graphs, tables, illustrations, etc, availability of back files availability should be checked. Following criteria also might state that the resource:

1. Support the main research aims and goals of the organization;
2. Add depth or breadth to the existing collection supported by subject profiles; and
3. Meet out the requirements of the patrons.

Currency

It is important to see frequency of updation of contents, embargo and its period and moving wall on full text access of journal(s). Embargo, as it relates to aggregated databases, is a publisher imposed delay on the availability of full text contents. Some publishers put embargos six months to two years. A journal subscription or an individual article purchase fee would be required to access the materials before this embargo period ends. The purpose of this is to protect subscription income / revenue of the publisher. Moving wall is time lag between current issue published and the journal available in electronic format. It is specified by publishers in their license agreements with databases, and generally ranges from several months to several years. A "moving wall" of one year, therefore, means current issues are not available online but any issues older than one year will be.

Impact Factor of Journals

Impact factor is an important consideration for evaluation of journals. Impact factor of an academic journal is a measure reflecting the average number of citations to articles published in the journal. These measures apply only to journals, not individual articles or individual author. It helps to evaluate the use and reputation a journal.

User Interface

User interface is a space where interaction between humans and machines occurs. Librarian should evaluate user interface and its features such as stability, consistency, searching options such as use of Boolean operators, field specific search, multiple year searching, thesaurus / subject searching, lateral searching, limiting, save search history, e-mailing and printing, easy to navigate and intuitive, etc. Possibility of customization of searching options should also be explored. Design of a user interface affects the amount of effort the patrons put to provide input and how much effort it takes to learn how to do this.

Indexing

Librarians should determine whether electronic resource is indexed or not.

Technical Support

E-journals also present a number of technical issues that need to be considered that resources are compatible with existing library hardware and software, method of access, authentication, browser, etc.

Training Support

Publisher / aggregator should provide initial and ongoing training, including the provision of documentation / online manuals, presentations for better and effective use of the resource. This will reduce the burden of staff for training and development of documentation.

Response, Reliability and Availability

The system should be available 24x7. It should be stable with limited evidence of unscheduled downtime. The system should be technologically up-to-date and have the appropriate capacity and network infrastructure to support multiple users simultaneously and optimum response times.

Statistical Reporting

Availability of statistical reports is important to know how resources are being used and how cost effective compared to other products. This is particularly important in supporting renewal and cancellation of subscription. Hiller (2003) reported that academic libraries in North America are increasingly depending upon statistical data, including transactional information for e-resources usage, to assist and support library management decisions. There should be provision that different types of usage reports of different period can be generated and can also be scheduled. Publisher / aggregator should provide statistical reporting following recognized standards such as ICOLC (International Coalition of Library Consortia)'s Guidelines For Statistical Measures of Usage of Web-Based Information Resources and/or COUNTER (Counting Online Usage of Networked Electronic Resources)'s Code of Practice.

But COUNTER - communicates e-journal(s) usage reports count the number of article downloads of title(s). This measure does not address how articles were used after being downloaded, and it does not answer questions concerning how a particular article was chosen. It simply counts what was downloaded. In a 2008 survey of academic libraries, this report was "the usage statistic identified as most useful by survey respondents" (Baker and Read 2008).

Terms and Conditions of License Agreement

License agreement should reflect terms and conditions negotiated between the library and the publisher for the subscription of a resource. It is important to carefully read the agreement and its terms and conditions such as various restrictions, access to archived information, and definition of authorized users, off-campus access, etc before signing. Librarians should always attempt to obtain where possible, a standard model license agreement that describes the rights of the library in easy-to-understand and explicit language. In some countries such the United States, new approaches (e.g. SERU – A Shared Electronic Resource Understanding, which relies on existing U.S. copyright Law and a mutual agreement between resource provider and library to operate within a framework of shared understanding and good faith) are emerging as an alternative to a license agreement.

The license should permit fair use of resources for educational, and research purposes. The following considerations regarding fair use, user statistics and liability for unauthorized use should be addressed in any licensing agreement which a library, its parent institution, or its consortium signs:

1.   Terms of payment;
2.   Grace period for renewal;
3.   Governing laws;
4.   Resource providers authority to provide access;
5.   Method of access; and
6.   Liability for unauthorized use

It is recommended that the following points governing access by a library's patrons shall be covered by any licensing agreement which a library, its parent institution signs.

Authorized Users and Sites

'Authorized Users' and 'Authorized Sites' should be defined as broadly as possible.

Authorized users are all persons with a current, authenticated affiliation with the subscribing institution(s). This includes full- and part-time students and employees - faculty members, staff members. Visitors who have permission to use the institution's available computers should have access to the licensed resource. This is commonly known as 'walk-in use'.

Authorized sites should include all sites including satellite facilities in different geographic locations. Authorized users should also have access to the licensed resource from home, offices, or any other remote location, through the use of a proxy server, IP authenticated protocol, virtual private network (VPN) as provided by the subscribing institution. This is commonly referred to as 'remote use'.

Method of Access

Access should be permitted via IP authentication for the entire institution(s), including simultaneous access for multiple users, in different geographic locations, sites. Such access should be provided without requiring the use of a password or other code.

PURPOSE OF SUBSCRIPTION

Journals are learned publications requiring heavy investments and also include complexity in subscription. These need to be ascertained and clarified before making a final decision for subscription of e-resources:

1.   Examine the objectives for subscription of the resource;
2.   consider the impact and coverage of the resource;
3.   determine the subscription and other associated costs;

4. find out benefits of this subscription; and

5. find out alternatives and summarize the findings.

The above mentioned process determines a comparison of each potential resource as a valued resource based on observation and professional evaluation.

First step in examining an e-resource is to define the objectives for subscription of the resource. In simple terms, what is the purpose for the subscription? For it a true / false questionnaire can be developed to avoid individual bias in prioritizing. For example, resource enhances retrieval of citations, no self space required, maintenance, time saving, requirement of equipment, etc. This observation process develops a positive / negative scenario, where positive objective is compared to any potential negative variable. This evaluation of the proposed subscription can be expressed in terms of statements, why product 'A' is subscribed than product 'B' due to certain factors.

Next step in this evaluation process is to determine impact and coverage of the resource to be subscribed. This is a study of outcomes of the particular subscription will bring to the study. For example, the primary objective is to reduce maintenance and enhance searching capabilities, then impact of these objectives can be can be described in terms of changes in research time and staffs labour cost. This process can be accomplished examining each objective with a value ratio with a 1 – 5 range, 1 representing the lowest and 5 representing the highest.

COST-BENEFIT ANALYSIS

CBA has been used in business and industry over a long period as a tool to measure benefits. CBA can be defined as a tool to measure that helps to determine what are the benefits of a product in comparison to its costs.

Nas (1996) has defined CBA as a "methodology in which all potential gains and losses from a proposal are identified, converted into monetary units, and compared on the basis of decision rules of determine if the proposal is desirable."

The McGraw Hill Encyclopedia of Professional Management defines CBA as determining "... the ratio of the benefit of a given project to its costs, taking into account the benefits and costs that can not be directly measured in dollars" (Bittel, ed, 1978). A closely related concept of cost effective analysis (CEA) "... is defined as a way of finding the least expensive means of reaching an objective or a way of obtaining the greatest possible value from a given expenditure" (Bittel, ed, 1978).

Encyclopedic Dictionary of Accounting & Finance (Shim and Siegel, 1989), cost-benefit analysis is an analysis to determine whether the favourable results of an alternative are sufficient to justify the cost of taking the alternative. Cost-benefit analysis attempts to decide whether the result justifies the expense. Benefits are typically defined in terms of an organization being better off and, ideally, cost should be measured in the same terms.

Businesses typically use one of three common CBA models: return on investment (ROI), present value analysis, or payback period. ROI models determine the amount of profit, or return, from a product or service and compare this figure to its cost. Present value analysis models compare the cost of the product or service to its future estimated annual rate of return. Payback period models look at how long it will take before the profit or return pays for the cost of the product or service, and compares this time period to the estimated life of the product or service.

There are several problems while applying these models in libraries. Libraries are non profit organizations. All these three models rely on the use of return / profit the product / service generates. The benefits that arise from products / services in libraries are very difficult to quantify. How can 'value' of information be quantified? How it is difficult to put a figure on such non-tangible benefits as faster search / delivery of information, patron's satisfaction? Moreover, measuring benefits is very difficult as asking from patrons directly is usually not possible because they typically do not quantify value of information. Accurately measuring benefits over a period also is very difficult, if not impossible.

Not only measuring benefits is very difficult but calculating costs accurately is also difficult. Although direct costs (subscription costs, equipment costs, etc) are easy to calculate, indirect costs (staff time in assisting patrons, training and instruction time, troubleshooting, etc) are much difficult to calculate. In addition, the concepts of fixed, variable, and marginal costs need to be considered. *Fixed costs* are costs that do not change regardless of level of service or number of patrons. An example is the cost of keeping a building open and running. *Variable costs* are costs that increase with each level of output. For example, every time another page is photocopied, the costs for paper and toner increase. *Marginal costs* are related to variable costs and are the measure of each additional unit of output. Finally, there is an inherent bias in looking at costs versus benefits. Whereas costs typically are more immediate and somewhat more accurately known, benefits are much more difficult to measure and typically are spread out over a much longer time period.

COST-BENEFIT ANALYSIS IN LIBRARIES

What is the method for calculating CBA in a library? A framework for conducting CBA consists of the following components: purpose, method, data collection, analysis of data, results, policy changes, and future studies (see Figure 1). The first thing to consider is the reason for conducting the CBA. What is expected to be determined from the study? Second, and most important, is the method

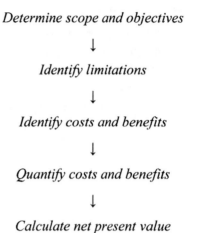

Figure 1. The process of cost benefit analysis

Determine scope and objectives

↓

Identify limitations

↓

Identify costs and benefits

↓

Quantify costs and benefits

↓

Calculate net present value

for conducting the study. The method chosen will ultimately determine the type of data collected, their analysis, and the type of results. Data collection depends directly on the methodology used. Results are a function of method and data collection. In addition to satisfying the purpose of the study, results potentially can lead to meaningful policy changes and ideas for future study.

CBA requires a study of both costs and benefits, or potential costs and benefits, of a product or service. As mentioned earlier, direct costs are relatively easy to identify. However, indirect costs are just equal important to identify. Factors such as time, tangential costs such as paper or ink cartridges (or any other somewhat hidden costs), costs for training and materials, or any other factors that add to the cost of providing a service or product are considered indirect costs. An exact figure for indirect costs is difficult to calculate. Estimates of the exact costs, both direct and indirect, are necessary to more accurately calculate the total cost of the product or service. Some data, such as salaries and fringe benefits, may be difficult to obtain due to employee confidentiality.

Measuring benefits in a not-for-profit environment can be even more difficult. Basically, there are two schools of thought: the first attempts to place a figure on the benefits derived, and the other measure benefits as a decrease in costs in other areas. The accuracy of the first method is somewhat questionable, so the second method is usually the primary choice. Most CBAs use a blend of both methods.

Griffiths and King (1983) offer a library perspective as stated in their manual *Library Cost Benefit Analysis*: Cost and benefits should be described in terms of the unfavorable (i.e costs) and favorable (i.e. benefits) outcomes of input and output and consequences such as effectiveness. Thus, cost and benefits (of a component, activity, service or product, function of the library) are expressed in terms of input expenditures and other resources, and output results in terms of performance and attributes, and effectiveness.

Another library perspective on cost-benefit analysis is presented by Cummins (1989):

The concept of cost-benefit analysis is best appreciated if its motivation is understood. The key is whether reallocation of resources results in being better off and certainly not being worse off. The simplest way is to ask those who will be affected; for example, library patrons might be polled on whether they would be willing to pay for a new program and, if so, how much. Cost-benefit analysis is not an attempt to convert decision making into a formula, but it does provide a framework for decision making. This analysis creates a method of listing and quantifying the pros and cons of a problem or opportunity in order to weigh the importance of each. As a tool for better fiscal control, it supplements but does not replace judgment or political acumen.

PROCESS OF COST BENEFIT ANALYSIS

Process of CBA can be summarized by a flow diagram:

Costs tend to be bunched and up front. They include capital expenditures, operating costs and maintenance costs. Benefits tend to be spread out, and arrive in future

REVIEW OF REVELANT LITERATURE

Most studies of the costs and benefits of library services have focused on the collections and staffing of libraries. In his review of the cost analysis literature of librarianship, Mick (1979) divided the studies he found into four types: those that study a function or service, those that look at the organization, those that examine the structure within which the library is located (university, town, or corporation), and those that compare costs across similar types of libraries. However, his review predates the advent of electronic services within libraries.

Library services and products have associated costs, direct and indirect costs, and decision to acquire or provide a particular product or service should involve an examination of its costs and benefits to library customers. One technique for analyzing cost-effectiveness is to perform a CBA. CBA involves analyzing the benefits, or potential benefits, of offering a product or service and comparing them to the costs of offering that product or service.

Harrington and Stovall (2011) discussed that cost and usage have been consistent elements among both serials decision databases and commercial decision support systems, and the cost per use calculation had become a well-established criterion for assessing electronic subscriptions. However, it is just a numerical value until it can be plotted along several axes related to its components. Mapping these calculated values within and across platforms and subjects allows them to be read through multiple contexts to define what is relatively "high" or "low," and establishing the relative averages and benchmarks within these multiple contexts informs the difficult serials decisions often faced. This presentation looks at ways in which cost per use, as well as other cost and use calculations, has been incorporated into Virginia Tech's relational database for serials decisions in order to arrive at an understanding of what those values mean in both the immediate context and the larger picture.

Daniels (2010).presented a case study at a pediatric hospital system to cut journal costs while increasing value for patrons. First, the worth of the libraries was proven to system leaders using a cost-benefit analysis. Then, librarians used a survey of library users and analysis of usage patterns to reevaluate the number and format of individual journal subscriptions. The results included cutting substantial costs and unpopular resources, adding more relevant resources, and garnering the respect and support of hospital leaders.

Pan and Fong (2010) described the cost-benefits and the return on investment of one consortium comprised of five separately administered libraries in the University of Colorado (CU) System. With a long history of collaboration, the libraries have developed an ideal cooperative arrangement for acquiring electronic content that is accessible across all campuses. The size and flexibility of this institution-based consortium allows it to be responsive and successful in collaborating across four campuses despite different sized budgets and unique local and institutional constraints. To demonstrate the value of jointly leveraging library budgets to university administrators, the authors conducted a consortium level cost-benefit analysis and describe the methodology used to quantify return on the university's investment. This paper addresses both qualitative and quantitative outcomes and underscores how consortial participation has become an essential way of doing business.

Fortini (2007) discussed the results of a survey of academic librarians and details the problems and concerns that arise during an e-journal project, the issues that persist throughout e-journal acquisition and management, and the phases in which these problems arise. The study found that librarians considering a switch to electronic access must be prepared to face continuing problems with access, archiving, cost, staffing/workflow, and technology. The study also indicates a lack of consensus between the different levels of administration regarding problems and concerns with e-journal management, suggesting a need for better administrative communication.

Prabha (2007) study tracked journal subscription and format data for a sample of 515 journals in the Association of Research Libraries (ARL) university member libraries from 2002 to 2006. During this period, subscriptions to journals in print format decreased by 32 percentage points, whereas journals obtained in electronic format increased by 34 percentage points. Findings show journal collections in ARL university libraries reached a "tipping point" between 2005 and 2006 and that, for the first time, electronic journals dominate print subscriptions.

Franklin (2005) discussed some of the early efforts to develop cost per use data for electronic collections and discusses some of the ways libraries, consortia, and publishers currently use unit cost information to make management decisions. Emerging trends in the standardization of electronic usage statistics and concurrent utilization of cost per use data to manage electronic collections hold tremendous potential for libraries and library consortia to increasingly employ reliable cost and use data to support collection development and management decisions.

Odlyzko (1999) was unusual in his focus on non-subscription costs. In a 1999 article, he pointed out additional factors to consider in evaluating the impact of journal growth on libraries:

Journal subscription costs were only one part of the scholarly information system... . internal operating costs of research libraries were at least twice as high as their acquisition budgets. Thus for every article that brings in $4,000 in revenues to publishers, libraries in aggregate spent at least $8,000 on ordering, cataloging, shelving, and checking out material, as well as on reference help. The scholarly journal crisis was really a library cost crisis. If publishers suddenly started to give away their print material for free, the growth of the literature would in a few years bring us back to a crisis situation.

White and Crawford (1998) discussed that library services and products have associated costs, direct and indirect costs, and decision to acquire or provide a particular product or service should involve an examination of its costs and benefits to library customers. One technique for analyzing cost-effectiveness is to perform a CBA. CBA involves analyzing the benefits, or potential benefits, of offering a product or service and comparing them to the costs of offering that product or service. Described in study in which CBA was used to examine the cost-effectiveness of an electronic database. Librarians can use the results of CBA studies to justify budgets and acquisitions and to provide insight into the true costs of providing library services.

Hawbaker and Wagner (1996) performed a CBA in which they compared the costs of providing full-text access to two full-text business databases, *Business ASAP* and *Business Index*, with the costs of owning or subscribing to the periodicals included in these sources. They found that providing access to both indexes increased access from the 242 periodicals to which their library subscribed to 513 periodicals at a cost increase of approximately 15 percent. This tradeoff of increased costs versus increased access is an issue that every library must address. Hawbaker and Wagner indicated that other issues, such as savings from increased shelving availability or increased costs from computer hardware and software, also should be studied.

Friend (1996) made the case that economic models for evaluating the cost/benefit for e-journals subscriptions were imperative and offered a tentative cost per use model for e-journals similar to those traditionally employed to evaluate print journal titles. He noted that many costs such as the cost of shelving were taken for granted and were never included in library economic models. He then discussed both the direct and indirect assumptions that are implicit in a valid economic model and the difficulties inherent in making comparisons and in calculating the true value to the user.

Hawbaker and Wagner (1996) also computed only subscription costs when comparing the costs of journal subscriptions to online access of full-text. They concluded that, for a fulltext business database, the University of the Pacific's library could offer more than twice as many journals for a 15-percent increase in expenditures.

Bane (1995) conducted a user survey and discussed the impact of acquiring BPO in library at Penn State University's Great Valley campus. Users identified the following items as positive aspects: availability of full-text articles, timely access, ease of use, access to a large number of journals, immediate feedback, and lengthy abstracts. The downsides included system downtime, time limits (imposed by the library), lack of downloading capability, lack of total full-text availability (approximately 50% of the indexed articles are full text), lack of remote access, limited time coverage (full image coverage begins with 1987 journal issues), and the manual loading of CDs. She also looked at the impact on ILL in the library. In 1994, BPO provided access to approximately 12,000 articles that otherwise would have been acquired through ILL. Bane estimated that this would have cost $360,000 that year, whereas BPO costs approximately $20,000 per year. Other issues she addressed were the potential for periodical cancellations, increased expectations of users (especially the reluctance to return to print indexes), and additional labor in training and using electronic resources.

Meyer (1992) did a cost-benefit comparison of mediated searching, end user searching, and locally mounted databases at Clemson University. He computed a cost-per-hour and cost-per-search figure for each electronic resource used in the library and then compared each figure to a baseline established in the library to determine which resources would be offered.

Browning and Haas (1991) conducted a cost analysis and user survey of Business Periodicals Ondisc (BPO). They analyzed the costs of BPO, including subscription costs, supplies, and royalty fees (which are no longer included in the price of BPO). They also addressed various methods of paying for the database through donations or charging patrons for printing, or by cutting costs, for example, through periodical cancellations. A survey showed that 78 percent of BPO users were business majors. Some disadvantages addressed included system downtime, system crashes, and length of time to print articles. Advantages discussed included ease of use, quality of the final product, and convenience.

Libraries that go online may cancel their print subscriptions, although some have chosen to retain print titles "as a safety net". Subscription costs are rising, forcing some libraries to choose between the two formats. Potential criteria for canceling print subscriptions include licensing concerns, electronic providers, local politics (e.g., consortia, faculty, user and institutional preferences), publication structure, technological considerations, and local resources, such as cost, space and staffing limitations (Rupp-Serrano et al., 2002). Li and Kopper (2005-2006) reported that the University of California; Davis libraries thought of print journals as duplicates when electronic access was available, and chose to cancel the print subscriptions.

Projects like JSTOR, which builds journal back files, do address building-related costs. One of the JSTOR objectives is "To reduce long-term capital and operating costs of libraries associated with the storage and care of journal collections." By guaranteeing online availability of back files, JSTOR not only makes these files more accessible, but also allows libraries to discard old journal runs without decreasing service to their users.

Odlyzko figured that the library's non-subscription (i.e., operational) costs were on average double the subscription costs. His figures were derived from the Association of Research Libraries (ARL) (2000) statistics. This was a macro level measurement that did not take into account, for example, the different processing costs for books and journals or library costs unrelated to the collections which might cause the non-subscription

figure to be over-estimated. On the other hand, ARL statistics did not report the considerable costs associated with constructing and maintaining library buildings, a factor which if added to Odlyzko's number would lead to a higher estimate of non-subscription costs. But even if off by a factor of 100 percent, Odlyzko's estimate was astounding to consider, and points out the importance of looking at how these operational costs shift in the transition to an electronic model.

REASONS TO SHIFT IN E-JOURNALS

Libraries derive several benefits from e-journals. Searching expedites the retrieval of full-text articles. Electronic access permits patrons to search by different approaches like subject, author, or title, and complex search resulting large number of hits. Boolean operators allow to frame complex search queries, resulting more relevant hits. Remote access to e-journals has removed boundaries of time and space: patrons can download articles from their home or office computers, avoiding need to visit to the library. Furthermore, e-journals can be manipulated into various formats, such as MS Word and MS Excel, through simple copy and paste functions. A major and obvious advantage of electronic information is that it takes no space in the library as it stored on servers with publishers.

Raising Subscription Cost of Print Journals

Cost of print journals has been raising more than a rate exceeding inflation, especially in the sciences. For example, between 1982 and 1990, the cost of chemistry and physics journals rose 131.9 percent, those in engineering 125.6 percent, and those in political science 91.9 percent (Quandt 2003). This trend continued into the 1990s. Mathematical journals subscription costs increased at an annual rate of 15 percent during this time, when inflation rates were at an historic low of 2 percent (Barnett 2004). Other studies have confirmed this trend continuing into the twenty-first century. According to the U.S. Periodical Price Index, the average periodical's price rose 7.7 percent in 2003, slightly higher than increases in the previous two years (Dingley 2003). Quandt (2003) wrote that libraries have reduced their print subscriptions in response to these rising costs. He called this trend the "library crisis" since it threatens the provision of scholarly resources, a primary function of the academic library.

Lower Non-Subscription Costs

Due to increase in prices of print journal(s), it is not surprising that libraries have shifted to e-journals from print. Librarians have been optimistic that a shift towards e-journals and full-text databases would offer significant reductions in non-subscription costs. It has been assumed that transition to electronic format would reduce in non-subscription expenditures such as cataloging, shelving, check-in/check-out, binding, and shelving space. Libraries can indeed realize significant savings in non-subscription costs of electronic access, as Schonfeld et al. (2004) found in their study, which will be examined below.

SUBSCRIPTION COSTS OF PRINT VS. ELECTRONIC JOURNALS

Comparisons of print and e-journal subscription costs have been complicated by varying deals offered by publishers and aggregators. Ketcham-Van Orsdel and Born (1998), "The result is a confusing array of choices and limitations that have librarians wondering if the electronic revolution is leading them where they want to go." One complication resulting from this situation is the frequent inability to make a one-to-one switch from purchasing print journals to their electronic equivalents.

Often libraries are forced to buy a greater number of journals when replacing a set of print editions with their electronic counterparts. Therefore, it is difficult to directly compare the subscription prices of print and e-journals.

Non-Subscription Costs

Roger C. Schonfeld, et. al. (2004) discussed in detail non-subscription costs of a digital and paper library. The study included eleven U.S. academic libraries, varying in size and degree of transition to digital resources. The goal of the study was to calculate and compare the non-subscription cost per print title to the cost per electronic title. By comparing these per title costs, this study goes beyond the one described above.

This study (Schonfeld, et al. 2004) measured non-subscription costs of print and e-journals, which are significant. Schonfeld's quote of a librarian participating in the study points to some of these non-subscription costs, "A not unsubstantial amount of our staff time is devoted to making sure print issues get to the shelf. Mail handling, issue check-in, security taping, bar coding, stamping, and shelving the issues are labor intensive activities that absorb entire job descriptions or multiple staff hours every day." While much has been written about electronic subscription prices (Chen 2001; Quandt 2003), there had not been a detailed study of non-subscription costs. This study is important in that it gives librarians previously unavailable non-subscription cost data. These activities include: collections development, negotiations and agreement, subscription processing, receipt and check-in, routing of issues and table of contents, cataloguing, physical processing, stack maintenance, circulation, user instruction, preservation, and other.

Impact on Staff and Other Costs

Relevant content at affordable price are the offerings a quality e-journals collection but the resources needed to provide access to the content must also be factored in the cost equation. In this section, the impact on the materials budget and changes in each area of the library operations will be discussed in detail with particular attention to the changes in the staffing patterns and shifts in costs. Table 1 summarizes these operational effects:

Infrastructure

The impact of e-journals on the infrastructure is outlined in Table - 1. While space is the most important requirement for the print journals, networks, computer hardware / software and systems staffs are required to provide access to e-journals. Fortunately theses days, for libraries these items are rapidly becoming key components in all academic institutions, as they are essential for so many other reasons. None of the Library systems are used for e-journals exclusively since provide access to the entire web, databases, electronic mail, a library management system with a web-based catalog, application software and several specialized applications.

Space

Print journals require additional space every year to shelve bound volumes. The transition to e-journals eliminates space concerns as contents are saved on publishers' server.

Administration/Management

Journals have always required serious attention from librarians. In science and technology libraries, journal costs usually represent most of the materials budget. Traditionally, the decision to subscribe to a new journal has required careful consideration because of the long-term implica-

tions. And, for the last two decades as prices escalated so drastically, librarians became increasingly involved in advocating for additional funding to pay for journals. Often, in recent years as costs skyrocketed, they oversaw time-consuming annual journal evaluation processes and implemented severe cost-cutting measures. E-journals raise new issues which require the librarian's involvement to an even greater extent.

Staffing

Many times libraries create a new position, Electronic Resources Manager (ERM), to provide a focal point for integrated development of all electronic resources. He initiates contacts with vendors to negotiate favorable pricing and packaging and arranges trials for each new service considered for purchase. He also reviews licenses and contracts and negotiate appropriate amendments and corrections to these documents. For example, one of our goals is to always provide remote access to content we make available to our users; initially some contracts do not allow this. The ERM also interacts with consortia for purchase of electronic resources and evaluates the cost / benefits of going with a particular group offer. The ERM manages the overall content for our web site and looks at how new content affects the current design and implementation. He also collaborates closely with the Webmaster in designing and populating our e-journal database. Finally, gathering and organizing use statistics for electronic resources is a major aspect of his responsibilities.

The transition from print to e-journals has had a large impact on the workload and involvement of the library's administration. It is always more difficult and time consuming to manage change than maintain the status quo.

Technical Services

In the Technical Services Section, the transition to e-journals has had a direct impact on the day-to-day work of each staff member. Changes in workflow

Table 1. Transition from print to e-journals: changes in staffing, infrastructure and others

Activity	Print Journal	E-Journal	Impact
ICT Infrastructure			
Computer (Servers and workstations)	Not required	Purchase of computers	↑ Increased capital cost
Application Software's	Not required	Required to use computes	↑ Increased capital cost
Computer systems – h/w and s/w – maintenance	Not required	Installing s/w, AMC	↑ Increased capital cost
Providing access	Not required	New activity, requires troubleshooting	↑ Increased capital and staffing
Printers for printing	Not required	Increased activity	↑ Increased capital cost
Space	Additional space required every year	Content stored remotely	↑ Reduce space needs
Administration and Management			
Negotiating contracts		Specialized work	↑ Increased work, may require additional staff
Managing the change			
Technical Services			
Check in of issue(s)	Every issue arrival to be recorded	Not required	↓ Reduce workload, may reduce staff
Claiming	Some issue(s) for claiming	Not required	↓ Reduce workload, may reduce staff
Bindery	Every volume to be bound	Not required	↓ Reduce workload, may reduce staff
Classification and cataloguing	Every volume to be classified	Not required	↓ Reduce workload, may reduce staff
Circulation / Access			
Check in / out of issue(s)	Some issue(s) for checked in / out	Not required as in e-format	↓ Reduce workload, may reduce staff
Display of new arrival	Every new issue to be displayed	Not required as in e-format	↓ Reduce workload, may reduce staff
Shelving of current / bound volumes	Every volume shelved	Not required as in e-format	↓ Reduce workload, may reduce staff
Stack maintenance	Required as some issues are taken out	Not required as in e-format	↓ Reduce workload, may reduce staff
Document Delivery			
Faculty copy service	Photocopying and maintaining file	Sending pdf	↓ Reduce workload, may reduce staff
Inter-library loan	Photocopying and courier	Sending by e-mail	↓ Reduce workload, may reduce staff
Information Services			
User literacy	Not much required	Specialized training and continuous support required	↑ Increase workload, may require additional staff

and procedures are drastic, with very large shifts in costs. It is clear that the significant decrease in print titles has directly decreased workload for tasks related to the print format, for example, time is needed to check in print issues, claim non-arrivals, replace missing pages, and prepare and receive bound volume. Bindery charges are also reduced over the time since binding fewer items.

Offsetting the decrease in activity levels and costs related to the print format is a very large increased workload for both the serials acquisitions and cataloging functions related to providing access to e-journals. Updating the e-journal maintenance database that now creates our e-journal lists is a major new task transferred to the Technical Services Department. The e-journal collection is much more volatile than a print collection: links break, coverage changes and sometimes the e-journals themselves are available through a new distributor. An advantage of electronic distribution that creates extra work is that we are not tightly linked to calendar year only subscriptions; so journals are added continuously and sometimes cancelled during the year. Maintaining access points to e-journals both in our e-journal database and soon in the library catalog, requires a different set of skills than the activities associated with maintaining a print journal collection.

CONCLUSION

It is very important for librarians to keep up-to-date on various changes and developments taking place and implement them in their respective libraries. E-journals have made a big change in academic libraries. They are transforming librarians into 'cybrarians'. Increase in availability and demand for electronic resource(s), libraries need to subscribe good number of electronic resource(s) to keep pace and meet out its patrons demand. Decision to subscribe the resource should be team decisions consist of librarians and subject experts. And it is librarian's responsibility to maintain balance between print and e-journals. Subscription of e-journals is just access, not ownership. But e-journals have many added value features that justify their subscription. Probably the most important is that they are accessible anytime and anywhere simultaneously by more than one patron. But selecting and acquiring relevant bunch of e-journals is extremely difficult as every bunch there is overlapping of some journals. The cost of subscription of e-journals has increased budgets overall, but unit costs have significantly decreased since library provides a collection many times larger. And librarians know that they are obtaining a better return on investment by migrating print to e-journals.

REFERENCES

Association of Research Libraries. (2000). *Statistics and measurement program*. Retrieved February 29, 2000 from http://www.arl.org/stats/index.html

Baker, G., & Read, E. J. (2008). Vendor supplied usage data for electronic resources: A survey of academic library. *Learned Publishing*, *21*(1), 48–57. doi:10.1087/095315108X247276.

Bane, A. F. (1993). Business periodicals ondisc: How full-text availability affects the library. *Computers in Libraries*, *15*(5), 54–56.

Barnes, J. (1997). Electronic archives: An essential element in complete electronic journals solution. *Information Services & Use*, *17*(1), 37–47.

Barnett, J. B. (n.d.). Marine science journal prices: A case study. *Journal of Educational Media & Library Sciences, 41*(3), 315 – 323.

Bittel, L. R. (Ed.). (1978). *Encyclopedia of professional management*. New York: McGraw Hill..

Boyd, N. (1997). Towards access service: Supply times, quality control and performance related services. *Interlending and Document Supply*, *25*(3), 118–123. doi:10.1108/02641619710170537.

Brand, A. (1996). Standardisation of electronic document delivery: A practical example. *Interlending and Document Supply*, *24*(2), 12–18.

Brown, D. J. (2003). *Electronic publishing and libraries: Planning for the impact and growth*. London: Bowker-Saur..

Browning, M. W., & Hass, L. M. (1991). Is business periodicals ondisc the greatest thing since sliced bread? A cost analysis of user survey. *CD-ROM Professional*, *4*(1), 37–41.

Daniels, K. (2010). Got value? Journal collection analysis is worth the effort. *Medical Reference Services Quarterly*, *29*(3), 275–285. doi:10.1080/02763869.2010.494521 PMID:20677068.

Dingley, B. (2003). U.S. periodical prices – 2003. *Library Resources & Technical Services*, *47*(4), 363–371. doi:10.5860/lrts.47n4.192.

Franklin, B. (2005). Managing the electronic collection with cost per use data. *IFLA Journal*, *31*(3), 241–248. doi:10.1177/0340035205058809.

Friend, F. J. (1996). Economic models for electronic libraries: Electronic documents and information: From preservation to access. In *Proceedings of 18th International Essen Symposium*. Essen: Essen University Library.

Griffiths, J., & King, D. (1983). *Library cost benefit analysis: A SUNY/OCLC workshop manual*. Albany, NY: SUNY/OCLC Network Office of Library Services, State University of New York..

Harrington, M., & Stovall, C. (2011). Contextualizing and interpreting cost per use for electronic journals. In *Proceedings of the Charleston Library Conference*. Retrieved December 13, 2001, from http://docs.lib.purdue.edu/cgi/viewcontent.cgi?article=1200&context=charleston

Hawbaker, A. C., & Wagner, C. K. (1996). Periodical ownership versus full-text online access: A cost benefit analysis. *Journal of Academic Librarianship*, *2*(22), 105–109. doi:10.1016/S0099-1333(96)90176-7.

Heting, C. (1999). *Electronic journals: Promises and challenges for academic libraries.*

Hiller, S. (2003). But what does it mean? Using statistical data for decision making in academic libraries. *Occasional Paper, 32*, 10-23.

JOSTOR. (n.d.). *The need*. Retrieved from http://www.jstor.org/about/need.html

Kidd, T. (1997). Electronic journals management: Some problems and solutions. *Managing Information*, *4*(10), 25–26.

Li, X., & Kopper, C. (2006). Cancellation of print journals in the electronic era: A case study. *Against the Grain, 17*(6), 1, 18, 20, 22.

McMillan, G. (n.d.). *Management of serials in libraries*. Eaglewood, IL: Libraries Unlimited.

Meyer, R. W. (1992). Locally mounted databases: Making information as close to free as possible. *Online, 16*(1), 15–24.

Mick, C. K. (1979). Cost analysis of information systems and services. *Annual Review of Information Science & Technology, 14*, 37–64.

Nas, T. F. (1996). *Cost-benefit analysis: Theory and application*. London: Sage..

Nisonger, T. E. (1996). Collection management issues for electronic journals. *IFLA Journal*, *22*(3), 25–31. doi:10.1177/034003529602200311.

Odlyzko, A. M. (1995). On the road to electronic publishing. *European Bulletin, 2*(1), 49–60.

Odlyzko, A. M. (1999). Competition and cooperation: Libraries and publishers in the transition to competition electronic scholarly journals. *Journal of Electronic Publishing, 4*(4), 163–185. doi:10.3998/3336451.0004.411.

Pan, D., & Fong, Y. (2010). Return on investment for collaborative collection development. *Collaborative Librarianship, 2*(4), 183–192.

Prabha, C. (2007). Shifting from print to electronic journals in ARL university libraries. *Serials Review, 33*(1), 4–13. doi:10.1016/j.serrev.2006.12.001.

Quandt, R. E. (2003). Scholarly material: Paper or digital? *Library Trends, 51*(3), 349–375.

Reitz, J. M. (2004). *ODLIS: Online dictionary of library and information science*. Retrieved February 10, 2013 from http://lu.com/odlis/index.cfm

Rupp-Serrano, K., Robbins, S., & Cain, D. (2002). Canceling print serials in favor of electronic: Criteria for decision making. *Library Collections, Acquisitions & Technical Services, 26*(4), 369–378. doi:10.1016/S1464-9055(02)00274-9.

Schonfeld, R. C., King, D. W., Okerson, A., & Fenton, E. G. (2004). *The non-subscription side of periodicals: Changes in library operations and costs between print and electronic formats*. Washington, DC: Council on Library and Information Resources..

Shim, J., & Siegel, J. (1989). *Encyclopedic dictionary of accounting and finance*. Englewood Cliffs, NJ: Prentice-Hall..

White, G. W., & Crawford, G. A. (1998). Cost-benefit analysis of electronic information: A case study. *College & Research Libraries, 59*(6), 502–509.

APPENDIX

Conferences

Many conferences are available to library staff and faculty that will facilitate a better understanding of the profession; allow the attendee to network, speak with vendors on the vendor floor during individual events scheduled by the vendor, or Learning the Basics of Electronic Resource Management at a prescheduled one-on-one meeting; and keep up on what is going on in the profession. The following are three suggestions for readers who want to have a rewarding experience and learn a lot about electronic resources.

ER&L

ER&L (Electronic Resources and Libraries) is a conference designed to offer opportunities for communication and collaboration of information professionals and topics related to managing electronic resources. The conference is held in different locations around the country and generally lasts for three days. In her article "Keeping Current in Electronic Resources and Libraries," Mary Moore offers many insights about the ER&L conference, including many of the benefits of attending the conference. Moore states, "No other conference seemed to appeal to all individuals working to develop, deliver, and assess e-resources" For more information on ER&L, visit www.electroniclibrarian.com.

Charleston Conference

Charleston, as it is referred to by those attendees who have attended in past years, is a conference that started out primarily as an acquisitions librarian's conference. However, Charleston is now arguably one of the best conferences for any librarian to attend, due to the wide range of session topics covered on a yearly basis, not to mention the large vendor floor. Speaking as a multiyear attendee, the Charleston Conference offers sessions on a wide range of issues, including many that relate directly to electronic resource management. The conference is large enough to facilitate sessions and discussions on a large number of topics, but small enough to get to know your fellow professionals and to speak with vendors one-on-one, and the venue of Charleston is breathtaking and engaging. For more information on the Charleston Conference, visit www.katina.info/conference/.

LITA Forum

The Library and Information Technology Forum is an annual event held to facilitate networking and the sharing of ideas between professionals in the library community. Held in various locations around the country each year, the forum seeks to showcase some of the leading technologies in the field and give professionals ideas on how they may be able to implement these technologies in their home institutions. Like the LITA organization, the conference is highly respected in the library community. For more information on the LITA Forum, visit www.ala.org/lita/conferences/forum/2011/.

Electronic Mailing Lists

Electronic mailing lists are a great way to keep up with conversations going on within the library community. The following electronic mailing lists provide information and discussions, as well as job advertisements and information on current trends. While not all of the following relate directly to electronic resources, they will all assist a professional in this field.

LITA-L

LITA-L is a list sponsored by LITA, a subgroup of the American Library Association. It is a list dedicated to the discussion of issues related to library information technology. For more information on LITA-L and other ALA mailing lists, visit http://lists.ala.org/sympa/

Liblicense

Liblicense is a mailing list hosted by Yale University Libraries that provides a discussion forum for issues relating to licensing library content. It is especially helpful when advice is needed on the wide-ranging issues that may arise when reviewing licensing for content. For more information, visit www.library.yale.edu/~llicense/

SERIALST

SERIALST is a forum moderated by Birdie MacLennan of the University of Vermont that discusses serials related issues. This resource is a good place to start for questions relating to print and electronic journal content. For more information, visit www.uvm.edu/~bmaclenn/serialst.html

ERIL-L

ERIL-L is a list hosted by Binghamton University that is devoted to the discussion of topics relating specifically to electronic resources. For more information, visit http://listserv.binghamton.edu/archives/eril-l.htl.

AUTOCAT

AUTOCAT is an electronic mailing list hosted by Syracuse University that is devoted to the discussion of topics relating to the cataloging of resources in any format. This a great place to go if questions should arise about how to catalog an electronic resource. For more information, visit www.cwu.edu/~dcc/Autocat/AutocatFAQ-2.html

Chapter 6
Copyright and Licensing Essentials for Librarians and Copyright Owners in the Digital Age

Anne Moon
University of the Western Cape, South Africa

ABSTRACT

So much of what we as librarians do involves some aspect of copyright, whether it is document delivery, electronic reserves, online learning tools, and course management systems (e.g. Blackboard), or online modules that allow one to share one's references and full-text attachments with others (e.g. RefShare). It is therefore important that we become involved in copyright- and licensing negotiations with our online content providers. We also have an obligation to not only familiarize ourselves with but also to tutor our library patrons in terms of copyright legislation, bearing in mind that they may be held personally liable for their use of copyrighted materials through digital interfaces (Graveline, 2011).

INTRODUCTION

This chapter provides a brief introduction to copyright and licensing in the digital environment, especially as it pertains to academic libraries. It seeks to facilitate an understanding of best practices in fair use of copyrighted materials in academic libraries. It aims, furthermore, to highlight the most important lessons learned from the well-documented Georgia State University (GSU) copyright lawsuit, which was filed in 2008, and to also provide ideas on how to launch a successful copyright education programme.

BACKGROUND

As academic librarians we know that our clients make and/or transmit thousands of copies of documents and images they find in libraries and

DOI: 10.4018/978-1-4666-4761-9.ch006

on the Internet. The question that can be asked in each of these cases is "Is that copy legal?" The answer lies in Copyright legislation. This varies from country to country, especially in terms of its term which, in most countries, is the duration of the author's life plus either 50 years or 70 years.

The definition of Copyright, according to *BusinessDictionary.com* is as follows:

Legal monopoly that protects published or un-published original work (for the duration of its author's life plus 50 years) from unauthorized duplication without due credit and compensation. Copyright covers not only books but also advertisements, articles, graphic designs, labels, letters (including emails), lyrics, maps, musical compositions, product designs, etc. According to the major international intellectual-property protection treaties (Berne Convention, Universal Copyright Convention, and WIPO Copyright Treaty) five rights are associated with a copyright: the right to: (1) Reproduce the work in any form, language, or medium. (2) Adapt or derive more works from it. (3) Make and distribute its copies. (4) Perform it in public. (5) Display or exhibit it in public. To acquire a valid copyright, a work must have originality and some modicum of creativity. However, what is protected under copyright is the 'expression' or 'embodiment' of an idea, and not the idea itself. A copyright is not equivalent of legal-prohibition of plagiarism (which is an unethical and unprofessional conduct, but not an offense), and does not apply to factual information.

Some of the five rights are immediately clear, especially nos. 3-5 above. Others, however, require some explanation. The copyright owner's exclusive right to reproduce a work in any form or medium implies, amongst other things, that we need to seek permission, should we wish to have the work transcribed into Braille or an audio-recording for visually disabled or illiterate users. The second right is one which many of us are familiar with by virtue of the much publicized

lawsuit involving Shepard Fairey's copyright infringement in his design of the Obama 'Hope' *poster during the* presidential *campaign*. The poster, which consisted of a stencil portrait of Obama in solid red, beige and blue, led to sales of hundreds of thousands of posters, mugs, tote bags and t-shirts, and became so much in demand that copies signed by Fairey were purchased for thousands of dollars on eBay. The poster was based on a photograph owned by the Associated Press (AP), which Fairey took off the Internet without permission and without credit for its originator. The AP held that Fairey should not have used the photograph as the basis for his portrait without compensating them or, at the very least, crediting them. In terms of the United States Copyright Act of 1976 their photograph of Obama was, after all, protected from "un-authorized duplication without due credit and compensation". The civil lawsuit was settled out of court with the two parties agreeing to financial terms that were not disclosed (Italie, 2009; Kennedy, 2012). It is known, however, that part of the private settlement included a split in the profits for the work (moonlighter1965, 2013)

Copyright laws are vague, ambiguous, and frequently misunderstood. A case in point is the Georgia State University (GSU) copyright lawsuit, in which three publishers, Cambridge University Press, Oxford University Press and SAGE Publications, sued GSU for 74 alleged instances of copyright infringement involving GSU Library's electronic reserves collection.

Approximately two years later, only 5 of the 74 claims succeeded.

The remaining 69 claims failed due to the following reasons:

- Ten of them failed because the copying was de minimise, for example because it was a supplemental reading assignment that no student actually downloaded;
- Sixteen of them failed because the plaintiffs were unable to prove ownership of

copyright in the specific chapters copied and thus could not make a prima facie case;
- Forty-three of them failed because the copying was fair use. (Kluft, 2012)

At first glance, the victory on the part of GSU seems overwhelming (approximately 93%). On closer inspection, however, it was really only a 58% victory, i.e. only 43 of the 74 rulings were clear-cut victories in GSU's favour. (Kluft, 2012)

Petruska (2012) outlines three important lessons to be learned from the GSU copyright case, viz. the following:

"Lesson 1: Universities and departments have a responsibility to educate faculty and student teachers about Fair Use and official policy regarding copyright" (Petruska, 2012)

Where the 5 claims of outright copyright infringement were concerned, the Court held that GSU's electronic reservess policies and practices caused this infringement because GSU failed to provide sufficient guidance to the professors. (Petruska, 2012)

"Lesson 2: Teachers need to be aware that they may be personally liable for their use of copyrighted materials through digital interfaces." (Petruska, 2012)

"Lesson 3: This case highlights the limits of the symbiotic relationship between academic scholar and the academic publisher." (Petruska, 2012)

Petruska (2012) mentions, in illustration of lesson 3 (above), that one of the professors called to testify in this case was asked about her classroom use of an essay she herself wrote. This professor did not hold the rights to her work, though, so the publisher alleged that her provision of that essay for her students through the library's E-reserves was a violation of the publisher's ownership of the content she produced.

Issues, Controversies, Problems, Recommendations and Solutions

If something is copyrightable in print, it is also copyrightable in electronic form. In a single webpage, there can be a multitude of different copyrights. For example, each photograph, caricature or map may have a different copyright holder. The consent of the copyright holder is required for each act of copying. Many library patrons mistakenly assume that what can be copied and pasted from the Internet is free of copyright protection, especially as they are frequently unaware that much of what they are able to access on-campus, via institutional IP authentication, is purely due to the fact that their institution has paid for the relevant content (e.g. an e-journal or e-book). Frequently, their institution has signed a license agreement with the publisher of the content, agreeing to ensure that said content will be used in accordance with international copyright legislation and, furthermore, for academic purposes only and not for commercial gain. This is where the library's branding of its subscription databases with the university's logo has an important role to play.

Another clause that frequently appears in license agreements for content in electronic format is the clause stipulating that the content may not be shared with anyone outside the university community, except in the context of document delivery (inter-library lending) for a strictly non-commercial purpose. For example, articles may not be embedded in *RefShare* folders that are going to be forwarded to research partners at for-profit organizations. In an age of increasing globalisation, internationalisation, cross-disciplinary research collaboration and shared degree offerings, sometimes across two or more continents, this restriction can pose a challenge. The problem is, however, not insurmountable provided that negotiations are entered into timorously between the publisher and the other relevant parties. This is where Academic Liaison Librarians (ALLs) have a role to play. They need to keep abreast of impending changes to the curricula and envisaged collaborative degree offerings between universities. If course material needs to be shared across two or more universities offering shared degree programmes, the ALLs need to communicate the fact that there is a need to get the ball rolling in terms of having the existing license agreement amended, at a slightly increased cost to take into account the increased student numbers. According to Cooke (2011), "a study undertaken at a United Kingdom university found that, in terms of services that Academic Library Liaisons provide, academic staff appears most to value assistance with copyright matters and institutional repositories." In order to increase their visibility on campus, ALLs would hence be well advised to kept abreast of copyright legislation and licensing essentials.

E-reserves staff, together with cataloguing staff, has an equally important role to play. They can help create awareness about how to legally keep copyright clearance costs for e-reserves to a minimum and, at the same time, ensure that the library does not pay for the same content twice. Many academic libraries spend a fortune on copyright clearance fees for journal articles that academics ask to have placed on short loan. Very often the university holds online subscriptions for the very same online journals from which photocopied articles are being requested. What academics are not always aware of is the fact that it should never be necessary to obtain copyright clearance for students to access e-content the library already subscribes to. Instead, they should simply request that these articles be catalogued and made available via the online public access catalogue (OPAC). Cataloguing staff are able to add a proxy-prefixed link to the 856 field to make the online content of the full-text article accessible from on-campus as well as off-campus. An e-reserves scope can be added to the OPAC to enable students to limit their searches to e-reserves content only. It should be possible for students to search the OPAC for short-loan articles via at least two search fields, e.g. Course Code and Lecturer Name. There is nothing illegal about students downloading e-reserves articles via the OPAC in cases where the library subscribes to this e-content. No copyright clearance is required, as long as it is only the article URL which is embedded in the catalogue record, and not a digitized or PDF version of the article itself. It goes without saying, of course, that it is not permissible to add a link that points to a pirated version of a file or a plagiarised article When electronic reserves staff receive requests for articles to be copied, they should establish via the library's A-to-Z e-journals list, whether these articles are available in any of the library's subscribed databases. If so, the next step is to liaise with the cataloguing staff and relevant academic to have the required online articles catalogued and made available via an 856 link in the catalogue. This saves the library from incurring unnecessary copyright costs and also makes it easier for off-campus students to acquire short-loan articles without having to physically visit the library.

Another area where Academic Liaison Librarians and Information Literacy Librarians could make a difference is in terms of the kind of embedded librarianship that requires of student editors to update the free *Wikipedia* online encyclopedia, for assignment purposes, on topics decided by their professors and relevant library personnel. Librarians could provide the necessary guidance in terms of citation styles and copyright issues. They could refer student editors to an excellent copyright reference guide from Wikimedia Commons at http://bit.ly/13hhMAz. This guide provides an overview of copyright laws around the world. The table in the guide makes it easy to establish whether a work is suitable for upload to Wikipedia. It is important to note that works can be uploaded only if they are in the public domain in both their source country and in the

United States. The table provides conditions under which most works will be in the public domain in both countries.

Copyright legislation is continually changing, especially now that we have entered the digital age. One example of a change, or provision, to the Copyright Act is the "window" for terminating a copyright transfer agreement, which opened at the beginning of 2013. Section 203 of the US Copyright Act of 1976 is a provision, which allows the original authors of creative works to terminate any transfer or licensing agreement 35 years after the license was signed and reclaim their copyrights. They have a window period of 5 years in which to do so, provided they give advance notice to the publisher within a specified period of time before the proposed termination date. This provision went into effect on 1 January 1978, so the window for terminations opened on 1 January 2013. The law applies only to license- or transfer agreements that were signed after 1 January 1978.

Pike (2012) points out that Section 203 has come into effect at a time of increased options for self-publishing, and the emergence of e-books. This provision gives authors "a second bite of the apple" and enables them to renegotiate with their original publisher or seek out a new publisher after a period of 35 years has elapsed.

We, as academic librarians, need to keep abreast of the legislation to be able to tutor our patrons in terms thereof. By fulfilling this role, we are also able to raise our visibility as library professionals. Our authored patrons who wish to exploit self-publishing options, open access options, DRM-free options, or options to make their work available in other languages or in a format or medium accessible to visually disabled users, should be made aware of their right to do so. If they have transferred their copyright to the publisher of their original work, they may need to wait 35 years after publication of the work to exercise this right. For those academics who are already close to retirement age, however, the wait may not be long at all. We need to ensure that they know about this right.

We also need to alert our patrons to the perils of relinquishing too many of their rights to publishers and to be especially wary of click-through copyright-transfer agreements as these can be very rigid, and frequently make no provision for self-archiving of open-access pre-prints or post-prints in an institutional repository. Many publishers are open to negotiation but, in reality, it is the author who needs to initiate these negotiations. We, as librarians, need to educate our users in this regard (Carpenter, 2013).

Graveline (2011) provides some useful pointers in terms of embarking on a successful copyright education programme. Of course, before we can enlighten our patrons or even our colleagues, we need to familiarise ourselves with copyright legislation. There are a number of excellent sources that can provide us with a "crash course" in copyright education. In addition to ensuring that we are conversant with all the *Key Terms and Definitions* included in this chapter, we should consult as many as possible of the *References* and *Additional Readings*, especially the ones by *Adler et al.* (2012), Crews (2012), Lipinski (2013), Petruska (2012), Pike (2012) and Russell (2004).

Once we have mastered the basics of copyright, we will be in a position to organize a series of brown-bag sessions, at which we will be able to use our newly acquired copyright knowledge to provide professional development to our colleagues, and also practice fielding questions on the topic. Each week a different aspect of copyright can be covered, e.g. copyright basics and terminology in week one, fair use in week two, creative commons licenses in week three, open access and the public domain in week four, Digital Rights Management (DRM) in week five, accounts of famous copyright infringement cases in week six, and guidelines for training academics to add proxy-prefixed article links to course management systems (e.g. *Blackboard*) in week seven. Staff that should be invited are inter-library lending personnel, cataloguers, information literacy librarians, academic liaison librarians, electronic resources librarians and faculty librarians.

Once we are comfortable with delivering presentations to our library colleagues and fielding questions, we will be ready to address our academics, either during their Faculty meetings or at the Library. We will advise them about in-depth tutorials that we can arrange in order to assist them with adding proxy-prefixed links to the university's online course management system, and we will also talk to them about the possibility of assigning Wikipedia editing tasks to their students with the assistance of the library. Moreover, we will discuss with them the rationale for providing an e-reserves service, as opposed to a traditional (print copies) one, for which we must spend an enormous sum of money on copyright clearance fees, for content we already own.

Copyright permissions are handled centrally within the Cape Higher Education Consortium (CHEC) of which my own library is a member. The Publishing Liaison Office is located at the CHEC Offices in Cape Town and handles copyright permissions for all four of the university libraries within the CHEC. The Director of this unit sometimes delivers copyright presentations at the four campuses, which are all in close proximity of each other. On 9 November 2011, she and I delivered a joint presentation to library staff at the University of the Western Cape. Her presentation dealt with copyright as it pertains to print materials while mine dealt with licensing issues pertaining to electronic resources. Among the guidelines I provided to my library colleagues on that day, were the following:

- If you are copying from the Internet or a database because you want to include it in a different site, e.g. an online course management system or a LibGuide, then rather

than copying the content (journal article or e-book chapter), you should simply quote the appropriate URL or link to it and let your readers consult the source material online (in another window on the site).

- To make content from a subscription database accessible to bona fide members of the University community from off-campus, you can prefix the URL with http://ezproxy.uwc.ac.za/login?url= You should draw your users' attention to any copyright notice on the target site.

- Never upload a PDF copy of an article to a server that is not secure, i.e. a server that can be accessed from outside (a particular IP range) by unauthorized users. It is always preferable to use simply the proxy-prefixed URL and let your readers retrieve the source material themselves.

- The downloading of content from online databases is governed by the terms of the license agreement from the supplier under service contract. The license is usually pretty clear as to how much you may copy, the purposes for which you can do that copying and for what you can and cannot subsequently use the material. For example, you can use it to fulfil interlibrary loan requests within the boundaries of fair use and provided it is solely for education- and/or research purposes and that the copies are going to be transmitted to a not-for-profit institution. However, you cannot use the content e.g. French grammar and literature books, in online format, to provide French tuition to private clients at a profit.

- You should never give your login credentials to anyone else.

- You should not republish the material in any form without the copyright holder's permission. For example, do not translate a work without permission. Some licenses do, however, make provision for content to be transformed into Braille format.

- Most publishers make provision for database articles to be transmitted via Ariel inter-library loan software to another not-for-profit institution, provided that the principle of fair use is not violated.

FUTURE RESEARCH DIRECTIONS

What is apparent from the literature on copyright infringement cases is that copyright violations can land you in court, damage your reputation and cost you time and money. The literature also makes it clear that library patrons can be held personally responsible for copyright violations. The GSU copyright lawsuit is a case in point. There are some important lessons to be learned from copyright infringement lawsuits. In illustration hereof, see http://bit.ly/15nE1Y7, which summaries five famous copyright infringement cases and what we can learn from them (moonlighter1965, 2013).

Librarians need to follow the literature on copyright infringement cases. We, as librarians, are fortunate to have access to many of the subscription resources that provide access to these cases. These include databases such as *LexisNexis* and *Westlaw* as well as the *OCLC FirstSearch Service* (with *WorldCat* and *ArticleFirst*) and *ProQuest's Dissertations & Theses Full Text (PQDT)* database.

There are also blogs on the Internet that one can follow, e.g. the *Kluwer copyright Blog*, accessible at http://kluwercopyrightblog.com/ and *The Scholarly Kitchen*, published by the Society for Scholarly Publishers, at http://scholarlykitchen.sspnet.org/. The latter mentioned focuses on copyright issues, as well as a host of other topics, and provides thoughtful analysis on timely issues. There is also the blog "*Copyright and Access to Information (A2K) Issues*", which one can subscribe to. It is accessible at http://bit.ly/18QcsbF and is maintained by Denise Nicholson, an A2K activ-

ist in South Africa. Many universities maintain *LibGuides* that provide copyright guidelines for staff and students. Some of these are maintained by well-known experts in the field of copyright legislation. For an example of one such guide, see http://bit.ly/ZKA2ne, created by Nicholson (2013). Twitter is another rich source of current information on matters pertaining to copyright and intellectual property.

The *State of America's Library Report 2012* highlights the fact that 2012 was "a complex year of copyright issues", in terms of e-books and libraries Since "e-books are the future of book consumption and, therefore, in many ways, the future of libraries", it stands to reason that libraries should focus their attention on especially copyright issues that pertain to e-books. (American Library Association, 2012).

CONCLUSION

We, as librarians, need to be greatly involved in copyright- and licensing negotiations with our online content providers, keeping in mind that it is very rarely that vendors refuse to negotiate their terms, especially now that the publishing industry is experiencing such tough times. We also have an obligation to not only familiarize ourselves with, but to also tutor our library patrons in terms of copyright legislation, bearing in mind that they may be held personally liable for their use of copyrighted materials through digital interfaces. This lesson is borne out through the recent Georgia State University lawsuit. Last, but not least, we need to counsel our patrons, especially our budding young researchers, in terms of their rights as emerging authors. By fulfilling these roles, we are also able to raise our visibility as library professionals and become an invaluable part of our university.

REFERENCES

Adler, P. S., Aufderheide, P., Butler, B., & Jaszi, P. American University Washington College of Law, & Andrew W. Mellon Foundation. (2012). Code of best practices in fair use for academic and research libraries. Washington, DC: Association of Research Libraries..

American Library Association. (2012). Ebooks and copyright issues. In *The state of America's libraries: A report from the American Library Association*. Chicago, IL: American Library Association..

Carpenter, T. A. (2013, March 6). Copyright transfer as a click-through – It's so easy to sign away your rights. *The Scholarly Kitchen*. Retrieved May 30, 2013 from http://bit.ly/WIOHIG

Commons, W. (2013). *Commons: International copyright quick reference guide*. Retrieved June 4, 2013 from http://bit.ly/13hhMAz

Cooke, L., Norris, M., Busby, N., Page, T., Franklin, G., Gadd, E., & Young, H. (2011). Evaluating the impact of academic liaison librarians on their user community: A review and case study. *New Review of Academic Librarianship*, *17*(1), 5–30. doi:10.1080/13614533.2011.539096.

Crews, K. D. (2012). *Copyright law for librarians and educators: Creative strategies and practical solutions*. Chicago: American Library Association..

Dusollier, S. (2012). DRM at the intersection of copyright law and technology: A case study for regulation. In E. Brousseau, & M. Merzouki (Eds.), *Governance, Regulations and Powers on the Internet* (pp. 297–317). Cambridge, UK: Cambridge University Press. doi:10.1017/CBO9781139004145.019.

Graveline, J. D. (2011). Launching a successful copyright education program. *College & Undergraduate Libraries*, *18*(1), 92–96. doi:10.1080/10691316.2011.550534.

Italie, H. (2009). AP accuses Obama artist Shepard Fairey of copyright infringement. *The Huffington Post*. Retrieved from http://huff.to/LJU1

Kennedy, R. (2012, September 7). Shepard Fairey is fined and sentenced to probation in Hope poster case. *The New York Times*. Retrieved from http://nyti.ms/10OWoyX

Kluft, D. (2012). *The devil's in the details: Dissecting the 350-page Georgia State University electronic reserves copyright ruling*. Retrieved June 2, 2013 from http://bit.ly/14q3tZT

Lipinski, T. A. (2013). *The librarian's legal companion for licensing information resources and services*. Chicago: Neal-Schuman..

moonlighter1965. (2013a, June 4). *Are European orphans about to be freed?* Retrieved June 4, 2013 from http://www.twitter.com/moonlighter1965

moonlighter1965. (2013b, June 4). *Five famous copyright infringement cases (what you can learn)*. Retrieved June 4, 2013 from http://www.twitter.com/moonlighter1965

Nicholson, D. R. (2013). *Copyright and related issues*. University of the Witwatersrand. Retrieved June 5, 2013 from http://libguides.wits.ac.za/Copyright_and_Related_Issues

Petruska, K. (2012a). *The GSU copyright case: Lessons learned part 1*. Retrieved January 30, 2013 from http://bit.ly/JwtpXg

Petruska, K. (2012b). *The GSU copyright case: Lessons learned part 2*. Retrieved January 30, 2013 from http://bit.ly/KNGIE7

Pike, G. H. (2012, December 6). Window for terminating a copyright transfer agreement opens in 2013. *Information Today.*

Russell, C., Buttler, D. K., & American Library Association. (2004). *Complete copyright: An everyday guide for librarians.* Chicago: American Library Association.

UWCLibrary. (2013a, January 29). *When including attachments in RefShare, please ensure that content sharing is not prohibited by copyright restrictions.* Retrieved from http://bit.ly/11JNZls

UWCLibrary. (2013b, May 24). *MT @waynestatelib copyright guidelines for posting online documents to blackboard & similar course management systems.* Retrieved from http://on.fb.me/19vEWX1

ADDITIONAL READING

Beebe, B. (2008). An Empirical Study of US Copyright Fair Use Opinions, 1978-2005. *University of Pennsylvania Law Review*, 549–624.

Bently, L. (2010). *Global copyright: Three hundred years since the Statute of Anne, from 1709 to cyberspace.* Cheltenham [u.a.: Elgar].

Brassil, J. T., Low, S., & Maxemchuk, N. F. (1999). Copyright protection for the electronic distribution of text documents. *Proceedings of the IEEE*, *87*(7), 1181–1196. doi:10.1109/5.771071.

Butler, R. P. (2011). *Copyright for teachers & librarians in the 21st century.* New York: Neal-Schuman Publishers..

Cheung, O., Thomas, D., & Patrick, S. (2010). *New approaches to e-reserves: Linking, sharing and streaming.* Oxford: Chandos. doi:10.1533/9781780630441.

Erickson, J. S. (2003). Fair use, DRM, and trusted computing. *Communications of the ACM*, *46*(4), 34–39. doi:10.1145/641205.641228.

Felten, E. W. (2003). A skeptical view of DRM and fair use. *Communications of the ACM*, *46*(4), 56–59. doi:10.1145/641205.641232.

Fulkerson, D. M. (2012). *Remote access technologies for library collections: Tools for library users and managers.* Hershey, Pa: IGI Global..

Gadd, Elizabeth. (2001). *Clearing the way: copyright clearance in UK libraries.* Loughborough University / © Elizabeth Gadd.

Gordon, W. J. (1989). An Inquiry into the Merits of Copyright: The Challenges of Consistency, Consent, and Encouragement Theory. *Stanford Law Review*, 1343–1469. doi:10.2307/1228805.

Harvard Law School., & eIFL.net. (2012). *Copyright for librarians: The essential handbook.* Cambridge, Mass.: Berkman.

Herrington, T. A. K. (2010). *Intellectual property on campus: Students' rights and responsibilities.* Carbondale: Southern Illinois University Press..

Kingston, Paula, Gadd, Elizabeth, & Goodman, Richard. (1997). *Developing and evaluating an electronic 'short loan' collection in a university library.* Aslib in association with the International Institute for Electronic Library Research © Elizabeth Gadd.

Klemchuk, D. M., Ross, M., & Stallion, M. E. (2012). *Navigating the legal issues surrounding social media: Understanding and avoiding the legal risks associated with social media services.* Boston, Mass: Thomson Reuters/Aspatore..

(n.d.). Kramer [Digital Rights Management: Pitfalls and Possibilities for People with Disabilities. University of Michigan.]. *Elsa F.*.

Landes, W. M., & Posner, R. A. (1989). An economic analysis of copyright law. *The Journal of Legal Studies*, *18*(2), 325–363. doi:10.1086/468150.

Litman, J. (2001). *Digital copyright: Protecting intellectual property on the Internet.* Amherst, N.Y: Prometheus Books..

Loren, L. P. (2006). Building a reliable semicommons of creative works: Enforcement of creative commons licenses and limited abandonment of copyright. *George Mason Law Review*, *14*, 271.

Montanez, S. (2009, September 29). Espresso Book Machine raises copyright issues. *The Maneater*. Retrieved June 2, 2013 from http://bit.ly/nOD97

Nicholson, D. R. (2012). *Accommodating persons with sensory disabilities in South African copyright law.* Retrieved June 2, 2013 from http://wiredspace.wits.ac.za/handle/10539/12525.

Nikolaidis, N., & Pitas, I. (1996, May). Copyright protection of images using robust digital signatures. In *Acoustics, Speech, and Signal Processing, 1996. ICASSP-96. Conference Proceedings., 1996 IEEE International Conference on* (Vol. 4, pp. 2168-2171). IEEE.

Nimmer, M. B. (1978). *Nimmer on copyright: A treatise on the law of literary, musical and artistic property, and the protection of ideas.* M. Bender..

Patterson, L. R., & Lindberg, S. W. (1991). *The nature of copyright: A law of users' rights.* University of Georgia Press..

Poe, J., & McAbee, S. (2008). Electronic reserves, Copyright, and CMS Integration–Six Years Later. *Journal of Access Services*, *5*(1-2), 251–263. doi:10.1080/15367960802198879.

Polak, F. M. (2010). *Copyright and digital music collections in South Africa* (Doctoral dissertation).

Potter, K. D. (1999). *An educator's guide to finding resources in the public domain.* Bloomington, Ind: Phi Delta Kappa Educational Foundation..

Reichman, J. H. (1994). Legal hybrids between the patent and copyright paradigms. *Columbia Law Review*, *94*(8), 2432–2558. doi:10.2307/1123143.

Rich, J. (2006). *Self-publishing for dummies.* Hoboken, N.J: Wiley Pub.

Ruanaidh, J. Ó., Dowling, W. J., & Boland, F. M. (1996). Watermarking digital images for copyright protection. *IEE Proceedings. Vision Image and Signal Processing*, *143*(4), 250–256. doi:10.1049/ip-vis:19960711.

Smith, K. L., McDonald, S. J., & Academic Impressions (Firm). (2011). *Libraries and copyright in a digital age.* Denver, CO: Academic Impressions. University of Pretoria. Copyright. Retrieved June 5, 2013 from http://www.ais.up.ac.za/copyright/

Wagner, V. H. (2008). Processing reserves, seeking permissions and engaging the campus: How the library serves as the copyright touchstone. *Journal of Interlibrary Loan. Document Delivery & Electronic Reserves*, *18*(2), 247–254. doi:10.1300/10723030802099970.

KEY TERMS AND DEFINITIONS

Blackboard Online Course Management System: *Blackboard* is a tool that enables faculty to add resources for students to access online. *LibGuides*, *Powerpoint*, *Captivate*, video, audio, animation, and other applications are created outside of Blackboard and added into Blackboard courses for students to enhance teaching and learning efforts. Links to *RefShare* folders and online course reserves (e-reserves, accessible via the

Library's OPAC) can also be added. It is important to note that the full-text documents themselves should not be added, but simply the links to these documents. The links should be proxy-prefixed so that they are also accessible from off-campus. Academic Liaison Librarians have an vital role to play in training academic and e-learning personnel to add proxy prefixes to stable URLs for full-text course material in e-journals and e-books.

Creative Commons: *Creative Commons* (CC) licenses are on a continuum between full copyright, in which no use is permitted without permission, and public domain, where permission is not required at all. Creative Commons *licenses* do not *replace copyright*, but are based upon it. The Creative Commons licenses consist of four usage conditions, which can be mixed and matched to form one of six licenses. The four usage conditions are (1) attribution, (2) share-alike, (3) non-commercial and (4) no-derivatives. For more information, visit the Creative Commons website at: http://creativecommons.org/licenses/.

Derivative Work: A new work that translates or transforms one or more original copyrighted works (e.g. a movie made from a book, e.g. *The Help* or a book translated into another language or medium, e.g. print to audio-cassette or braille), or a photograph transformed into a stencil portrait, e.g. the *Obama Hope Poster*.

Digital Rights Management: *Digital rights management (DRM)* is a controversial access control technology used by copyright holders to control the use of digital content after procurement, whether by sale or subscription. DRM schemes seek to control copying, printing and altering of works. Frequently no more than five percent of a work may be copied or printed. DRM has a number of pros and cons. The technology is frequently too crude to distinguish between a fair use and an unfair use of a work. For example, it can restrict users from doing something perfectly legal, such accessing works in the public domain, or using copyrighted materials for research and education under fair use laws. (Fair use in an education or research setting allows for more than 5% of copying or printing, yet DRM frequently does not). As Dusollier (2012) points out "The scope of copyright is no longer decided according to what its proper scope should be but according to what technology can do."

Electronic Access Field (856 Field): The *856 field* is an Electronic Access entry that is added to a catalogue record or MARC holding record. The 856 entry contains information required to locate an electronic resource. By inserting an 856 tag, with correctly formatted data, users can link to full-text content outside the catalogue. It they double-click the hyperlinked 856 entry message in the record, they can view the resource through the Online Public Access Catalogue (OPAC). Hyperlinked 856 messages in OPAC records typically read something along the lines of: "If you are from [name of university], click here for full-text access, via [name of database]", or simply "Click here for online access via the publisher's website", if it is an Open Access title.

Electronic Reserves: *Electronic Reserves (E-reserves)* are sometimes referred to as course reserves. They are prescribed- or recommended readings in electronic format, which have been selected by faculty for use in specific university courses. E-reserves are in electronic format and are usually comprised of journal articles and book chapters. In cases where full-text content is digitized and uploaded to the e-reserves server, copyright clearance needs to be obtained beforehand. If, however, journal articles or book chapters are catalogued and made available via a proxy-prefixed 856 link in the OPAC, then no copyright clearance is required, since no copying of material has taken place. This is consequently the most economical way of maintaining e-reserves. It also facilitates accurate reporting of a library's electronic resources usage. E-reserves, as opposed to traditional course reserves (in print format), does, however, require a certain level of computer literacy on the part of the student accessing the content.

Fair Use: In an educational setting, copyright policy and practices should be based on *fair use*. The four factors that help to establish whether copying can be considered fair use or not, are (1) the purpose and character of the use, (2) the nature of the work being used, (3) the amount of the work being used, and the (4) impact on the potential market for or the value of the original work.

License: Permission granted by the copyright holder to copy, distribute, display, transform and/or perform a copyrighted work.

Orphan Works: These materials are called "orphan works" because they remain copyrighted under U.S. law, but have no identifiable copyright owner to contact for permission to digitize, reprint, translate, or otherwise transform. Consequently they are, at present, lost to the digital revolution. There are indications, however, that European orphans are possibly about to be freed (moonlighter1965, 2013).

Public Domain: Works that are not restricted by copyright and do not require a license or fee to use. Works can enter the public domain automatically because they are not copyrightable, have been designated as Open Access works in the public domain by the creator (author or artist), or have become part of the public domain because the copyright term has expired.

RefShare: *RefShare* is a module of *RefWorks*, a web-based bibliography and database manager that allows one to create one's own personal database by importing references from commercial databases and search engines (like *Google Scholar*). Like the name implies, RefShare, allows one to easily *share* a *folder* of references. One can also *share* any file *attachments* stored with one's references. When collaborating on a research project with colleagues or fellow students at another institution, it is important to ensure that one does not contravene any copyright legislation (UWCLibrary, 2013).

Chapter 7
Comparative Analysis of Electronic Resource Management Systems (ERMS):
A Web Study

Nihar K. Patra
National Institute of Food Technology Entrepreneurship & Management, India

Shiv S. Jha
National Institute of Food Technology Entrepreneurship & Management, India

ABSTRACT

Electronic Resource Management Systems (ERMSs) have been developed to manage e-resources by several proprietary and open source products, which are now available on the market. The main purpose of these ERMSs is to manage the workflow of e-resources, access, centralize data, and improve administrative interfaces, etc. This chapter compares and analyzes the 16 ERMSs' information available on their respective Websites. The comparison covers on ERMSs' functionality, use of standards and compatibility, distinguish features, modules, etc. These 16 ERMSs are Innovative Interface's Innovative ERM, TDNet's TDNet ERM Solutions, Ex Libris's Verde ERM, OCLC's Web-Share License Manager, SemperTool's SMDB, University of Notre Dame's CORAL, MIT's VERA, SerialsSolutions's 360 Resource Manager, HARRASSOWITZ's HERMIS, The Johns Hopkins University's HERMIES, Colorado Alliance's Gold Rush, WT Cox's Journal Finder, EBSCO's EBSCONET ERM Essentials, Simon Fraser University Library's CUFTS, SIRSI Corp's E-Resource Center, Priory Solution's Research Monitor. This comparison found that basic features and standards adopted are more or less common in all ERMSs. However, the modules, programming language, and platform used in the ERMSs are somewhat unalike. This study concludes with usefulness of ERMSs for librarians and end-users.

DOI: 10.4018/978-1-4666-4761-9.ch007

INTRODUCTION

Does your library have an electronic resource (e-resources) which includes databases, e-journals, e-books, free e-resources etc? Does your library face a growing challenge to adequately access and manage the diverse e-resources such as evaluation, selection, acquisition, renewal/cancellation, license agreement, open access and institutional archives, access rights, usage statistics, single access point, implementation and administration. If so, it is required to have your library an Electronic Resource Management System (ERMS).

An ERMS is a software that assists the library in managing the details access and manages the e-resources. An ERMS is basically a tool for librarians, but its impact relates to end-users. The information gathered in the ERMS can serve as a starting point for user's interaction with e-resources. Further, ERMS addressed the issues on new standards and protocols.

ERMS are used "… to keep track of a library's digital titles, subscription and vendor/publisher information, and link resolution with more accuracy and less duplication" (McCracken, 2007). ERMS are systems designed to manage the details involved in the acquisitions of e-resources, including subscription and licensing details, usage, cost, and access tracking and data gathering. In general, an ERMS is used for record keeping and budgeting activities, while Content Management Systems (CMS) are used for access and authority control. In some respects these are functions can overlap. Several good stand-alone ERMS both commercial and open source are available and many ILS (Integrated Library System) integrate some form of ERMS (Breeding, 2008; Fons and Jewell, 2007).

In 2002, the Digital Library Federation (DLF) and the National Information Standards Organization (NISO) co-sponsored a workshop that eventually led to the Electronic Resource Management Initiative (ERMI). The landmark ERMI report published in 2004 (http://www.diglib.org/pubs/dlf102/) articulated the challenges of e-resource management and offered a blueprint, of sorts, to companies and individuals engaged in building new or expanding current electronic resource management (ERM) systems. The original work of the ERMI evolved into ERMI, Phase II, which continued to explore the variegated issues associated with e-resource management, such as data standards and usage statistics (http://www.diglib.org/standards/dlf-erm05.htm). Bob McQuillan noted in a January 12, 2011, presentation at a NISO webinar (The Three S's of Electronic Resource Management: Systems, Standards, & Subscriptions, http://www.niso.org/news/events/2011/nisowebinars/erm/) that the early challenges for librarians dealing with e-resource management were four-fold: e-resource data existed in many formats and locations, was not centralized, was often stored and accessed in a variety of silos, and was not integrated with the Integrated Library System (ILS). To what extent have we solved these challenges and what obstacles remain? (Collins and Grogg, 2011)

Generally, ERMS has a one-stop solution of e-resource management which contains two parts includes "management" and "access" for both librarians and end-users, compliance with specific standards and compatibility.

The features and functions includes in "management" aspect of ERMS are:

1. **Workflow Management:** ERMS support e-resource workflow (Life cycle) such as selection, acquisitions, trial, review/renewal/cancellation, usage statistic, cost, and administrative data etc. Workflow management helps to keep track of task assignments throughout the e-resource life cycle.

2. **Licensing Management:** It manages license details with central storage of all license agreements. It is also manage number of users and permission to make copies, printouts,

and interlibrary loans etc. Enabling libraries to compare and standardize licensing terms and defined uniformity and compliance.

3. **Usage Management:** It supports to gather the usage statistics of e-resources. The standard codified by both COUNTER and SUSHI helps the quality of usage statistics and the method of gathering them which helps in evaluation and decision making throughout the life cycle of electronic products, including new purchases, renewal, and cancellation of projects (Hults, 2008).

4. **Administration Management:** ERMS support the functions like User and Admin ID/Password, authority-controlled resource names, contact information for sales and technical support, overall information about resources (holdings/coverage, URL), selection and trail process tracking and documentation, access parameter of each resources: access dates, limits on concurrent users if any, physical limitation on access etc.

5. **Acquisition Management:** Within the workflow management, acquisition is an important part of ERMS. The report of CUNY ERM System committee, 2008 submitted that the functionalities of ERM module should be multiple funds and discretionary accounts, shared cost allocations, tracking of purchase orders, renewal tracking including reminder emails or other alerts to staff to begin evaluation at an appropriate date and methods of recording decision process, trial tracking reminder emails or other alerts to staff to begin evaluation at an appropriate date and methods of recording decision process, tracking system for communications with vendors including sales staff, technical support staff and others, history of payments on a particular resource to chart price increases at the resource level as well as globally, user-friendly report generation capabilities to produce on-the-fly reports about the budget from the local college and global perspective

The second part of ERMS is 'access management'. Once e-resources received in the library the final step is to make it accessible to the users easily. Access management includes IP address management, Discovery search management, A to Z list management, authentication setups on both the library and publisher sides, user ID setups, OpenURL knowledgebase management, Link resolvers and whatever setup or policies are needed to ensure license compliance.

Use of standards is inevitability in any ERMS. To manage all steps in the life-cycle of electronic resources, ERMS must interoperate with existing Integrated Library Management System (ILMS) other applications and services use in the library. The specifications published by the Digital Library Federation's (DLF) Electronic Resource Management Initiative (ERMI) (DLF-ERMI www.diglib.org/standards/dlf-erm02.htm) in 2004 have become the de facto standard for the development of ERMS (Kasprowski, 2007). Although ERM software leverages and expands earlier standards work (MARC, Onix for Serials, openURL, metasearch, etc.), most contemporary ERMS are built using the DLF-ERMI specification as the underlying guide for data element and functional requirements. In the second phase, the group ERMI-2, a major objective is to develop standards for the collection of license information and usage statistics, which would reduce the administrative costs of both data sets. The recent effort, such as Standardized Usage Statistics Harvesting Initiative (SUSHI) and the License Expression Work Group, are defining new standards and protocols to address new ERM issue.

For the Standard for licensing information, ONIX for Publications Licenses (ONIX-PL) that created encoded exchange of licensing terms, NISO's License Expression Working Group that mapped the license syntax between ERMI and ONIX, and NISO's Shared E-Resources Understanding (SERU) that provided guidelines for those who want to forego negotiated licenses. To track usages of e-resources, the development of the COUNTER Codes of Practice to standardize what was counted and how. The success of COUNTER resulted in NISO's SUSHI, a protocol to automate the harvesting of COUNTER data. Another significant new capability with e-resources was OpenURL linking. OpenURL evolved into a formal standard (ANSI/NISO Z39.88) and generated another project, the NISO/UKSG Knowledge Base and Related Tools (KBART) initiative. They issues first of their recommendation practices earlier this year to improve the quality of OpenURL knowledge bases and their metadata. Another NISO project, Improving OpenURLs Through Analytics (IOTA) is looking at how to measure this metadata quality. Systems-related standards efforts for ERM include NISO's Cost of Resource Exchange (CORE) project to develop a protocol for exchanging financial between an ILS and an ERM, and a project to develop best practices for Single-Sign-On Authentication so users don't have to log in over and over. Some of these projects have had tremendous success and are being rapidly adopted in the community. SUSHI and SERU are two examples whose success points to the underlying reasons why standards are adopted generally. In the case of SUSHI, it was the gathering of usage data from several dozen to as many as a few hundred content suppliers. For SERU it was the effort to negotiate licenses, which becomes completely unsalable when the number of licenses reaches a few dozen (Carpenter. http://www.niso.org/apps/group_public/download.php/5258/).

BACKGROUND

Since this chapter is focused on ERMS, it is necessary to review the work carried out, analyze, evaluating the development of latest trends on the same area. In this context, very appropriately Grover & Fons (2004) in their paper brings the works and information of Innovative Interfaces, Inc. in coordination with several libraries in a development partnership to create an electronic resource management (ERM) system. The new ERM system is designed to track licensing and purchasing information about electronic resources, define relationships among aggregators, publishers, or vendors and the resources they provide, and to selectively display information in the Web OPAC for public services staff and patrons. The librarians took advantage of the opportunity to contribute to the functional requirements, field definitions, and public display characteristics of ERM. The vendor, in turn, took advantage of the opportunity to create architecture to meet new system requirements. Together they created a new tool that broadens the choices for management of electronic resources now available to libraries, whereas Tonta (2005) in his paper overview of a wide variety of electronic information management issues ranging from infrastructure to the integration of information technology and content, from personalization of information services to "disintermediation". It discusses the issues of description, organization, collection management, preservation and archiving of electronic information. However, Cotter, Carroll, Hodge & Japzon (2005) discussed in their paper on development in the factors and strategies affecting collection management and access. It discusses major trends in electronic user services including electronic information delivery, information discovery and electronic reference. Finally, it addresses the challenges in user and personnel education in response to this electronic environment and an increasingly information literate user population. Murdock (2010) discuss the problems related to management of electronic resources including the job requirements for ER personnel methods and means used to acquire and manage them, their licenses, their access, etc. Appleton, Regan, England & Fu (2011), discussed about effective approaches to ERM processes and how automation of the acquisition process for new electronic resources has greatly improved workflow coordination and communication between library departments. In this case study, authors discover not only how to best use an ERMS to record workflow, but also to generate and communicate that workflow. Silton & LeMaistre (2011) represented in their paper on the results of a survey on Innovative Interfaces' Electronic Resource Management System (III's ERM). The survey contained seventeen questions that focused on three themes i.e. satisfaction with implementation, impact on workflow, and impact on patrons. The results indicated that difficulty with implementation caused some dissatisfaction with staff workflow, although a majority of informants indicated that III's ERM improved staff workflow to some degree. The major benefits of III's ERM were listed in terms of the product's impact on patrons. Hartnett & Price (2011) in the their innovative paper find the solution of managing e-resources while in tour/move or out of the office for conferences or other obligations, those who manage e-resources must often take their work with them. With the advent of Apple's iPad, the authors made the decision to investigate the possibilities and potential offered by this new device for mobile management of electronic resources. To accomplish this, the authors used iPads to test the various systems and tools utilized every day to manage and maintain the library's electronic resources to find out what worked, and what didn't. While the results vary by system, overall, the iPad is a useful but limited means for electronic resource management. In the paper wherein authors Cukadar, Tuglu & Gurdal (2012) share their hands on experience gained at the Anatolian University Libraries Consortium (ANKOS), which was originally established to coordinate university libraries' electronic serials purchases. In order to selecting, providing access to, managing and evaluating, measuring the usage rate, conduct cost analyses and to use the findings in strategic planning cycles of both the institutions and the consortium of e-resources, a New Electronic Resources Management System (ERM) has been developed by ANKOS. In this study, the authors also explain how the new system was developed, its technical features, data entry and collection, the system's contribution to the collection of institution and usage statistics, and its impact on strategic planning. Stone & Emery (2012) projected to encourage open peer commentary and crowd sourcing of areas of best practice for each of the stages of the e-resources lifecycle. The project aims to become a reference point for those who are new to e-resource management and for those who may want to implement its recommendations of best practice. Collins (2008) provides the information based on survey responses of nine ERMS i.e. the CUFTS ERM (an open source ERMS developed by Simon Frasier University), EBSCO's ERM Essentials™, ExLibris' Verde, Colorado Alliance's Gold Rush, HARRASSOWITZ's HERMIS, Innovative ERM, Serials Solutions 360 Resource Manager, Swets-Wise eSource Manager and TDNet Open ERAM. Each profile describes availability, development, use of standards, compatibility, functionality and distinguishing features.

The full story for electronic collection management and electronic information services has yet to be told. There are number of articles that do not address recent empirical developments on functions, features, standards & compatibility of ERMS. Only one paper talked about the comparison nine ERMS. Keeping in view, this chapter explores the concept of ERM and compared modules, features, standards and workflow management of sixteen ERMS available recently.

SCOPE AND LIMITATION

In this chapter an analysis in comparison of 16 ERMS has been made to know the modules, features, standards, workflow management etc. that have been implemented in these softwares. These 16 ERMS are Innovative Interface' Innovative ERM, TDNet' TDNet ERM Solutions, Ex Libris' Verde ERM, OCLC' Web-share License Manager, SemperTool' SMDB, University of Notre Dame' CORAL, MIT' VERA, SerialsSolutions' 360 Resource Manager, HARRASSOWITZ' HER-

MIS, The Johns Hopkins University' HERMIES, Colorado Alliance' Gold Rush, WT Cox' Journal Finder, EBSCO' EBSCONET ERM Essentials, Simon Fraser University Library' CUFTS, SIRSI Corp' E-Resource Center, Priory Solution' Research Monitor. Information has been taken from the websites of 16 ERM companies as well as from the articles published from different sources.

OBJECTIVES

The aims and objectives of the present study are:

- To find out the goodness of ERMS, comparing amongst 16 ERMS.
- To know and articulate the utilities of ERMS.
- To know the standards, features, functions available in ERMS.
- To understand the function of entire life-cycle of e-resources available in ERMS.
- To know the usefulness of ERMS for Librarians and End-Users.

COMPARISON OF ERMS

The following table indicates the comparison of 16 ERMS which covers its functionality, use of standards and compatibility, distinguish features and modules etc.

INNOVATIVE ERM (http://www.iii.com/products/electronic_resource.shtml)

Innovative Interface developed its Innovative ERM in 2004 for managing electronic resources. It saves time, improves collection analysis, and makes the most of scarce budgetary resources by centralizing and assimilating all of the technical and administrative details of electronic resources.

Features

- Offers the Content Access Service (CASE)
- Provides tools for patron access such as Spell Check.
- Integrated Really Simple Syndication (RSS) feeds.
- Faceted search results.
- Ability to maintain resources, track licenses, and manage coverage data etc.

Standards and Compatibility

ANSI/NISO search and Retrieval Protocol, COUNTER, Excel & Text Format, MARC, ONIX and SUSHI are the standards and compatibility adopted the Innovative ERM.

Functions and Modules

The modules available in this software are Acquisitions, Serials, Cataloguing, Circulation, Management Reports.

TDNET ERM SOLUTIONS (http://web.tdnet.com/)

TDNet ERM Solution is proprietary product of TDNetInc developed in 2000. It offers a broad spectrum of e-Resource Access & Management (ERAM) solutions for the academic, corporate, government, and healthcare communities.

Features

- Full neutrality towards all content providers without exception on a global scale.
- Flexibility and customization of management and A-Z holdings.
- Scalable, multi-level customization & personalization.
- Federated searching of internal repositories and of external databases.

Table 1. Comparison of ERMS

Sr. No.	Name of Software	Developed By	Version	Functions/ Modules	Year of Development	Who Implemented	Open Source/ Proprietary	Standards and Compatibility	Platform, Programming Language, Database	Features	URL Link
1	Innovative ERM	Innovative Interface		Acquisitions, Serials, Cataloging, Circulation, Management Reports	2004	University of Washington Libraries (Approx 300 Users)	Proprietary	ANSI/NISO search and Retrieval Protocol, COUNTER, Excel & Text Format, MARC, ONIX and SUSHI	Linux Java PostgreSQL	It offers the Content Access Service (CASE), tools for patron access such as Spell Check, integrated Really Simple Syndication (RSS) feeds, faceted search results, ability to maintain resources, track licenses, and manage coverage data.	http://www.iii. com/products/ electronic_ resource.shtml
2	TDNet ERM Solutions	TDNetInc		Comprehensive Knowledgebase, eJournal and eBook management, Holdings Manager, TOU Resolver, Searcher Analyzer, New Acquisitions Module	2000	NA	Proprietary	COUNTER Delimited, Excel and Text format support, Full text resolver, MARC NISO ONIX, OpenURL, SOH (Serial Online Holdings), SUSHI, XML,	NA	Flexibility of ILL, presentation of A-Z holdings, multi-level customization & personalization, federated searching, eBook Manager, link resolver, partners with the Copyright Clearance Center (CCC)	http://web.tdnet. com/
3	Verde ERM	Ex Libris	2.4	Verde task, KB Manager, KB Tools, Admin, Info Gateway, Universal Gateway, SFX, User module	2004	Iowa State University, Loughborough University, University of East Anglia(Approx.160 Users)	Proprietary	ANSI/NISO COUNTER and SUSHI, MARC, ONIX OpenURL, Simple Object Access Protocol (SOAP), Unicode, XML (Extensible Markup Language)	Linux, Window	Verde KnowledgeBase assists staff in easily finding latest titles, where they are available, and how they are packaged, Staff can easily derive cost-per-use metrics, Easily analyze cost, usage, and licensing information, Libraries can quickly analyze actual expenditure vs. budget.	http://www. exlibrisgroup. com/category/ VerdeOverview

continued on following page

Table 1. Continued

Sr. No.	Name of Software	Developed By	Version	Functions/ Modules	Year of Development	Who Implemented	Open Source/ Proprietary	Standards and Compatibility	Platform, Programming Language, Database	Features	URL Link
4	Web-share License Manager	OCLC	NA	Matadata, Integrated Acquisition, Licenses, Circulation, Admin, Help.	NA	https://www.oclc.org/news/releases/2011/201128.en.html	Proprietary	COUNTER, Ezproxy, OCLC MARC Format, OpenURL link resolver, Z39.50 search and Retrieval Protocol	NA	Interlibrary loan, Course reserves, Archival materials, Perpetual access, Remote access, Post-cancellation access, Copying and sharing, A to Z journal list, A citation finder tool for articles, An API Web Service for the WorldCat knowledge base, Evaluative content, Mobile access, OCLC's partnerships,	https://www.oclc.org/license-manager.en.html
5	SMDB	SemperTool	NA	Products, providers, resources, publishers, subjects, organizations, reports, users & setup.	NA	100 universities in Europe, Africa	Open sources	SUSHI	Window, LAMP (Linux, Apache, MySQL, Perl)	Product description, Price information, Renewal notification, Subscription history, Provider contact information, Resource management, Availability holding information, Library holding information, File upload feature, Access control, General reports, Renewal reports	http://www.sempertool.dk/?func=loadTemplate&template=smdbMore
6	CORAL	University of Notre Dame's Hesburgh Libraries	1.2	Resource, Licensing, Organizations, Usage Statistics	2010		Open sources	HTML, LDAP(Lightweight directory access protocol), MySQL, ONIX-PL	Linux, Window, Mac JavaScript, PHP5, MySQL5,	It's a workflow management tool,	http://erm.library.nd.edu

continued on following page

Table 1. Continued

Sr. No.	Name of Software	Developed By	Version	Functions/ Modules	Year of Development	Who Implemented	Open Source/ Proprietary	Standards and Compatibility	Platform, Programming Language, Database	Features	URL Link
7	VERA	MIT	NA	Licensed details, licensed list, admin details, admin list, subject list, maintainer list & reports	2000	Massachusetts Intitutes of Technology	NA	COUNTER and SUSHI, DLF-ERMI Standards MARC, NISO, ONIX, SOAP, XML,	Linux, Window, Mac '=	Vera is a Multi-Search interface,	http://vera.mit.edu/
8	360 Resource Manager	SerialsSolutions	NA	Advanced 360 resource manager tools, assessment tools, manager your products, manage your library	2005	NA	Proprietary	COUNTER and SUSHI, CrossRef DOI Linking, MARC, NISO,1 OAI-PMH, ONIX SRU/SRW, OpenURL, SOAP, SOH, XML,	NA	E-Journal Portal, A-to-Z Title List, cited journal anywhere in your collection, Identify overlapping journal coverage within a collection of databases, Customize the content of the e-Journal portal, Control individual administrator access,	http://www.serialssolutions.com/en/services/360-resource-manager
9	HERMIS	HARRASSOWITZ	NA	NA	NA	NA	NA	COUNTER and SUSHI, DLF-ERMI standards MARC, NISO, ONIX (Online Information eXchange), SOH (Serial Online Holdings), SPS (Serial Products and Subscription), SRN (Serial Release Notification), XML,	NA	Detailed information on all periodical print and electronic and electronic only, E-Resources News/Offers are announced on his website, License analysis based on library licensing requirements, A-Z lists, tables of contents service, Access verification	http://www.harrassowitz.de/subscription_services/hermis.html

continued on following page

Table 1. Continued

continued on following page

Sr. No.	Name of Software	Developed By	Version	Functions/ Modules	Year of Development	Who Implemented	Open Source/ Proprietary	Standards and Compatibility	Platform, Programming Language, Database	Features	URL Link
10	HERMIES	Johns Hopkins University libraries	NA	Authentication, Authorization, Selection, Acquisitions, Catalog Interface, Library Computing Services, Public Display, Administrative Search, Report, Scheduled Notifications, Automated Subject Indexing	2004	Johns Hopkins University	NA	LDAP (Lightweight directory access protocol), XML,	Web-based application (Macromedia ColdFusion) Python	Provide automatic notification to appropriate staff of changes of status and scope in e-resource ordering and licensing, provide for link management for e-resources, including the automatic updating of URLs in the backend database,	http://www.ala. org/lita/ital/22/1/ cyzyk
11	Gold Rush	Colorado Alliance	NA	Reports, holdings, subscriptions, cataloguing and setting	2003	(Approx.37 Users) http://www. coalliance.org/grinfo/ node/18	Proprietary	OpenURL link resolver with full compliance for NISO 1.0 and 0.1 standards, SOAP Protocol, Support Excel format, SUSHI, XML,	Linux, PHP5, Perl	Gold Rush has a large body of open access journals that can be selected and added to your holdings at no additional cost, Control your own style sheets and results page templates Public search interface, Public search interface (A-Z), Content Comparison, create a customized interface	http://www. coalliance.org/ grinfo/
12	Journal Finder	WT Cox	NA	NA	2008	University of North Carolina	Proprietary	Link Resolver	NA	ILL(Inter Library Loan), document delivery, Automatically updated list content, Hosted by WT Cox -- no server headaches at your site	http://www. wtcox.com/ journal-finder. cfm

Table 1. Continued

Sr. No.	Name of Software	Developed By	Version	Functions/ Modules	Year of Development	Who Implemented	Open Source/ Proprietary	Standards and Compatibility	Platform, Programming Language, Database	Features	URL Link
13	EBSCONET ERM Essentials	EBSCO	NA	My collection, Renewal, Upload, Reminders, Tasks, Options and Reports.	2010	75 customer	proprietary	ANSI/NISO, CORE (Cost of Resource Exchange) HTML Format, MARC, ONIX, OpenURL link resolver, Support Excel format, support proxy, XML,	Web-based	EBSCO Integrated Knowledge Base, EBSCO's OpenURL link resolver, maintains approx. 100 highly customizable data fields for e-packages, single-point access to manage critical e-resource data, Create your own reports, Customize fields, hide fields that aren't relevant for your processes, and create fields specifically for your library	http://www2. ebsco.com/en-us/ ProductsServices/ ERM/Pages/ index.aspx
14	CUFTS	Simon Fraser University Library	3.0	Local resources, site setting, statistics, tools, Account setting	2009	Lee College & Chapman University, Simon Frasier University	Open source	COUNTER and SUSHI, MARC, ONIX, OpenURL Link solver XML,	Linux, Window Perl	A-to-Z database search, direct to article OpenURL resolving, As a knowledgebase of over 575 full text resources, an integrated journal A-Z database, It provides some powerful publicly-accessible services (Resource Comparison & Journal Search)	http://researcher. sfu.ca/cufts
15	E-Resource Central	SIRSI Corp			2011	More than 3,600 customers worldwide		MARC, ONIX, XML	Linux, Window	E-content management,	http://www. sirsidynix.com/ eresourcecentral

continued on following page

Table 1. Continued

Sr. No.	Name of Software	Developed By	Version	Functions/ Modules	Year of Development	Who Implemented	Open Source/ Proprietary	Standards and Compatibility	Platform, Programming Language, Database	Features	URL Link
16	ResearchMonitor	Priory Solution	6.0	Usage Analysis, Access control, Client validation, Cost recovery, Contract management	NA	NA	NA	NA	NA	Facilitate contract, negotiations, Reduce costs, Improve management reporting, Improve cost allocation, Improve usage patterns, No impact on how users access services, All client reference codes are validated, Dramatically increase recovery rates using your existing processes, Easy and fast to use, Simplify introduction of RSS feeds onto the intranet, Control online costs, Automatic contract renewal notices via email	http://www.priorysolutions.com/ResearchMonitor

Figure 1. Innovative ERM

- On-the-fly post search analysis; alternatively classification-based analysis.
- Availability of eBook Manager.
- Option available for print resources in same database.
- Advanced statistics data facility starting at end-user up to the level of the organization, per product, per provider, per time slot, etc.

Standards and Compatibility

Standards compatible with TDNET ERM solutions are COUNTER, Delimited, Excel and Text format support, Full text resolver, MARC, NISO, ONIX, OpenURL, SOH (Serial Online Holdings), SUSHI, XML,

Functions and Modules

It provides unique functions such as single point of maintenance; eBook management, Public display functions, Collection evaluation, Authentication Management, Reporting etc. It manages access permissions via IP / access details / access notes / support specific access solutions (Athens). Access can be differentiated by user identity, e.g., when belonging to a pre-defined group.

VERDE ERM (http://www. exlibrisgroup.com/category/ VerdeOverview)

Verde ERM is developed by Ex Libris in 2004. It is commercial software. Approximately 160 Users are used Verde ERM software. Verde is a centralized repository through which all e-resource workflows—acquisitions, trial, usage, cost, access, and administrative data—are managed.

Features

- Tools for effectively managing expanding e-collections throughout a resource's life

Figure 2. TDNet ERM Solutions

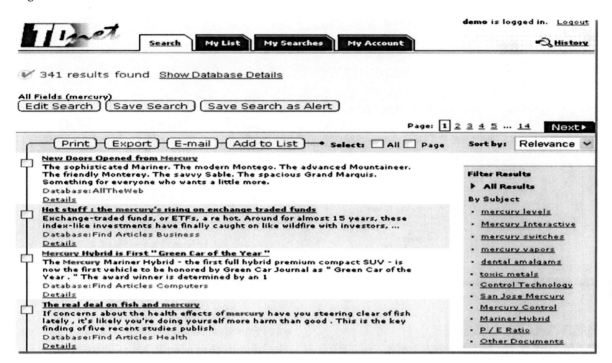

cycle from evaluation, selection, and acquisition through renewal and cancellation.

- Facilitates collection development decision making and cost analysis for single institution and consortia.
- Ready to access to prevailing license terms, such as printing permission.
- A standalone product that can be integrated with existing library applications such as SFX, OPACs, A-Z list, applications that handle acquisitions and more.
- Assistance in managing electronic journals with no duplication of effort for SFX customer.
- Easily analyze cost, usage, and licensing information, Libraries can quickly analyze actual expenditure vs. budget.
- The MetaLib gateway and metasearch system—allows users to simultaneously search multiple databases and receive combined results in a uniform format.

Standards and Compatibility

Verde is an open architecture and support for industry standards such as ANSI/NISO, COUNTER and SUSHI, MARC, ONIX OpenURL, Simple Object Access Protocol (SOAP), Unicode, XML (Extensible Markup Language), adhere to the DLF ERMI model, with additional consortia support and tools for cost analysis.

Functions and Modules

In Verde, end users can access e-resources via an A-Z list, library portal, library OPAC, or link server. It provides the functionality such as acquisition, cost analysis, admin, Verde Task, KB Manager, KB tools etc. Verde interact not only with Ex Libris products but also with similar products provided by other vendors based on industry standards.

Figure 3. Verde ERM

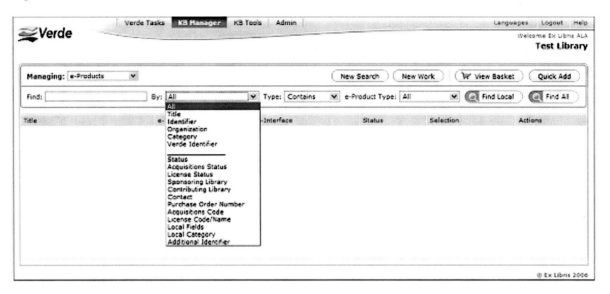

WEB-SHARE LICENSE MANAGER (https://www.oclc.org/license-manager.en.html)

Web-share License Manager developed by OCLC. It manages divergent e-content workflows and put everything in one place, which saves time and money, and makes collection development easier too.

Features

- It's a unique ERM solution that consolidates the management of link resolution with vendor, licensing and subscription management, centralized acquisition, budgeting, ordering.
- Managing access to all library resources in a single location.
- Allows library staff and others to create applications that enhance current features and bridge information to other systems.
- Provides analytics that inform library management decisions. COUNTER-compliant statistics are aggregated in the OCLC statistics portal.

- Provides customizable workflows that accommodate negotiation of licenses with content providers, evaluation of trial subscriptions, registration and configuration of access credentials, including support for EZproxy.

Standards and Compatibility

The standards compatible with Web-share License Manager are COUNTER, Ezproxy, OCLC MARC Format, Open URL link resolver, Z39.50 search and Retrieval Protocol.

Function and Modules

The screenshot mentioned below represents that the modules of World-Share License manager are metadata, acquisitions, Licenses, circulation, admin, and help. It delivers, an OpenURL link resolver, management of terms of use by type of resource, including interlibrary loan, course reserves, archival materials, perpetual access, remote access, post-cancellation access, copying and sharing, A to Z journal list, citation finder tool for articles, API Web Service for the WorldCat knowledge base.

Figure 4. Web-share License Manager

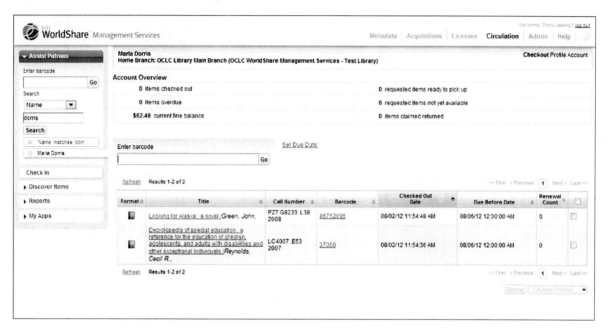

SMDB (http://www.sempertool. dk/?func=loadTemplate&t emplate=smdbMore)

SMDB is open source ERM software developed by SemperTool. SMDB is a LAMP (Linux, Apache, MySQL, Perl) system. It uses its own module called webUtil to deal with web forms and templates. SMDB is an ERMS for the products you buy or subscribe to, a single institutions or consortia solution, manages any media type.

Features

- SMDB provides product description, price information, renewal notification, subscription history, provider contact information, resource management, availability holding information, library holding information.
- It also offers features like file upload feature, access control, general reports, renewal reports etc.

Standards and Compatibility

SMDB support the standards such as SUSHI.

Functions and Modules

From the screenshot of SMDB it is stated that the functions and modules are products, providers, resources, publishers, subjects, organizations, reports, users and setup. In addition to that it includes managing product and resources types & also manage agent and currencies.

CORAL (http://erm.library.nd.edu)

CORAL is an open source ERMS available on GitHub and developed by the University of Notre Dame's Hesburgh Libraries, released in the year 2010. CORAL called as centralizes Online Resources Acquisition and Licensing. It runs on PHP 5, MySQL 5 and webserver. CORAL resources

Figure 5. SMDB

aids in the management of the electronic resource workflow from the initial request through the acquisition process and into ongoing support and maintenance.

Features

- Supports the completion workflow processes with a convenient task-based queue in which automated email alerts indicate to staff when new tasks are available.
- Provides both search and A to Z browse access to the resource records.
- Licensing management store current and past license information, including uploading the actual documents.
- Statistic management provides usage statistics for all resources.
- Includes acquisitions information, contacts, account information and access information. E-mail alerts can be set up to remind before the licenses are up for renewal with a custom time period.

Standards and Compatibility

CORAL compatible with the standards such as HTML, LDAP(Lightweight directory access protocol), MySQL, ONIX-PL.

Functions and Modules

CORAL E-Resources Management has four major Modules that are Resource, Licensing, Organizations and Usage Statistics.

VERA MIT (http://vera.mit.edu/)

VERA is a project of MIT (Massachusetts Institutes of Technology) for managing the e-resource and launched in 2000. The VERA program was created using FileMaker Pro software.

Features

- It develops for both front-end and back-end system. The front-end, or patron view, allows searches by title, subject, keyword, or provider. The back-end, or staff view, allows staff to enter data into the Web-enabled version of FileMaker Pro.
- Web-based VERA allows librarians sitting anywhere can make changes to the title database without downloading software to their computers.
- In VERA, the icon appears on the search results screen, assisting the patron to understand the access restrictions and permissions in a visual format.

Figure 6. CORAL

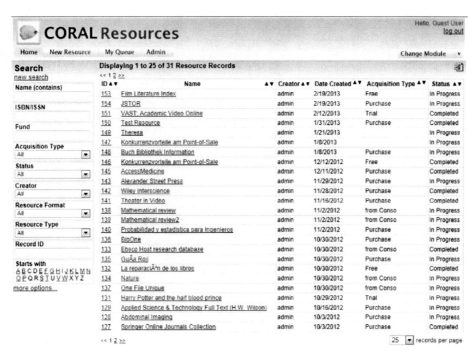

- Librarians activate the appropriate icons from the back-end view of VERA in order to display them to the public.

Standards and Compatibility

Standards compatible with VERA ERMS are COUNTER and SUSHI, DLF-ERMI Standards, MARC, NISO, ONIX, SOAP, XML.

Functions and Modules

Modules based on screenshot are licensed details, licensed list, admin details, admin list, subject list, maintainer list and reports.

360 RESOURCE MANAGER (http://www.serialssolutions.com/en/services/360-resource-manager)

360 Resource Manager is proprietary ERM software developed by Serials Solutions in 2005.

360 Core is powered by KnowledgeWorks, the authoritative e-resource knowledgebase provides consistent and accurate e-resource access and facilitate simple, streamlined management.

Features

- It includes E-Journal Portal A-to-Z title List, different types of searching (titles, ISSN/ISBN, subject etc.) of e-Journals and e-Books are all included in a webpage interface that is fully localized, customizable, and updated. It also uses single search interface regardless of format.
- Journal Linker Link from abstracts and indexes to the cited journal anywhere in e-resources collection.
- Identify overlapping journal coverage within a collection of databases and download summary and results sets of analyzed data to use for library-specific queries and comparisons. Search statistics identify the number and type of searches by the users.

Figure 7. VERA MIT

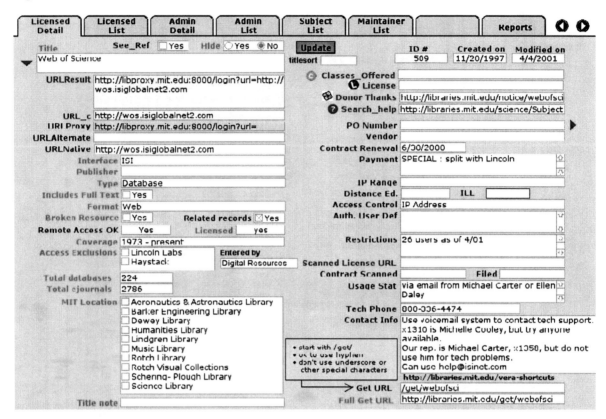

- Usage statistics generates report which journals and databases are accessing by users, and aggregate the click counts at the holding, journal, database and provider levels.
- Add custom URLs, proxies, database names, coverage dates, and more to ensure data reflects local needs. Add custom notes to resources at the holding, database, and journal levels to keep patrons informed of special access requirements.
- Control individual administrator access within the administrative website, Serials Solutions client center, while enabling administrators to pick the language they prefer to see when using the Client Center.

Standards and Compatibility

The standards compatible with 360 resource manager are COUNTER and SUSHI, CrossRef DOI Linking, MARC, NISO, OAI-PMH, ONIX SRU/SRW, OpenURL, SOAP, SOH, XML.

Functions and Modules

The 360 E-Discovery and E-Management Services control e-resources collection and provide easy access to end-users by the function such as advanced 360 resource manager tools, assessment tool, manage the products and manage library by its accounts & settings.

Figure 8. 360 Resource Manager

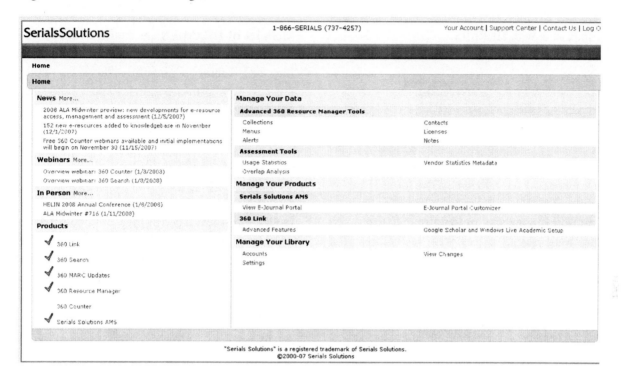

HARRASSOWITZ ELECTRONIC RESOURCES MANAGEMENT AND INFORMATION SOLUTIONS (HERMIS) (http://www.harrassowitz.de/ subscription_services/hermis.html)

HERMIS is developed by HARRASSOWITZ, a Bookseller and subscription agent since 1872.

Features

- Resource Identification and Evaluation: detailed information on all resources, notifications of changes in online availability of publications, changes in publishers' e-journal policies, e-resources news/offers etc.
- License management: license analysis based on library licensing requirements, negotiation with publishers, online repository for signed licenses etc.

- Ordering and payment, renewals and cancellations of e-resources.
- Automatic activation and status of e-resources.
- Public resource discovery and access: A-Z lists, link resolvers, tables of contents service, and MARC records available through HARRASSOWITZ's industry partners.
- Access verification and technical access management includes notification of URL changes and to publisher for IP changes.
- Usage tracking which links in OttoSerials to COUNTER statistics on publishers' websites.

Standards and Compatibility

COUNTER and SUSHI, DLF-ERMI standards, MARC, NISO, ONIX (Online Information eXchange), SOH (Serial Online Holdings), SPS

(Serial Products and Subscription), SRN (Serial Release Notification), XML, are the standards compatible with HERMIS.

HERMIES (http://www.ala.org/lita/ital/22/1/cyzyk)

HERMIES (Hopkins Electronic Resource Management System) an electronic resource management system is developed by The Johns Hopkins University (JHU) libraries. It provides an easy and time-saving tool to identify and access the electronic resources, as well as facilitate the process of selecting, purchasing, and managing e-resources.

Features

- It provide automatic notification to appropriate librarian for changes of status and scope in e-resources ordering and licensing, provide for link management for e-resources, including the automatic updating of URLs in the backend database.
- Provide a full workflow and approvals process to support the selection, procurement, and implementation of e-resources.
- Enable dynamic generation of e-resource information for public display.
- Provide librarian with a unified, web-based means for viewing, updating, reporting, and administering e-resources, including custom report generation.
- Interoperable with existing and future systems, including the integrated library system, the campus proxy server, and web sites of the various campus libraries.

Standards and Compatibility

HERMIES compatible with standards are LDAP (Lightweight directory access protocol), XML.

Functions and Modules

Modules of HERMIES are Authentication, Authorization, Selection, Acquisitions, Catalogue Interface, Library Computing Services, Public Display, Administrative Search, Report, Scheduled Notifications, Automated Subject Indexing.

GOLD RUSH (http://www.coalliance.org/grinfo/)

Gold Rush is developed by the Colorado Alliance of Research Libraries in 2003 to help libraries for managing electronic resources and provide improved access to these resources for their patrons.

Features

- It is centrally hosted and requires no programming or management of a local server. It interoperates with any integrated library system and can be folded into library's website.
- Open access journals that can be selected and added to library's holdings at no additional cost, control own style sheets and results page templates, public search interface (A-Z), content comparison and create a customized interface.

Standards and Compatibility

Standards compatible in GOLD RUSH are OpenURL link resolver with full compliance for NISO 1.0 and 0.1 standards, SOAP Protocol, Support Excel format, SUSHI, XML.

Functions and Modules

Modules available in GOLD RUSH ERMS are Reports, Holdings, Subscriptions, Cataloguing and Settings.

Figure 9. Gold Rush

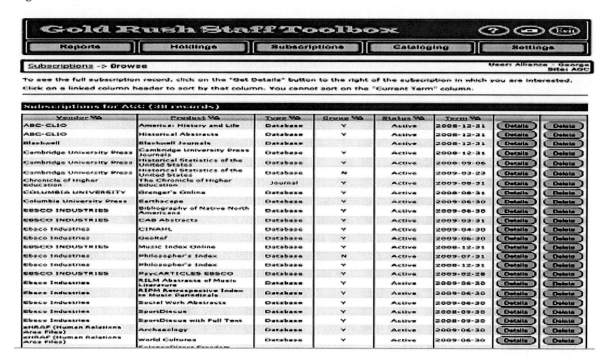

JOURNAL FINDER (http://www. wtcox.com/journal-finder.cfm)

Journal Finder was developed by the University of North Carolina - Greensboro in 2000 and was the first OpenURL Link Resolver in the United States. It's a complete A-Z List, Link Resolver and ERM solution and provides library users on easy access to electronic content with a user friendly interface.

Features

- All e-resources can be searchable at one single access point.
- Automatically updated contents list.
- Hosted by WT Cox so no server needed. Completely customizable to complement the library website. Easy to use administration for maintaining content.

- Option available for generating management reports.
- Ability to link from a citation in one commercial database to the library catalog or to the full text article in another database.

Standards and Compatibility

In Journal Finder, standards compatible with Link Resolver.

ERM ESSENTIALS (http:// www2.ebsco.com/ en- us / ProductsServices / ERM / Pages / index.aspx)

EBSCONET' ERM Essentials is developed by EBSCO in 2010. It is a full-featured electronic resource management tool that maintains ap-

Figure 10. Journal Manager

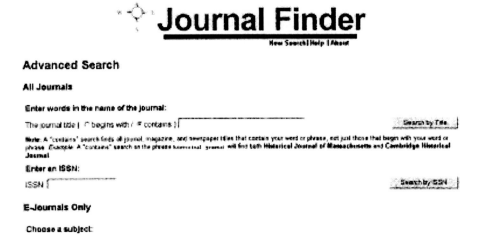

proximately 100 highly customizable data fields for e-journal and e-package orders.

Features

- Reduce the complexity of managing e-journals and e-packages with single-point access to manage critical e-resource data.
- It facilitates the management of e-resources development decisions by trials, evaluations, licensing management, orders and renewals.
- Simplify workflows and streamline e-resource management processes by setting statuses, creating reminders and assigning tasks.
- Generate different types of reports.

Standards and Compatibility

EBSCONET ERM ESSENTIALS compatible with standards such as ANSI/NISO, CORE (Cost of Resource Exchange), HTML Format, MARC, ONIX, OpenURL link resolver, Support Excel format, support proxy, XML.

Functions and Modules

Modules available in this ERM Essential based on screenshot are My collection, Renewal, Upload, Reminders, Tasks, Options and Reports.

CUFTS (http://researcher.sfu.ca/cufts)

CUFTS is open source software developed at the Simon Fraser University Library. Originally it was developed to provide full-text link resolving for GODOT. In 2005, COPPUL funded an expansion of CUFTS to facilitate the creation of publicly-accessible A-Z serials databases (CJDB) as well as for basic electronic resource management (ERM) functionality.

Features

- Facilitate A-to-Z database search, MARC record of each title and direct to article OpenURL resolving and Electronic resource management tools.
- Resource Comparison & Journal Search.

Figure 11. ERM Essential

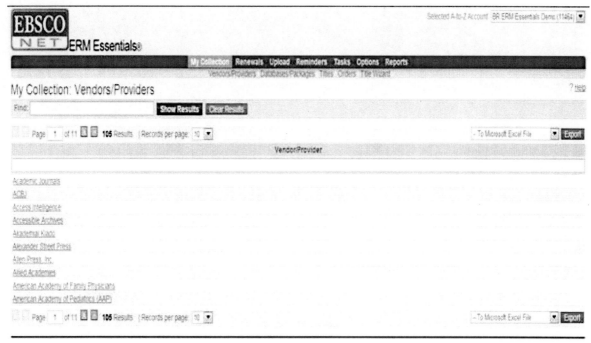

Standards and Compatibility

Standards available in COUNTER and SUSHI, MARC, ONIX, OpenURL Link solver, XML.

Functions and Modules

From the below screenshot it is found that the modules of CUFTS are Local resources, site setting, statistics, tools, change site, account setting.

E-RESOURCE CENTRAL (http://www. sirsidynix.com/eresourcecentral)

E-Resource Central, a next generation electronic resource management solution for libraries developed in the year 2011 by SirsiDynix. eResource Central bridge the gap between content providers

and users, enabling libraries to manage and deliver e-resources seamlessly and cost-effectively.

Features

- It provides access to all library resources, including e-books and e-journals, via a single user interface.
- Enables cost savings and simplifies the process of delivering content of disparate sources and formats to users by managing licensing and access rights; maintaining MARC records and metadata for library e-resources; integrating e-resource usage into circulation reporting; and managing electronic content acquisition and creation.
- Provide end-user tools to simplify the e-resource access and download process.
- SirsiDynix technology is architected to be open, scalable and robust, offering a com-

Figure 12. CUFTS

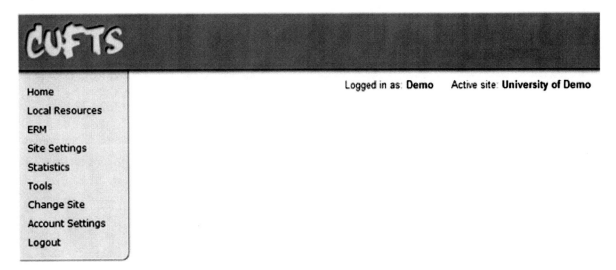

plete solution out-of-the-box, and unparalleled flexibility through APIs and web services.

Standards and Compatibility

Standards compatible with eResource central are MARC, ONIX, XML.

RESEARCHMONITOR (http://www.priorysolutions.com/ResearchMonitor)

It is developed by Priory Solution in 2004. It is a modular solution that will help manage external online database subscriptions as well as internal intranets and knowledge base portals.

Figure 13. E-Resource Centre

Features

- A user-friendly database with many useful features such as translation into 10 different languages, forecasts, ability to export the reports into PDF, Excel and power point formats, split screen facilities etc. No registration is needed to access the data, although doing so gives the user enhanced functionality, and there is unlimited access to content for all users.
- Records online usage, consistent usage reports across all online services. Reports usage down to an individual level or summarized by practice area, office, job title, etc. Also records details of how people use services, such as search terms, databases accessed and documents viewed.
- Validates client references entered in any online service against current matter list. Ensuring only valid references are used

can dramatically increase recovery rates without changing your existing processes.
- Provides single sign-on by automatically logging users on to online services they should have access to. People no longer need to remember passwords and you can control access to services on an individual or group level where needed.
- Records online charges as they occur and seamlessly feeds the information to billing system, eliminating unnecessary manual effort and maximizing recovery rates. Allows rate-cards to be configured, so you can determine what charges you pass on to your clients.

Functions and Modules

The modules of RM are Usage Analysis, Access control, Client validation, Cost recovery, Contract management.

Figure 14. Research Monitor

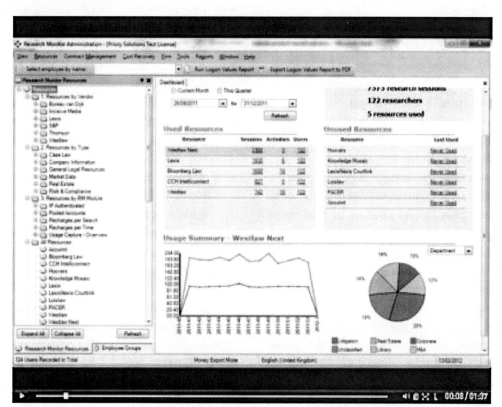

CONCLUSION

Growth of electronic resources is exponential and brought a herculean challenge to the library professionals for managing the e-resource. Necessity is mother of invention; in light of this different tools and technology have been developed to counter these challenges. This chapter concludes that different ERMS facilitate the management of e-resources covering its workflow (life-cycle) such as selection, acquisitions, trial, review/renewal/cancellation, usage statistic, cost and access.

ERMS proves its usefulness for the librarian and the users by providing basic features such as:

- Tools for effectively managing and expanding e-collections throughout a resource's life cycle from evaluation, selection, and acquisition through renewal/review and cancellation.
- Ability to maintain resources, track licenses, and manage coverage data and A-Z holdings etc.
- Assistance in managing electronic journals with no duplication of effort.
- Easily analyze cost, usage, and licensing information, Libraries can quickly analyze actual expenditure vs. budget.
- Allows users to simultaneously search multiple databases and receive combined results in a uniform format.
- Consolidates the management of link resolution with vendor, negotiation license with content provider, evaluation of trial subscriptions, subscription management, centralized acquisition, budgeting, ordering.
- Statistic management provides usage statistics for all resources.
- Includes acquisitions information, contacts, account information and access information. E-mail alerts remind before the licenses are up for renewal with a custom time period.

- Access verification and technical access management includes notification of URL changes and to publisher for IP changes.
- Provide automatic notification to appropriate librarian for changes of status and scope in e-resources ordering and licensing, provide for link management for e-resources, including the automatic updating of URLs in the backend database.
- Facilitate A-to-Z database search, MARC record of each title and direct to article OpenURL resolving and Electronic resource management tools.

Though, the above basic features of ERMS are beneficial to both the librarians and the users there are certain perils needs to be addressed in these ERMS which are:

- The main weakness of most of the ERMS is that the diversity of the digital collection such as digital images, streaming video sound file etc. are still to dealt with.
- Implementation of ERMS system leads to a huge additional cost since most of the proprietary ERMS are costly.
- A group of professionals with their technical skills/expertise is required for implementing ERMS.
- Redundancy rate is very high in case of personnel, technology after implementing ERMS .
- Although most of the functions are inimitable in all ERMS but the paramount issue i.e. basic structural features / modules are unlike.
- Integration of electronic resources in ERMS is a mountainous job which takes longer time.

This chapter tried to compare and evaluate the standards, features, functions use in ERM software designed especially for managing the electronic resources. Authors also mentioned general benefits and weakness of ERMS. Based on this comparison, librarians can take this as a ready reference to match their needs facilities offered by ERMS. This will be very handy tool in making right choice & decision for selecting ERMS for efficient management of e-resources. This comparative study also finds some gaps and scope for further innovation and study in terms of development of single software which should be in combination of integrated library management software, digital library software and ERM Software. The advance technology like the mobile management technology for ERM would also be for further direction. Study on continuous technological advancement of ERMS needs to be done for cost effectiveness. Now authors would like to conclude this chapter for further study on practical aspects of users / librarians benefits.

REFERENCES

360 *Resource Manager*. (n.d.). Retrieved May 09, 2013, from http://www.serialssolutions.com/en/services/360-resource-manager

Appleton, B., Regan, S., England, L., & Fu, L. (2011). *Improving electronic resources management (ERM), critical work flow and operations solution*. Lafayette, IN: Purdue University..

Breeding, M. (2008). Helping you buy: Electronic resource management systems. *Computers in Libraries*, 28(7).

Carpenter, T. (n.d.). *Standard columns – Electronic resource management standardization - Still a mixed bag*. Retrieved March 30, 2013, from http://www.niso.org/apps/group_public/download.php/5258/

Collins, M. (Ed.). (2008). Electronic resource management systems (ERMS) review. Elsevier, 267..

Collins, M., & Grogg, J. E. (2011). At ERMS length: Evaluating electronic resource management systems. *Library Journal*, 136(4), 22–28.

CORAL. (n.d.). Retrieved May 06, 2013, from http://erm.library.nd.edu

Cotter, G., Carroll, B., Hodge, G., & Japzon, A. (2005). Electronic collection management and electronic information services. *Information Services & Use*, 25, 23–34.

CUFTS: Open Source Serial Management. (n.d.). Retrieved May 03, 2013, from http://researcher.sfu.ca/cufts

Cukadar, S., Tuglu, A., & Gurdal, G. (2012). Perspectives on new electronic resources management system for the ANKOS consortium. *Journal of Academic Librarianship*. doi:10.1016/j.acalib.2012.11.011.

E-Resource Central: SirsiDynix. (n.d.). Retrieved May 04, 2013, from http://www.sirsidynix.com/eresourcecentral

EBSCONET: ERM Essentials. (n.d.). Retrieved May 02, 2013, from http://www2.ebsco.com/en-us/ProductsServices/ERM/Pages/index.aspx

Fons, T. A., & Jewell, T. D. (2007). Envisioning the future of ERM systems. *The Serials Librarian*, 52(1-2), 151–166. doi:10.1300/J123v52n01_13.

Gold Rush. (n.d.). *Electronic resource management and discovery*. Retrieved May 09, 2013, from http://www.coalliance.org/grinfo/

Grover, D., & Fons, T. (2004). The innovative electronic resource management system: A development partnership. *Serials Review*, 30(2), 110–116. doi:10.1016/j.serrev.2004.03.003.

Hartnett, E., & Price, A. (2011). iPotentila: Mobile electronic resource management an iPad. *Library Collections, Acquisitions & Technical Services*, 35(4), 118–128. doi:10.1016/j.lcats.2011.06.001.

HERMES: The Hopkins Electronic Resource Management System. (n.d.). Retrieved April 07, 2013, from http://www.ala.org/lita/ital/22/1/cyzyk

HERMIS. (n.d.). Retrieved May 06, 2013, from http://www.harrassowitz.de/subscription_services/hermis.html

Hults, P. (2008). Electronic usage statistics. In H. Yu, & S. Breivold (Eds.), *Electronic Resource Management in Libraries: Research and Practice* (pp. 29–46). Academic Press. doi:10.4018/978-1-59904-891-8.ch003.

Innovative. (n.d.). Retrieved May 06, 2013, from http://www.iii.com/products/electronic_resource.shtml

Journal Finder. (n.d.). Retrieved May 09, 2013, from http://www.wtcox.com/journal-finder.cfm

Kasprowski, R. (2007). *Standards in electronic resource management*. Retrieved May 09, 2013 from http://www.asis.org/Bulletin/Aug-07/kasprowski.html

McCracken, E. (2007). Description of and access to electronic resources (ER): Transitioning into the digital age. *Collection Management, 32*(3-4), 259–275. doi:10.1300/J105v32n03_02.

Murdock, D. (2010). Relevance of electronic resource management systems to hiring practices of electronic resources personnel. *Library Collections, Acquisitions & Technical Services, 34*(1), 25–42. doi:10.1016/j.lcats.2009.11.001.

OCLC WorldShare License Manager. (n.d.). Retrieved May 09, 2013, from https://www.oclc.org/license-manager.en.html

Report of the CUNY Electronic Resource Management System Committee. (n.d.). Retrieved April 1, 2013, from https://www.google.co.in/url?sa=t&rct=j&q=&esrc=s&source=web&cd=1&cad=rja&sqi=2&ved=0CC8QFjAA&url=http%3A%2F%2F128.228.178.102%2Fexport_test5%2Fmain%2Fabout%2Fadministration%2Foffices%2FOLS%2FERMS012008.doc&ei=vOFWUf_bM4KrrAfhzoDoAw&usg=AFQjCNHLDK_vTVk6AOaufrUf449BjuazIg&sig2=zn8Km2M1r2HBvK1f1y4HlA&bvm=bv.44442042,d.bmk

ResearchMonitor: Priory Solutions. (n.d.). Retrieved May 09, 2013, from http://www.priorysolutions.com/ResearchMonitor

Samper Tool: SMDB. (n.d.). Retrieved May 09, 2013, from http://www.sempertool.dk/?func=loadTemplate&template=smdbMore

Silton, K., & Lemaistre, T. (2011). Innovative interfaces electronic resources management system: A survey on the state of implementation and usage. *Serials Review, 37*(2), 80–86. doi:10.1016/j.serrev.2011.01.002.

Stone, G. (2012). *Techniques for electronic resource management*. Retrieved May 08, 2013, from http://eprints.hud.ac.uk/12972

TDNet: E-Resource Management Solution Libraries. (n.d.). Retrieved May 09, 2013, from http://web.tdnet.com/

Tonta, Y. (2005). Internet and electronic information management. *Information Services & Use, 25*(1), 3–12.

VERA. (n.d.). *Jump start your library research: MIT libraries*. Retrieved May 09, 2013, from http://vera.mit.edu/

VERDE. (n.d.). *The library solution for efficient electronic resource management*. Retrieved May 09, 2013, from http://www.exlibrisgroup.com/category/VerdeOverview

Chapter 8
Knowing Protection of Intellectual Contents in Digital Era

Priyanka Vishwakarma
Banaras Hindu University, India

Bhaskar Mukherjee
Guru Ghasidas University, India

ABSTRACT

New technological innovations have made the publishing of ideas easy, while maintaining protection of the published content has become a concerning issue. Plagiarism is an emerging issue in the digital era. The intention of writing this chapter is to explore various tools and projects that enable an author to know: 1) that their work is original; 2) The best possible options to maintain rights on intellectual work; 3) the publishers' policies while archiving your document in an institutional repository; and 4) the ethics of publishing. To handle such issues, the authors identify ways to avoid plagiarism and mention the use of anti-plagiarism software. Attempts are also made to explore how far a scholarly work can be treated under the periphery of "fair use." The various derivatives of creative commons are also explained regarding copyright issues in the digital era. The essence of projects like SHERPA/RoMEO and COPE are also discussed.

INTRODUCTION

The ongoing acceleration in the field of information technology has given wide opportunity to flourish ideas on a multitude of platforms, both print and digital. Enormous ways of self publishing, storing, accessing and making it available to numerous people throughout the world can be easily possible through the new applications of information communication technology. Obviously, this may be considered as one side of coin, the other side may be the increasing number of rejections and retractions in scholarly submission due to scholarly misconduct. Dr. Everett, an editor

DOI: 10.4018/978-1-4666-4761-9.ch008

at the *International Dairy Journal*, mentioned in its web site *"Of the 450 articles submitted to the journal, we publish approximately 150. So 300 of them go into the great wash, and we occasionally see them ending up in online journals - some of lesser quality. The increasing rejection rate has led to a market to establish new journals online, and in my opinion there are far too many of them."* So, there is a need to gain proper knowledge about the use of web enabled tools and literate yourself ongoing activities on scholarly publishing.

In general, there are many laws are available for the protection of creators work such as copyright, intellectual property right etc. When it came to the protection of an author's work in a country other than it was produced then the need of a universal law was felt and in 1886 Berne convention for Literary and artistic works, which is also called Berne convention, evolved in a convention held at Berne city of Switzerland. Now it comes under one of the 25 treaties administered by WIPO, especially for protection of intellectual property. Before the commencement of this Berne convention it was very difficult to protect the intellectual property outside the country. It has provided protection statements and made essential for all its members to look after and take preventive measures against the violation of copyright of literary and artistic works produced in each others' territory. Berne convention consists of 38 articles with separate headings providing clear guidelines to its signatories for the protection of intellectual property of an author beyond the boundaries of the country. It provide all guidelines about, creating a union for the protection of rights of an author, what will be considered as literary and artistic work, what kind of work will be considered under violation of rights of an author according to this convention, criteria for eligibility for protection for authors, rights for translation, reproducing literary works etc. not only rights but it also include the limitations regarding the protection of certain artistic work. Apart from this Berne convention, there are several other prominent codes and legisla-

tions, such as the WIPO Internet Treaties (WCT art.11 and WPPT art. 18), the Digital Millennium Copyright Act (DMCA sec. 1201), the European Copyright Directive (EUCD, art. 6 and art. 8), and the respective implementations of the EUCD into the laws of EU Member States, are formed to protect the content from stealing in this digitally equipped era (Gasser, 2006).

The intension of writing this piece of work is to explore various tools and projects other than these laws, rights and institutions of international level, which enables author to know: i) how far their work is original; ii). best possible option to maintains rights on intellectual work; iii). the publishers' policies while archiving your document on some institutional repository; and iv). the ethics that is important while publishing especially in digital environment.

INTELLECTUAL PROPERTY AND PLAGIARISM

One of the greatest problems of 'sudden increase' of information causes information explosion, which made it very difficult to judge right information for right users at right time. The very common reason for enormous information explosion may be due to empowerment of every person to create and publish new ideas, thoughts etc. When human being created such ideas using their intellect for the benefit of society, then it is called intellectual property. According to World Intellectual Property Right Organization (WIPO) *"intellectual property (IP) refers to creations of the mind: inventions, literary and artistic works, and symbols, names, images, and designs used in commerce."*

Although creation for the betterment of society is one of the basic mottos for scholarly communication, when the intentions of the scholarly communicator turns to publish anyway just because of not-to-perish, the possibility of committing plagiarism came into the picture. Now, Internet exists everywhere and nowhere simultaneously. It is now become a *de facto* medium for accessing and dissemination of intellectual property at an unprecedented speed. At the same time, with the help of ICT tools it become easy for the swindlers to pilfer someone else work and use it for their own benefit by cut, copy and paste the contents. Charles Caleb Colton in 1802 commented that 'imitation is the sincerest form of flattery', this flattery, however, turn to the greatest moral offence day-by-day in academia and industry domain. There is evidence that the idea of plagiarism existed well before the Romantic Era of the eighteenth century (Green, 2002), in the internet age this has now become a cause of concern. McKenzie (1998) once said:

The New Plagiarism requires little effort and is geometrically more powerful. While the pre-modem student might misappropriate a dozen ideas from a handful of thinkers, the post-modem student can download and save hundreds of pages per hour. We have moved from the horse and buggy days of plagiarism to the Space Age without stopping for the horseless carriage.

'Plagiarism' derives from the Latin word plagiarius, meaning 'kidnapper' or 'abductor'. The first person to use the term "plagiarism" in connection with literary works was the Roman poet Martial, who lived in the first century C.E. Under Roman law, the term *plagiori* referred to the stealing of a slave or child (Robinson, 1995). *Webster's College Dictionary* defines plagiarism as "the unauthorized use of the language, thoughts of another author and pretending them as one's own" and the Oxford English Dictionary defines plagiarism as the "wrongful appropriation" or "purloining and publication as one's own of the ideas or the expression of ideas (literary, artistic, musical, mechanical, etc.)". Plagiarism is also termed as academic dishonesty in which one person intentionally captures someone else ideas, words, and design etc and present them as his / her belongings. The incidence of Plagiarism is

increasing due to the easy availability of document in electronic form.

In order to protect creators own intellectual activities from plagiarism various rights came in to force. Intellectual property right (IPR) refers to such legal rights given to person over the creations of their minds for a certain period of time. IPR divided into two categories: industrial property and copyright. Being part of information manager our concern mostly for copyrights and preservation of information in library setup. Due to that in the next we will proceed only with the issues of copyright leaving aside industrial aspect. Copyright in fact enacting by governments is a legal concepts for giving the creator of an original work exclusive right to it. It does not cover the ideas expressed in such works; it covers the way ideas are expressed. Copyright protections are automatically provided to the author of both published and unpublished works at the moment they are affixed in a tangible medium. Copyright protects a person's work from being used without the express permission of the copyright holder. Plagiarism is misrepresenting someone else's work as your own and can include the taking of their words, ideas or other creations. Even if you give permission for someone to use your work for a specific purpose and he uses it for another without acknowledging you, thus misleading the audience, its plagiarism. "Plagiarism" is not mentioned in any current statute, either criminal or civil. Some cases may be treated as unfair competition or a violation of the doctrine of moral rights. The increased availability of intellectual property due to a rise in technology has furthered the debate as to whether copyright offences are criminal. In short, people are asked to use the guideline, "...if you did not write it yourself, you must give credit." Plagiarism is not the same as copyright infringement. While both terms may apply to a particular act, they are virtually different concepts. Copyright is a legal issue that can be enforced in a court of law. Plagiarism is not in itself a legal issue, but is best described as a "respect and integrity" issue. IP violations are not always a legal issue.

TYPES OF PLAGIARISM

There are different types of plagiarism based on the intensity of plagiarism and some of them are as follows:

- **Complete Plagiarism:** Complete plagiarism takes place where content are presented without making any change in the language, thoughts, flow, and even punctuation. Experts believe this is the act of a person having a little knowledge on the define subject.
- **Partial/Substantial Plagiarism:** When content are present with some sort of modification, complying different sources, using synonyms, adding more details in the text, changing the patterns of the text and the technique of rephrasing, it is known as partial or substantial Plagiarism.
- **Minimalistic Plagiarism:** This kind of plagiarism mostly takes place in academic sector, where students plagiaries someone else concept, ideas, thought, or opinions in their own words and in a different flow.
- **Source Citation:** There are certain cases where user quotes the original sources, but the information or material provided in the articles are not match with the source provided at the end of the article. While in other cases user copy the information and merge all at one and provide the false reference.
- **Sources Not Cited:** Under this category user copy the information from different sources, regroup the word combination, rephrase the paragraph, add words and make the whole new article.
- **Self-Plagiarism:** This form of plagiarism is also known as "recycling fraud". When

the user uses significant, identical, or nearly identical portions of his own work in another article without giving the credit to the original sources is known as selfplagiarism. Publishing the same material through different mediums without referencing it correctly is a very common habit among many writers.

WAYS TO AVOID PLAGIARISM

Internet and other various networking technologies open immense possibilities to copy and paste material and publish it with one's name. Detection of plagiarism of such cases is relatively a simple process but preventing it a difficult task. Here are some of the way to prevent plagiarism:

- **Use Templates:** It is better to use templates, because copying of template is a difficult task and if anyone wants to copy he/she can easily identified by the original contributor. Suppose if you want to post something in online journal use image of the same colour matching with background behind the text and if someone copies your text from the page and publish it with their own name he easily detected online. What the original contributor has to do just change the image and plagiarized material also show the same changed image. Use of the Digital Millennium Copyright Act with a file and takedown notice is the most common method of dealing with plagiarism.
- **Preserve Evidence:** Preserving the evidence is another option to overcome plagiarism. Use a bookmarking site like Furl to keep a cached copy of the plagiarist's site. This is good for user's own records and if a dispute comes up later. Though it is not a full proof evidence but it is useful in future.

- **Use Licensing Wisely:** By using Creative Commons Licensing users can avoid persuing people that are merely reusing your content and focus on those that are plagiarizing it or using it for commercial gain. Though this isn't right for everyone, it can reduce the burden of fighting content theft while increasing legitimate distribution.
- **Take Help from Copyright Attorney:** Though the vast majority of plagiarism cases on the Web can be easily resolved without an attorney. But cases involving large sums of money and very large distribution may resolve with the help of copyright attorney.

1. MAKING YOUR WORK 'ORIGINAL'

Before submitting work for consideration in publication, one should be very fair that his work is original. Present day, every scholarly publisher is looking for original research and at their first step they always check how far submitted work is plagarised-free. Because, plagiarism is a severe problem growing over WWW these days. There are many plagiarism detecting solutions available on the web including iThenticate, Turnitin, Crosscheck, plagiarism.org, Copytracker, Plagium, Seesources, etc. Among them iThenticate is one of the most popular and widely used plagiarism detecting software on the web which is accessible on subscription. In the next paragraph we will see about the tool.

Detecting Plagiarism through iThenticate

iThenticate is a online plagiarism detecting software developed by Turnitin, widely used in scholarly publishing to ensure the originality of written work before publication. it is a online tool which helps to the editors, authors and researchers prevent

misconduct by comparing manuscript against 32 billion web pages and 125 million content items, including 34 million published work from over 365 scholarly publishers participants crosscheck. In present day world top publishers including IEEE, Elsevier, Willey Blackwell, Oxford, APS, AIP, are using iThenticate for detecting originality of submitted article.

In order to use iThenticate, user ID and password is needed, which can be received by purchasing/registering iThenticate. Through log in and password this online tool provides a platform to upload a file from local computer. Automatically it detects percentage of similarity from its database and provides a similarity report in two columns. While the left column mention the source text, the right column explain the number of words along with percentage of similarity and hyperlinked the source from which the similarity is based. In order to handle properly the right column and left column both it uses numeric number to show relationship between submitted article and source of matches. It also indicates over all percentage of similarity in terms of similarity index. Greater the similarity index, greater possibilities of plagiarism.

Present day there is a wide concern about should copyright take a back seat in the race of law and technology or how to protect electronic rights of authors of scholarly content? In fact, the same copyright protections also exist for the author of a work in electronic form regardless of whether the work is in a database, CD-ROM, bulletin board, or on the Internet. If you make a copy from an electronic source, such as the Internet or WWW, for your personal use, it is likely to be seen as fair use. However, if you make a copy and put it on your personal WWW site, it less likely to be considered fair use. The Internet IS NOT the public domain. There are both non-copyrighted and copyrighted materials available on internet.

Figure 1. Screenshot of iThenticate summary

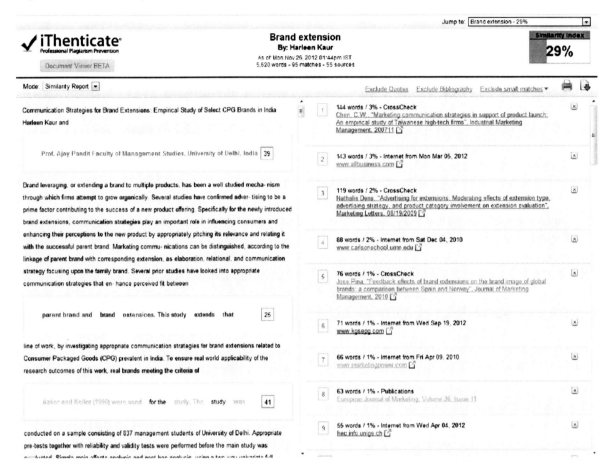

Fair Use

Fair use, the term originated in the United States, which simply means, use of any copyrighted works, reasonably be judged as fair, in non profitable purposes without obtaining permission. Here extend of fair must not creating harm to creators original work and curtails the profits reasonably expected by the owner. ALA defines Fair use as "limitations on the exclusive rights of the copyright holder", which provides the users with a permission to infringe the copyright of others with legal acceptance to it, because it has been observed that strict application of the copyright law disrupts the further development and use of the work or intellectual property under copyright. It makes a balance of the right between copyright owner and public. The extent to understand limits of use as fair should weighed four factors:

1. **Purpose and Character:** If your use is for teaching at a nonprofit educational institution, this is a factor favoring fair use. The scale tips further in favor of fair use if access is restricted to your students.

2. **Nature of Copyrighted Work:** Is the work fact based, published, or out-of-print? These factors weigh in favor of fair use.

3. **Amount Used:** Using a small portion of a whole work would weigh toward fairness. But sometimes it may be fair to use an entire work (such as an image) if it is needed for your instructional purpose.

4. **Market Effect:** A use is more likely to be fair if it does not harm the potential market for or value of the copyrighted work. But if it does, this could weigh more heavily against fair use than the other factors.

General Fair Uses

Subject to some general limitations discussed later in this article, the following types of uses are usually deemed fair uses:

- **Criticism and Comment:** If user commenting upon or critiquing a copyrighted work — for instance, writing a book review — fair use principles allow to reproduce some of the work to achieve the purposes. Some examples of commentary and criticism include:

  ○ Quoting a few lines from a Kishore Kumar's song in a music review.
  ○ Summarizing and quoting from a medical article on prostate cancer in a news report.
  ○ Copying a few paragraphs from a news article for use by a teacher or student in a lesson.
  ○ Copying a portion of a Sports Illustrated magazine article for use in a related court case.

The underlying rationale of this rule is that the public reaps benefits from one's review, which is enhanced by including some of the copyrighted material. Additional examples of commentary or criticism are provided in the examples of fair use cases.

- **Parody:** A parody is a work that ridicules another, usually well-known work, by imitating it in a comic way. Judges understand that, by its nature, parody demands some taking from the original work being parodied. Unlike other forms of fair use, a fairly extensive use of the original work is permitted in a parody in order to "conjure up" the original.

- **News Reporting:** Summarizing an address or article, with brief quotations, in a news report.

- **Research And Scholarship:** Quoting a short passage in a scholarly, scientific, or technical work for illustration or clarification of the author's observations.

- **Nonprofit Educational Uses:** Photocopying of limited portions of written works by teachers for classroom use.

In most other situations, copying is not legally a fair use. Without an author's permission, such a use violates the author's copyright.

- **Non-Commercial Use Is Often Fair Use:** Violations often occur when the use is motivated primarily by a desire for commercial gain. The fact that a work is published primarily for private commercial gain weighs against a finding of fair use.

- **Benefit To The Public May Be Fair Use:** A commercial motive doesn't always disqualify someone from claiming a fair use. A use that benefits the public can qualify as a fair use, even if it makes money for the user.

For example, in its advertising a RO Water purifier manufacturer was permitted to quote from a *Consumer Reports* article comparing vacuum cleaners. Why? The ad significantly increased the number of people exposed to the *Consumers Reports'* evaluations and thereby disseminated helpful consumer information. The same rationale probably applies to the widespread practice of quoting from favorable reviews in advertisements for books, films, and plays.

What Counts as Fair Use

While writing article, the primary attention should be to cite all materials that are used someway or other way. However one might be used following extends for academic reasons under fair use for a limited period of time:

- A chapter from a book (never the entire book).
- An article from a periodical or newspaper.
- A short story, essay, or poem. One work is the norm whether it comes from an individual work or an anthology.
- A chart, graph, diagram, drawing, cartoon or picture from a book, periodical, or newspaper.
- Poetry
    - Multiple copies of a poem of 250 words or less that exist on two pages or less or 250 words from a longer poem.
- Prose
    - Multiple copies of an article, story or essay that are 2,500 words or less or excerpts up to 1,000 words or 10 percent of the total work, whichever is less.
- Illustrations
    - Multiple copies of a chart, graph, diagram, drawing, cartoon, or picture contained in a book or periodical issue.

- Use of clip from a major motion picture, relevant to the researcher's subject during final meeting of academic association.
- Using of Audio-clip (probably all are copyrighted) for preparation of open courseware for wide visibility.

However, fair use a limitation to copyright law and it doesn't provide any hard and fast provisions to consider use of a work as fair use. The guidance for fair use is provided by a set of factors outlined in copyright law. These factors were weighed in each case to determine whether a use qualifies as a fair use or not. Unfortunately, if the copyright owner disagrees with the fair use interpretation, the matter may have to solve by legal institutions. And if it's not proved a fair use, then the users are considered for infringement of the copyright of author and may be liable for damages.

In India fair use is known as "fair dealing" doctrine, it is equitable to fair use doctrine, and statutorily entrenched under section 52 of the Indian Copyright Act, 1957 and has been amended thrice. According to clause 31 the fair dealing changes may help to a certain fact about fair dealing in India, vis-a-vis fair dealing in the rest of the world. India has specific usages provided as statutory provision. Unless the usage is not provided for under these provisions, the defense of fair dealing may not be used by the user of the work (Saikia, 2010). Sharma (2009) observes that, fair dealing cases have been rare in India until the recent decades which, even then, generated only a mere handful of cases. One must again be mindful that the Indian Copyright Act does not contain any list of factors to consider in determining fair dealing. Nonetheless, given the limited Indian decisions, navigating these decisions using American system of factors analysis provides at least some framework of orientation. It is simpler to conclude that the provision of fair dealing in the Indian Act is brief and does not define the meaning or the application of the defense. Clause 31 of the Amendment Bill proposes amendments to Section 52(1) (a) of the Act by way of inserting public and private use to the work for fair dealing. This allows the provision to have a more expansive nature as opposed to the limited nature offered by it now.

Furthermore, the rising trend of incidental storage of works in digital format while they are being viewed have been negated and established as fair dealing. It is proposed to insert an explanation to modification to section 52(1) that storing of any work in any electronic medium for the aforesaid purposes, public or private, including the incidental storage of any computer programme which is not itself an infringing copy for the said purpose, shall not constitute infringement.

It is imperative to note that the new subsection (b) of section 52 seeks to provide that the transient and incidental storage of a work or performance purely in the technical process of electronic transmission or communication to the public shall not constitute an infringement of copyright. Further amendments seek to provide that transient links, access or integration, where such links have not been expressly prohibited by the rights holder, unless the person responsible is aware or has reasonable grounds for believing that such storage is of an infringing copy shall also not constitute an infringement of copyright. The meaning of this amendment is that Internet Service Providers and Content Hosts shall have diminished liabilities in cases of creative works hosted or linked by them, provided they prove no knowledge or infringement (See Napster Case and other American decisions stating the same. The knowledge of ISP is hard to establish). The Indian Copyright Act does provide for an exception to use of any matter published by the government of India,(Section 52(1) (k), The Indian *Copyright Act*, 1957.), however such matters are limited to merely orders, reports, statutes etc in the official gazettes and acts of parliament. The government website or journals are hence open to copyright restrictions, which are not pursued in interest of public interest, but still have a risk of infringement to them. Hence it

would benefit if the government of India also, in all .nic databases make available content on CC license, like Netherlands Government.

Copyleft

The concept copyleft was initiated in 1983 when Richard Stallman started GNU Project in order "to develop a complete free Unix-like operating system." This concept was developed to give the freedoms of reuse, modification and reproduction of a work or its derivatives to be kept for all. Although, normal copyright asserts ownership and identification of the author, any form of distortion of original version, but it also carries other restrictions — such as restricting the reproduction or modification of a work. Copyleft contains the normal copyright statement, asserting ownership and identification of the author. Additionally, it then *gives away* some of the other rights including free rights to redistribute and change the work. However, you cannot claim to have written the original work, nor can you claim that these changes were created by someone else. Finally, all derivative works must also be placed under these terms. The left in copyleft is not a reference to the verb "to leave"- only to the direction which is the inverse of "right" in copyright. It ensure that public retains the freedom to use, modify extend and redistribute a creative work and all its derivatives. The success of copyleft is evidence by a vast number of copyleft projects and its output as copyleft software including Linux, MySQL, Open office, Ruby and Blender.

In India there is a foundation known as Free Software Foundation of India which follow this copyleft concept.

2. KNOWING 'RIGHTS' ON INTELLECTUAL CONTENTS

With the emergence of digital technology it was hope that scholarly communication would be more valuable and sharing of scholarly researches would be more easy however it was observed that contemporary copyright law has become so restrictive that it risks impeding future creation and innovatively. Sammuelson (n.d.) in this regard mention that today major copyright industries fearing a substantial loss of control over copyrighted material because of technological developments have lobbied to gain more control over customers than they have ever had before. Similarly Boyle (2004) stated that contemporary intellectual property policy is "in the sway of a maximalist 'rights-culture' which leads debate astray." By using Open Content Licensing users can avoid persuing people that are merely reusing your content and focus on those that are plagiarizing it or using it for commercial gain. Though this isn't right for everyone, it can reduce the burden of fighting content theft while increasing legitimate distribution. One of very popular open cont license is Creative Commons.

Creative Commons License

The birth of creative commons (CC) is closely related to the concern that the attempts of copyright holders to protect ownership are treating user's freedom. Launched in 2002, crafted by Stanford university law Prof. Lawrance Lessig, creative common license is a license that develops support and stewards legal and technical infrastructure that maximizes digital creativity, sharing and innovation. Commons is generally understood to be a legal regime where "multiple owners are each endowed with the privilege to use a given resource and no one has the right to exclude another". Since its inception this license has been enthusiastically adopted by many creators, authors and other content producers throughout the world to adopt the license of a copyrighted text.

Publishing under CC license needs choosing a condition for publishing: attribution, non- commercial, share alike, no derivative.

- Attributions means you allow people to copy distribute, display, perform and remix your copyrighted work as long as they give you credit. All CC licenses contain this property.
- By non-commercial a creator allow people to copy, distribute, display, perform and remix his copyrighted work for non-commercial purpose only.
- By share alike license creator allow people to create remix and derivative work based on his work as long as they only distribute them under the same CC license that original work belongs to.
- By no derivatives creator allow people to copy, distribute, display, and perform only verbatim copies of original work not derivative work based on it.

After choosing a proper cc license among above the website of CC (creativecommons.org/license) provides user with several lines of computer code that the user can copy and paste at his/her website. Visitors of that website will see a CC logo and a sentence under the logo indicating the condition and jurisdiction, it specifies, of that license. The logo and the sentence are embedded with link that directs visitors to commons deed, a quick and easy summary of the full license. Another click from the deed takes the visitor to the full license.

Meanwhile, a user who is looking for content to use under less restrictive conditions than traditional copyright law can go to the CC website and find appropriates. In fact creative commons licensing suite consist of public standardized license that allow authors to decide whether other may make commercial use of their work or whether to make their work shared or derivate. The license is expressed in three different ways: 1) human readable format; 2) lawyer readable format; 3) machine readable format. The third format enables online content and information to search

Figure 2. Screenshot of Creative Commons licenses (Source: http://creativecommons.org/)

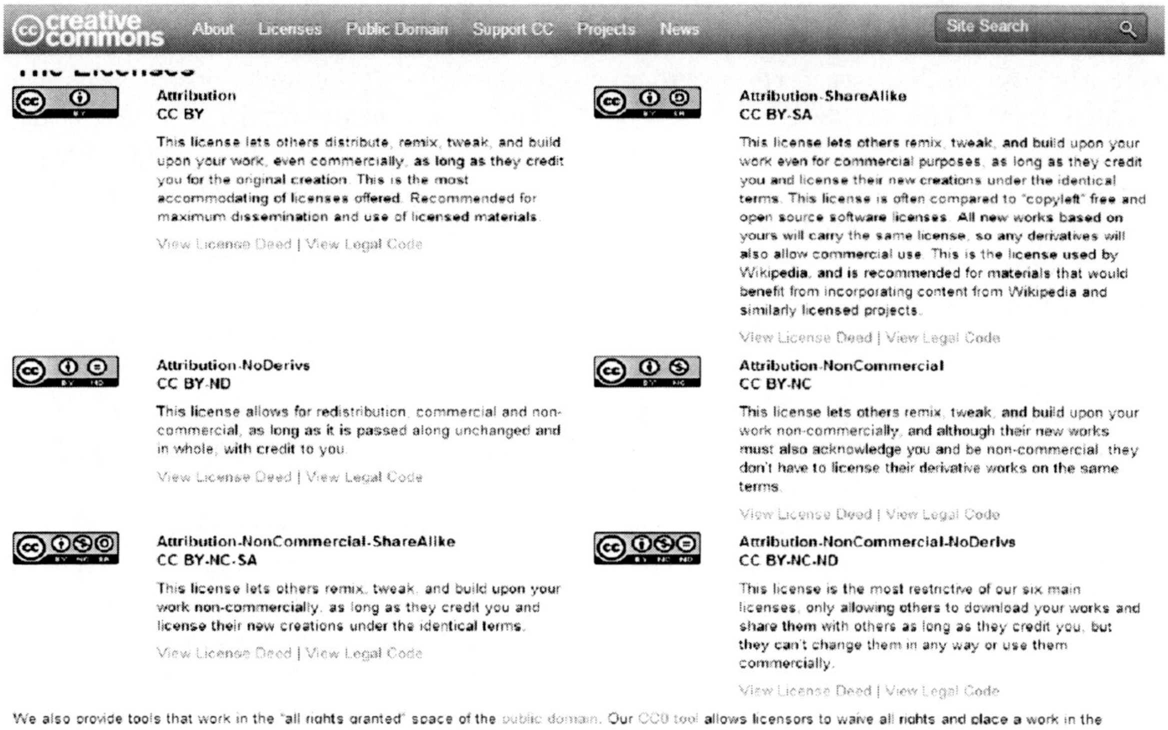

for an indentified based on the works licensing terms. The three different layers of CC distinct this license from other open content license such as GNU Free Documentation License.

In fact creative common consist of a set of copyright licenses and tools that creates a balance inside the traditional "all right reserve" setting that copyright law creates with the creators intention of "some rights reserve" approach of his creativity. CC enables one's creative educational and scientific content instantly more compatible with the full potential of the Internet. When the creator of a work may not one to exercise all of the rights generated by the copyright law, especially it is a creative activity; choosing creative common is the best possible way.

Although CC is seems to have the potential to provide solutions for the copyright issues of the creator up to an extent, but it must satisfy three conditions: 1) it must reflect the ways people pro- duce creative works; 2) it must serve the private interest of creators; and 3) it must serve the public interest of users.

Copyright law in India is seem to protect the expression and not the idea of the creative work in fact creativity hasn't inbound relationship with nature as Lessig has pointed out "Disney read creativity from the culture around him, mix that creativity with his own extraordinary talent and then burned that mix in to the soul of that culture". The Indian contract act, section 30 reads that the owner of the copyright in any existing or perspec- tive of copyright in any future work may grant any interest in the license in writing signed by him or his duly authorized agent: Provided that in the case of a license relating to copyright in any future work the license shall take effect only when the work comes into existence. As bare appraisal of license definition under Indian copyright act one may see that it not necessary to give the name of license, so much so that the author is free to license it to the public as a whole. Accepted is not required as on use of such work the user becomes a licensee and can be proceeded against under the provision of copyright law. Limited public licenses may be granted as well, and insertion of conditions into a license does not make it a contract. The term of copyright enforce by East India company was lifetime of the author plus 7 years postmortem, not exceeding 42 years. The government could grant the compulsory license if the owner of the copyright, after the death of the owner, refuse to publish. During revision in the year 1994 the postmortem time of copyright was increased from 50 years to 60 years. In general practice it has observed that proper control over the work are generally maintained by the promoters of the work that is publisher and not by the author of the work. So, copyright, which is basically meant for owner of intellectual creativity, is not remain useful for the actual creator of the work. In this view point it must be useful if an author choose creative commons license rather than copyright. In the new amendment of 1994 under clause 9 of section 21(1) it has allowed relinquishment, partly or wholly, of rights by an author, by way of notice to the registrar of copyright as well as by way of public notice, as appose to only the former option in a specified format. This minor procedural change is beneficial for a license of creative commons as they require partial relinquishment of the author's right in his works, and where applicable right even wholly relinquished. In the new bill the public notice does not need any specified format which becomes easy to the author. There is commercial exploitation of a CC licensed work possible as long as it has been granted on the Non-Commercial terms (nc), hence the authors may be required to ensure that their works secure them royalty where a non-commercial use of their work has been made. Clause 18 of the bill amends the Act in such manner that only authors shall be allowed

register a copyright society, hence eliminating creative content managers or intermediaries from the equation116. This makes it all the more convenient for authors of CC licensed works to appropriate commercial benefits from their works effectively while keeping to the core essence of CC licenses to keep out creative industry intermediaries from the creative work process, as is also shown by the clause as it amends section 35 of the Act to put the control of the copyright society from owner of the works to the author of the works.

3. KNOWING PUBLISHER'S POLICY

Presently, access to scholarly literature through commercial publishers/aggregator is mostly based on subscription of vendor databases through IP address. It is unrealistic that author/user have enough funds to subscribe various database for use. Generally, users access the database of the vendors through some institution where accessibility to that database is allowed. Vendors never give you the guarantee that access to that database is permanent. As a result, discontinue of subscription for a while or permanently stop accessing of the database for that particular period too on which the organization has already paid subscription charges. So, it is always better to submit research findings (pre-print or post-print of original article published in journal) to institutional archive. It is widely accepted that submitting work in institutional archive helps to facilitate the rapid and efficient worldwide dissemination of research. However, before submitting the work in institutional repository it is recommended to check the publisher policies of archiving. SHERPA/RoMEO is on of the award wining project which helps author to know the archiving policies of journal where author is willing to submit his/her paper.

SHERPA/RoMEO Project

SHERPA is a project drew from research-led universities with an active interest in establishing an example of an open access institutional repository. Presently, under this project 32 higher educational institutions, the *Science and Technology Facilities Council* (STFC) and the British Library are involved. Higher educational institute range from smaller specialized bodies such as The *School of Oriental and African Studies* (SOAS), to Universities like Cambridge and Oxford. The partners like British Library and the Arts and Humanities Development Service excelling their skills and experience in intellectual property rights, data preservation and collection management. This strong and varied consortial background of all its participant institutions offers the ideal environment for exploring and testing ideas for repository development, which can be evaluated and disseminated to the wider community. While the majority of institutions use EPrints software, three partners use DSpace for their principle repositories and one uses an in-house system.

Table 1. Various colour code and archiving policies

RoMEO Colour	Archiving Policy	Publishers	%
Green	Can archive pre-print and post-print	339	28
Blue	Can archive post-print (ie final draft post-refereeing)	392	32
Yellow	Can archive pre-print (ie pre-refereeing)	97	8
White	Archiving not formally supported	384	32

Figure 3. Screenshot of the growth of the SHERPA/RoMEO database
Source: http://www.sherpa.ac.uk/romeo/

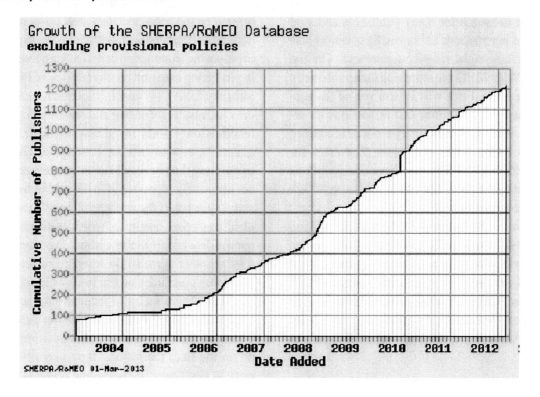

RoMEO is part of SHERPA Services based at the University of Nottingham. Presently RoMEO development is funded by Joint Information Systems Committee (JISC) at the University of Loughborough to investigate the rights issues surrounding the self-archiving of research in the UK community under the Open Archive Initiative Protocol for Metadata Harvesting (OAI-PMH). The Wellcome Trust has also given generous support to the work of SHERPA/RoMEO. Journal information used within the service is provided by the British Library Zetoc service, hosted by MIMAS (a Centre of Excellence based at The University of Manchester). Through surveying the academic community it ascertained how give-away research literature and metadata was used and how it should be protected. From this work, the RoMEO project created a list of publishers' conditions for self-archiving.

SHERPA/RoMEO project developed an outcome into a database-driven searchable service and knowledge bank of information, which details the rights given to authors by the major publishers of peer-reviewed academic journals. It is now possible to search for many publishers and find out what permissions are normally given as part of each copyright transfer agreement. On the SHERPA/RoMEO site searching for a publisher's name or journal title will inform you of the pre- and post-print conditions and restrictions on archiving. Each publisher's entry is coded according to one of four colour categories. The entry for each publisher also lists conditions or restrictions imposed by the publisher which govern archiving rights or activities.

There are 31 Indian publishers name enlisted in the SHERPA/RoMEO database. 14 of them are coded with blue (Can archive post-print (ie final draft post-refereeing) or publisher's version/PDF) and green (Can archive pre-print and post-print or publisher's version/PDF) colour each, and 3 are white (Archiving not formally supported) colour.

4. KNOWING ETHICS OF PUBLICATION

Although publication has always been one of the driving forces of scholarly research, the potential negative impact of not getting published on a regular basis is pushing some researchers to publish at any cost. Dr. Elizabeth Wager, the Chair of the Committee Publication Ethics (COPE), *"Promotion, appointments, and academic careers are really relying on publication and while that is in some ways good for the publishers and opens up some opportunities, I think there is always a concern that if the pressure is too high it will create an atmosphere in which the temptation to commit research or publication misconduct is increased."*

Moreover, academic institutions have made the criteria for appointment and promotion of a scholar on the basis of their number of publications in notable journals. When this kind of pressure is too high it definitely leads to the situation of large number of research and research misconduct too. One another possible reason for research misconduct is, in some countries "cash for papers" is offered to the scholars. Research misconduct is defined as" fabrication, falsification, or plagiarism in purposing, conducting or reviewing a research or in producing research results (Office of Research Integrity, USA)." Where fabrication is making up data and results recording and representing them; falsification stands for manipulating research materials, equipments, or process, or changing or omitting data or result such that the research is not accurately represented in the research record; and plagiarism is the appropriation of an author's idea, processes results or words without giving appropriate credit to the author. The question is why scholars agree to do research misconduct? Dr. Hanig concludes on the basis of his observation that "There's a lot of incentive for people to cut corners, to try and get something published. Their job, their career and their reputations could be on the line. Everything they may do for the next 30 years may be contingent on them getting one particular article into one particular journal. In order to do that, things take place that are not ethically sound". The pressure of publishing is not only on the scholars but also on the institutions like universities which have the aim of proving themselves as the top most among the universities all over the nation and world. This is the way they can show their efficiency to their government for getting funds and facilities for research, increase in reputation and the number of enrollment of student. However, number of research papers increased and the publishers are getting more and more submission of papers daily, but the number of paper publish decreased in comparison to submission. And the publishers give research misconduct as a reason for the retraction of a big percentage of papers as they are not up to the quality and original product of an author.

In order to make publishing process more ethical, there is a need to agree upon standards of expected ethical behavior for all parties involved in the act of publishing: the author, the journal editor, the peer reviewer, the publisher. There are few international projects working on ethical issues in publishing. Two most common are Elsevier's Publishing Ethics Resource and Committee on Publication Ethics. We are discussion here one of them.

COMMITTEE ON PUBLICATION ETHICS (COPE)

The cause for this level of misconduct and un-ethical behavior must be the lack of knowledge about research and publication ethics. Committee on Publication Ethics (COPE) aimed to promote integrity in research publication and discus the ethical issues related to the publication in biomedical journal. It was started in 1997 as an informal forum of a group of editors in UK. It has developed a code of conduct for the journal editors, providing them with a set of a minimum standards to which all its member are expected to follow. The Best Practice Guide for journal editors comes under the code of conduct for them. It tells them how

to conduct their duties in best manner and guide them about the wide range of increasingly complex ethical issues. It publishes the Code of Conduct and Best Practice Guide in two languages English and Chinese. All the member editors are expected to follow the guidelines, although not mandatory to follow but voluntary. Code of conduct for an editor and Best Practice Guide broadly include these 17 headings: 1) general duties and responsibilities of editors, 2) relation with reader, 3) relation with authors, 4) relation with editors, 5) relation with editorial board members, 6) relations with journal owners and publishers, 7) editorial and peer review processes, 8) editorial and peer review processes, 9) protecting individual data, 10) encouraging ethical research (research involving animals and human), 11) dealing with possible misconduct, 12) ensuring the integrity of academic records, 13) intellectual property issues, 14) encouraging debates regarding published work in a journal, 15) complaints (respond to the complaints), 16) commercial considerations (advertising should not affect editorial decision), 17) conflicts of interest.

COPE was started by a small group of medical journal editors in UK (and registered as a charitable company limited by a Memorandum of association on 3rd Oct. 2007 (updated 2011) but now it has 7000 plus members worldwide from each academic field. Any academic journal or journal interested in publication ethics are invited to be the member of this organization. Many among the world's most prominent Publishers such as Elsevier, Wiley–Blackwell, Springer, Taylor & Francis, Palgrave Macmillan and Wolters Kluwer are member of this organization.

COPE not only provide code of conduct and best practice guide but it also provide flowcharts to assist members and non-members on managing ethical issues available translated into Italian, Spanish, Chinese, Croatian, Japanese, Persian (Farsi) and Turkish – more planned). It is downloadable from the website of COPE; archive of all cases related to ethical issues presented at forum-about 400 cases together with the advice given by COPE with a list of recent cases at the right on

Figure 4. Screenshot of authors' link in COPE
Source: http://www.publicationethics.org

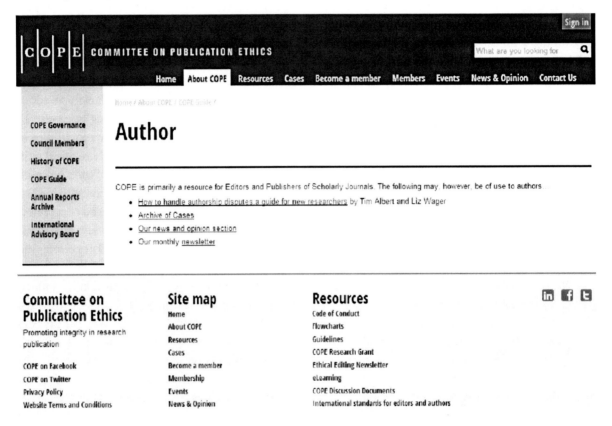

case page; guidelines and discussion documents; an e learning course for members only, to give them deep understanding of publication ethics and practical guidance how to detect, prevent and handle misconduct in research; audio, video and power point slides of seminar presentations of past few years.

COPE not only provides code of conduct, but it also provide grants up to £5000 to a cope member for conducting research in field of publication ethics twice in a year.

Many journals and publishing organizations from all over the world follow the code of conduct and Basic Practice guide set forth by COPE. The list of all such countries and organizations is given on the web site of COPE in alphabetical order.

COPE in Indian Perspective

There are 76 journals from India which are following this code. The journals are of different subjects and from different publishers. Journals from the field of medicine, management, science & technology and engineering etc. are following this code of conduct more predominently.

WEB RESOURCE FOR ETHICS AND PLAGIARISM ISSUES

http://online.northumbria.ac.uk/faculties/art/
information_studies/Imri/Jiscpas/site/jiscpas.asp

The JISC-funded Plagiarism Advisory Service provides general advice to institutions, academics and students, a portal to online resources on the issue of plagiarism, and an electronic detection service.

http://www.academicintegrity.org

The Center for Academic Integrity (CAI) aims to provide a forum to identify and affirm the values of academic integrity.

http://www.plagiarism.phys.virginia.edu

This is a free plagiarism detection program. It cannot search the Web to find matching documents, but it can make comparisons between locally stored files.

http://www.umuc.edu/distance/odell/cip/links_ plagiarism.html

The Center for Intellectual Property at the University of Maryland University College (UMUC) maintains one of the most comprehensive websites in the world on plagiarism-related issues.

CONCLUSION

Digital content doctrine has shown its widespread expansion throughout the world. With the new social conditions that have emerged with the widespread use of ICTs, plagiarism has now become an inevitable part of contemporary culture. There is enough testimony in the various websites, media reports, conferences and symposia to the amount of intellectual energy currently being dedicated to the topic of internet plagiarism. Simultaneously, there are various proprietary and freeware anti-plagiarism packages available for detecting plagiarism now. However, at this stage what is more important is that along with prevention we have to deterrence towards plagiarsm where we never feel motivated to plagiarise. There is and there will be increased external pressure to succeed. Publication for promotion is essential for our endeavour but at the same time we have to prove ourselves ethically correct.

According to Stewart Home, an author and satirist that plagiarism 'saves time and effort, improves results, and shows considerable initiative on the part of the plagiarist' (cited in Duguid, 1995). This line of thinking may reveal that there is nothing sinister about the liberal use of other people's ideas. However, there should be proper acknowledgement. Being an author its our intellectual honesty to maintain best practices of the followings:

1. While writing an article be sure your concepts are original. Area of research may be the same but there should be at least longitudinal difference with earlier research.
2. The piece of writing you submit should be referenced in internationally recognised referencing system (e.g. the American Psychological Style Manual).
3. At all times, ensure that you acknowledge all sources and text that consist of more than x words [as per institution's regulations] that are not your own.

In order to encourage digital rights management few new strategies are started. DTCP and HDCP are two of the most widely adopted methods of protecting digital entertainment content. While Digital Transmission Content Protection, or DTCP, is a digital rights management (DRM) technology that aims to restrict hooking televisions signals by encrypting interconnections between devices, the High-bandwidth Digital Content

Protection (HDCP) developed by Intel Corporation is a way to prevent copying of digital audio and video content as it travels across connections. Before sending data, a transmitting device checks that the receiver is authorized to receive it. If so, the transmitter encrypts the data to prevent eavesdropping as it flows to the receiver.

The digital licensing strategy of Creative Commons license is accurately reflect the ways people produce creative works, serve the private interests of creators, and serves the public interests of users by providing a pool of cultural works that everyone can use and by facilitating later creations. This is a unique development for authors to protect their digital content as per their choice. This license has the provision to differentiate different kinds of creators in the digital era and provided them with various degrees of freedoms.

REFERENCES

American Library Association. (n.d.). *What is fair use?* Retrieved February 27, 2013, from http://www.ala.org/Template.cfm?Section=cop yrightarticle&Template=/ContentManagement/ContentDisplay.cfm&ContentID=26700

Berne Convention for the Protection of Literary and Artistic Works. (n.d.). Retrieved March 28, 2013, from http://www.wipo.int/treaties/en/ip/berne/trtdocs_wo001.html

Cabanes, A. (2010). *Copyright vs copyleft: Short introduction to these licenses.* Retrieved February 22, 2013, from http://aintzane.wordpress.com/2010/01/28/copyright-vs-copyleft-a-short-introduction-to-these-licenses

Creative Commons. (n.d.). Retrieved February 19, 2013, from http://creativecommons.org/icense/by/3.0

Duguid, B. (1995). *The unacceptable face of plagiarism? Pop parody panic.* Retrieved 23 March 2013 from http://downlode.org/Etext/plagiarism.html

Gasser, U. (2006). *Legal frameworks and technological protection of digital content: Moving forward towards a best practice model.* Retrieved 3 April 2013 from, http://www.ftc.gov/bcp/workshops/techade/pdfs/Gasser1.pdf

Green, S. P. (2002). Plagiarism, norms, and the limits of theft law: Some observations on the use of criminal sanctions in enforcing intellectual property rights. *Hastings Law Journal, 54*(1). *iThenticate users guide.* (2012). Retrieved 20, 2013, from http://www.ithenticate.com/Portals/92785/media/iThenticate_qs_guide.pdf

James, B. (2004). A manifesto on WIPO and the future of intellectual property. *Duke Law & Technology Review.* Retrieved February 23, 2013, from http://scholarship.law.duke.edu/dltr/vol3/iss1/6/

Kapur, P. (2011). *Creative commons: Impact on Indian copyright law.* Retrieved February 19, 2013, from http://papers.ssrn.com/sol3/papers.cfm?abstract_id=2047662

Kim, M. (2007). *The creative commons and copyright protection in digital era: Use of creative commons licenses.* Retrieved February 20, 2013, from http://jcmc.indiana.edu/vol13/issue1/kim.html

Know Your Copy Rights. (n.d.). *Using works in your teaching*. Retrieved February 27, 2013, from http://www.knowyourcopyrights.org/bm~doc/kycrbrochurebw.pdf

Maracke, C. (2010). *Creative commons international: The international license porting project*. Retrieved February 26, 2013, from http://www.jipitec.eu/issues/jipitec-1-1-2010/2417/dip-padm1268743811.97.pdf

McKenzie, J. (1998). The new plagiarism: Seven antidotes to prevent highway robbery in an electronic age. *From Now On: The Educational Technology Journal, 7*(8).

Mukherjee, B. (2012). *Information communication and society*. New Delhi, India: ESS ESS Publication..

Robinson, O. F. (1995). *The criminal law of ancient Rome*. Academic Press..

Saiaki, N. (2010). *The Bollywood amendment: Film, music and copyright (amendment) bill*. Retrieved February 19, 2013, from http://papers.ssrn.com/sol3/papers.cfm?abstract_id=1566350

Samuelson, P. (2004). *Tightening the copyright noose: Why you should be worried about the white paper on intellectual property rights and the national information infrastructure*, Retrieved February 26, 2013, from http://www.eff.org/IP/?f=tightening_copyright_noose.article.text

Sharma, A. (2009). Indian perspective of fair dealing under copyright law: Lex Lata or Lex Feranda? *Journal of Intellectual Property Rights, 14*, 523–531.

Williams, J. B. (2005). *Plagiarism, deterrence, detection and prevention*. Retrieved February 24, 2013, from http://www.economicsnetwork.ac.uk/handbook/printable/plagiarism.pdf

World Intellectual Property Organization. (n.d.). *What is intellectual property?* Retrieved February 20, 2013, from www.wipo.int/about-ip/en

KEY TERMS AND DEFINITIONS

COPE: Committee on Publication Ethics is an ethics in publishing which need to adhere while writing intellectual work.

Copyleft: A concept by which author gives the freedoms of reuse, modification and reproduction of a work or its derivatives to be kept for all.

Creative Commons: A form of license mostly prevail in digital era for giving proper rights to the author of an intellectual work.

Digital Era: An era where most of the intellectual work is available in digital form.

Fair Use: Use of any copyrighted works, reasonably be judged as fair, in non profitable purposes without obtaining permission.

Intellectual Property Rights: A rights to the author for his/her work (intellectuality) from any type of infringements. By this lawful rights author can claim his rights if somebody violate the law.

iThenticate: A software for detecting percentage of plagiarism in the intellectual work.

SHERPA/RoMEO: A project which maintains publisher's copyright policies & self-archiving. RoMEO is part of SHERPA Services based at the University of Nottingham.

Chapter 9
Open E-Resources in Libraries

Vesna Injac-Malbaša
National Library of Serbia, Serbia

ABSTRACT

In general, electronic resources include articles, online journals, e-books, e-theses, databases, Websites, portals, gateways, blogs, etc. The author distinguishes Open Access (OA) resources mainly intended for researchers and open digital heritage mainly intended for the general public. The author's objective is to present the background of OA resources, different OA initiatives and software, first institutional repositories, open archives browsers and harvesters, open access registries, activities in Europe and UNESCO, and personalities who are the most important advocates of OA. Concerning the open digital heritage, the author's objective is to present the most important international and national projects like the European Library, Europeana, the World Digital Library, Gutenberg Project, Google Books Project, Hathitrust Digital Library, Digital Public Library of America, International Children's Digital Library, the Library of Congress Digital Library, Gallica of the French National Library, National Digital Library of China, etc. The author's opinion is that libraries have to accept all challenges of the open e-resources for researchers and open digital heritage and that the future of open access for all users is not impossible. The world's knowledge should be accessible as a public good to every citizen of the planet.

INTRODUCTION

In general, electronic resources include: articles, online journals, e-books, e-theses, databases, web sites, portals, gateways, blogs, etc. Electronic resources management is the practices and software systems used by libraries to keep track of important information about electronic informa-tion resources. Electronic resources are accessible in libraries as licensed (paid) services and open (free) e-resources. We can say that other name for open e-resources is open access resources. We can distinguish OA resources (articles, journals, books, thesis, databases etc.), mainly intended for researchers, and open digital heritage (journals, books, non-book material, audio and video ma-

DOI: 10.4018/978-1-4666-4761-9.ch009

terial, etc.), mainly intended for general public. Concerning OA resources for researchers our objective is to present the background of open access resources, different OA initiatives and software, first institutional repositories, open archives browsers and harvesters, open access registries, activities in Europe and UNESCO and personalities who are the most important advocates of OA. Concerning the open digital heritage our objective is to present the most important international and national projects like The European Library, Europeana, The World Digital Library, Gutenberg project, Google books project, Hathitrust digital library, Digital public library of America, International children's digital library, The Library of Congress Digital Library, Gallica of the French National Library, National Digital Library of China etc.

1. OPEN ACCESS RESOURCES

Open Access Resources Background

Open access (OA) is an extremely actual topic in today's librarianship and information sciences, although it is not so new. OA literature is digital, online, free of charge and free of most copyright and licensing restrictions. OA removes price barriers (subscriptions, licensing fees, pay-per-view fees) and permission barriers (most copyright and licensing restrictions).The legal basis of OA is the consent of the copyright holder (for newer literature) or the expiration of copyright (for older literature).

Since 1991, a physicist Paul Henry Ginsparg created software that allowed authors to enter by themselves their papers in the pre-print archive called arXiv. Ginsparg was a junior fellow and taught in the physics department at Harvard University until 1990. The pre-print archive was developed while he was a member of staff of Los Alamos National Laboratory, 1990–2001. Since 2001, Ginsparg has been a professor of Physics and Computing and Information Science at Cornell University. The e-print arXiv (where "e-print" means self-archiving by the author) since its inception in 1991 has become a major forum for dissemination of results in physics and mathematics. The arXiv is an example of a service created by a group of specialists for their own use: when researchers create such service, the results often differ from the services provided by publishers and libraries. The original objective of the e-print arXiv was to provide functionality that was not otherwise available, and to provide a level playing field for researchers at different academic levels and different geographic locations - the reduction in cost of dissemination came as an unexpected advantage.

In 1994, Stevan Harnad suggested at the Princeton University that all researchers should independently store an electronic copy of each published paper on university servers and make them available free of charge. Harnad's research interests are in cognitive science and open access. He is currently Canada Research Chair in cognitive science at Université du Québec à Montréal and professor of cognitive science at the University of Southampton. Harnad is an active promoter of open access and his opinion is that the research access and impact problems arise because journal articles are not accessible to all users and researchers are losing potential impact. The solution is to make all articles open access, free for all. OA articles have significantly higher citation impact than non-OA articles. There are two roads to OA: the "golden" road (publish the article in an OA journal) and the "green" road (publish the article in a non-OA journal but also self-archive it in an OA archive). Only 5% of journals are gold, but over 90% are already green (publishers given their authors the green light to self-archive); yet only about 10-20% of articles have been self-archived. To reach 100% OA, self-archiving needs to be mandated by researchers' employers and funders, as the United Kingdom and the United States have recently recommended, and universities need to implement that mandate.

For researchers and their institutions the main goal is to maximize access to research information and it is not just promotional slogan. Why? Because without OA everyone is at loss: users lose their access, authors lose their impact, and research fails to progress further. In April 2013 Harnad requests not to have different colors of OA as "diamond," "platinum" and "titanium", as some authors proposed. In his work *Paid Gold OA Versus Free Gold OA: Against Color Cacophony* (2013) Harnad states (Harnad, 2013):

And, before you ask, please let's not play into the publishers' hands by color-coding OA also in terms of the length of the publisher embargo: 3-month OA, 6-month OA, 12-month-OA, 24-month-OA, millennial OA: OA means immediate online access.

Harnad also proposed the transition utopian scenario:

- Mandatory self-archiving (in institutions and those who finance research).
- 100% Green OA - problems of access for users, the impact of researchers and absence of research progress.
- Institutions interrupt subscription to online journals because all is in OA.
- No more printed or online versions - it is not necessary because everything is available in institutional repositories.
- The only things that cost are peer-review and maintenance and development of servers and software and that costs institutions may pay instead of subscribing to online journals.

- Data archiving and providing access to a global network of institutional repositories is possible.
- All online journals are transferred to Gold OA.
- Funds for journals subscriptions are released for paying Gold OA.

We can not know in advance whether this Harnad's utopia will come true, but we know that statistics show that in 2011 about 25% of published and peer-reviewed articles could be found in open access.

Harnad talks also about Gratis OA and Libre OA. Gratis OA is free of charge access, but users must seek the permission, so the price barriers are removed, but not permission barriers. Libre OA is free of charge and also free of some copyright and licensing restrictions, so Libre OA removes price barriers and at least some permission barriers too.

Open Access Initiatives and Software

Activities related to open access are also followed by open access initiatives: the Budapest Open Access Initiative (2002), Bethesda Statement on Open Access Publishing, Maryland (2003), Berlin Declaration on Open Access to Knowledge in the Sciences and Humanities (2003), so-called 3 BBB initiatives.

The Budapest Open Access Initiative

The Budapest Open Access Initiative (2001), arises from a small but lively meeting convened in Budapest by the Open Society Foundations on December 1-2, 2001. The purpose of the meeting was to accelerate progress in the international effort to make research articles in all academic fields freely available on the Internet. The participants represented many points of view, many academic disciplines and many nations, and had experience with many of the ongoing initiatives that make up the open access movement. In Budapest they explored how the separate initiatives could work together to achieve broader, deeper and faster success. They explored the most effective and affordable strategies for serving the interests of research, researchers and the institutions and societies that support research. Finally, they explored how Open Society Institute and other foundations could use their resources most productively to aid the transition to open access and to make open access publishing economically self-sustainable. The initiative has been signed by the Budapest participants and a growing number of individuals and organizations from around the world who represent researchers, universities, laboratories, libraries, foundations, journals, publishers, learned societies. The Budapest Open Access Initiative was signed by 5734 individuals and 655 organizations. The new recommendations are the result of a meeting organized by the Open Society Foundation to mark the tenth anniversary (2012) of Budapest Open Access Initiative and these recommendations are translated to many languages.

The Bethesda Statement on Open Access Publishing

The Bethesda Statement on Open Access Publishing (2003), is a 2003 statement which defines the concept of open access and then supports that concept. On 11 April 2003, the Howard Hughes Medical Institute held a meeting for 24 people to discuss better access to scholarly literature. The group made a definition of an open access journal as one which grants a "free, irrevocable, worldwide, perpetual right of access to, and a license to copy, use, distribute, transmit, and display the work publicly and to make and distribute derivative works, in any digital medium for any responsible purpose, subject to proper attribution of author-

ship" and from which every article is "deposited immediately upon initial publication in at least one online repository". The Bethesda Statement builds on the Budapest Open Access Initiative by saying how users will enact open access. Specifically, open access practitioners will put content online with a license granting rights for reuse including the right to make derivative works.

The Berlin Declaration on Open Access to Knowledge in the Sciences and Humanities

The Berlin Declaration on Open Access to Knowledge in the Sciences and Humanities (2003), is a major international statement on open access and access to knowledge. It emerged in 2003 from a conference on open access hosted in Berlin by the Max Planck Society. Organizations that commit to implementing this definition of open access can sign on to the declaration. By 31 January 2013, 417 organizations had signed the declaration.

The Berlin declaration noted that the mission of disseminating knowledge is only half complete if the information is not made widely and readily available to the society. New possibilities of knowledge dissemination not only through the classical form but also and increasingly through the open access paradigm via the Internet have to be supported. It defines open access as a comprehensive source of human knowledge and cultural heritage that has been approved by the scientific community. It promotes new open access paradigm to gain the most benefit for science and society. They encourage researchers and grant recipients to publish their work according to the principles of the open access paradigm, the holders of cultural heritage to support open access by providing their resources on the Internet, develop means and ways to evaluate open access contributions and online journals in order to maintain the standards of quality assurance and good scientific practice, advocate that open access publication be recognized in promotion and tenure evaluation, advocate the intrinsic merit of contributions to an open access infrastructure by software tool development, content provision, metadata creation or the publication of individual articles.

Naturally, there is also open code software for creating institutional repositories such as DSpace, EPrints, and Fedora.

First Institutional Repositories

PubMed

PubMed Central (2013) is a free digital database of full-text scientific literature in biomedical and life sciences, launched in February 2000. It grew from the online Entrez PubMed biomedical literature search system. PubMed Central was developed by the U.S. National Library of Medicine (NLM) as an online archive of biomedical journal articles. The full-text of all PubMed Central articles is free to read, with varying provisions for reuse. Some participating publishers delay the release of their articles on PubMed Central for a set time after paper publication (often six months). A UK version of the PubMed Central system, UK PubMed Central (UKPMC), has been developed by the Wellcome Trust and the British Library as part of a nine-strong group of UK research funders. This system went live in January 2007. The Canadian member of the PubMed Central International network, PubMed Central Canada, was launched in October 2009. As of January 2013, the archive contains approximately 2.6 million items, including articles, editorials and letters. It appears to be growing by at least 7% per year.

BioMed Central

BioMed Central (2013) is an STM (Science, Technology and Medicine) publisher of 251 open access, online, peer-reviewed journals. The portfolio of journals spans all areas of biology and medicine and includes broad interest titles, such as *BMC Biology* and *BMC Medicine* alongside specialist journals, such as *Retrovirology* and *BMC Genomics*. All original research articles published by BioMed Central are made freely and permanently accessible online immediately upon publication. Authors publishing with BioMed Central retain the copyright to their work, licensing it under the Creative Commons Attribution License which allows articles to be re-used and re-distributed without restriction, as long as the original work is correctly cited. BioMed Central is owned by Springer Science+ Business Media, and also hosts the Springer Open platform.

The Public Library of Science

The Public Library of Science (PLOS, 2013) is a nonprofit open access scientific publishing project aimed at creating a library of open access journals and other scientific literature under an open content license. It launched its first journal, *PLOS Biology*, in October 2003 and publishes seven journals, all peer-reviewed, as of April 2012. PLOS announced their new initiative in April 2013, the PLOS Text Mining Collection, to assist researchers in easily retrieving and extracting information from a digital text format. To fund the journals, PLOS charges a publication fee to be paid by the author or the author's employer or funder. In the United States, institutions such as the National Institutes of Health and the Howard Hughes Medical Institute have pledged that recipients of their grants will be allocated funds to cover such author charges. The Global Participation Initiative was instituted in 2012, by which authors in group one countries are not charged a fee, and those in group two countries are given a fee reduction. PLOS core objectives are to provide ways to overcome unnecessary barriers to immediate availability, access, and use of research; pursue a publishing strategy that optimizes the openness, quality and integrity of the publication process and develop innovative approaches to the assessment, organization and reuse of ideas and data.

Research Papers in Economics

Research Papers in Economics (RePEc, 2013) is a collaborative effort of hundreds of volunteers from over 1.400 archives in 75 countries to enhance the dissemination of research in economics. The heart of the project is a decentralized database of working papers, pre-prints, journal articles and software components. The project started in 1997. Its precursor NetEc dates back to 1993. Using its IDEAS database, RePEc provides links to over 1.200.000 full-text articles. Most contributions are freely downloadable, but copyright remains with the author or copyright holder. It is among the largest Internet repositories of academic material in the world. Materials to RePEc can be added through a department or institutional archive or, if no institutional archive is available, through the Munich Personal RePEc Archive. Institutions are welcome to join and contribute their materials by establishing and maintaining their own RePEc archive. Leading publishers, such as Elsevier and Springer, have their economics material listed in RePEc. It collaborates with the American Economic Association's EconLit database to provide content from leading universities working paper or pre-print series to EconLit. Over 1.500 journals and over 3.300 working paper series have registered, for a total of over 1.2 million articles, the majority of which are online.

Digital Access to Scholarship at Harvard

Digital Access to Scholarship at Harvard (DASH, 2013) is the Harvard University's central service for sharing and preserving researcher's work. In addition to the scholarly journal articles targeted by Harvard's several open access resolutions, the DASH can be used to self-archive manuscripts and materials. DASH is established at 2009 and supports a variety of file formats and encourages researchers to deposit related materials with their manuscripts. When researcher deposits his work in DASH, it becomes visible to colleagues around the world by virtue of metadata harvesting, Google Scholar and other indexing services. Higher visibility leads to higher rates of citation and impact. When researcher posts early versions of his work, before publication, he establishes intellectual priority sooner. The researcher acts in his own best interests by taking part in the University's mission to share and preserve the knowledge produced here. Because Harvard now has a prior, non-exclusive license to faculty journal articles in schools with open access policies, those faculty members are required to act accordingly when publishing journal articles, either by attaching an addendum to their publication agreement or obtaining a waiver. They then must deposit the publication in DASH.

J-Gate

J-Gate (2013) is an electronic gateway to global e-journal literature. Launched in 2001 by Informatics India Limited, J-Gate provides seamless access to millions of journal articles available online offered by 10.209 publishers. It presently has a massive database of journal literature, indexed from 32.451 e-journals with links to full-text at publisher sites. J-Gate also plans to support online subscription to journals, electronic document delivery, archiving and other related services. Currently, J-Gate offers different types of products and services: J-Gate Portal - Table of Contents (TOC - for 32.451 e-journals); Database (comprehensive searchable database with 33.455.044 articles, with 4,000+ articles added every day); J-Gate Customized Services - J-Gate Custom Content (JCC - Local Intranet/Internet solution to libraries, providing e-access for subscribed journals); J-Gate Custom

Content for Consortia (JCCC - JCC extended to a homogeneous group of libraries for sharing "subscribed" journal resources.) J-Gate is a truly e-journal portal, it excludes journals that are not available online. It is portal with largest number of e-journals (32.451 e-journals), as well as access to 4.447 e-only-journals and 13.395 open access online journals, links to 6.533.588 open access articles, full-text links to largest number of 10.209 publisher sites etc.

The OAPEN Library

The OAPEN Library (2013), established by Oapen Foundation in The Hague, contains freely accessible academic books, mainly in the area of humanities and social sciences. OAPEN works with publishers to build a quality controlled collection of Open Access books and provides services for publishers, libraries and research funders in the areas of dissemination, quality assurance and digital preservation. OAPEN combines the advantages of an independently operating commercial venture with the benefits of being embedded in the scholarly community. Joining the OAPEN network involves no membership costs, while giving the privileged access to information-sharing and lobbying that are an important part of the initiative. OAPEN is open to publishers with a focus on the humanities and social sciences who would like to explore OA; to research institutions with an existing publishing program or an interest in publishing; to research funders with programs for the humanities and social sciences. OAPEN is also open to cooperation with other partners, as long as their business goals are consistent with OA. OAPEN is a mission-driven network dedicated to promoting OA publishing as an essential service to the academic community. OA publishing is in the public interest and should be seen as an essential service to the scientific community and to society at large.

CogPrints

CogPrints (2013) is an electronic archive in which authors can self-archive papers in any area of cognitive science, including psychology, neuroscience, linguistics and many areas of computer science, philosophy, biology, medicine, anthropology, as well as any other fields of the physical, social and mathematical sciences that are pertinent to the study of cognition. CogPrints is moderated by Stevan Harnad. The archive was launched in 1997 and now contains over 2.000 freely downloadable articles. Some cite CogPrints, along with the physics archive arXiv as evidence that the author self-archiving model of open access can work - although under the influence of the Open Archives Initiative and its OAI-PMH, the emphasis in self-archiving has since moved away from such central repositories in the direction of distributed self-archiving in institutional repositories. CogPrints was first made OAI-compliant, and then the software was converted into the GNU Eprints software at the University of Southampton by Rob Tansley who then went on to design DSpace. GNU Eprints is now maintained by award-winning developer Christopher Gutteridge at Southampton. The site is powered by EPrints3, free software developed by the University of Southampton.

Open Archive Browsers and Harvesters

The Scholarly Publishing and Academic Resources Coalition

Scholarly Publishing and Academic Resources Coalition (SPARC) (2013) initiative was made in 1998 by the American Association of Research Libraries (ARL). SPARC is an international alliance of academic and research libraries working to correct imbalances in the scholarly publishing system. Its pragmatic focus is to stimulate the emergence of new scholarly communication models that expand the dissemination of scholarly research and reduce financial pressures on libraries. Action by SPARC in collaboration with stakeholders – including authors, publishers, and libraries – builds on the unprecedented opportunities created by the networked digital environment to advance the conduct of scholarship. Leading academic organizations have endorsed SPARC in the beginning: the Association of American Universities (AAU), the Association of American University Presses (AAUP), the Big 12 Chief Academic Officers, Association of College and Research Libraries, Association of Universities and Colleges of Canada, Australian Vice-Chancellors Committee, Canadian Association of Research Libraries, Joint Information Systems Committee (JISC) from United Kingdom, National Association of State Universities and Land Grant Colleges, Standing Conference of National and University Libraries, etc.

Today membership in SPARC numbers nearly 800 institutions in North America, Europe, Japan, China and Australia. SPARC worked with the Ligue des Bibliothèques Européennes de Recherche (LIBER) and other European organizations to establish SPARC Europe. SPARC also is affiliated with major library organizations in Australia, Canada, Denmark, New Zealand, the UK and Ireland, and North America.

OAIster

OAIster (2013) was a project of the Digital Library Production Service of the University of Michigan University Library started at 2001. Its goal is to create a collection of freely available, previously difficult-to-access, academically oriented digital resources that are easily searchable by anyone. OAIster harvests from Open Archives Initiative, (OAI) compliant digital libraries, institutional repositories and online journals using the Open Archives Initiative Protocol for Metadata Harvest-

ing (OAI-PMH) protocol. In early 2009, OCLC formed a partnership with the University of Michigan in order to provide continued access to open archive collections through OAIster.

OAIster is a union catalog of millions of records representing open access resources that was built by harvesting from open access collections worldwide using the OAI-PMH. Today, OAIster includes more than 25 million records representing digital resources from more than 1.100 contributors. OAIster.worldcat.org is a freely accessible OCLC site for searching the millions of OAIster records alone. The records will continue to be indexed in OCLC's WorldCat and will be integrated in WorldCat.org search results along with records from thousands of libraries worldwide.

Securing a Hybrid Environment for Research Preservation and Access

Securing a Hybrid Environment for Research Preservation and Access (SHERPA, 2013) is a project team, originally set up in 2002 to run and manage the SHERPA Project. This was an initiative to support the establishment of a number of open access institutional repositories based in UK universities. SHERPA, the organization, is sometimes erroneously referred to as the SHERPA Project. SHERPA is managed by Bill Hubbard. As well as a staff team based at the University of Nottingham, 33 research institutions and organizations comprise the SHERPA Partnership. The makeup of this partnership includes many of the most active and significant institutions in the UK and provide practitioner led experience to the project team. SHERPA's work in supporting open access and repositories on a nationals and international level was recognized in 2007 with the award of the SPARC Europe Award for Outstanding Achievements in Scholarly Communication.

The SHERPA Plus project is a major initiative to support repository development in all UK Higher Education institutions. The project is addressing the practical tasks of cultural change and effective advocacy. It is looking at the issues generated by the extension of repository use to a variety of new content-types - datasets, learning objects, multimedia, etc. It is looking at the requirements of institutional stakeholders in the establishment of new repositories and in the further population of existing archives.

CiteSeer

CiteSeer (2010) was a public search engine and digital library for scientific and academic papers, primarily in the fields of computer and information science that has been replaced by CiteSeerX. Many consider it to be the first academic paper search engine. It became public in 1998 and had many new features unavailable in academic search engines at that time. It was created by researchers Lee Giles, Kurt Bollacker and Steve Lawrence in 1997 while they were at the NEC Research Institute, Princeton, New Jersey. CiteSeer's goal was to actively crawl and harvest academic and scientific documents on the web and use autonomous citation indexing to permit querying by citation or by document, ranking them by citation impact. After NEC, in 2004 it was hosted as CiteSeer.IST on the World Wide Web at the College of Information Sciences and Technology, The Pennsylvania State University, and had over 700.000 documents. For enhanced access, performance and research, similar versions of CiteSeer were supported at universities such as the Massachusetts Institute of Technology, University of Zürich and the National University of Singapore. However, these versions of CiteSeer proved difficult to maintain and are no longer available. CiteSeer had not been comprehensively updated since 2005 due to limitations in its architecture design.

To overcome some of these limitations, a modular and open source architecture for CiteSeer was designed - CiteSeerX. It continues to support the goals outlined by CiteSeer to actively crawl and harvest academic and scientific documents on the public web and to use a citation index to permit query by citations and ranking of documents by the impact of citations. Recently, a table search feature was introduced. It has been funded by the National Science Foundation, NASA and Microsoft Research. CiteSeerX continues to be rated as one of the world's top repositories and was rated number 1 in July 2010. It currently has over 2 million documents with nearly 2 million unique authors and 40 million citations.

DAEDALUS

DAEDALUS (2013) has established a number of different services for research material at the University of Glasgow. This approach has enabled to explore an institutional repository model which uses different software (ePrints, DSpace and PKP Harvester) for different content, including published and peer-reviewed papers and pre-prints, grey literature and theses. The project has also developed an open access e-Journal (JeLit) and a subject based repository for erpanet: ERPAePRINTS. The Glasgow ePrints Service was launched on 9 June 2004. DAEDALUS is funded by the Joint Information Systems Committee (JISC) of the Higher Education Funding Councils, as part of its Focus on Access to Institutional Resources Program (FAIR). DAEDALUS is establishing a range of Open Digital Collections which enable members of the University of Glasgow (and beyond) to deposit and access scholarly output such as published and peer-reviewed academic papers, pre-prints and e-theses.

Connecting Repositories

Connecting Repositories (CORE, 2013) aims to facilitate free access to content stored across Open Access repositories. CORE is a large aggregator of content (several million publications from hundreds of open access repositories) on top of which value added services are provided. It is developed by Knowledge Media institute, The Open University, Milton Keynes, United Kingdom.

The missions of CORE are to:

- Support the right of citizens and general public to access the results of research towards which they contributed by paying taxes.
- Facilitate access to OA content for all by targeting general public, software developers, researchers, etc., by improving search and navigation using state-of-the-art technologies in the field of natural language processing and the semantic web.
- Provide support to both content consumers and content providers by working with digital libraries and institutional repositories.
- Contribute to a cultural change by promoting OA.

Scientific Electronic Library Online

Scientific Electronic Library Online (SciElo, 2013) is a bibliographic database and a model for cooperative electronic publishing in developing countries originally from Brazil, supported by the Foundation for Research Support of the State of Sao Paulo and the National Council of Scientific and Technological Development in partnership with the Latin American and Caribbean Center on Health Sciences Information. The database contains 985 scientific journals from different countries in free and universal access, full-text format of 27.037 issues, 403.932 articles and 8.818.492 Citations. The SciELO Project's stated aims are to "envisage the development of a common methodology for the preparation, storage, dissemination and evaluation of scientific literature in electronic format." All journals are published by a special software suite which implements a scientific electronic virtual library accessed via several mechanisms, including a table of titles in alphabetic and subject list, subject and author indexes and a search engine.

African Journals OnLine

African Journals OnLine (AJOL, 2013) is a non-profit organization dedicated to improving the online visibility of and access to the published scholarly research of African-based academics. By using the internet as a gateway, AJOL aims to enhance conditions for African learning to be translated into African development. The mission of AJOL is to support African research and counter the "North-South" and "West-East" inequality of information flow by facilitating awareness of and access to research published in Africa. AJOL provides an online system for the aggregation of African-published scholarly journals and offers global access to and visibility of the research output of the continent. AJOL hosts African-published, peer-reviewed scholarly journals for free – and includes both open access and subscription-based journals. The meta-data of all participating journals is open access on the AJOL website. AJOL also provides an article download service for researchers to access full text of individual articles. AJOL hosts over 450 peer-reviewed journals from 27 African countries covering a variety of disciplines including health, education, agriculture, science and technology, the environment, and arts and culture. AJOL contains 7607 issues, 83.391 abstracts and 75.280 full-text articles. The number of participating journals and researchers using the service is growing continuously. AJOL hopes to eventually include all quality, peer-reviewed journals on the continent. The AJOL website receives over 100.000 visits per month from over 190 countries around the world. African Journals Online participates in the WorldWideScience global science gateway.

Chinese Open Access Portal

Chinese Open Access Portal (2013) is established by the National Science Library (NSL) at the

Chinese Academy of Sciences (CAS) at 2009. The NLS has been leading the way in the development of open access in China. With a staff of over 470 and a collection about 11.5 million items, the National Science Library serves more than 100 CAS institutes in over 24 cities across China. As the key member of the National Science and Technology Library (NSTL), a consortium established in 2000 by the Chinese Ministry of Science and Technology, it initiates strategic planning and system development projects for NSTL, organizes dissemination of its resources to the public, and collaborates with major domestic and foreign libraries for resource sharing and research collaboration. Besides, NSL set up the Chinese Open Access Portal as one of methods to sustainable support for open access. NSL defines its roles as a clearinghouse of international OA knowledge to support OA research and implementations, a study center for OA models, policies, and supporting mechanisms, a support base for OA training for OA implementers, policy makers and administrators, as well as general public, and a connection center for international cooperation in OA research and implementation.

Open Access Registries

Directory of Open Access Repositories

Directory of Open Access Repositories (OpenDOAR, 2013) service provides a quality assured listing of open access repositories around the world. OpenDOAR staff harvest and assign metadata to allow categorization and analysis to assist the wider use and exploitation of repositories. Each of the repositories has been visited by OpenDOAR staff to ensure a high degree of quality and consistency in the information provided. OpenDOAR is maintained by SHERPA Services, based at the Centre for Research Communications at the University of Nottingham.

The initial OpenDOAR was developed and maintained by the University of Nottingham as part of a portfolio of work in OA and repositories under the SHERPA umbrella. OpenDOAR was started and initially developed by the University of Nottingham, UK and Lund University, Sweden, home of the DOAJ.

The founders of the OpenDOAR project (OSI, JISC, SPARC Europe and CURL) asked the SHERPA team at the University of Nottingham to complete the original development work and since then the service has been based at the University, most recently (2009) being included within work at the Centre for Research Communications.

By 2003, a multiplicity of OA research archives had grown up around the world, confusing in response to calls by scholars, researchers and open access advocates to provide open access to research information. There were then a number of different lists of repositories and open access archives, but no single comprehensive or authoritative list which recorded the range of academic OA repositories.

Beyond these basic listings there was a need to move from cumulative lists to a more structured information service, cataloguing and describing repositories. Users need to know the scope and comprehensiveness of the information they find and be given features which facilitate the use of that information. For example, features to search, filter, analyze and query the descriptions of each repository.

Repositories need to be categorized with clear information on their policies regarding tagging peer-reviewed/non-peer-reviewed material, their subject coverage, the constituency they draw on for content, their collection and preservation policies, etc. Where this information does not exist, repositories should be encouraged to provide it as a means to further improve their visibility and the use of the content that they hold.

Therefore, there was a need for a dependable listing of the academic e-print research repositories that were available worldwide, to underpin the outreach of the OA movement. OpenDOAR was been set up to provide this service and has grown consistently since then. One key point about OpenDOAR is that this information is of use not only to users wishing to find original research papers but also for third-party service providers, like search engines or alert services, who need easy to use tools for developing tailored search services to suit specific user communities.

Directory of Open Access Journals

Directory of Open Access Journals (DOAJ, 2013) is web site, which lists open access journals and is maintained by Infrastructure Services for OA. Until January 2013, the DOAJ was maintained by Lund University. The project defines OA journals as scientific and scholarly journals that meet high quality standards by exercising peer-review or editorial quality control and "use a funding model that does not charge readers or their institutions for access." The Budapest Open Access Initiative's definition of OA is used to define required rights given to users, for the journal to be included in the DOAJ, as the rights to "read, download, copy, distribute, print, search, or link to the full-texts of these articles". The aim of the DOAJ is to increase the visibility and ease of use of OA scientific and scholarly journals, thereby promoting their increased usage and impact. The DOAJ aims to be comprehensive and cover all OA scientific and scholarly journals that use a quality control system to guarantee the content. In short, the DOAJ aims to be the one stop shop for users of OA journals.

As of April 2013, the database contains 9.049 journals, 4.615 journals searchable at article level, 120 countries and 1.081.472 articles. Each day an average of four journals are added. The aim of DOAJ is to increase the visibility and ease of use of OA scientific and scholarly journals thereby promoting their increased usage and impact.

The Open Society Institute funded various OA related projects after the Budapest Open Access Initiative and DOAJ was one of those projects. After the first Nordic Conference on Scholarly Communication in 2002, Lund University became the organization to set up and maintain the DOAJ.

DOAJ participated in the Europeana Libraries project 2010-2012. DOAJ is included in the portal which was launched in Tartu, Estonia on June 27, 2012. Offering free online access to high quality full-text content, plus excellent search tools, the portal enables researchers to find, use and re-use a vast range of materials. The content of DOAJ will be even more visible and disseminated through this portal.

Registry of Open Access Repositories

Registry of Open Access Repositories (ROAR, 2013) is a searchable international portal which is indexing the creation, location and growth of OA institutional repositories and their contents. ROAR was created by EPrints at University of Southampton in 2003 and is made possible by funding from the JISC. ROAR is part of the EPrints.org network. To date, 2.500 institutional and cross-institutional repositories have been registered in ROAR. An institutional repository is an online locus for collecting, preserving and disseminating, in digital form, the intellectual output of an institution, particularly a research institution. For a university, this would include materials such as research journal articles, before (pre-prints) and after (post-prints), undergoing peer-review, and digital versions of theses and dissertations, but it might also include other digital assets generated by normal academic life, such as administrative documents, course notes or learning objects.

The four main objectives for having an institutional repository are:

- To provide OA to institutional research output by self-archiving it;
- To create global visibility for an institution's scholarly research;
- To collect content in a single location;
- To store and preserve other institutional digital assets, including unpublished or otherwise easily lost ("grey") literature (e.g., theses or technical reports).

Registry of Open Access Repositories Mandatory Archiving Policies

Registry of Open Access Repositories Mandatory Archiving Policies (ROARMAP, 2013) is a searchable international registry charting the growth of OA mandates adopted by universities, research institutions and research funders that require their researchers to provide OA to their peer-reviewed research article output by depositing it in an OA repository. ROARMAP was created by EPrints at University of Southampton in 2003. As of April 2013, OA mandates have been adopted by over 200 universities and over 80 research funders worldwide.

In spite of growth in polices, there are still many thousands of universities, research institutes and research funders across the world that have not yet implemented an Open Access policy – and without policies deposit levels (self-deposit) for repositories remain obstinately low at around 20-30% of total scholarly works (research outputs). Evidence has unequivocally demonstrated that to have real effect policies must be mandatory, whether institutional or funder policies. Mandatory policies at institutions succeed in accumulating content in their repositories, averaging 60% of total output after a couple of years of the policy being in place. Evidence shows that researchers are quite happy to be mandated to act in this way. When OA policy is voluntary, the growth of deposited research works is very small.

European Union

Open Access Infrastructure for Research in Europe

Open Access Infrastructure for Research in Europe (OpenAIRE) is the project initiated by the European Union (EU) in 2009 which is developing mechanisms for identification, deposit, access

and supervision of storing of all research articles financed through the EU's Seventh Framework Program.

Currently the European Commission (EC) has two policies on OA in practice. Both aim to ensure that research results funded by the EU citizen are made available to the population at large for free. In this way, OA is considered a way to improve the EU's return on research and development investment.

In December 2007, the ERC Scientific Council published his Guidelines for Open Access, as a follow up of the 2006 Statement on Open Access. In August 2008, the European Commission launched the Open Access Pilot in FP7 that will run until the end of the Framework Program.

Open Access to research articles helps to increase the impact of the European Union's investment in research and development and to avoid wasting time and valuable resources on duplicative research. With access to a wider selection of literature, researchers can build upon this knowledge to further their own work. Small and medium sized businesses and entrepreneurs can also benefit from improved access to the latest research developments to speed up commercialization and innovation.

OpenAIRE builds on and provides access to the network of open access repositories already developed; and in cooperation with other stakeholders, like COAR, SPARC Europe, and LIBER, it supports further expansion, so that authors have the possibility to comply with the EC Open Access Pilot and ERC Guidelines on Open Access within their own local context. OpenAIRE ties the publication to key research project data, so that it can be identified as an FP7 or ERC-funded project.

Most of the EU member states have built expertise on OA. OpenAIRE capitalizes on this by establishing a network of National Open Access Desks (NOADs), who can provide support to researchers, institutions and repository managers in their own country seeking to comply with the EC Open Access Pilot and ERC Guidelines on Open Access.

The OpenAIRE network of Open Access desks is structured similarly to the Europe-wide information network on European Research Programs. The focus of the Open Access Desks activities is on support for compliance with the EC Open Access Pilot. The Open Access desks can be contacted for all questions on Open Access, depositing, the EC Pilot, etc. on the national level.

Open Access Publishing in European Networks

Open Access Publishing in European Networks (OAPEN LIBRARY) is an initiative in Open Access publishing for humanities and social sciences monographs. The consortium of University-based academic publishers who make up OAPEN believe that the time is ripe to bring the successes of scientific Open Access publishing to the humanities and social sciences. The OAPEN partners are all active in the Open Access movement already, with details available on their pages on this site and on their own web sites.

The project will find useful, exciting and beneficial ways of publishing scholarly work in OA, enhancing access to important peer-reviewed research from across Europe. Most importantly it will find a financial model which is appropriate to scholarly humanities monographs, a publishing platform which is beneficial to all users and create a network of publishing partners across Europe and the rest of the world.

OAPEN consists of a number of European university presses and universities, and is open to new partners. The publishing partners are all scholarly presses predominantly active in Humanities and Social Sciences and book publishing. Jointly the members have digital publishing programs, conduct experiments with OA, make use of digital repositories, publish in different European languages, have a worldwide distribution network (including the USA), and cooperate closely with university libraries.

At the request of the European Commission, these partners have developed a joint proposal in the category Targeted Projects in the eContentplus program. The 30 months project aims to develop and implement an OA publication model for academic books in the Humanities and Social Sciences. The project aims to achieve a sustainable European approach to improve quantity, visibility and usability of high-quality OA content. It will foster the creation of new content by developing future-oriented publishing solutions, including an online library dedicated to Humanities and Social Sciences. In order to expand the content of the online library and achieve critical mass, OAPEN will also aggregate content from other publishers in Humanities and Social Sciences.

The OA model that will be developed (the first of its kind) aims to create an OA-publishing platform in combination with an online library that can be used by academic publishers and research funding institutes, based on their respective needs. In this sense OAPEN will play an integrating and marketing role for OA publishing of Humanities and Social Sciences books. It will develop and foster the visibility of this publishing model to all stakeholders, readers and authors, institutions, publishers, librarians and research funding organizations.

The basic e-publishing infrastructure already exists. In order to establish an online library for Humanities and Social Sciences publications, funding is needed for scientific studies, development of OA models and e-publishing services, and the development of tools and services connected to the publication infrastructure.

The OA publications will be thoroughly peer-reviewed and subject to the usual publishing restrictions of each press, and they will be made available as printed books globally.

UNESCO

UNESCO (2013) adopted in 2011 a strategy for promoting OA for scientific information and research. Scientific information is both a researcher's greatest output and technological innovation's most important resource. UNESCO promotes and supports OA - the online availability of scholarly information to everyone, free of most licensing and copyright barriers - for the benefit of global knowledge flow, innovation and socio-economic development.

UNESCO promotes OA, with particular emphasis on scientific information (journal articles, conference papers and datasets of various kinds) emanating from publicly funded research. Working with partners, UNESCO works to improve awareness about the benefits of OA among policy makers, researchers and knowledge managers. Through its global network of Field Offices, Institutes and Centers, UNESCO facilitates the development and adoption of OA enabling policies. In addition, UNESCO engages in global OA debates and cooperates with local, regional and global initiatives in support of OA.

UNESCO's OA program pays particular attention to African and other developing countries where, notwithstanding important gains in ICT availability, OA prevalence, both in terms of output and usage, remains low. OA benefits researchers, innovators, teachers, students, media professionals and the general public.

UNESCO published 3 very important publications on OA: *Guidelines for open education resources (OER) in Higher Education* (2011), *A Basic Guide to Open Educational Resources* (2011), *Policy Guidelines for the development and promotion of open access* / by Alma Swan (2012).

UNESCO's Policy Guidelines for the development and promotion of open access (Swan, 2012) are to serve to decision makers and funders of scientific research, and form a part of UNESCO's strategy plan for Open Access. The paper, written by Alma Swan, one of the leading experts in the field of Open Access, the co-maker of Open Access Map and a team member of Open Oasis group, also serves the whole community as a smaller overview of recent and crucial issues in making Open Access a reality and a gateway to a wider, bigger ecosystem of Open.

The UNESCO document first serves as a guideline paper for funders that wish to create OA policies and institutions that wish to mandate them. The policy framework section states (Swan, 2012, p. 46):

Policy development is of critical importance to the progress of Open Access and a structured process is the best way to ensure a good policy outcome. Policy support is necessary even where advocacy is at its most effective.

Swan even adds a short historical overview of first policies created on institutional, national and funders level (Swan, 2012):

- The first policy to have any real effect was the mandatory one adopted by the School of Electronics and Computer Science at the University of Southampton, UK, in 2002. This required authors in that School to place their post-prints (the authors' final version of their peer-reviewed articles) in the School's repository.
- Research funders, too, have been introducing policies over the past 5 years or so. The first was the Welcome Trust, a London-based funder of biomedical research worldwide. It adopted its policy in 2005, quickly followed by the National Institutes of Health (NIH) in the USA.
- As well as institutional and funder policies, there has been some development of policy at national level. The first national policy was in the Ukraine in 2007.

By the end of the document, Swan calls to action (Swan, 2012, p. 54):

Research funders play a crucial role in policy making with respect to Open Access. Where funders are disbursing public money they will wish to ensure that the results of their funding are disseminated as widely as possible and used by all who can benefit. Open Access increases the visibility, usage and impact of research, and enables it to reach all constituencies that can benefit, including the education, professional, practitioner and business communities, as well as the interested public. The return on public investment in science is thereby maximized. Research funders are therefore encouraged to develop and implement an Open Access policy.

Some Other Important Advocates of Open Access

Berners-Lee (2013), the father of the Internet, believes that the open Internet is a key to continuous success. He argues that all metadata should be open, mutually linked and freely available on the web. He is the president of the Open Data Institute

Peter Suber is a leading voice in the open access movement. He is the Director of the Harvard Open Access Project, a senior research professor of philosophy at Earlham College, the open access project director at Public Knowledge, a senior researcher at SPARC (Scholarly Publishing and Academic Resources Coalition), and a Fellow at Harvard's Berkman Center and Office for Scholarly Communication. He is a member of the Board of Enabling Open Scholarship, the Advisory Boards at the Wikimedia Foundation, the Open Knowledge Foundation, and the advisory boards of other organizations devoted to open access and an information commons.

Suber participated in the 2001 meeting that led to the world's first major international open access initiative, the Budapest Open Access Initiative. He writes Open Access News and the SPARC Open Access Newsletter, considered the most authoritative blog and newsletter on open access.

He is also the founder of the Open Access Tracking Project, and co-founder, with Robin Peek, of the Open Access Directory (OAD).

Suber believes that the Internet offers us an excellent opportunity to exchange our works around the world and that we should use this revolutionary advantage and make our knowledge available. He states (Suber, 2010):

Open access does not imply only exchange of knowledge; it also speeds up research as it assists authors and readers to find each other... Knowledge has always been a public good, in a theoretical sense. Open access makes knowledge a public good in practice.

His new book, published by MIT in 2012 *Open Access* is one of the most important publications on open access, the Bible of OA. In the chapter on OA Future, Suber concludes (Suber, 2012):

The first irony of our still-short history is that OA has been impeded by the turbulence of its own success. The changes wrought by the mere passage of time point up a sad second irony. Nobody is surprised when cultural inertia slows the adoption of radical ideas. But cultural inertia slowed the adoption of OA by leading many people to mistake it for a more radical idea than it actually is.

Alma Swan, a famous open access researcher, believes that the global network has ensured means by which researchers will be able to make their research available to anyone, anywhere and at any time. In 2011, she initiated a project "Open Access Map", already mentioned ROAR MAP and states (Swan, 2011):

OA is now a global movement and initiatives are springing up across the world. It is important to have a single location where OA initiatives can be discovered. The OA Map allows users to conduct searches or obtain overviews of Open Access

developments around the world. This will help to prevent duplication, enhance collaboration and generally enable an approach where new projects properly build upon existing or completed ones.

Stevan Harnad, already mentioned above, is really one of the most important advocates of open access. He is the author of some of the most well-known terms of open access, as Gold and Green OA, Libre and Gratis OA etc. In addition, he founded Psycoloquy (an early electronic journal sponsored by the American Psychological Association), CogPrints (an electronic eprint archive in the cognitive sciences hosted by the University of Southampton), and the American Scientist Open Access Forum (since 1998). Harnad is an active promoter of open access (EPrints, Enabling Open Scholarship (EOS), Open Access Scholarly Information Sourcebook (OASIS), SPARC Campus Open Access Policies.

Subbiah Arunachalam, expert from Swaminathan Research Foundation, Chennai, India, was called by Stevan Harnad, in his blog post at 2003, "India's and the Developing World's great advocate for open access". Arunachalam had then been named as Co-Director of the CogPrints Archive. Arunachalam has argued that research performed in India, and funded by Indian taxpayers, is reported in a few thousand journals, both Indian and foreign. But since some of these journals are very expensive, "many Indian libraries, including sometimes the author's own institutional library, are not able to subscribe to them. As consequence, other Indian scientists working in the same, or related, areas are unable to read these papers. This is a problem common to all developing countries." Arunachalam's view is that "if all these papers were published in OA journals, or if the authors made them freely available on the web by self-archiving them — either in institutional OA archives or in central archives like arXiv and CiteSeer — then the problem would vanish." He is known to favour the self-archiving route for Indian researchers.

Aaron Swartz is one of the most intriguing advocates of the open access. He was an American computer programmer, writer, political organizer and Internet activist. Swartz was involved in the development of the web feed format RSS, the organization Creative Commons, the website framework web.py and the social news site Reddit, in which he was an equal partner after its merger with his Infogami company. Swartz also focused on sociology, civic awareness and activism. In 2010, he became a research fellow at Harvard University's Edmond J. Safra Research Lab on Institutional Corruption, directed by Lawrence Lessig. He founded the online group Demand Progress, known for its campaign against the Stop Online Piracy Act. On January 6, 2011, Swartz was arrested by MIT police on state breaking-and-entering charges, in connection with the systematic downloading of academic journal articles from JSTOR. Federal prosecutors eventually charged him with two counts of wire fraud and 11 violations of the Computer Fraud and Abuse Act, charges carrying a cumulative maximum penalty of $1 million in fines plus 35 years in prison, asset forfeiture, restitution and supervised release. On January 11, 2013, two years after his initial arrest, Swartz was found dead in his Brooklyn apartment, where he had hanged himself. A long-time supporter of Open Access, Swartz wrote in his *Open Access Guerilla Manifesto* (Swartz, 2008):

Information is power. But like all power, there are those who want to keep it for themselves. The world's entire scientific and cultural heritage, published over centuries in books and journals, is increasingly being digitized and locked up by a handful of private corporations... The Open Access Movement has fought valiantly to ensure that scientists do not sign their copyrights away but instead ensure their work is published on the Internet, under terms that allow anyone to access it... With enough of us, around the world, we'll not just send a strong message opposing the privatization of knowledge — we'll make it a thing of the past. Will you join us?

2. OPEN DIGITAL HERITAGE

Many international and national projects are initiated concerning digital collections of library material held in libraries worldwide. These digital libraries consist mainly of precious library material which is in public domain. Because of that, most of them are in open access.

The European Library

The European Library is led by three major library associations: CENL (Conference of European National Librarians), LIBER (Ligue des Bibliothèques Européennes de Recherche) and CERL (Consortium of European Research Libraries).

It operates out of offices in The Hague, Netherlands, and was established by CENL in 1997, when the GABRIEL (Gateway and Bridge to Europe's National Libraries) project set out to establish a joint web portal of European national libraries. At a basic level, the portal provided information about each library's collections and access to their online public access catalogues (OPACs).

GABRIEL was followed by the TEL (The European Library) project, which ran from 2001-2004. It created a framework for access to key national and deposit collections within Europe. The project was part-funded under the Fifth Framework Program of the European Commission.

The national libraries involved in the TEL project were those of Finland, Germany, Italy (Florence), Italy (Rome), Netherlands, Portugal, Slovenia, Switzerland and United Kingdom. This led to the launch of the first portal under the web address www.theeuropeanlibrary.org in 2005. The National Library of Serbia became full partner in the project in July 2005.

Between 2005-2007, the TEL-ME-MOR project helped to incorporate 10 more national libraries from new European Union member states as full partners of The European Library. By the beginning of 2008, a further nine national librar-

ies within the European Union and the European Free Trade Association had joined the service.

This was followed by FUMAGABA project (2008-2009), which aimed at integrating the collections of national libraries in Eastern Europe: The Former Yugoslav Republic of Macedonia, Ukraine, Moldova, Albania, Georgia Armenia, Bosnia and Herzegovina, and Azerbaijan.

The European Library took a further step towards its enlargement with the EDLproject, during which national libraries continued to join The European Library. The project also focused on multilingualism, undertook the first steps towards a European Metadata Registry and created a roadmap for potential digitization efforts in the national libraries.

Through the single search box, everyone can freely search the resources of Europe's leading national and research libraries. This includes all of the bibliographic records of Europe (the Union Catalogue), plus over 24 million pages of full-text content and 10 million digital objects in more than 400 different digital collections from 48 European national libraries.

The European Library has 200 million resources in total and they come from prestigious network of institutions, including all of Europe's 48 national libraries and an increasing number of research libraries, such as the University of Oxford's Bodleian Library.

EUROPEANA

EUROPEANA (2013) is an Internet portal that acts as an interface to millions of books, paintings, films, museum objects and archival records that have been digitized throughout Europe. More than 2.000 institutions across Europe have contributed to Europeana. The partners are libraries, museums archive and audiovisual institutions. Together, their assembled collections let users explore Europe's cultural and scientific heritage from prehistory to the modern day.

The catalyst for Europeana was a letter sent by Jacques Chirac, President of France, together with the premiers of Germany, Spain, Italy, Poland and Hungary to the President of the European Commission, José Manuel Durão Barroso, in April 2005. The letter recommended the creation of a virtual European library, to make Europe's cultural heritage accessible for all.

The letter added resonance to the work that the European Commission's Information Society and Media Directorate had been engaged in for over a decade, with programs such as Telematics for Libraries. It gave strong political endorsement to the Directorate's strategy, *i2010: communication on digital libraries*, which was published on 30 September 2005. The strategy announced the intention to promote and support the creation of a European digital library, as a goal within the European Union, which aims to foster growth in the information society and media industries.

The project that began the building of Europeana was called the European Digital Library Network (EDLnet) and was aimed at building a prototype of a cross-border, cross-domain, user-centered service. It was funded by the European Commission under its eContentplus program, one of the research and development funding streams of i2010.

The prototype was launched on 20 November, 2008. At its beta launch, the site gave access to 4.5 million digital objects – more than double the initial target – from over 1.000 contributing organizations, including world famous national library, gallery and museum collections from the capitals of Europe.

In February 2009, the successor of EDLnet – Europeana version 1.0 – began. This 30-month project was to develop the prototype into a fully operational service. In 2010, the project accomplished its objective of giving access to over 10 million digital objects. Early in 2011, new features

on the site included a translation tool and the ability to expand on information by automatically transferring the search term to Wikipedia and other services.

Europeana gives access to different types of content from different types of heritage institutions. The digital objects that users can find in Europeana are not stored on a central computer, but remain with the cultural institution and are hosted on their networks. Europeana collects contextual information – metadata – about the items, including a small picture. Users search this contextual information. Once they find what they are looking for, if they want to access the full content of the item, they can click through to the original site that holds the content.

Different types of cultural heritage organizations – libraries, museums, archives and audiovisual collections – catalogue their content in different ways and to different standards. Approaches also vary in different countries. In order to make the information searchable, it has to be mapped to a single common standard, known as the Europeana Semantic Elements. This metadata standard at present takes a lowest common denominator approach to the integration of different types of digital content. However, the introduction of a richer metadata standard, the Europeana Data Model, will help to give users more and better information.

In its Strategic Plan for 2011–2015, which was published in January 2011, Europeana outlines four strategic tracks that will shape its further development:

- **Aggregate:** To build the open trusted source for European cultural and scientific heritage content;
- **Facilitate:** To support the cultural and scientific heritage sector through knowledge transfer, innovation and advocacy;

- **Distribute:** To make heritage available to users wherever they are, whenever they want it;
- **Engage:** To cultivate new ways for users to participate in their cultural and scientific heritage.

The Europeana Foundation is the governing body of the Europeana service. Its members are the presidents and chairs of European associations for cultural heritage and information associations. The Foundation promotes collaboration between museums, archives, audiovisual collections and libraries so that users can have integrated access to their content through Europeana and other services.

The Foundation is incorporated under Dutch law as Stichting Europeana and is housed within the Koninklijke Bibliotheek, the National library of the Netherlands. It provides a legal framework for the governance of Europeana, employing the staff, bidding for funding and enabling the sustainability of the service.

GALLICA of the French National Library

GALLICA (2013) of the French National Library is one of the richest European digital library which was established in 1997. As of January 2012, Gallica made available on the web about 1.600.000 documents, 320.000 books, 36.000 maps, 19.462 manuscripts, 410.000 images, 830.000 newspapers and magazines, 7.000 sheets music. About 50% of all content in Europeana is from Gallica and French cultural heritage.

The World Digital Library

The World Digital Library (WDL) (2013) is an international digital library operated by UNESCO and the Library of Congress. The WDL has stated that its mission is to promote international and intercultural understanding, expand the volume and variety of cultural content on the Internet, provide resources for educators, scholars, and general audiences, and to build capacity in partner institutions to narrow the digital divide within and among countries. It aims to expand non-English and non-western content on the Internet, and contribute to scholarly research. The library intends to make available on the Internet, free of charge and in multilingual format, significant primary materials from cultures around the world, including manuscripts, maps, rare books, musical scores, recordings, films, prints, photographs, architectural drawings, and other significant cultural materials. At launch, the library had 1.236 items. By November 2012, the library had 6.506 items.

After almost twenty years of absence, the United States re-established its permanent delegation to the UNESCO in 2003. Dr. James H. Billington, Librarian of Congress, was nominated as a commissioner of the U.S. National Commission to UNESCO and was invited to give a plenary speech at its inaugural conference in June 2005. His speech, entitled *A View of the Digital World Library*, described a vision in which the rich collections that "institutions, libraries, and museums have preserved could be given back to the world free of charge and in a new form far more universally accessible than any forms that have preceded it."

In December 2006, forty-five national library directors, library technical directors and cultural and educational representatives from UNESCO met in Paris to discuss the development of the World Digital Library. The working groups presented their findings to the larger WDL group in July 2007. Findings from this planning process were presented at the thirty-fourth session of the UNESCO General Conference in October 2007 in Paris, France.

In early September 2008, the Organization of American States (OAS) agreed to join with the Library of Congress in developing the World

Digital Library. The World Digital Library was launched on April 21, 2009 at UNESCO headquarters in Paris, France.

Project Gutenberg

Project Gutenberg (PG) (2013) is a volunteer effort to digitize and archive cultural works, to "encourage the creation and distribution of eBooks". It was founded in 1971 by Michael S. Hart and is the oldest digital library. Most of the items in its collection are the full-texts of public domain books. The project tries to make these as free as possible, in long-lasting, open formats that can be used on almost any computer.

Wherever possible, the releases are available in plain text, but other formats are included, such as HTML, PDF, EPUB, MOBI, and Plucker. Most releases are in the English language, but many non-English works are also available. There are multiple affiliated projects that are providing additional content, including regional and language-specific works.

Starting in 2004, an improved online catalog made Project Gutenberg content easier to browse, access and hyperlink. Project Gutenberg is now hosted by Ibiblio at the University of North Carolina at Chapel Hill.

As of February 2013, Project Gutenberg claimed over 42.000 items in its collection, with an average of over fifty new e-books being added each week. These are primarily works of literature from the Western cultural tradition. In addition to literature such as novels, poetry, short stories and drama, Project Gutenberg also has cookbooks, reference works and issues of periodicals. The Project Gutenberg collection also has a few non-text items such as audio files and music notation files. Most releases are in English, but there are also significant numbers in many other languages. As of February 2013, the non-English languages most represented are: French, German, Finnish, Dutch, Portuguese, and Chinese.

Project Gutenberg is intentionally decentralized. For example, there is no selection policy dictating what texts to add. Instead, individual volunteers work on what they are interested in, or have available. The Project Gutenberg collection is intended to preserve items for the long term, so they cannot be lost by any one localized accident. In an effort to ensure this, the entire collection is backed-up regularly and mirrored on servers in many different locations

Google Books Project

Google Books Project (2013), previously known as Google Book Search and Google Print, is a service from Google Inc. that searches the full-text of books and magazines that Google has scanned, converted to text using optical character recognition, and stored in its digital database. The service was formerly known as Google Print when it was introduced at the Frankfurt Book Fair in October 2004. Google's Library Project, also now known as Google Book Search, was announced in December 2004.

A click on a result from Google Books opens an interface in which the user may view pages from the book, if out of copyright or if the copyright owner has given permission. Books in the public domain are available in "full view" and free for download. For in-print books where permission has been granted, the number of viewable pages is limited to a "preview" set by a variety of access restrictions and security measures, some based on user-tracking. For books where permission for a "preview" has been refused, only permission for "snippets" (two to three lines of text) may be permitted, but the full-text of the book is searchable on this limited basis. Where the owner of a book cannot be identified, a "snippet" view may be implemented. For other books that have neither a "full view" nor "preview", the text is not searchable at all, and Google Books provides no identification of content beyond the book title.

Most scanned works are no longer in print or commercially available. For those which are, the site provides links to the web site of the publisher and booksellers.

In December 2004 Google signaled an extension to its Google Print initiative known as the Google Print Library Project. Google announced partnerships with several high-profile university and public libraries, including the University of Michigan, Harvard University Library, Stanford Green Library, Oxford Bodleian Library and the New York Public Library. According to press releases and university librarians, Google plans to digitize and make available through its Google Books service approximately 15 million volumes within a decade. The announcement soon triggered controversy, as publisher and author associations challenged Google's plans to digitize, not just books in the public domain, but also titles still under copyright.

In November 2005, Google changed the name of this service from Google Print to Google Book Search. Its program enabling publishers and authors to include their books in the service was renamed Google Books Partner Program and the partnership with libraries became Google Books Library Project.

In August 2006 the University of California System announced that it would join the Books digitization project. This includes a portion of the 34 million volumes within the approximately 100 libraries managed by the System. In September 2006 the Complutense University of Madrid becomes the first Spanish-language library to join the Google Books Library Project. In March 2007 the Bavarian State Library announced a partnership with Google to scan more than a million public domain and out-of-print works in German as well as English, French, Italian, Latin and Spanish. In July 2007 Keio University became Google's first library partner in Japan with the announcement that they would digitize at least 120.000 public domain books. In September 2007 Google debuts a new feature called "My Library" which allows

users to create personal customized libraries, selections of books that they can label, review, rate or full-text search. In December 2008 Google announces the inclusion of magazines in Google Books. Titles include *New York Magazine*, *Ebony*, *Popular Mechanics*, and others. In December 2009 a French court shut down the scanning of copyrighted books published in France saying it violated copyright laws. It was the first major legal loss for the scanning project. In May 2010 it is reported that Google will launch a digital book store termed as Google Editions. It will compete with Amazon, Barnes and Noble, Apple and other electronic book retailers with its very own e-book store. Unlike others, Google Editions will be completely online and will not require a specific device (such as kindle, Nook, iPad, etc.). In August 2010 it was announced that Google intends to scan all known existing 129.864.880 books by the end of the decade, accounting to over 4 billion digital pages and 2 trillion words in total. In April 2013 Google's database encompasses more than 30 million scanned books.

The Google Books initiative has been hailed for its potential to offer unprecedented access to what may become the largest online body of human knowledge and promoting the democratization of knowledge, but it has also been criticized for potential copyright violations.

Hathitrust Digital Library

Hathitrust Digital Library (2013) is a large-scale collaborative repository of digital content from research libraries including content digitized via the Google Books project and Internet Archive digitization initiatives, as well as content digitized locally by libraries.

HathiTrust was founded in October 2008 by the thirteen universities of the Committee on Institutional Cooperation and the University of California. The partnership includes over 60 research libraries across the United States and Europe, and is based on a shared governance structure. Costs are shared by the participating libraries and library consortia. The repository is administered by Indiana University and the University of Michigan. As of January 2012, HathiTrust comprises over 10 million volumes, over 2.7 million of which are public domain (at least in the U.S.A.). HathiTrust provides a number of discovery and access services, notably, full-text search across the entire repository. Hathi, pronounced "hah-tee", is the Hindi word for elephant, an animal famed for its long-term memory.

The Digital Public Library of America

The Digital Public Library of America (DPLA) (2013) is a project aimed at bringing about a large-scale public digital library. It was launched by Harvard University's Berkman Center for Internet and Society in 2010, with financial support from the Alfred P. Sloan Foundation and several other funders. It aims to unify such disparate sources as the Library of Congress, the Internet Archive, various academic collections, and presumably any other collection that would be meaningful to include. They have yet to decide such issues as how near to the present their catalog will come. There is an ongoing dispute regarding so-called orphan works and other questions of copyright.

Among the critiques of the project: its vagueness, lack of internal cohesion, potentially redundant overlap with similar efforts, and potential to redirect financial support away from existing public libraries. It has been suggested that in contrast to the brick-and-mortar public library, a digital public library may not be suitable for providing adult literacy training or fostering young children's development. Some public librarians have also expressed a concern that a national digital library will divert and reduce traditional public library funding which received a fast response from the DPLA.

A proposed future project of the DPLA is the idea of the Scannebago, a mobile scanning unit that would travel the United States in order

to digitize and curate local historical materials. Harvard staff is coordinating a broad-based team that built a digital library platform, which launched on April 18, 2013.

International Children's Digital Library

International Children's Digital Library (ICDL) (2013) is a free online library of digitized children's books in many languages from various countries. Designed specifically for use by children ages 3 to 13, the Library is a housed by the International Children's Digital Library Foundation and was originally developed in the College of Information Studies and the Human-Computer Interaction Laboratory at the University of Maryland, College Park.

Children can search for books by location, color, length, intended age group, content type, and emotional quality, among other qualifiers. An advanced search option is also provided for more experienced or older users, and all users can register to save search preferences and favorite books.

Books are selected based on quality and appropriateness and are presented in their original language with copyright permission from publishers or authors. The Library's ultimate goal is to foster a love of reading, a readiness to learn, and a response to the challenges of world literacy.

The International Children's Digital Library was initially launched in November 2002 under the direction of University of Maryland Computer Science professor Dr. Allison Druin and in collaboration with researchers from other fields, such as information studies, art, psychology, and education, in order to better understand children's online habits and to encourage a love of reading and increased literacy.

The 2002-2005 phase of development saw a working model of the Library accessed by over one million users around the world and home to 1.000 books. Funding initially came from the National Science Foundation and the Institute of Museum and Library Services. In April 2006, the International Children's Digital Library became part of the newly formed International Children's Digital Library Foundation, a non-profit corporation under the leadership of Tim Browne as Executive Director. The Library's principal support comes from the Library of Congress, National Science Foundation, the Institute of Museum and Library Services and Microsoft Research.

The ICDL has been visited by over three million unique visitors since its launch in November, 2002.

Today the ICDL collection includes 4.642 books in 61 languages. Users come from 228 different countries.

The Library of Congress National Digital Library Program

The Library of Congress National Digital Library Program (NDLP) (2013) is assembling a digital library of reproductions of primary source materials to support the study of the history and culture of the United States. Begun in 1995 after a five-year pilot project, the program began digitizing selected collections of Library of Congress archival materials that chronicle the nation's rich cultural heritage. In order to reproduce collections of books, pamphlets, motion pictures, manuscripts and sound recordings, the Library has created a wide array of digital entities: bitonal document images, grayscale and color pictorial images, digital video and audio, and searchable e-texts. To provide access to the reproductions, the project developed a range of descriptive elements: bibliographic records, finding aids, and introductory texts and programs, as well as indexing the full-texts for certain types of content.

The reproductions were produced with a variety of tools: image scanners, digital cameras, devices that digitize audio and video, and human labor for creating key words and encoding texts. American Memory employs national-standard and well established industry-standard formats for many digital reproductions

The Library of Congress is trying to extend its library services to include services to the entire web. While the original Library was focused on the needs of the U.S. Congress, dealing with the whole world through the Internet is something it is still struggling with. The collection includes an eclectic mix of documents, images, videos and sound recordings. Images include maps, sheet music, handwritten documents, drawings and architectural diagrams. The goal of a Library of Congress Digital Library should be to provide access to those materials unique to the Library of Congress, and a clear guide to any Internet materials related to the United States. The Library of Congress Global Gateway has about 200.000 documents currently, and the American Memory site has about 350.000 documents.

The National Digital Library Project of China

The National Library of China in Beijing is the largest library in Asia and one of the largest in the world with a collection of over 30 million volumes of books. It holds the largest and among the richest worldwide collections of Chinese literature and historical documents. Beginning in 1995, the National Library of China has followed the development of digital libraries in the international community, marking the beginning of Chinese digital library development. Although China started late compared to the US and other developed countries, its development has been quickly catching up. Generally speaking, the development of Chinese digital library efforts can be viewed in three developmental phases: the conceptual introduction phase (between 1995 and 1996), the technical exploration phase (from 1996 to 2000), and the application development phase (from 2001 to now). Each of these phases has a unique development pattern and set of achievements. (Xihui Z., 2010) The National Digital Library Project was established in 2002, and started its implementation phase in 2005. The goal of the project was to establish a digital library service that provides all the functionality of the Chinese National Library, and implements mechanisms and procedures for collection, digitization, and archiving of Chinese information resources, accumulates a very large amount of high quality digital resources, provides access to those resources over the Internet, establishes the largest and most complete digital Chinese information collection and provides services for it. By the end of 2009, the digital library of the Chinese National Library had established an index of more than 27 million items, accumulated more than 320 TB of digital resources and made them accessible via the library website. The NDLP massive collections enable the NLC to provide information service to the central government and other governmental organizations, educational, scientific, and research institutions, and the general public. It includes electronic books, dissertations, Min Guo documents, on-line lectures, oracle bones, Dunhuang materials, rubbings, digital chronicles, New Year pictures, etc. (Wei and Sun, 2010).

FUTURE RESEARCH DIRECTIONS

It is not possible to predict in which extent the Internet will be developed for long-term. Some authors think that we are living in the first minute of the development of the Internet and that its future is very uncertain. We have to be aware that we live with Internet just over 20 years. In the web site of popular science, Gizmodo, we can find what happens in only 60 seconds on the Internet: 694.445 search queries in Google, 168 million emails are sent, 60+ new blogs, 1500+ blog posts, 70+ new domains registered, 600+ new videos on You-Tube, 13.000+ iPhone applications downloaded, 370.000+ minutes voice calls on Skype, 320+ new Twitter accounts, 98.000+ new tweets, 100+ new LinkedIn accounts, 6.600+ new pictures on Flickr, 695.000+ Facebook status updates etc. Internet

is indeed immense and unpredictable. We should try to take advantage of Internet benefits without being hooked to this great network. In February 2013 the BBC is launching a series of programs about what the world might be in future, and holding a global competition inviting audiences to create their own vision of the future. The BBC also recently published an infographic looking to the future — 2013 to 50 years to 100 years out (What Happens…, 2012). Using predictions from thinkers, scientists and pundits, the graphic also outlines the odds of the events taking place. In the field of computing and robotics: in 2017 people can touch one another through their phones and our computer has a sense of smell, in 2025 we can upload the contents of our brain to our computer, in 2037 we can log in to our computer directly from our brain, in 2045 the singularity has taken place – there exist machines with greater than human super-intelligence. In the field of science and nature: in 2017 the first immortal mouse has been created, in 2020 the high resolution bionic eyes are on sale, in 2070 the first cloned humans have appeared and in 2090 the new ace age has begun. In 2150 a human being has lived to older than 150 years. When we see all these predictions, we can be really excited and a little afraid. In order to reach such a world in the future, knowledge of the world has to be free and open. We are going back now to the near future and our topics of open access and open digital heritage.

Concerning open access resources for researchers, it would be necessary to develop the mandatory policy in many universities, libraries and other funding institutions. It is desirable that mandatory policy of open access is introduced in national level, if possible by government of different countries. Institutional repositories should be established in all institutional levels (universities, libraries, publishers, funders etc.) and for all types of material (articles, journals, books, thesis etc.). Self-archiving by researchers should be also mandatory. It is not real to have in the early future all researches in open access, but it is not inconceivable. Harnad's utopia has good arguments to become the reality.

Concerning the open digital heritage, we believe that Bibliotheca Universalis is possible, as digital library of the world's cultural heritage, open to every citizen of the planet. It should be necessary to coordinate all activities in international level, as well as in national levels. The real world digital library, as a comprehensive collection of all nations cultural and scientific digital heritage is not possible without implementation of same standards of digitization, metadata formats and selection principles. It is also necessary that the developed countries help developing countries in order to overcome the digital divide. The world cultural and scientific heritage can not exist without heritage from all countries around the world.

CONCLUSION

Libraries must accept all challenges of the open e-resources for researchers and open digital heritage. They should first create the lists of open access e-resources in their web sites, they should establish the institutional repositories and promote the mandatory policy of self-archiving. Of course, they will continue to license the e-content with commercial publishers, but in the same time they have to try to reduce the costs and to find another ways of services for their users, services of open access. As Peter Suber told, the knowledge is the public good and open access makes knowledge a public good in practice. Without open knowledge accessible to every citizen of the Earth, there is no progress and future.

REFERENCES

African Journals OnLine. (2013). Retrieved May 25, 2013 from http://www.ajol.info/

Berners-Lee, T. (2013). *Linked data: Web science and the semantic web*. Retrieved April 10, 2013 from, http://www.edge.org/conversation/linked-data

Berners-Lee, T., De Roure, D., Harnad, S., & Shadbolt, N. (2005). *Journal publishing and author self-archiving: Peaceful co-existence and fruitful collaboration*. Retrieved March 20, 2013, from http://eprints.soton.ac.uk/261160/

BioMed Central. (2013). The open access publisher. *Springer Science+Business Media*. Retrieved March 5, 2013, from http://www.biomedcentral.com/about

Brody, T. (2006), *Evaluating research impact through open access to scholarly communication*. Retrieved March 20, 2013, from http://eprints.soton.ac.uk/263313/

Brody, T., Carr, L., Hey, J. M. N., Brown, A., & Hitchcock, S. (2007). PRONOM-ROAR: Adding format profiles to a repository registry to inform preservation services. *The International Journal of Digital Curation*, 2(2).

Budapest Open Access Initiative. (2001). Retrieved March 10, 2013 from http://www.opensociety-foundations.org/openaccess

Chinese Open Access Portal. (2013). *The national science library (NSL) at the Chinese academy of sciences (CAS)*. Retrieved May 25, 2013 from http://www.open-access.net.cn

CiteSeer. (2010). *The college of information sciences and technology, the Pennsylvania State University*. Retrieved March 5, 2013, from http://citeseerx.ist.psu.edu/index

CogPrints. (2013). Retrieved March 5, 2013, from http://cogprints.org/

CORE. (2013). *Connecting repositories, knowledge media institute*. Retrieved March 10, 2013, from http://core-project.kmi.open.ac.uk/

DAEDALUS. (2013). Retrieved March 5, 2013, from http://www.lib.gla.ac.uk/daedalus/

DASH. (2013). *Digital access to scholarship at Harvard*. Retrieved March 15, 2013, from http://dash.harvard.edu/

Digital Public Library of America. (2013). Retrieved March 20, 2013, from http://dp.la/

Directory of Open Access Journals (DOAJ). (2013). Retrieved March 10, 2013, from http://www.doaj.org/

Directory of Open Access Repositories (OpenDOAR). (2013). Retrieved March 10, 2013, from http://www.opendoar.org/

DOAJ. (2013). *The directory of open access journals*. Retrieved March 10, 2013, from http://www.doaj.org/

European Library. (2013). Retrieved March 20, 2013, from http://www.theeuropeanlibrary.org/tel4/

EUROPEANA. (2013). Retrieved March 20, 2013, from http://www.europeana.eu/

GALLICA. (2013). Retrieved March 20, 2013, from http://gallica.bnf.fr/

Ginsparg, P. (2001). *Creating a global knowledge network*. Retrieved March 20, 2013, from http://people.ccmr.cornell.edu/~ginsparg/blurb/pg01unesco.html

Gizmodo. (2012). *What happens in 60 seconds on the internet*. Retrieved 25 May, 2013 from http://gizmodo.com/5813875/what-happens-in-60-seconds-on-the-internet

Google Books Project. (2013). Retrieved March 20, 2013, from http://www.google.com/google-books/library/index.html

Gutenberg Project. (2013). Retrieved March 20, 2013, from http://www.gutenberg.org/

Harnad, S. (2013). Paid gold OA versus free gold OA: Against color cacophony. Open Access Archivangelism. Retrieved March 20, 2013, from http://openaccess.eprints.org/index.php?/archives/1003-Paid-Gold-OA-Versus-Free-Gold-OA-Against-Color-Cacophony.html

Harnad, S., Brody, T., Vallieres, F., Carr, L., Hitchcock, S., & Gingras, Y. et al. (2004). The access/impact problem and the green and gold roads to open access. *Serials Review*, *30*(4). doi:10.1016/j.serrev.2004.09.013.

Hathitrust Digital Library. (2013). Retrieved March 20, 2013, from http://www.hathitrust.org/

Howard Hughes Medical Institute. (2003). *The Bethesda statement on open access publishing*. Retrieved March 10, 2013 from http://legacy.earlham.edu/~peters/fos/bethesda.htm

International Children's Digital Library. (2013). Retrieved March 20, 2013, from http://en.childrenslibrary.org/

J-Gate. (2013). *The e-journal gateway*. Retrieved March 5, 2013, from - http://www.jgate.in/

Library of Congress. (2013). *Digital collections*. Retrieved March 20, 2013, from http://www.loc.gov/library/libarch-digital.html

Max Planck Society. (2003). *Berlin declaration on open access to knowledge in the sciences and humanities*. Retrieved March 10, 2013 from http://oa.mpg.de/lang/en-uk/berlin-prozess/berliner-erklarung/

OAIster. (2013). *OCLC*. Retrieved March 5, 2013, from http://www.oclc.org/oaister.en.html

Oapen Library. (2013a). *Publishing in European network*. Retrieved March 5, 2013, from http://www.oapen.org/home

Oapen Library. (2013b). Retrieved March 10, 2013 from http://project.oapen.org/

Open Access. (2013). *Infrastructure for research in Europe*. Retrieved March 10, 2013, from http://www.openaire.eu/index.php?lang=en

Open Access Directory. (2013). Retrieved March 5, 2013, from http://oad.simmons.edu/oadwiki/Timeline

Open Access Infrastructure for Research in Europe. (2013). Retrieved March 10, 2013, from http://www.openaire.eu/index.php?lang=en

OpenDOAR. (2013). *Directory of open access repositories*. Retrieved March 10, 2013, from http://www.opendoar.org/

Peter Suber Website. (2013). Retrieved March 10, 2013, from http://legacy.earlham.edu/~peters/hometoc.htm

Public Library of Science (PLOS). (2013). Retrieved March 5, 2013, from http://www.plos.org/

PubMed Central. (2013). *The U.S. national institutes of health's national library of medicine (NIH/NLM)*. Retrieved March 5, 2013, from http://www.ncbi.nlm.nih.gov/pmc/

RePEc. (2013). *Research papers in economics*. Retrieved March 5, 2013, from http://repec.org/

ROAR. (2013). *Registry of open access repositories*. Retrieved March 10, 2013, from http://roar.eprints.org/

ROARMAP. (2013). *Registry of open access repositories mandatory archiving policies*. Retrieved March 10, 2013, from http://roarmap.eprints.org/

SciElo. (2013). Retrieved May 23, 2013 from http://www.scielo.org/php/index.php?lang=en

Sherpa. (2013). *Securing a hybrid environment for research preservation and access*. Retrieved March 5, 2013, from http://www.sherpa.ac.uk/

Sherpa Plus. (2013). *Securing a hybrid environment for research preservation and access*. Retrieved March 5, 2013, from http://www.sherpa.ac.uk/projects/sherpaplus.html

SPARC. (2012). *The scholarly publishing and academic resources coalition*. Retrieved March 5, 2013, from http://www.sparc.arl.org/

Suber, P. (2010). *Knowledge as a public good*. Retrieved April 10, 2013 from http://legacy.earlham.edu/~peters/fos/newsletter/11-02-09.htm

Suber, P. (2012). *Open access*. Cambridge, MA: MIT..

Swan, A. (2005). *Open access: Briefing paper*. Retrieved April 10, 2013 from http://eprints.soton.ac.uk/261005/

Swan, A. (2010). *Modeling scholarly communication options: costs and benefits for universities*. Retrieved April 10, 2013 from http://repository.jisc.ac.uk/442/2/Modelling_scholarly_communication_report_final1.pdf

Swan, A. (2011). *Open access map: Charting the growth and development of open access globally*. Retrieved April 10, 2013 from http://www.openaccessmap.org/about/

Swan, A. (2012a). *Policy guidelines for the development and promotion of open access*. Retrieved March 20, 2013, from http://unesdoc.unesco.org/images/0021/002158/215863e.pdf

Swan, A. (2012b). *Open access briefing paper from SCONUL*. Retrieved April 10, 2013 from http://blogs.warwick.ac.uk/libresearch/entry/open_access_briefing/

Swartz, A. (2008). *Guerilla open access manifesto*. Retrieved May 25, 2013 from http://archive.org/stream/GuerillaOpenAccessManifesto/Goamjuly2008_djvu.txt

Tomorrow's World Infographic from the BBC Lays the Odds on the Future. (2013). Retrieved May 27, 2013 from http://www.33rdsquare.com/2013/01/tomorrows-world-infographic-from-bbc.html

UNESCO. (2011a). *A basic guide to open educational resources*. Retrieved March 20, 2013 from http://unesdoc.unesco.org/images/0021/002158/215804e.pdf

UNESCO. (2011b). *Guidelines for open education resources (OER) in higher education*. Retrieved March 20, 2013, from http://unesdoc.unesco.org/images/0021/002136/213605e.pdf

UNESCO. (2013). Retrieved March 15, 2013, from http://www.unesco.org/new/en/communication-and-information/access-to-knowledge/open-access-to-scientific-information/browse/1/

Wei, D., & Sun, Y. (2010). The national digital library project. *D-Lib Magazine, 16*(5/6).

World Digital Library. (2013). Retrieved March 20, 2013 from http://www.wdl.org/en/

Xihui, Z. (2010). Overview of digital library development in China. *D-Lib Magazine, 16*(5/6).

Chapter 10
Riding the Waves of Change for Electronic Resources at the Library and Learning Commons, Monash University Sunway Campus[1]:
From Vision to Reality

Sossamma K. T. George
Monash University – Sunway Campus, Malaysia

ABSTRACT

This chapter contributes to the topic of electronic resources. The purpose of this chapter is to share with fellow professionals the experience and challenges that the Library and Learning Commons, Monash University Sunway Campus Malaysia faced in progressing electronic resources at the Sunway campus. It discusses two major actions undertaken, namely (1) the implementation of an e-book acquisitions policy and (2) the implementation of Search, a Web resource discovery service undertaken in collaboration with Monash University Library Australia. The intent of the chapter is to share the experience of the Information Resources Section that undertook to implement these actions as part of the Section's annual development plan for 2011 and 2012. The ensuing initiatives to realize the action plans and the progress made are discussed here. More importantly, the outcomes and the learning experiences are shared, in the understanding that by sharing, they contribute to enriching the field and empowering and challenging ourselves to progress further.

DOI: 10.4018/978-1-4666-4761-9.ch010

INTRODUCTION

Monash University Sunway Campus is a branch campus of Monash Australia. The unique experience of being located in Malaysia as a branch campus of Monash Australia and providing students across campuses with similar e-resource is an ongoing challenge. In general the Sunway Campus Library and Learning Commons manages a budget for its local acquisitions of print books, serials and audio visual materials. However, for electronic resources, access is provided by Monash University to most of the e-resource. Providing access to e-resource in a changing learning environment that is encouraging e-resource has seen rapidly changing acquisitions practices as well as raised concerns and issues of costs, access and usage of e-resource at the Malaysian campus.

This chapter is essentially a descriptive case study that addresses the research question of "how" in the pursuit to progress e- resources for collection development. In 2010, an E-resource Taskforce was set up at MUSC and some of the recommendations of the E-resource Taskforce report were given closure by the actions undertaken and implemented by the Library and Learning Commons, Sunway Campus. The objectives of this chapter are to share the experiences of the two major strategic actions undertaken by the Library and Learning Commons, Sunway Campus to progress electronic resources. These are:

1. The implementation of an e-book acquisitions policy.
2. The implementation of *Search,* a web resource discovery service undertaken in collaboration with Monash University Library Australia. With *Search,* staff and students can now use *Search* as a single point of access to the library's catalogue, to e-books and

e-journals and to journal articles in many of the databases that Monash staff and students have access to.

BACKGROUND TO STRATEGIC ACTIONS PURSUED

In 2010, an E- Resources Taskforce was established and in November 2010 a report entitled "Report of the Monash University Sunway Campus (MUSC) Taskforce on: Contemporary Collection Development Policy and Procedure at MUSC for E-Book Resources "was presented. The Taskforce comprised 8 members and their purpose was to provide advice to the MUSC President and Chief Executive on how the Library and Learning Commons (LLC) at MUSC may develop a contemporary collection development policy and procedure for E-resource. The E-resource Taskforce Report noted the expanding use of E-resource in higher education which had implications for the whole system i.e. the people, processes and practices. With regards to the people, the whole community, i.e. students, teaching staff, library staff and researchers are affected by the shift and expansion to electronic resources. In relation to processes, accessing and utilizing knowledge in the context of teaching and learning will also change and as for practices, training students and staff in the use of new features, gadgets or innovations, policies of the LLC and IT Services Department and the University at large will also see changes. The report noted literature purporting the great potential for e-resource (e.g. Rowlands et al, 2007) and its advantages in terms of accessibility, enhanced searchability, cost savings particularly on multiple copies, up-to-date or current data and increased visual appeal provided by still and moving graphics, video clips and interactivity. Given the competitive environment on the Sunway Campus and leveraging on the strength of e-resource provided through MUA, the push to transition from print to e-books was seen as advantageous, cost effective over time and allowed for optimal access in the future as recommended in the Report.

E-Books Acquisition Policy

One of the recommendations of the Taskforce was for the acquisitions of e-books and the promotion of e-resource to be given priority at the Sunway Campus. In relation to this recommendation, the paradigm shift of acquisitions from print to e-books and e-resource was implemented through a Library Book Acquisitions Charter as suggested by the President and Pro-Vice Chancellor for Sunway Campus. The experience of the Information Resources Section that undertook to implement the acquisitions of e-books and e-resource to progress the recommendations of the Taskforce will be shared as well as outcomes and the learning experiences.

Implementation of *Search* Service, the Web Resource Discovery Service

The other strategic action undertaken was the implementation of *Search Service,* the resource Discovery Service that promotes e-resource in an unassuming manner. This action and implementation was undertaken in September 2011 for Sunway campus and continued into early 2012 as part of the Section's annual development plan, in collaboration with colleagues at Monash University Library Australia.

Both these actions have provided new opportunities for engagement and learning, particularly during the time of the implementation of the project plan and has led to both job enrichment and increased efficiencies.

PROGRESSING E-RESOURCE MANAGEMENT THROUGH STRATEGIC ACTIONS

Implementation of the Library Book Acquisitions Charter and Initiatives Undertaken

As explained earlier in 2010, an E-resource Taskforce was established in Sunway campus and one of the recommendations of the Taskforce report was for the acquisitions and promotion of e-books and e-resources. To action the Taskforce recommendation to implement e-book acquisitions, the Information Resources team needed to address a number of issues that required actively engaging and demonstrating qualities of leadership, communication, teamwork and an open and willing spirit to learn and make changes. This was carried through by implementing specific action plans laid out in the Annual Development Plan of 2011. This commitment was reflected by setting a target for the Information Resources Section (IRS) in its 2011 ADP, which was the successful implementation of the Library Book Acquisition Charter.

Hence as one of the recommendations put forward by the e-resource Taskforce, namely the acquisitions of e-books and e-resource to be given priority, it was actioned by the Library and reflected through a Charter that reads,

This library acquires books based on demonstrated need. We undertake to get any book needed for your academic studies or research. If we don't have it, and you can show us an online seller that has it in stock, we undertake to order it within one week and expedite delivery.

Simply fill out the Staff Request Form for Library Materials or Student Request Form for Library Books and we will notify you as soon as it arrives.

Figure 1. The library book acquisition charter

Library Book Acquisition Charter

This library acquires books based on demonstrated need. We undertake to get any book needed for your academic studies or research. If we don't have it, and you can show us an online seller that has it in stock, we undertake to order it within one week and expedite delivery.

Simply fill out the request form available from our website or at the One-Stop Information Centre, and we will notify you as soon as the book arrives.

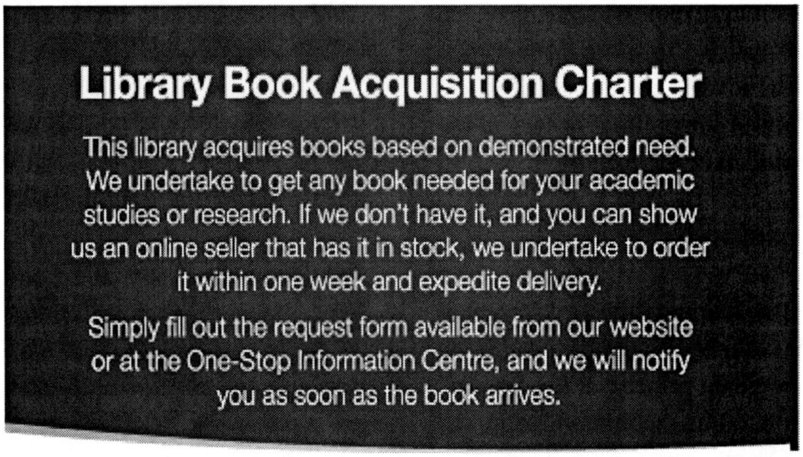

The implementation of the Library Book Acquisition Charter was effected on 24th December 2010, whereby e-books were given priority over print formats and orders placed within a week or 7 working days. The challenges that the Information Resources (IRS) team faced, particularly the Acquisitions team, in transitioning this change included the following:

- Shifting acquisitions based on a 'collection building' mode to purchasing based on "demonstrated need"
- Shifting priority toward e-books and engaging with Monash Library Australia on e-book orders and licenses
- Processing orders within 7 days and engaging with the Purchasing Department, Finance and vendors
- Communicating and engaging across teams at LLC, with vendors, with counterparts in MUA and patrons as work processes changed, and,
- Monitoring the Charter and providing feedback to Management

INITIATIVES UNDERTAKEN TO AFFECT THE LIBRARY CHARTER

Revising the Request Form

In early January 2011, with the Charter announced and placed on the website as well as displayed on stands and plaques on all levels of the library, the old request forms had to be revised with regards to details and differentiated for staff and students. Furthermore, the old form was in a PDF format on the website which was considered to be not user friendly. This was because users had to print out the forms and fill it in and submit it to the Library for order processing.

To address this issue of revising and converting the form to be more interactive, the IRS team engaged with staff from the IT Department to explore alternative software. A new fillable PDF software called Adobe Acrobat Xpro10 was found after investigations and discussions. This was then purchased and used to create fillable PDF forms. With this new form, staff and students could type in details, save and email the form to the acquisitions team. This has provided for better student and staff experience and the team has also received positive feedback for these efforts. (See Figure 2)

Figure 2. The old request form (Till 23 Dec 2010)

REQUISITION FOR BOOKS & AUDIO VISUAL MATERIALS

REQUEST NO.:

NOTES

1. Please check the online catalogue (http://voyager.monash.edu.my) before submitting a request. Your item may be held or on order in the library system.
2. Prescribed and Recommended Texts will be purchased according to the library formula 1 copy for every 15 students with a maximum of 12 copies.
3. Email notifications on arrival of requested items will be sent only for request of teaching copies, research and urgent materials.
4. Kindly submit completed forms to Acquisitions Librarian, Library & Learning Commons.

STAFF/STUDENTS

Request Type *(select one)*	☑ Normal request ☐ Urgent request		
Name	Dr Ngim Chin Fang	School / Dept.	\
Email	ngim.chin.fang@med.monash.edu.my	Ext / Mobile No.	07-2170624
Category *(select one)*	☑ Academic staff ☐ Admin. staff ☐ Postgraduate students ☐ Honours students ☐ Undergraduate students		

REQUEST DETAILS

Item Details & Purpose	Copies and Location
Title: Chicken soup for the soul. Campus Chronicles 101 inspirational, supportive and Humorous stories about life in college. Author: Jack Canfield, mark Victor Hansen Publisher: Chicken soup for the soul ISBN: 9781935096344 Year: 2009 Edition: 1 Purpose *(select one)*: ☐ Prescribed Text ^ ☑ Recommended Text ^ ☐ Research ☐ Collection Building ^ *If course related reading, please complete the following:* Unit code: med 3051/3062; No. of student: 90	Open Shelf: 1; Reserve * (4 hours / 7 days): ; Teaching copy: * Expiry date in Reserve: ** Name of lecturer(s) requesting teaching copy: 1. 2. 3. 4.
Title: Chicken Soup for the Soul: The cancer Book: 101 Stories of courage, support and love Author: Jack Canfield, mark Victor Hansen Publisher: Chicken soup for the soul ISBN: 9781935096306 Year: 2009 Edition: 1 Purpose *(select one)*: ☐ Prescribed Text ^ ☑ Recommended Text ^ ☐ Research ☐ Collection Building ^ *If course related reading, please complete the following:* Unit code: med 3051/3062; No. of student: 90	Open Shelf: 1; Reserve * (4 hours / 7 days): ; Teaching copy: * Expiry date in Reserve: ** Name of lecturer(s) requesting teaching copy: 1. 2. 3. 4.

Figure 3. 1ˢᵗ revision (24 Dec 2010)

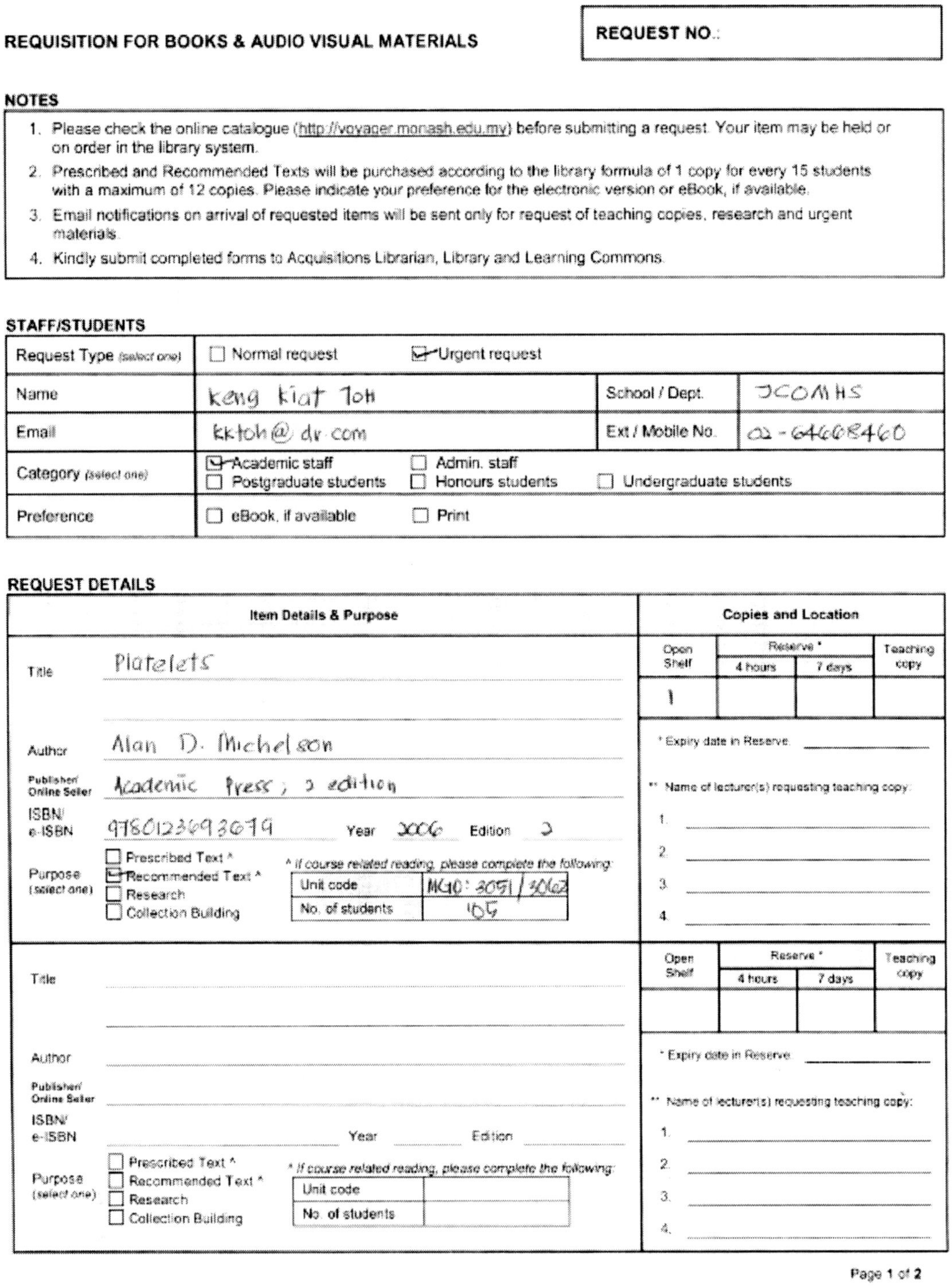

REQUISITION FOR BOOKS & AUDIO VISUAL MATERIALS

REQUEST NO.:

NOTES

1. Please check the online catalogue (http://voyager.monash.edu.my) before submitting a request. Your item may be held or on order in the library system.
2. Prescribed and Recommended Texts will be purchased according to the library formula of 1 copy for every 15 students with a maximum of 12 copies. Please indicate your preference for the electronic version or eBook, if available.
3. Email notifications on arrival of requested items will be sent only for request of teaching copies, research and urgent materials.
4. Kindly submit completed forms to Acquisitions Librarian, Library and Learning Commons.

STAFF/STUDENTS

Request Type *(select one)*	☐ Normal request ☑ Urgent request		
Name	keng kiat Toh	School / Dept.	JCOMHS
Email	kktoh@ dr.com	Ext / Mobile No.	03 - 64608460
Category *(select one)*	☑ Academic staff ☐ Admin. staff ☐ Postgraduate students ☐ Honours students ☐ Undergraduate students		
Preference	☐ eBook, if available ☐ Print		

REQUEST DETAILS

Item Details & Purpose		Copies and Location			
		Open Shelf	Reserve * 4 hours / 7 days		Teaching copy
Title	Platelets	1			
Author	Alan D. Michelson	* Expiry date in Reserve: _____			
Publisher/ Online Seller	Academic Press, 2 edition	** Name of lecturer(s) requesting teaching copy:			
ISBN/ e-ISBN	9780123693679 Year 2006 Edition 2	1. _____			
Purpose *(select one)*	☐ Prescribed Text ^ ☑ Recommended Text ^ ☐ Research ☐ Collection Building	^ If course related reading, please complete the following: Unit code MG10: 3051 / 3062 No. of students 105	2. _____ 3. _____ 4. _____		
Title		Open Shelf	Reserve * 4 hours / 7 days		Teaching copy
Author		* Expiry date in Reserve: _____			
Publisher/ Online Seller		** Name of lecturer(s) requesting teaching copy:			
ISBN/ e-ISBN	Year Edition	1. _____			
Purpose *(select one)*	☐ Prescribed Text ^ ☐ Recommended Text ^ ☐ Research ☐ Collection Building	^ If course related reading, please complete the following: Unit code No. of students	2. _____ 3. _____ 4. _____		

Page 1 of 2

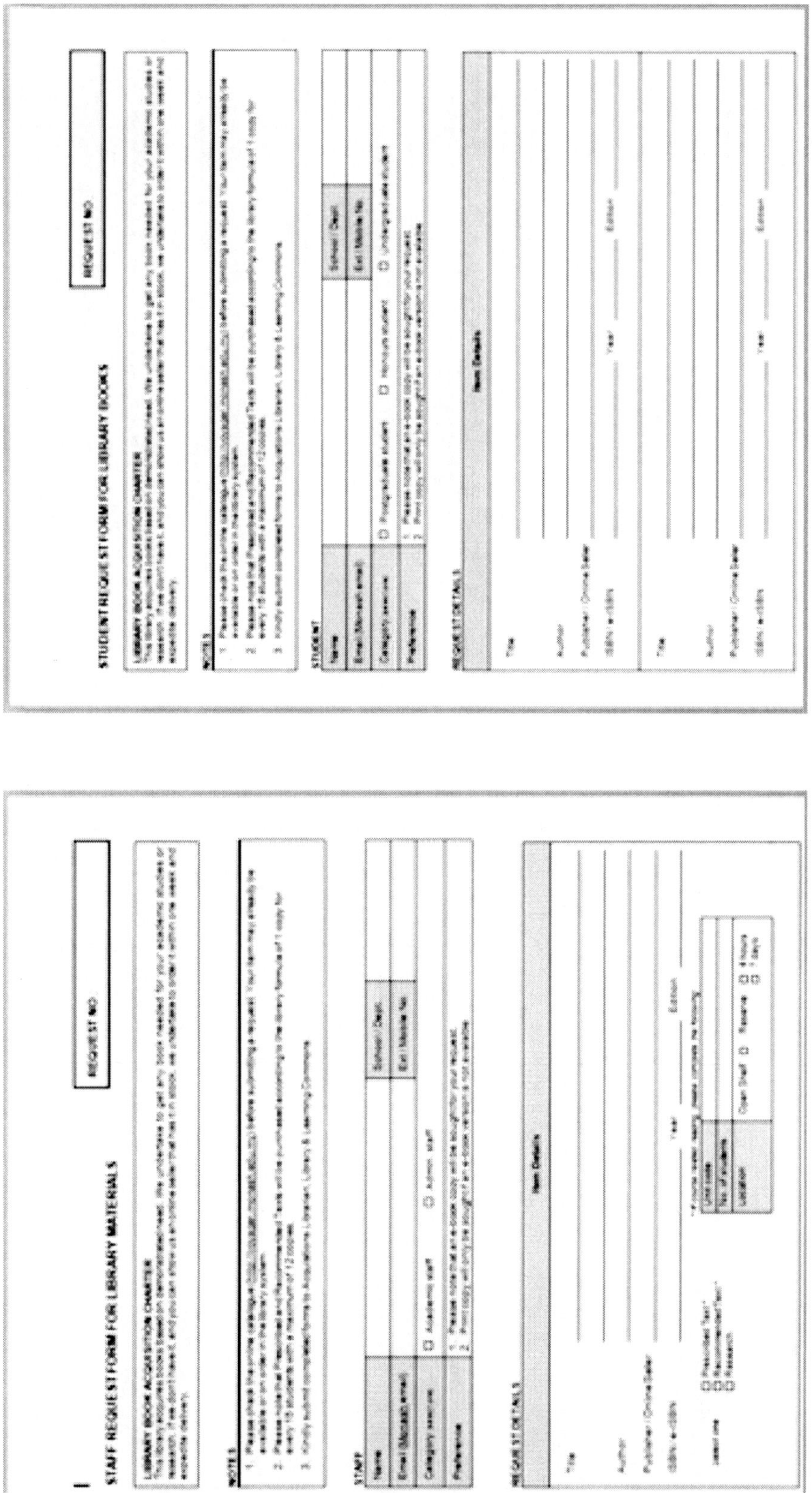

Figure 4. 2nd revision (24 February 2011)

Figure 5. form Currently Used (19 May 2011)

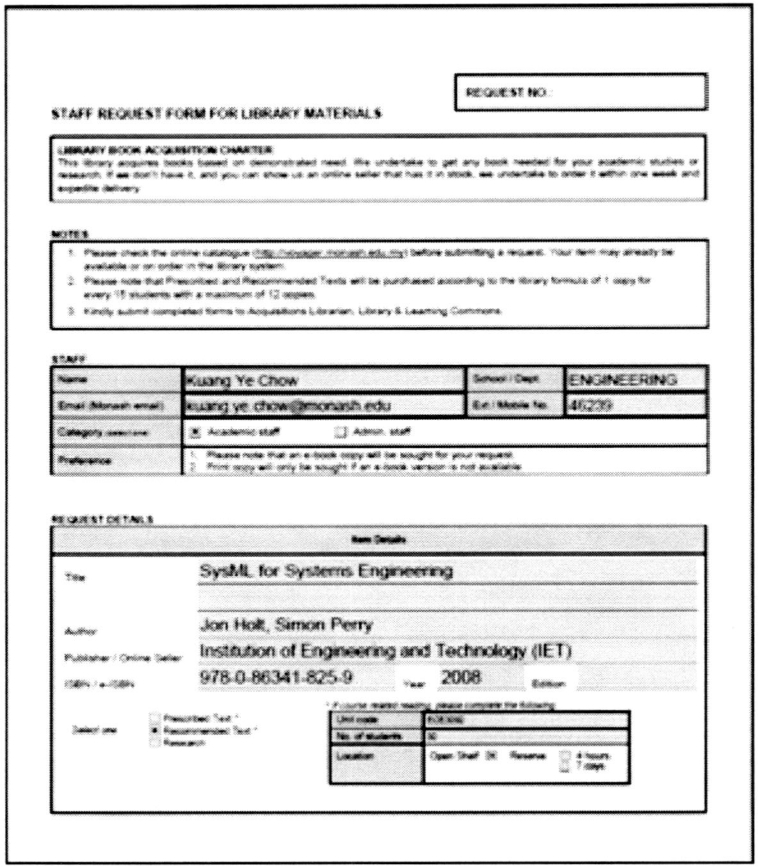
STAFF REQUEST FORM FOR LIBRARY MATERIALS

REQUEST NO.:

LIBRARY BOOK ACQUISITION CHARTER

NOTES

STAFF

Name	Kuang Ye Chow	School / Dept	ENGINEERING
Email (Monash email)	kuang.ye.chow@monash.edu	Ext / Mobile No.	46239

REQUEST DETAILS

Item Details

Title: SysML for Systems Engineering

Author: Jon Holt, Simon Perry

Publisher / Online Seller: Institution of Engineering and Technology (IET)

ISBN / e-ISBN: 978-0-86341-825-9 Year: 2008 Edition:

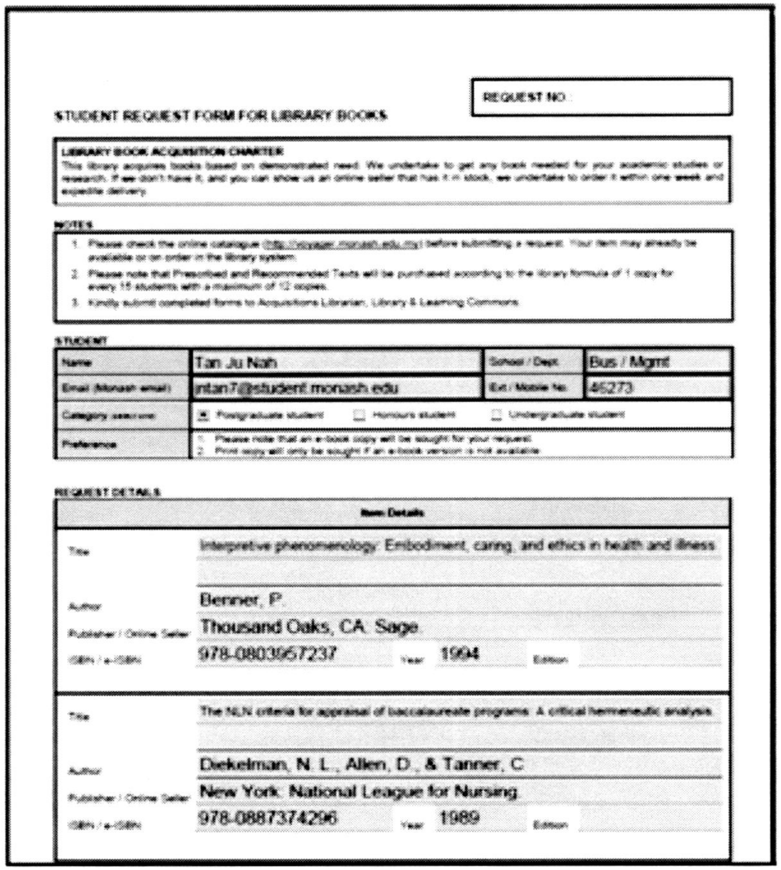
STUDENT REQUEST FORM FOR LIBRARY BOOKS

REQUEST NO.:

LIBRARY BOOK ACQUISITION CHARTER

NOTES

STUDENT

Name	Tan Ju Nah	School / Dept	Bus / Mgmt
Email (Monash email)	jntan7@student.monash.edu	Ext / Mobile No.	46273

REQUEST DETAILS

Item Details

Title: Interpretive phenomenology: Embodiment, caring, and ethics in health and illness

Author: Benner, P.

Publisher / Online Seller: Thousand Oaks, CA: Sage

ISBN / e-ISBN: 978-0803957237 Year: 1994 Edition:

Title: The NLN criteria for appraisal of baccalaureate programs: A critical hermeneutic analysis

Author: Diekelman, N. L., Allen, D., & Tanner, C.

Publisher / Online Seller: New York: National League for Nursing

ISBN / e-ISBN: 978-0887374296 Year: 1989 Edition:

Communicating the Charter to Patrons

Communicating the Charter to patrons had its related challenges. Initially, although old forms were cleared and replaced with the new, it was found requesters were submitting old forms from copies they held in stock or in softcopy. Thus this provided the team the opportunity to inform patrons about the Charter and to use the new form. In general despite the recommendation of the Taskforce, it was found that print requests were generally preferred. Hence although the Charter gave priority to the e-book, many requesters indicated their preference for the print format. This was also seen in the statistics of print requests received. The School of Arts and Social Sciences for instance informed the library that they were unanimously opposed to the Charter through their academic representative at the Library Committee. Reactions such as this was taken in stride and was not considered a setback as discussions with academics, MUA counterparts as well as general reading of the literature led us to understand and accept that not all users and disciplines are inclined towards electronic resources. It was noted that the Sciences, Medicine and Technology were inclined to electronic resources in comparison to the Arts and for the Arts and Social Sciences, which are still stronger in their print publications. Nonetheless, overtime the team continued to implement and monitor the Charter while taking into consideration the need for flexibility in approach and for parallel purchasing where justifiable.

Restructuring the Acquisitions Workflow

One of the first issues faced by the team was that of restructuring the acquisitions workflow. With the Charter, the workflow was revised to give priority to e-books meaning requests had to be checked to determine if an e-book was available in the market, sourced and orders placed in 7 days with vendors who could provide the requested title. This gave rise to another challenge with regards to e-book acquisitions and licenses, which is explained in the section below on engaging with counterparts. As acquisitions staff could not continue using the previous work procedures, the team needed to rethink the ordering process and a new workflow was drawn up to help track procedures and put into practice. The new workflow took into account giving priority to check for the e-book, sourcing directly from approved vendors and set a 3 day timeline to obtain quotations for the requested item. The new workflow is in Figure 6.

Engaging with Purchasing Department, Finance and Vendors

Another challenge faced was in obtaining quotations. We found that we were not able to place orders in 7 days. Reasons identified for this were (i) a reduction in staff numbers as the team was reduced from 4 to 3 members due to a staff resignation and recruiting staff pitched at higher skill levels is an on going struggle, (ii) receiving long lists of requests for 300 or more titles which were beyond the working capacity of the team to achieve the Charter and (iii) the time taken in receiving quotations from vendors.

To address this issue of quotations, as we were still bound by company purchasing practices for print acquisitions, cooperation and collaboration was sought by meeting and discussing with counterparts at the Purchasing Department. As a result of a meeting on 7th April 2011, where the expectations of the Charter was explained and our new workflow shared giving priority to the e-book, it was agreed that titles requested may be sent for quotations either directly to approved or preferred vendors or to the Purchasing Department. This was to expedite the process and purchase orders would be placed based on prompt quotations received. A timeline of 3 working days for receiving quotations was agreed from the supplier sourced either directly or through the Purchasing

Figure 6. Restructuring the ordering workflow

Proposed Acquisitions Flowchart for Request and Ordering with Book Charter in View

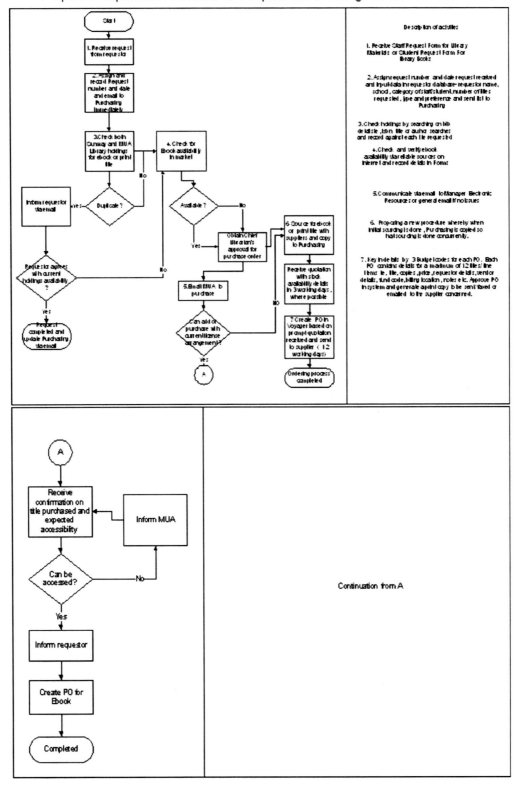

Department to facilitate and ensure the objectives of the Charter are achieved. With this cooperation and successful engagement, more requests were placed as direct orders.

Engaging with Counterparts at Monash University Library Australia on E-Book Orders and Licenses

Email discussions and engagement with our MUA counterparts were pursued for e-book orders. For e-book orders we had to consider the costs of e-books and more importantly, the considerable costs of platforms and licenses. Furthermore, in view of existing license arrangements with MUA that include LLC, Sunway, we explored this option first as there was no good financial reason to be paying for duplicate licenses for the common vendors for e-books and e-resources. With communication and engagement between the e-book vendor and colleagues at MUA Library, an account for Sunway's e-book selections in the vendor's database and procedures were set up and put in place. We began making selections against the agreed e-book vendor account that was set up for Malaysia. By the end of 2011, we had some 80 e-book titles that were requested and selected in GOBI, in collaboration with MUA. These e-book orders were used as a test case for MUA to investigate and provide an overview of costing and resources for our collaboration. In June 2011, a discussion paper was prepared by Monash University Library Australia on the acquisition of electronic resources. It was agreed that for e-book orders, in view of existing licenses, collaborating with MUA for the purchase of electronic resources was our preferred option under a OneMonash model. It was also agreed that for print purchases, the local vendors were generally better able to facilitate print orders. Furthermore it was also agreed that given the scenario for electronic resources purchasing, it was more viable for Sunway

campus to consider the title-by-title selection for e-books as MUA Library had existing purchases by collections as this was the more competitive option for e-resource. .

Engaging with Ex Libris (Vendor Customer Support) to Effect Email Notifications to Requestors for New Titles Purchased as per Charter

Another challenge that came with the Charter was to notify requesters as soon as the item was available. The practice at that time was for new titles requested and received, emails via Microsoft Office were sent out by the Lending team, using a template, to the respective staff or student email. This task was shifted to Information Resources Section due to a shortage of casual staff at Lending sometime in March 2011. This posed an added task to the Information Resources team that was also reduced in numbers and challenged to meet the objectives of the Charter. Circumstances necessitated exploring more efficient and innovative systems. For this, engagement with an ExLibris trainer was sought to automate the notifications. With the vendor's advice, the Library Systems Officer created and tested a new policy called AcqHold. This is currently now used to automatically generate notifications of new titles purchased to requestors.

Monitoring and Providing Feedback to Management

Given these challenges, the team monitored orders as per the Charter and provided feedback to top Management on a monthly basis. From the tracking and monitoring, it was noted and reported that 32% were ordered in 7 days at 15 May 2011. It was also noted that a majority of requests were for the print format. This in turn was reported at the campus level meetings, that is the Library and

Learning Commons Committee meeting and the Library Reference Group meeting, and one of the outcomes of this has been to recognize the need for both e- resources and print resources and to acquire the format that is wanted or required.

IMPLEMENTATION OF *SEARCH* SERVICE, A WEB RESOURCE DISCOVERY SERVICE

Background, Implementation and Completion

The project to implement *Search* at Sunway began as an initiative in 2011 and was carried through into the 2012 Annual Development Plan. The implementation of *Search* at Monash University Australia was initiated in 2010 with careful and detailed project planning and management by the Primo/Search Steering Committee (PSC) established at Monash University Library Australia.

In 2011, the Sunway Search Working Group began participating via videoconference in the Primo/Search Steering Committee. After the launch and roll out of *Search* in Australia in February 2011, the Primo/Search Steering Committee moved to commit time and resources for the implementation of Search at its overseas campuses. For Monash University Sunway Campus (MUSC), the participation in the Primo/Search Steering Committee began in 2011 via videoconference meetings between the Sunway library staff who were co-opted into the Primo/Search Steering Committee established at Monash Australia.

In September 2011, details of the Sunway *Search* implementation project were discussed and planned including configuring, harvesting and testing of Sunway library records, testing the staging site for Sunway using harvested records and testing of user accounts on a staging site. Based on guidelines from colleagues at MUA, a communication plan for the implementation of *Search* for Sunway's timelines was prepared. This

was followed through with conducting a *Search* demo on the staging site to library staff and *Search* Reps to familiarize key Sunway library staff. In line with the project plans, the results in the staging site were confirmed which led to affirmation for colleagues in MUA to run *Search* in the production site in early January 2012. Following this, and keeping to project plans, a library staff training session was carried out and finally, on 30th January 2012, *Search* was successfully launched and went live at Sunway campus and the Clinical School Johor Bahru. Notices were posted for new and returning students and staff through the library website and through the campus broadcast system. The project was noted as completed in the Primo/Search Steering Committee meeting held in MUA on 7th February 2012.

Going forward with a OneMonash model in resource discovery and user experience, the management of key stages of the project were carried through and all Sunway library records and user accounts were harvested and went live on the production site on 19th January. On 30th January 2012, *Search* was successfully launched and went live at Sunway campus and the Clinical School Johor Bahru whereby all of Monash University Malaysia's library catalogue and holdings records were loaded to *Search* and the new url replaced the links to the old library catalogue. With the implementation of *Search* service, improved access to information resources for both local content and hosted content, i.e. resources within the library catalog and beyond has been achieved and librarians at Client Services continue to conduct training and user support.

With *Search*, a web scale discovery service has been implemented and staff and students can now use *Search*, a single point of access to the library's catalogue, to e-books and e-journals and to journal articles in many of the databases that Monash staff and students have access to. *Search* is also designed to be intuitive and simplifies searching with added features such as facet searching, e- shelf and more. As noted by Bunkell, (2009), it is important to put e-books on a highly accessible and familiar research platform as access is optimized by putting books online. In this sense, the implementation of *Search* at Sunway Campus has also optimized access and discoverability of resources and allows for a richer and dynamic research experience.

OUTCOMES OF ACTIONS UNDERTAKEN AND PROGRESS

In general the outcomes from the implementation of the Library Book Acquisitions Charter and the implementation of *Search* within a relatively short span of time, has meant that the team has had to cope with various issues at various levels which required taking responsibility, working with and across teams, exploring new and innovative systems and managing and transitioning the change; in short riding the waves of change and transitioning change positively.

In terms of achieving the Charter objectives, at 8th July 2011, 45% of orders were placed in 7 days. To date at end November 2012, the team is happy to report some 82% of orders are placed within 7 working days. As for shifting acquisitions towards e-books, collaboration and engagement with colleagues at MUA has brought about significant progress to set up and align processes using GOBI, the online ordering system of a common vendor for our libraries. At end 2011, the year the Charter was implemented, 276 e-titles were ordered and to date at end 2012, we note an increase for e-book orders to 318 e-titles. The e-preferred policy has made in roads at the Monash University Sunway campus particularly among postgraduates in the disciplines of science, technology and medicine.

The outcomes for these actions may be summarized as:

- Contributing to a shared vision where e-resource is the future realm and raising awareness to purchasing practices and benchmarks and using e- resources among academics and students at MUSC.
- Developing new skill sets of the team members and improving group dynamics as they demonstrated leadership, communication, collaboration on difficult and divisive issues and engaging for better results.
- Campus level committees acknowledged results reported and in turn recognized the need to make adjustments to the Charter as it has been noted at top campus level committees that it is a time of change and at this stage of development, it was advisable to maintain print purchasing while pursuing electronic book purchasing in parallel.
- Actively engaging with MUA and collaborating for better methods of acquiring e-resource, particularly building upon vendor relationship through service level agreements rather than continuing the Request For Tender (RFT) practices and in the process gaining efficiencies for electronic and print materials acquisitions as evidenced by integration of operating processes between the vendor and the library, better services, increased efficiencies and cost effectivenes.
- Team members have learnt much personally and professionally through this experience in that they have upgraded their skills and understanding of e-resource, from the technicalities of acquisitions processes and practices, platforms and licensing issues to interacting and communicating across teams locally and internationally, staff involvement and participation in Committees in MUA and working together in a multicultural environment. This has strengthened ties between the Monash libraries in

Australia and Malaysia and led to better collegiallity in general.

- The implementation of *Search* has also transformed the visibility and access of electronic resources for Monash libraries as users are now able to use this discovery tool and filter by the facets available, save on their e-shelf and more

- With *Search,* patron driven acquisitions has also become more significant as arrangements with vendors for EBL records by MUA are loaded into the system and integrated for seamless acquisitions based on actual use.

- Facilitating access to e-resource by providing loans of mobile computing devices namely laptops and tablets and enabling supportive wireless access and web printing has contributed to progressing e-resource at Sunway campus.

- Working collaboratively with the IT Services team, Purchasing and Finance teams to effect changes positively and cater for enchanced student / client experience.

CONCLUSION

Progressing e-resource in the Library and Learning Commons, Monash University Sunway Campus has been one lead by Campus directions and the persona of top management played a vital role in moving e-resource forward. E-resource has found a new niche with regards to diversified practices for print and electronic acquisitions practices and accessing e-resource. This is definitely a new feature in resources and collection development and is now noted as having a shared budget and cost implications. These actions undertaken progressed successfully because of the strategic support, infrastructure and teamwork amongst the teams concerned and between the Australian and Monash campuses. Our commitment towards adapting to new technology and trends to meet user's needs provides the drive for us to continue progressive trends in e-resource.

ACKNOWLEDGMENT

Special acknowledgements and thanks to the Head of Library and Learning Commons & Chief Librarian, Sunway Campus, Ms. Rohani Zainal Abidin, the Information Resources Section team (Hariyani, Noraini, Sofia, Kevin, Belinda, Azrul and Irma) and colleagues at LLC, who rose to the challenge and provided support, dedication, encouragement and commitment in their various roles and operations undertaken. Much thanks also to the Monash University Library Australia colleagues and partners namely Monash University Librarian, Ms. Cathrine Harboe-Ree and her team of librarians and colleagues at MUA for their guidance, expertise and continuous support.

REFERENCES

Bunkell, J., & Dyas-Correia, S. (2009). E-books vs. print: Which is the better value? *The Serials Librarian*, *56*(1-4), 215–219. doi:10.1080/03615260802698283.

E-Resource Taskforce Report. (2010). *Report of the Monash University Sunway Campus (MUSC) taskforce on contemporary collection development policy and procedure at musc for e-book resources.* (Unpublished / Restricted report).

JISC. (2009). *Libraries of the future*. Retrieved October 18, 2012, from http://www.jisc.ac.uk/publications/generalpublications/2009/librariesofthefuturebrochure.aspx

Renner, R. (2009). *E-books – Costs and benefits to academic and research libraries*. Retrieved October 18, 2010, from www.springer.com.cda/… /e-book+white+Paper.pdf

Shepperd, J., Grace, J., & Koch, E. (2008). Evaluating the electronic textbook: is it time to dispense with the paper text? *Teaching of Psychology, 35,* 2–5. doi:10.1080/00986280701818532.

Springer. (2009). *E-books – The end user perspective.* Retrieved October 21, 2012, from www.springer.com/.../e-books

University Leadership Council. (2011). *Redefining the academic library: managing the migration to digital information services.* Retrieved August 24, 2012, from http://www.educationadvisoryboard.com/pdf/23634-EAB-Redefining-the-Academic-Library.pdf

Yin, R. (2003). *Case study research: design and methods.* Thousand Oaks, CA: Sage Publications.

ADDITIONAL READING

Ruddock, B. (2012). *The new professional's toolkit.* London: Facet Publishing..

ENDNOTES

[1]   In October 2013, Monash University Sunway Campus was renamed Monash University Malaysia.

Chapter 11
Embracing Change:
How South Ayrshire Council Library Service Became a World Leader in Electronic Resources Management

Jean Inness
South Ayrshire Council, UK

ABSTRACT

This chapter outlines the successful management style that has proactively facilitated innovative changes to a range of library services. The changes discussed are those facing all contemporary libraries. Starting with an overview of service provision, staffing, the management team, and management style, it considers the factors required for the effective implementation of innovation in a range of services. The topics covered include creating a library "blog," the benefits of a library bookshop, e-book lending, e-book publishing, creating a library mobile app, and e-magazine lending. The aim of this chapter is to argue that fellow librarians can embrace change and facilitate innovation in ways that are efficient, cost-effective, and cutting-edge, whilst reinforcing the importance of libraries at the centre of our society.

BACKGROUND

South Ayrshire, a community in South West Scotland, has a population of 112,097 (UK 2001 census). It is one of thirty-two Scottish Local Authorities.

The area includes the towns of- Ayr, Prestwick, Troon, Maybole and Girvan. This largely rural area of 422 square miles (1,222 square km) extends from Troon and Symington in the North,

to Ballantrae and Loch Ryan in the South. From Burns Cottage to Culzean Castle, South Ayrshire has a rich history and culture. Scotland's National Bard, Robert Burns, was born in Alloway, on the outskirts of Ayr, in 1759. Burns cottage is the centrepiece of the Burns National Heritage Park that includes the Burns Monument, Brig O'Doon and Alloway Kirk, where Tam O'Shanter spied on witches and warlocks in the world-famous poem. South Ayrshire is also noted for its fine

DOI: 10.4018/978-1-4666-4761-9.ch011

golf courses, including the world-class Turnberry Ailsa course and Royal Troon– both of which have hosted the British Open on a number of occasions.

South Ayrshire Council (SAC) was established in 1996, when Scotland moved from the administrative model of district and regional administrative units, to a unitary authority structure.

The population of South Ayrshire is served by fourteen branch libraries and one mobile library. The largest branch is the Carnegie Library, which has thirty staff and is home to the Local History Library and a large "Cybercentre". There are six medium-sized "branch" libraries operating with more than one member of staff and six single-manned libraries which have part-time public access.

THE SERVICE

In most respects South Ayrshire's library service is similar to other Local Authority-run library services: we face the same challenges to deliver an attractive service within severe budget constraints. Staffing numbers and book-fund resources have both been reduced significantly in the recent past and these factors have forced a major rethink about how we can work "smarter" and optimise our use of resources.

There is a Management Team of seven staff- a Senior Library Manager and six specialist librarians. Each professional member of staff has a different area of expertise and carries out a diverse range of duties. The post descriptions are: Carnegie Librarian, Local Studies Librarian, Life-Long Learning Librarian, Acquisitions Librarian and Children's Services Librarian.

Although these are traditional job titles, the reality of the work carried out currently by post-holders bears little resemblance to that of similar "roles" in the past. Each post has a discreet objective, but, in fact, the area of overlap required

to meet overall objectives has been increasing exponentially. More than ever before, a librarian has to be a "master-of-all-trades" to deliver a specialist service.

The Library Service has always embraced innovation and change- with the aim of delivering the highest quality service. The Senior library staff are committed to shaping future developments. Effective leadership of a productive professional library team propels the Service forward. We are acutely aware that the future of our Service lies in our hands and that we must be radical in our approach, if we are to survive.

The use of social media, and other on-line resources, by professional staff, is mandatory. Staff awareness of current trends in all aspects of librarianship and information dissemination is expected. These resources also provide an invaluable source of staff development. The team of South Ayrshire Libraries is encouraged to take an entrepreneurial and enterprising approach to service delivery.

Staff meetings are a valuable management tool. Effective meetings are vital, if innovation is to take place effectively. Professional staff meetings are held every three weeks. Time is reserved for brainstorming, discussing current developments, articles read on Linkedin or Twitter, and prioritising future developments. This meeting provides a forum for professional staff to gain insights into what colleagues are doing, rather than merely noting items "for information". The staff are encouraged to "pitch-in" ideas that would enhance the Service or project. Staff morale within the team is high and what might otherwise be seen as a chore is turned into *fun*.

As previously stated, meetings are held every three weeks. Furthermore, monthly meetings are held with the staff in charge of branch libraries. In addition, the Carnegie Librarian holds a weekly staff meeting for our largest staff group. Like librarians the world over, we talk a lot! This model has served us well over the past six years, with many ideas and issues communicated from branch level, as well as being proposed at management level.

An example of a valuable contribution, from branch level, is a project designed to combat the growing problem of IT literacy amongst employment-age people. This illiteracy came to light at a local level, when the majority of Scottish employers, Councils included, moved to on-line job application procedures. Together with our colleagues in Adult Literacy, South Ayrshire Libraries submitted a successful bid for funds to provide a tutor who would support job applicants, at four of our libraries.

INNOVATION

This approach to staff involvement provided a forum and framework for discussion during all our major Library Service projects. In 2008 the Library Service tendered for a replacement Library Management system (LMS). Innovative Interfaces was appointed to supply their Millennium platform.

This decision was momentous for two reasons. The project management that was required was of a high level, and the IT and on-line potential that the new system offered us was inspiring. The purchase of the new system provided the software tool to allow facilitating innovation effectively. This was combined with an approach which ensured that four major projects were implemented effectively. The projects were- an e-book lending service, e-book publishing a library app and an e-magazine service.

With the additional remit of redesigning, adapting and future- proofing all of our service points, the new LMS project soon involved seven private companies- all of which had to be co-ordinated to deliver their work, site by site. With twelve sites to be converted in a progressive manner, and staff being trained at the same time, this became one of the most ambitious projects that the current library staff had undertaken. The project was successfully completed within the nine months specified and incurred only a small overspend. This overspend was due to the "unknowns" that can lurk beneath the facades of differently-aged buildings.

The successful completion of this challenging project provided an enormous confidence boost to all the library staff. The timescales and budgets had been very tight but everything worked out better than expected. More importantly, staff and users could see the benefits of both the new library environment and the new LMS. Our quiet, no-nonsense- just–get-on-with-it attitude had also impressed other Council colleagues.

From that point onwards, our plans for future Service developments were looked on favourably and with respect. One of the most important issues for all libraries is that they are often not in control of their IT destinies. However, by consulting with the Council IT Department from the outset, we impressed them with our knowledge and business-like manner. Consequently, the Council IT department has now delegated back to us the responsibility for our future IT provision. This does not happen in many cases. The demonstration of a sound knowledge of IT and a mature attitude towards IT use, paid huge dividends.

So, by 2009, we had faith in ourselves when it came to implementing change. What would be next? This is where the potential of the new LMS began to reveal itself!

LIBRARY BLOG

The positive "can-do" attitude of library staff paid dividends. Rather than being seen as fairly mundane task, customising the Millennium platform was grasped as a wonderful opportunity. We wanted our library website pages to look appealing, attractive and funky. We seconded a member of our Cybercentre staff to work full-time on getting the "look and feel" of our website and user-experience just right. Our Library Blog was launched in 2010 and this began our love affair with the digital age.

The uptake of the Library "Blog" - 250,000 hits a year and rising - was encouraging. Our interest in national projects was growing and we took part in the National Library of Scotland's initiative to digitise the Nation's Street Directories, in 2010.

Furthermore, in 2009, South Ayrshire Libraries were invited to be a member of a Knowledge Transfer Group. This Glasgow University / Kings College London / Edinburgh University-led project intended to digitise all of the Scottish medieval Charters and to make them freely accessible to the general public. (This database is called POMS (People of Medieval Scotland) and has now been successfully launched). Additional new funding should extend the digitisation of Charters from later centuries. Furthermore, this was formal acknowledgement that libraries, in particular public libraries, were key to information dissemination and essential to academia when reaching out for publicity, usage and uptake.

BOOKSHOP

We also gained a unique insight into the publishing and book trade in Britain via the creation of the South Ayrshire Book Shop. When the previous Kyle and Carrick Library Service became South Ayrshire Libraries in 1996 there was an increased emphasis on library income-generation. An Enterprise Officer post was created and, in 1997, South Ayrshire Book Shop was established.

South Ayrshire Bookshop has a showroom and is a book retailer, book wholesaler and book publisher. It deals directly with the publishing industry and has been the main supplier of textbooks to South Ayrshire schools since 1998. The Book Shop deals directly with all the major publishers (the big six) and with large distributors such as Gardners and Bertrams. There are regular visits from publisher's representatives and, on occasion, authors.

In 2010, after an analysis of budget and staffing costs, the Book Shop became South Ayrshire Libraries preferred library supplier. As far as we know, we are the only library service that operates this purchasing model.

News from our Book Shop arm chimed with the professional press and it became clear to us that publishing, book retailing and book wholesaling were not standing still. The publishing industry and its book supply mechanisms provide us with our raw materials, Libraries could not wait and watch the changes from afar. We needed to be part of the solution to ensure the future supply of information.

E-BOOK LENDING

In November 2009, South Ayrshire Libraries launched an eRead service. In July 2010 SAC became the first Scottish Local Authority to offer an e-book lending service to its users.

Our staff meetings and interest in librarianship made clear to us that changes were afoot in several areas. There was much talk of digitisation and the phenomena of e-books. There was a lot of confusing information in the media in 2009 / 2010 and we realised that we had to investigate all of the possibilities and come up with a plan.

We realised that four areas required development, namely: e-books, e-magazines e-publishing, establishing a library app, and that universal access to our services via electronic devices like tablets and smart phones, would be essential.

South Ayrshire Council's Libraries had been developing a 24/7 model of operation. Commitment to improving Library Services was also identified in South Ayrshire Library's business plan which set out the objective of improving and modernising library provision, while maximising the use of modern technology.

We maximise the use of our website which carries a copy of our catalogue, provides on-line reference tools and gives customers the facility to reserve books. In addition, many of our citizens experience difficulties, in relation to accessing library services. These issues are not unique to South Ayrshire Council. They typically arise for people who are geographically-isolated, socially-isolated, people with sensory impairments, shift-workers and the elderly. A range of initiatives, such a mobile library and flexible opening hours, which are aimed at widening access, had been introduced previously.

Other omens were good: Library Service patrons were comfortable with using innovative technology. In 2008 the Service had introduced pre-loaded digital audio-book players called "Play-away". These players were a great success Library staff felt that customer enthusiasm reflected the willingness of users to adopt new technology.

The 24/7 virtual library branch became our vision. We used the combined resources of the service to make it a reality. The provision of an e-book service was seen as the next step towards achieving these objectives.

The proven project team method of working was used again. This team carried out extensive research using a variety of mechanisms, including maximising the use of social media, such as Linkedin and Twitter, to review and monitor potential service-delivery models from around the world. This research identified an organisation called: "Overdrive Incorporated" as being market leaders in the provision of e-book services. Overdrive was chosen as the aggregator to deliver our e-book lending service and in January 2010 contracts were signed.

Budget for the project was identified from within the existing Book Fund. Analysis of book issues demonstrated that the borrowing figures for Large Print books were declining, annually. We decided to utilise part of the Large Print budget to fund these new developments.

The Project Team had clear objectives: to introduce an e-book lending service which would be accessible to all South Ayrshire Library users and to deliver this within existing resources. The Project Team reviewed a range of options, in relation to service provision and set the additional, ambitious target of providing this service free of charge. Research further identified that although some Councils in England were providing of e-books through their Library Services, none of the Councils was offering this service on a free basis. In addition, no Council in Scotland was, at that time, offering the provision of e-books

The Team developed a comprehensive Project Plan which included key milestones and targets. These included a redesign of the website and the integration of the e-book metadata with the existing catalogue. A comprehensive purchasing strategy for e-books, the integration of user tickets and Library user details, staff-training and system configuration and testing were also factored into this time-line. Significant work was completed within the timescales, in partnership with other Council Services. This ensured that the various ICT operating platforms were working in synergy and that all necessary protocols and procedures were in place.

Stakeholder consultation was a crucial element in the planning and design of this innovative service. The Council also recognised that consultation had to reach beyond current library users into the wider community. Consultation with young people was especially important. By using the school librarian network, the Library Service gathered a wide range of information in relation to the needs and expectations of this demographic group. Visually-impaired people can derive great benefits from the use of e-books. Specific consultation took place with this group, through a local Macular Degeneration Group.

Overdrive Inc. was also involved with the Project Team in delivering a series of staff-training sessions prior to the "soft launch", to allow comprehensive testing, before the official launch of the e-book service. Furthermore, a programme of ongoing training is provided to all staff, to help them to provide appropriate advice and guidance to customers. Updates on e-book developments are provided to the public via the Library Blog on the Council website and to all staff through team briefings and electronic bulletins. Finally, the team reviewed and amended the patron registration requirements and introduced on-line registration procedures for users.

The titles chosen were a mix of e-books in e-pub format and e-audio books in WMA format. The Project Team had researched the issue of compatibility and identified these formats as being the most popular e-book formats. Titles were also made available in PDF and Mp3.

The Project Team, in partnership with colleagues from South Ayrshire Council Communications Team, devised a full marketing and publicity campaign for the launch of the e-book service. The initial launch event was held at Prestwick Airport and attracted coverage on National Television, from both STV and the BBC. We also launched a radio campaign. Billboards advertised the new service and leaflets were distributed through the Council's information networks.

This successful, comprehensive publicity campaign led to the Service receiving the: "Overdrive International Outreach Program Award for 2010" which also included a prize of $1000 worth of e-book titles. This money allowed us to further develop our e-book collection. The project was also mentioned in the BBC "Audio Go" newsletter and was front page news on the CILIPS Information magazine. Both of these publications perform an important role in informing library professionals and the publishing trade nationally.

The e-reads service, incorporating both e-books and e-audio, was launched with 228 titles. As of December 2012 the e-reads service has 743 e-books and 364 e-audio books. The uptake was swift and by April 2012 the number of individual users was 1093 and the issue figures had overtaken those of our two smallest branch libraries. The number of total checkouts to date is 11,295, of which e-books comprised 8,139 and e-audio 3,156. This total included 1,230 checkouts to children and young adults- 65% of these for young adult materials.

In response to user demand, a "feedback button" has been added to the e-book catalogue. Users can e-mail suggestions on book purchases and improvements to the design of the site. The Library Service is currently rolling-out the public library catalogue and system to all secondary schools within South Ayrshire. This should maximise opportunities to engage with young people.

Although in its infancy, the e-book service is already proving popular with pupils. It was one of the principal reasons that South Ayrshire Libraries had for developing an App.

The next step was to publish our own e-book!

E-BOOK PUBLISHING

In June 2011, the Service decided to publish an e-book. "The Records of the Ayrshire Militia 1803 - 1883 was chosen. With a huge team effort, publication was achieved in November 2011.

SAC became the first Local Council in the world to publish an e-book.

South Ayrshire Libraries has a good track record of publishing local history books. It seemed logical that the next book to be published should be in e-format. Past titles include: "History of Ayr", by John Strawhorn and "History of Prestwick", also by John Strawhorn, "The Gaiety Theatre" by John Moore, and many other smaller publications. (Our e-audio book on Old Ayr was developed as a guided walk App. Currently under consideration is a series of local "tourist trails" with QR codes.)

Many of the library professional staff either have a History degree, or a deep interest in history and local history. The Carnegie Library in Ayr has a wonderful collection of archives dating back to the Middle Ages. It attracts scholars, interested amateur historians and family history researchers from around world.

The Service has hosted the annual "South Ayrshire History and Family History Fair" for the past seventeen years. The History Fair offers a full programme of lectures by nationally-acclaimed experts. It also offers delegates the opportunity to browse stalls of local history and family history organisations.

Ironically, the progressive trends seen in librarianship over the past 20 years have been to the detriment of local history services. Investment in IT was often funded by reducing the money spent on cataloguing or maintaining valuable, often unique, items. To many councils and libraries the local history service was an easy target. The conflict between pushing forward, while not neglecting past responsibilities was not lost on us. The Linkedin Group, "Scottish and Local History Enthusiasts", was founded precisely to focus attention on this subject. Our work with both the POMS site and the National Library of Scotland reinforced our conviction that digitising our materials and considering e-publishing were worth exploring.

The Library Team loves a challenge! When it became clear, from wide social media consultation, that no other public library service had published an e-book, we decided to learn the process, with a view to assessing the potential of an "in-house" publication.

Our Local Studies Librarian suggested that the privately-printed and now scarce publication, "The Records of the Ayrshire Militia 1802 – 1884" might be worth considering. This was ideal on three counts: information from it was often requested from overseas researchers, it was in a fragile state and it was a brief publication.

The costs for an e-publication are calculated on the number of pages reproduced. With a small publication, such as the one we had chosen, we would be able to achieve publication within the small budget.

We turned again to social media and discovered an e-book conversion company based near Ayr. Developing a sound working partnership was central to our success. After several productive conversations we quickly realised that, for a relatively small cost, publishing an e-book would be feasible. Although the body of the book would be the digital reproduction of the original, a new introductory chapter would be written and all the other areas involved with publishing an e-book would undertaken by this company.

A contract for the conversion of three books- the "Records", and the reprint of two books of Monumental Inscriptions, was awarded in July 2011. These books were to be supplied in the four formats required for publication as e-books, "Print on Demand" items and as items for borrowing by library users. The e-book covers were designed and ISBN numbers were procured. Trade accounts were opened with Amazon and with Lightning Source.

We now undertook the various tasks that all e-book self-publishers the world over are agonising over: ISBNs, cover designs, and formats. The most formidable challenge of all, we discovered, was dealing with and uploading to Amazon. There was no blueprint to follow and the Library Team had to work its way through the same barriers and challenges that are now facing authors and publishers alike- e-publishing formats, copyright legislation, legal issues, e-hosting, negotiating trade agreements, e-marketing and e-selling. It was a steep learning curve, which we tackled with relish.

When it came to making our e-publication available to the public, it was a much more difficult idea to market than our eRead launch. Although the event was re-tweeted several thousand times, mentioned on various Linkedin forums and generally thought to be a "good thing", it has been a difficult publication to market.

There are various reasons for this- with the vagaries and idiosyncrasies of Amazon being to the fore. Sometimes our publication is listed as "for sale" and other times it is not. Why? Where do we list our publication to its best advantage? We used several key terms, as many as are allowed, and yet they are not always picked up. Of course, we pay a monthly fee to Amazon, whether or not we sell any books. In this, we are no different to any other author using e-publishing for the first time. We are now fully able to identify with all the frustrations that self-publishing authors experience.

In November 2011 Professor Dauvit Brown, Chair of Scottish History at the University of Glasgow formally launched our e-book.

It was published in a range of formats. The e-book can be borrowed via the e-book lending service. It can also be purchased throughout the world, via Amazon and as a POD (Print on Demand) item in paper form. Simultaneously, the e-book was also made available for borrowing, and via Overdrive's community pages, available for any partner Overdrive library service throughout the world to access. Various libraries throughout the world have added the title to their catalogues. These include: West Virginia, Kentucky and South Dakota libraries.

It will never go "out of print". Although it can be accessed free of charge by all members of South Ayrshire Libraries, it has the potential to provide an income stream that could be used to further protect and preserve other vulnerable items in our local collection. A programme of archive digitisation is under development. This will lead to the conservation and preservation of a range of our most precious archival materials.

The impact of the SAC-published e-book has yet to be fully measured. However, we feel that, for a very small investment (£140), and a huge leap of imagination by the Project Team, the milestone publication of our first local history e-book title will blaze the trail for a change of attitude in the library world as to how the challenge of disseminating information and conserving archives is faced.

In September 2011 we published an e-audio book- "Crooks in the Nooks". This is the story of the more infamous crimes that occurred in the history of the town of Ayr, It is written and narrated by Tom Barclay, our Local Studies Librarian. The basis of the book is the guided town walk that Tom regularly conducts. It was uploaded onto our e-catalogue in September 2011 and is now in the top five of our most borrowed e-audio books.

This leads us to several conclusions: there is a huge appetite for local information; there is a willingness to adopt alternative means to access it and we have identified a possible income stream for the future. We are also alerting the public again to the resources we have and how we can still provide a relevant Service.

Through the development and launch of e-book lending and publishing, SAC demonstrated that a relatively small Council can be at the forefront of Library Service provision- leading on-service delivery, and delivering innovative new ways of working in an affordable way.

The launch of the new e-service has attracted a great deal of interest from other Local Authorities. They have approached us for guidance and advice on developing and implementing a similar service. The model that we have developed can be, and is currently being, adopted by other Local Authorities.

What have we learnt from the development of e-lending and e-publishing? The following recommendations became apparent:

1. The e-conversion company should be based locally.
2. That the publication is relatively small in pagination.

3. That the e-conversion company should complete the final upload of files to Amazon and Lightning Seed.

4. That the Authority's e-aggregator uploads the e-book onto the authority's own catalogue for borrowing purposes.

5. That the Authority's e-aggregator uploads the e-book onto the "Community Pages", or equivalent, to allow free download by partner libraries throughout the world.

6. That the Authority uses social media to advertise the product.

LIBRARY "APP" AND E-MAGAZINES

In July 2012, the Service launched its whole-service "App" and launched an e-magazine service. A library "App" (mobile application) was seen as the next, and very necessary, step to providing a digital service.

The South Ayrshire Council Library App was developed with a Scottish company called Solus. Although launching an App sounds like a reasonably simple thing to do, it required a number of months of staff time in design, development and testing. During the week after the launch we paid for an advertising slot on our local radio station, West Sound.

The time we had previously spent on customising our library website proved to be a wise investment, as the same bright, cheerful and modern graphics designed from 2009 onwards proved ideally-suited for use on mobile devices.

This is a project that will be monitored, changed and updated as software developments are rolled out. There is a short video on our library website which was commissioned to show our users the advantages of downloading our App. It can be seen at: http://www.south-ayrshire.gov.uk/libraries Currently under consideration is a series of local "tourist trails" with QR codes. The Library App is free to download from the App store etc.

E-MAGAZINE

In July 2012 we launched an e–magazine service, in conjunction with Zinio magazines. This is purchased through a third party in the UK- a company called FW Howes. It was not without its teething troubles, when it was first launched. An example of this was a delay due to a fire in USA premises! However, the service has now settled down and since September 2012, it has achieved 881 downloads to 144 users. The most popular e-magazines are: New Scientist, Hello, BBC Good Food and Digital SLR.

Four of the seven local schools which serve 11–18 year old pupils are now using our LMS and are able to download e-books and e- magazines. The other three schools will join within 18 months. The University of the West of Scotland has a campus in Ayr and the three Ayrshire Further Education Colleges are coming together to form one unit in 2013. Both of these bodies will use the LMS marketed by Innovative Interfaces in their respective libraries from 2013 onwards. This common platform gives us a tremendous opportunity to work together on a variety of integrated projects.

CONCLUSION

South Ayrshire Library's positive approach to the e-book revolution has demonstrated that e-books are not to be feared- they will not cause the demise of a library service. E-books should be embraced and incorporated into mainstream provision. Providing an e-book service also illustrates libraries' commitments to the digital up-skilling of its residents. It has further demonstrated that the public will wish to borrow e-books from their library, and that this additional service provision can be introduced without huge disruption, or, crucially, the need for extra or excessive funding.

Sadly, and this may only be a personal feeling, my feeling is that many in the profession are still, at best, lukewarm to the idea of e-books and e-publishing. Fear of the unknown is perhaps the root cause, with many librarians holding the erroneous perception that they do not have the necessary technical skills. Many only see e-books as part of an eventual loss of library services.

To date, South Ayrshire Libraries have been invited to speak on e–initiatives at various conferences and this has done much to dispel myths and misunderstandings around e-books.

Social media is invaluable as a tool for professional development. Crucially it is free. It is available to all librarians, irrespective of how long they have been in the profession, or at what level of post they currently hold. Social Media tends to be written in an inclusive, non- threatening manner. Most importantly, it allows new thinking and new research to be broadcast quickly and with enthusiasm. Writers do not have to endure the task of writing articles and chapters to get their message out. No costs are carried by either the giver or receiver of information. The traditional willingness of librarians to share data and good practice is ideally-suited to this medium.

On-line reference tools have been available to Scottish Libraries for several years. Purchased as a bundle via SLIC (Scottish Libraries and Information Council), we have access to sites such Credo and Know UK. However, despite extensive staff-training and direct advertising to the public, the uptake of the service by our patrons remains slow. Our recent use of digital media has restored our faith in the limitless possibilities it presents.

We have recently taken the decision not to renew many of our on-line subscriptions and instead concentrate on educating our patrons on using search engines such as Google, to their

better advantage. E-books, e-magazines, and on-line genealogy sites will carry out an important function in engaging the general population on all things digital. It may be the case that in a few years, on-line reference tools, such as those that we have temporarily abandoned, will take a place in everyday life.

Beyond any doubt, these e-book initiatives have raised the profile of all Scottish Libraries. Many more people realise that libraries can provide relevant services which meet changing demands and needs. Furthermore, this innovative approach has led to improved user access to our library catalogues and databases. We launched a History blog in April 2012 and it is already receiving hits from around the world.

Our new digital services have particularly benefited a range of identified groups of disadvantaged people. Consequently, these initiatives ensure that the Service contributes directly to the national ambition of ensuring that our public services are of high quality, efficient, continually improving, and are responsive to the needs of local people.

The Projects have had an impact nationally and internationally through Library and publications and the industry media, leading to debate about the best way forward. Through social media and professional networking, public libraries in New Zealand, Australia and the USA have all registered an interest in the publication of library-produced e-books. In partnership with Overdrive, the Council has developed a presentation on our experience. This can be used in various forums to advertise and evangelise on behalf of libraries.

The wider publishing world is grappling with the future. The changes in technology are driving the industry- often into areas it dislikes. The key players are ever-changing; devices are evolving rapidly; the business models transforming.

Where do libraries fit into this evolving publishing and reading picture? Can we influence it? Should we try to? I suspect that we should provide the steady pair of hands that our users need to get the best use of their library service.

Books- "where to buy them?" "In what format to buy them?" "Which ones to read?" These are the same questions that, as traditional librarians, we have always tried to answer.

Through navigating the e-publishing path, not only have we travelled the path with would-be authors and e-publishers, we have gained valuable insight into the publishing business in 2012. We can empathise with publishers, readers, booksellers and the general public.

We know that, given ease of use and a good product, library users of all ages are keen to adopt new technology. We also know that we have found a way forward to protect our most vulnerable local history items for posterity.

We also know that a small number of committed, enthusiastic librarians, with a small budget can implement major change effectively.

Our experiences in South Ayrshire Libraries lead us to believe that libraries should actively embrace e-books and e-technology.

REFERENCES

Ayrshire Post. (2010). *Council offers free ebook downloads*. Retrieved 2010 from http://www.ayrshirepost.net/ayrshire-news/scottish-news/2010/07/01/council-offers-free-ebook-downloads-102545-26766260/

Barclay, T. (2011). *Records of the Ayrshire militia from 1802 to 1883*. Retrieved 2011 from http://south-ayrshire.lib.overdrive.com

Bookseller Association. (2010). *Does anyone care about the impact of ebooks?* Retrieved July 2010 from http://bookseller-association.blogspot.com/2010/07/does-anyone-care-about-impact-of-ebooks.html

News, B. B. C. (2010). *E books launch*. Retrieved July 2010 from http://news.bbc.co.uk/1/hi/scotland/10474210.stm

Scotsman. (2010). *Coming soon to your computer*. Retrieved 2010 from http://news.scotsman.com/news

South Ayrshire Council. (n.d.a). *eReads*. Retrieved from http://www.south-ayrshire.gov.uk/ereads

South Ayrshire Council. (n.d.b). Retrieved from http:www.south-ayrshire.gov.uk

South Ayrshire Libraries. (n.d.b). *History blog*. Retrieved from http://sayrshirelib.wordpress.com

South Ayrshire Libraries. (n.d.a). Retrieved from http://www.south-ayrshire.gov.uk/libraries

UKwired News. (2010). *South Ayrshire Council launches ebooks service*. Retrieved 2010 from http://www.ukwirednews.com/news.php/71630-South-Ayrshire-Council-launches-ebooks-service

KEY TERMS AND DEFINITIONS

Blog: A contraction of the words web log. A blog is a discussion or informational site published on the World Wide Web and consisting of discrete entries (posts) typically displayed in reverse chronological order.

E-Book: A book length publication in digital form consisting of text, images or both and produced on, publishes through and readable on computers or other electronic devices.

Mobile App: Applications software for mobile devices.

Chapter 12
Towards Innovative Library Services:
A Case Study of Indira Gandhi National Open University, India

Parveen Babbar
Indira Gandhi National Open University, India

ABSTRACT

This chapter discusses emerging innovative technologies and examines how Indira Gandhi National Open University (IGNOU) Library is increasingly benefited by its new and future services. It discusses the National Open Distance Learners' Library and Information Network (NODLINET), a project of IGNOU Library created for distance learning libraries for sharing collections, e-resources, and services on a common platform. The chapter discusses how IGNOU Library is moving towards innovative Library Services by providing its users with updated contents and constantly strengthening service capability in network information environment. It also explains in detail the component of Remote Access to E-resources, which is a quick, easy, and convenient service to gain off-campus access to all IGNOU Library subscribed databases and other online resources. It also enumerates the copyright restrictions and licensing restrictions through Remote Access Service. There is also a discussion in detail on various other innovative initiatives taken by IGNOU Library like Cloud Computing, Course Reserves, Institutional Repository, Discovery, and AtoZ Services.

INTRODUCTION

Education aims to impart knowledge and makes good citizens. Libraries are the repositories of knowledge and form an integral part of education. They are the important setups for storing and spreading specific information sources and for providing services and education. Academic Libraries have always been offering an environment for high-quality information service and knowledge access through their bibliographic systems, trans-platform search and acquisition of distributive resources and virtual reference consultation. They are considered to be the

DOI: 10.4018/978-1-4666-4761-9.ch012

nerve centres of academic institutions, and must support teaching, research, and other academic programmes (Mahajan, 2005). Tao Xingzhi, a well-known Chinese educator, said: "A vigorous, stable, harmonious, healthy, and upbeat environment and atmosphere has an extensive educating effect". The University Library needs to provide healthy education environment and makes meticulous transformation to support education from its original and new facilities and services.

University libraries have always been important setups for storing and spreading information resources, and for providing support services. On the same lines IGNOU Library envisages to provide an environment for high-quality information service and knowledge access through its bibliographic systems, subject navigation, trans-platform search and acquisition of distributive resources, literature transfer network, long-distance study, and virtual reference consultation. IGNOU Library is focusing to be a distributing center with its reliable search portals of high-quality academic information for its users.

INDIRA GANDHI NATIONAL OPEN UNIVERSITY

The Indira Gandhi National Open University (IGNOU) was established by an Act of Parliament in 1985, and since than has continuously striven to build an inclusive knowledge society through inclusive education. It has been a source of increasing the Gross Enrollment Ratio (GER) by offering high-quality teaching through the Open and Distance Learning (ODL) mode. The University started with two academic programmes in 1987, i.e., Diploma in Management and Diploma in Distance Education, with a strength of 4,528 students and at present it serves the educational aspirations of over 4 million students in India and 36 other countries through 21 Schools of Studies and a network of 67 regional centres, around 3,000 learner support centres and 67 overseas centres.

The University is now offering about 490 certificate, diploma, degree and doctoral programmes, with strength of nearly 420 faculty members and academic staff at the headquarters and regional centres and about 36,000 academic counselors from conventional institutions of higher learning, professional organisations, and industry among others. (IGNOU – Profile, 2012).

The National Open University mandate is to provide access to higher education to all segments of the society and offer high-quality, innovative and need-based programmes at different levels, to all those who require them. The university is committed to reach out to the disadvantaged by offering programmes in all parts of the country at affordable costs; and promote, coordinate and regulate the standards of education offered through open and distance learning in the country. For achieving all this the University is widening access for all sections of society and providing continual professional development and training to all sectors of the economy, the University uses a variety of media and latest technology in imparting education. The formulated vision of IGNOU, keeping its objectives in focus, is to be the National Resource Centre for Open and Distance Learning, with international recognition and presence, and provide seamless access to sustainable and learner-centric quality education, skill upgradation and training to all by using innovative technologies and methodologies and ensuring convergence of existing systems for large-scale human resource development, required for promoting integrated national development and global understanding (IGNOU – Profile, 2012).

IGNOU Library and Documentation Division

The IGNOU library is the most resourceful information centre in the country in the field of Distance Education. The library has the largest collection of books, journals and other related materials in the field of Distance Education, throughout the country. It was established in 1986 in tune with the objectives of IGNOU. The primary mission of the library is to support the educational and research programmes of the University by providing physical and intellectual access to information. In accordance with the objectives of the University, the library aims to develop a comprehensive collection of documents, useful for the readers.

Library and Documentation Division of IGNOU is a hierarchical system with the Central Library at the Headquarters followed by libraries located at Regional Centres (RCL) and Study Centres (SCL) scattered around the country. The Central Library caters to the needs of Academic, Administrative and Supportive staff and students at the headquarters. The RCLs look into the library requirements of Staff, Students, Academic Counselors and Academic coordinators at Regional Centres and the SCLs to meet the needs of the students exclusively.

As the role of the Library within any University can be realized only in the context of the institution's philosophy of education, the basic objectives of the L&DD are in tune with those of the IGNOU. They are as follows:

- To develop appropriate collections in various disciplines for satisfying the needs of the diverse clientele of the libraries of the University, Regional and Study Centres.
- To provide reading, lending, reference, information and documentation facilities to all categories of staff and students.
- To develop a special collection of distance education books and journals at the libraries at the Headquarters as well as Regional Centres.
- To provide documentation and comprehensive reference/information services in areas related to distance education to other Open Universities of the world in general and in India in particular (IGNOU- Library, 2012).

In addition to above IGNOU Library nurtures a learning ecology by enhancing the learning experience of its users and develops specialized collections and learning objects. The library partner's with faculty and academics to develop a campus wide learning strategy. It has endeavored for development of integrated systems and tools to facilitate access to information, resources and services in support of teaching, learning and research. The IGNOU Library has been always keen to provide innovative new facilities and establish staffing levels and processes to enable teaching, learning and research.

National Open Distance Learners' Library and Information Network

National Open Distance Learners' Library and Information Network (NODLIENT) is a national network of distance learning libraries for sharing collections, e-resources and services on a common platform. Currently access to the network resources is open to IGNOU Community, and soon it would be extended to state open universities, and distance education institutes attached to conventional universities. NODLINET is mandated to offer 24 X 7 access to online electronic resources, anywhere, anytime to authorize members of the NODLINET network.

Some of the activities of the network include:

- Library automation on a centrally hosted system.
- Content digitization (of exam papers, course materials, course readings and institutional publications).
- Strengthening of ICT infrastructure in Libraries.
- Standards for library development.
- Information literacy tutorials.
- Linkages with consortium networks in the country.

The Open and Distance Learning System is vast and complex. NODLINET addresses issues of equity in the delivery of information services at par with conventional system to the millions of Open Learners-faculty, counselors, researchers and students in remote setting of the country. It is a platform for libraries and information centres of the Open and Distance Learning System of the country provisioning information resources and digitized content to its stakeholders form anywhere at anytime using advanced technologies to enhance the quality of education at par with the conventional education system.

The activities of the NODLINET are grouped as - VISDOL (Virtual Information System for Open and Distance Libraries) with its component CERDOL (Consortium of E-Resources for Open & Distance Libraries). Its activity components are:

1. E-Resources
2. Digitized content
3. Strengthening the ODL library setup
4. Convergence with conventional system
5. Linkage with other networks
6. System integration
7. Web Portal with access management and authentication
8. Integrated platform for library related and other diversified library related services as E-Library (IGNOU- NODLINET, 2012)

The University Library needs to enhance the services for which it has long been famous and valued, such as quality-controlled answers, provision of authoritative information, due diligence, and keeping users current for the digital era (Innovations range from interacting with users and delivering content and services to mobile devices to customizing alerts into on-point synthesized briefings).

We know that libraries are in a dynamic social environment. So they also need to adopt an open development mode, paying constant attention to the changes of user and environment, regarding user satisfaction, social value realization, and knowledge spreading and using as basic goals, and forming a constant, stable, coordinated, and effective development strategy scheme. Innovation in University Library involves many aspects. It includes not only the adoption of the advanced technologies to upgrade service standard and efficiency, but also another important feature – softness, which refers to such non-technical characteristics as method, concept, and mode.

The IGNOU Library is working with tools that utilize artificial intelligence and multitasking to assist learners in creating individualized information portfolios. The Library is communicating through Virtual Reality helmets and utilizing diagnostic tools to customize resources to individual profiles, and provide effective support for problem solving and discovery groups (Marcum, 2003)

IMPLEMENTATION OF TECHNOLOGIES AT IGNOU LIBRARY FOR INCREASING REACH TO ITS USERS

EZproxy: Remote Access Authentication Mechanism

Libraries and the information community have moved rapidly into an era of powerful networked scholarly world, large quantities of information accessible in electronic formats, and dispersed information sources connected to regional and national networks. This rich diversity poses new challenges for the provision of appropriate electronic services. Remote-access services in libraries have evolved beyond after-hours and essential users tools to become integral parts of libraries. In the present scenario the types of mobile devices used to access library data and information have also evolved to provide highly-capable multifunctional devices that deliver e-resources, databases of e-content, voice, video and data to the users. These emerging remote-access technologies are increasingly benefiting the Libraries from the extensive use of convergent mobile devices such as tablets and smartphones to enhance the use e-resource capabilities. The ubiquitous nature of the Internet and many web-based applications are also creating remote-access opportunities ranging from simple communication (email and web browsing) to enabling complex library control systems.

The Indira Gandhi National Open University of India have successfully implemented and tested a prototype solution to the problem of providing electronic resources to scholars who are accessing networked information resources and who are at locations remote from physical library. A virtual service was provided directly for information access and retrieval sessions, remotely assisting the user during the real-time, online process.

EZproxy helps provide users with remote access to Web-based licensed content offered by libraries. It is middleware that authenticates library users against local authentication systems and provides remote access to licensed content based on the user's authorization. Presently more than 2,500 institutions in over 60 countries are using EZproxy software. OCLC is offering the a new incremental release, EZproxy 5.6.3, resolves several issues identified in EZproxy 5.6 related to the Linux build and Shibboleth running on the Windows platform. In preparation for EZproxy v6.0, we need beta testers for each supported platform—Windows, Linux and Solaris. EZproxy is available for servers running Linux (x86 and x86_64), Solaris (x86) and Windows (2000, 2003, 2008, XP, XP Professional and 7) (OCLC, 2012).

EZproxy is a URL-rewriting proxy server which operates between the user's Web browser and the restricted service, intercepting both the Web browser's requests and the pages returned by the Web server. The requests come from an authorized IP address and are accepted as valid if it has come from genuine user. The server dynamically changes all the URLs on the Web

pages that returned from the restricted service. The URLs are rewritten as they're displayed on the user's Web browser with the base address of the EZproxy server. The rewriting makes the links will function correctly after passing through the proxy server. The mechanism works with the direct link if the access is from the IP range otherwise when used from outside the library's IP-address range, EZproxy prompts for their username and password.

As EZproxy provides access, it logs each use into a file generally in SQL database that can be utilized to create statistical reports. These statistics allows the library to monitor the use of specific electronic resources and the users who are accessing the resources. The statistics can also be used for renewal and cancellation decisions of e-resources for the next year.

The main advantage of using EZproxy is that library users don't have to make any changes to their browsers to access restricted resources. The library needs a front end of web pages generally in ASP or HTML or any other web based language for the users to have access to the portal (Breeding, 2001).

So the benefits of remote-access capability extend beyond supporting IGNOU Library users. Many job functions of Library are inextricably linked to institution applications and services and, as such, having an effective remote-access capability can provide institution with many tangible benefits by bringing the workplace to the employee. Effective remote-access capabilities can provide enhanced productivity and profitability by allowing Library Staff to respond quickly to Library users and client requests. It can also provide more flexible working arrangements for staff by allowing 24-hour, seven-days-a-week access to job functions. Apart from the benefits to an to Library Staff a well-designed and implemented remote access solution can assist an Library facing an emergency situation to maintain:

- Access to all the Library Services and Resources
- Financial viability through the continued provision of services
- Its reputation and brand equity with clients and users
- Compliance to regulatory obligations
- Protection from risk and security exposures

Remote Access to E-Resources (RATE)

Remote Access to e-resources is a quick, easy, and convenient service to gain off-campus access to all IGNOU Library subscribed databases and other online resources. It requires no prior computer or browser set-up. All is needed to do is to login using RATE Service username and password when prompted. It will also ask for security question answer. It is a service provided by the Library and Documentation Division of IGNOU for remote access to library-licensed content and supports a broad range of academic activities requiring remote authentication. (Staff Reporter, 2011)

Remote Access of IGNOU is a suite of e-library services by converting the existing service into e-services and exploring many other ways to support its distance education system such as increasing the scope of e-resources accessed, better methods of seeking information, saving time in the information search and delivery, and significant rise in the use of e-resource and article downloads by students and faculty.

Figure 1. Login Page of remote access to e-resources of IGNOU Library

Please enter your credentials to log in to E-Resources subscribed by IGNOU

User Email ID

Password

Sign In

Forgot Password?   New User? Register here

* The facilities is presently available for IGNOU faculties, Academics, Face to Face students, Researchers and Regional centre Academics

IGNOU Wiki | DEPSSA | IPS | Faculty |Alumni | PCF6 Conference | Brand Manual

IGNOU at a Glance | Profile | Mail Sevice| Intranet & ODL Soft Services | RTI Act | RSS | Virtual Classroom | Related Links | Sitemap | Employee Telephone

Directory | Feedback | On Demand Examination | Copyright | Privacy | Faculty Blogs | Register for SMS Alerts | Route Map | Student Satisfaction Survey | Community Colleges

Convergence Scheme | FAQ | IGNOU Online | IGNOU: A Sucess Story | Staff Corner| RC Serives | Science Olympaid | Eduaction Broadcast | Flexilearn | eGyankosh

e-Resources for Experts | Security Helpline (24 Hrs) | Placement Portal | Student Grievances Redressal Forum

Site Designed and Developed by Informatics (India) Limited

Existing Library and Information set up has limitations in ODL system in regards to the library facilities, printed information resources, infrastructure, space, storage, ICT provisioning and staff. Due to resource constraints and location in far flung areas, the students in the distance learning institutions do not have access to the same kind of library services as available to the campus based learners. In the ODL system the applications of ICT hold great potential to meet the challenge of bridging the gap between the libraries and the students at home, work place or anywhere. With this aim to create an integrated e-platform for scattered e-resources i.e. accessible e-books/journals of publishers this attempt is made. Through the network distance learning students have now access to library/learning resources and services, designed to support the specific programmes offered. The services/resources meet the same standard of academic qualities as the same information resources offered in traditional settings.

The service has overcome the challenge of accessibility to library resources, reaching out the unreached to support curriculum needs of faculty and IGNOU Distance Learning courses through its network of Regional Centers.

Over the past five years, the library collection of e-resources has grown to over 75000 approx full text e-journals, databases, and e-books all from leading publishers worldwide. The users of IGNOU are now able to access these e-resources from any computer connected to the campus network. Off campus users can access to e-resources from their homes. The service authenticates authorized users outside of the IGNOU campus IP range to login to e-resources (IGNOU Blogspot, 2011)

Copyright Restrictions through IGNOU RATE

IGNOU RATE service restricts the copyright to its users with

- Downloading, saving and printing of limited data or articles from e-resources is permitted for personal, academic use only.
- Reproductions of copyrighted materials, such as making copies of electronic articles for others is not permitted.

Licensing Restrictions (Terms of Use)

Access to the electronic resources subscribed by IGNOU Library and used through RATE are restricted to members of the IGNOU community

Figure 2. Screenshot of e-resources provided through remote access services

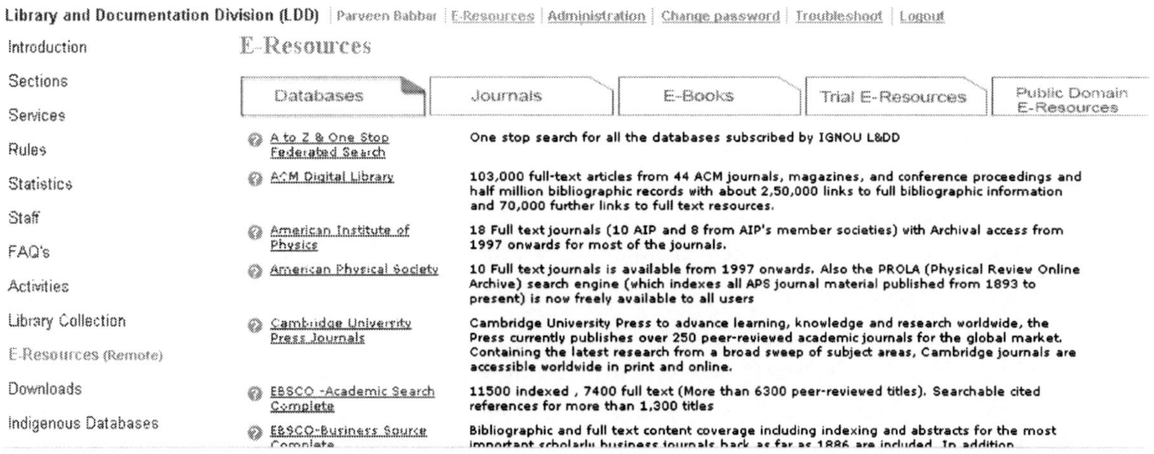

for the purposes of research, teaching, and personal study. Under IGNOU Library's license agreements for electronic resources, users may not:

- Share 'User ID and Password' with others.
- Download cover- to – cover full text of entire journal issue.
- Systematically download, distribute, or retain substantial portions of information such as entire journal issues or e-books.
- Use the licensed materials for commercial purposes.
- Re-distribute content to people other than IGNOU Faculty, staff and students.
- Share data with people other than IGNOU Faculty, staff and students.
- Post actual content or articles to web sites listservs.
- Modify or create a derivative work of the licensed materials without the permission of the licensor.
- Allow anyone other than an authorized user to use the licensed materials.
- Remove, obscure or modify any copyright or other proprietary notices included in the licensed materials.

Federated and Discovery Search Solutions

Search solutions like federated and discovery forms the integral component of an Information Portal of University Library, which provides the interface to diverse information resources. Individual end users benefits from the search technology which blends e-journals, subscription databases, electronic print collections, other digital repositories, and the Internet. It reduces the time to search, displays results in a common format and provide seamless access to the resources. The search solutions facilitate users to search multiple full-text and bibliographic databases subscribed by the library as well as open access e-resources, library OPAC, IRs, and other library resources

through a single search box. In addition to it provide link source and A to Z service for complete listing of resources. The major providers of one stop search are EBSCO's Discovery Service, Primo Central (Ex Libris), Summon (Serials Solutions), WorldCat Local (OCLC) and Encore Synergy (Innovative Interfaces).

IGNOU Library provides Single search window portal for the Student, Faculty, and Employee to quick access to key library resources and services: the catalog; course reserves; electronic resources; and library record In addition, a link to the Libraries' home page provides full access (pre-authenticated through the IGNOU Library login process) to all library web pages and licensed resources that are available from off-campus and require authorization. With the convenience of the pre-authentication mechanism of a one-time login via IGNOU RATE Service, users only need to login once during a single session on the library website.

A to Z Service

IGNOU Library provides complete resource listing which includes publisher packages, aggregated packages, or individually subscribed e-resources. It provides access to all of library's resources, including e-journals, titles in full-text databases, titles in publisher packages, eBooks, and other resources. It enables linked access to full text from popular research sites by utilizing A-to-Z's built-in Open URL link resolver. It also expands the library's collection by including the collection of subject-specific Open Access packages also.

Cloud Computing

Cloud computing is a new perspective and it gives rise to a totally new generation of Libraries with innovative features that goes beyond our dream for the Next Generation Computing. Cloud computing can help University Library in transformation and better services. An entire

Figure 3. Screen shots of single search window for all IGNOU subscribed resources (e-journals, e-books, e- databases & OPAC for print records)

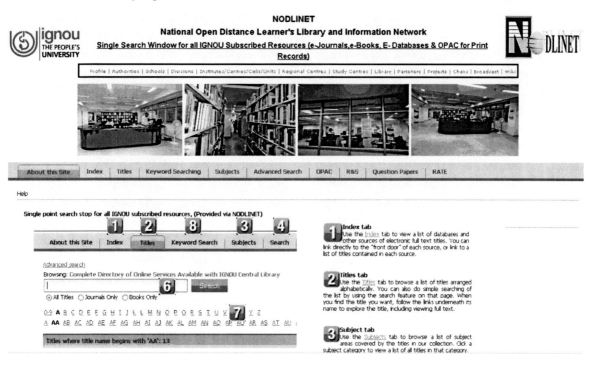

Figure 4. A to Z service

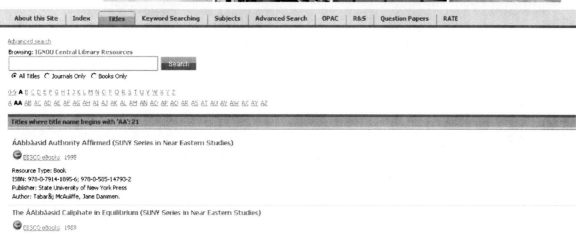

world of knowledge can now be made available to Users through cloud based services that can be accessed anytime, anywhere, from any device. It is often proposed as the biggest revolution since the internet. The concepts of cloud computing to not only relieve University Library from the need to maintain local hardware and software, but to also embrace new models of managing data and content that enable increased collaboration among libraries in the way that they manage their collections. They manage print, electronic, and digital resources in a way that avoids the need to operate different applications to manage each format of material (ICAL, 2013). IGNOU Library is making efforts to have server space in cloud to provide its services through cloud.

IGNOU Library is planning to use the cloud infrastructure, by procuring the server space on which it will build its applications. The library will also migrate its Integrated Library System to cloud in coming days. Aggregated subject gateways that support systematic unified web-scale resource discovery from EBSCO Discovery Service is already on trial at IGNOU Library. Further the Cloud based Services for e-resources of IGNOU Library include various online databases, e-books, research guides and online reference services that are already for use. Cloud external servers for electronic storage for institutional digital repositories and institutional archives are also in pipeline.

Institutional Repositories

An Institutional Repository (IR) is a digital archive where a university community's intellectual work is made accessible and preserved for posterity. The concept of IR suggests the tantalizing possibility of greater library influence over the full cycle of scholarly communication on campus, from research through publication, collection, and preservation. It represents an integral part of the

long-term strategies of the universities to redesign their publishing and library policies to take into account the totally new conditions created by the Internet. The University own production of theses and working papers can easily be put up on such repositories. A number of software packages both proprietary and free are available for archiving and managing digital collections. Various open source software packages such as Dspace developed by MIT and HP, E-prints developed by University of Southampton, Fedora developed by University of Virginia and Cornel University are driving the OA movement especially the development of IRs in the world. IGNOU has its one of the largest repository of IGNOU Course material called as E-gyankosh which is a National Digital Repository to store, index, preserve, distribute and share the digital learning resources developed by the Open and Distance Learning Institutions in the country. At present the community has 40736 documents under it and 1700 under Pan Africa e-network. In addition to this IGNOU Library is in process to create new repositories on Photo Albums of IGNOU, special collection on distance education and faculty publications.

Course Reserves: E & Print

IGNOU Library will set the course reserve service under its NODLINET programme to provide the full-text articles of course reading materials, course readings updates, and in addition to provide full-text of any other reading materials requested by faculty to support subjects offered at IGNOU. Course reserves of IGNOU will be mainly the reservoir of e-documents of suggested reading the IGNOU course material. Library shall take initiative to collect and digitize print materials, acquire relevant e-books for updates on course readings, and make such course readings accessible online on the Web within the framework of copyright laws. The project has been approved and Library is initially planning to start with MBA and MCA programme as pilot project.

Resource Sharing

Resource sharing has been always important and inevitable for University Libraries. Resource sharing from its elementary concept of inter-library lending, has included cooperative acquisition, collection development, shared cataloguing, centralized processing, exchange of content page of journals, sharing of bibliographical data, centralized periodicals collection, exchange of electronic documents and articles, obtaining photocopies of articles etc. Having resource sharing facilitate users to have the better access to library holdings and enable the users to be more aware regarding the resources not available in their own library. Thus only solution to the problem is the pooling and sharing of resources—print as well as electronic—by way of consortia and networks. New technology has provided great opportunities for delivery of services. More and more libraries must unite, which of course requires a change in the attitudes, practices, and policies to get the maximum benefit. IGNOU library is direct member of various institutions and is also taking Developing Library Network Services. It has extended this service to all its Regional Centers Libraries.

Selective Dissemination of Information

For Reaching out the Users with New and Innovative Technologies a range of services can be offered (face-to-face and at a distance). One of the important services is to package electronic documents and resources generated primarily by libraries. Selective dissemination of information and alert systems linked to a student's course management account and supported by virtual reference highlights library services. IGNOU library need to be ubiquitous, and with its range

of services it dramatically overpower the roles related to the traditional library as "place" with its books and printed materials.

The IGNOU library circulates content pages of current issues of periodical to the academic staff to promote the use of the periodicals. New accessions are displayed in the the library. Availability is acknowledged through news letter and through E-mails. List of Books are also provided to the users on request. Library keeps the users aware of E-journals, Databases and other E Resources to promote the use.

Assisted Technologies for Disabled

IGNOU Library is committed to providing accommodations for its users with disabilities. These technologies enable disabled users to efficiently use of the libraries facilities, materials and services. The IGNOU Library has already procured and is providing the services of JAWS, Kurzweil (Braille translation software), MAGic (screen magnification software), Braille embosser and scanners. In addition to this IGNOU Library is procuring for various Screen Reading Software, Magnification Software, Scanning Equipment and Braille Technology equipments.

Information Literacy and Competency Development

Information literacy and competency is the ability to identify information needs, seek out resources to meet those needs, and then analyze, evaluate, synthesize, and communicate the resulting knowledge. It is a core instructional pedagogy. The role of the ILCP in the context of a University Library is intended to encourage and facilitate life-long learning. In order to empower students in the pursuit of knowledge, the library professionals aim to teach them the skills of identifying, locating, and evaluating information. Among many other things, information literate students are competent, independent learners (Majumdar & Singh, 2007).

To create a more informed citizenry, any society and, in particular a university and its library, must be in a position of enabling its people to use the information effectively. Thus, ILC facilitates to seek and evaluate right sources of information and acquire it. The IGNOU Library is in process of launching its ILCP module for its users.

Multimedia Resource Centre

IGNOU Library is determined to provide quality education to its learners by providing various supplementary materials and multimedia resources in addition to Self Learning Materials (SLMs). The supplementary materials and multi-media resources (e.g. reference books, audio-video cassettes/CDs, etc.) are helpful for the learners at Learners Study Centres (LSCs). Therefore, IGNOU Library is initiating to establish IGNOU Multimedia Resource Centres (MRCS) in existing conventional University Libraries. Under the project the IGNOU Library will provide various supplementary materials and multimedia resources in addition to Self Learning Materials (SLMs). In addition to this it will provide Internet Facilities to the best utilized Learner Support Centres and books with nominal maintenance charges.

M-Libraries

Mobile computing has exploded around the world over the past several years and there are many exciting mobile technologies that University Library can capitalize on and highlight their collections, provide reference assistance and instruction, and simply make their collections and services more accessible to patrons wherever they are. So, IGNOU Library is also ambitious in offering new mobile services, such as mobile optimized IGNOU Library website and OPACs, mobile library applications that provide access to local digitized collections, and renewal notices and reference services via SMS. The m-library of IGNOU Library will also provide links to mobile-enabled Web 2.0

accounts, such as Twitter, Flickr, YouTube, and Facebook; News about library events; Content for download on podcasts, videos; Floor maps. Some of the popular m-library services already available are Mobile online public access catalogs, Mobile collections, Mobile library instruction, Mobile databases, Library Short Message Service (SMS) notifications and SMS Reference (Vollmer, 2010).

QR Codes

QR (quick response) Code is another kind of barcode that is gaining popularity in the library world and social media culture. The QR codes have its potential use in libraries and are beginning to make inroads in University Library. It is a matrix barcode readable by smartphones and mobile phones with cameras, sometimes referred to as 2d codes, 2d barcodes, or mobile codes. These codes can be linked to songs, videos, Web sites, surveys, contests, etc. or other information that augments the exhibits in University Library. IGNOU Library will use these codes in the library stacks/end caps or magazine/journal areas to point to online electronic holdings of print materials or related subject guides. Similarly the library is planning to link these codes to library audio tours for orientations and text that loads the library's text message reference service. QR codes will also be used for IGNOU Library video tutorials linked to a YouTube playlists of videos, through mobile home screen app that can be saved for easy access, as needed.

Gesture-Based Computing

Gesture-based technology has become very prevalent in recent years. From smartphones to tablets, people spend a great deal of time tapping and swiping away on their mobile devices. The current crop of gesture-based devices employs touch screens that require user contact, either with fingers or a stylus. Gesture recognition offers University library many practical applications, especially as assistive or enabling tools for students and users with disabilities. Gesture-based technology could give people with visual or other impairments much greater freedom in accessing a library's computers. And they won't be limited to just simple hand movements. Other gesture recognition interfaces are currently being developed (or improved) for reading facial expressions, sign language, head and body motion, and eye movements. IGNOU Library in future is planning to very soon introduce Gesture based technology in its library.

Mobile Augmented Reality

Mobile augmented reality (AR) applications represent a profound opportunity for increased access to print and digital library collections. Mobile augmented reality is also planned in IGNOU Library for augmenting physical book stacks browsing, library navigation, optical character recognition, facial recognition, and building identification mobile software for compelling library experiences and much more (Hahn, 2012).

Working with Network

Last but not the least, with collaboration as the key, IGNOU library staff needs to work closely with other libraries, information technology and computer science departments, instructional designers, and information architecture specialists to service student needs. Customization and personalization are seen as key value-added contributions. Multiple collections, some designed for a specific course, utilizing video clips and various media, simplifies the complex morass of information for the students and the learner. Providing access to preprints, software, listserv archives, websites and other currently overlooked resources will make the IGNOU library commonplace and necessary.

At present IGNOU Library is innovating and is moving towards use of cloud based information services, new forms of library software, virtualisation technology, augmented reality and gamification. Gamification is beginning to have a real impact on university library services, it is changing the way users interact with resources and services. The pioneering use of Augmented Reality (AR) is bringing special collections into the age of the app and enhancing their use by students. The availability of new technologies is making libraries need to rethink how they buy new apps and develops and roll out new solutions.

IMPLEMENTATIONS OF LATEST TECHNOLOGIES AND INTRODUCTION OF NEW SERVICES AT IGNOU: FUTURE PLANS

The IGNOU Library is stipulated by a series of new service measures and encouraged innovation and adjustment of concepts and methods during services. Some of the innovative services and technology implementations which IGNOU Library is going to implement are:

1. Adopting a pattern featuring extensive openness and service– prolonging service time, extending service site; providing readers with big rooms and open shelves; adopting one-door management and one-stop service; and realizing a five-in-one organic service mechanism in one service space, which involves storage, searching, borrowing, reading, and reference.

2. Offering quiet individual study areas, group discussion rooms, topic study rooms, and multimedia innovation labs; following internationally popular "immersive" education concept, establishing a "scene-based independent English learning center", creating a vivid learning and research atmosphere; offering duplicating and printing education and supporting self-help service.

3. Using Web 2.0 tools to establish "subject blog", offer RSS subscription, IM robot consultation; using open source software to

carry out setup storage construction; integrating system to establish a unified academic resources portal service platform.

4. Consultation instant response and scheduling: integrating telephone calls, e-mails, web sheets, IM software, and interactive videos in one work station through "network calling center", realizing consultation instant response and scheduling through intelligent calling distribution by program-controlled switchboard, integration of computer and telephone, and automatic answering system (Jing, & Jin, 2009).

INTERNSHIP PROGRAMME FOR FRESH LIBRARY GRADUATES

IGNOU Library has only not kept to the standards of innovation and technology implementation but has also been in frontier in benefiting the profession by providing training to the young professionals. Library of Indira Gandhi National Open University started the apprenticeship programme to Library trainees in 1990. The basic objectives are as below:-

- Train the Library & Information Professionals in Library operations/applications to help in further placement.
- Awareness to the trainees with the role of the library
- Provide an Opportunity to work in different sections of the Library & Documentation Division
- Training on the modern library management techniques and web based services
- Awareness to the trainees with the use of various reference sources to retrieve the information
- Conduct problem solving sessions so that trainees have to share their work, questions and suggestions for improving the training

- Provide the hands-on practice session in each areas of library & information services, and
- Provide ample of opportunities to exposure, work and learn on emerging IT tools and technologies.

IGNOU Library has so far provided training to more than 533 library professionals. During 2012-13, Thirty Three (33) Interns have been apprenticed. It is to inform that after obtaining training in

IGNOU library these interns have been well placed in good jobs in other organizations. These interns also compensate the shortage of library staff in library system.

CONCLUSION

IGNOU Library is undergoing through tremendous transition as it is moving to virtual services in response to changes in technology and the expectations of their patrons, and as they facilitate not only the use of existing information, but also production of new information through online communities and virtual spaces. The emerging technologies have brought enormous challenges and new work tasks. Social networks with their unstructured data have made its library work more challenging and innovative. But after the inclusion of semantic web, it has been possible to have structured data and thus making sense of the chaotic digital world. IGNOU Library has experienced improvements in user satisfaction and in the provision of timely, accurate access to electronic resources through the implementation of an RATE Service, Discovery Service and many more upcoming new services. It has improved in the use and access of electronic and print resources. Further the IGNOU Library is able to effectively help the users by rapidly diagnosing and remedying access problems. It has been seen that with implementation of various latest technologies, the use of library resources have substantially accelerated the research speed at the University.

So, the future of IGNOU library is not in the type of collections or a building, but it is the relationships with those they serve or the services they provide. The Library needs to continuously represent a community investment in a vision of a better tomorrow through sharing information, knowledge and, hopefully, wisdom. It is a knowledge hub that brings together the wisdom of the community, and shares it with the world. It is correctly said that while the format of resources may change, while access to information may change and while styles of service may change, the vision of high quality, service-oriented, information centres always fits the University library's mission.

REFERENCES

Blogspot, I. G. N. O. U. (2011, November 23). IGNOU e-library services. *IGNOU 4 U Blog.* Retrieved April 12, 2013, from http://www.ignou4ublog.com/2011/11/ignou-has-introduced-suite-of-e-library.html

Breeding, M. (2001). Offering remote access to restricted resources. *Information Today, 18*(4), 52–53.

Hahn, J. (2012). Mobile augmented reality applications for library services. *New Library World, 113*(9/10), 429–438. doi:10.1108/03074801211273902.

ICAL. (2013). The second international conference on academic libraries on cloud computing for libraries. *ICAL 2013 Newsletter.* Retrieved April 11, 2013, from http://www.ipu.ac.in/ical2013/icalnews220213.zip

IGNOU Library. (2012). *Introduction.* Retrieved April 22, 2013, from http://www.ignou.ac.in/ignou/aboutignou/division/ldd/introduction

IGNOU NODLINET. (2012). *NODLINET.* Retrieved May 1, 2013, from http://www.ignou.ac.in/NODLINET/aboutnodlinet

Jing, G., & Jin, C. (2009). The innovative university library: Strategic choice, construction practices and development ideas. *Library Management, 30*(4/5), 295–308. doi:10.1108/01435120910957959.

Mahajan, P. (2005). Academic libraries in India: A present-day scenario. *Library Philosophy & Practice, 8*(1), 1.

Majumdar, S., & Singh, R. (2007). *Information literacy and competency programme in academic libraries: a case study of DULS.* Paper presented at the 5th International CALIBER-2007. Chandigarh, India. Retrieved April 22, 2013, from http://ir.inflibnet.ac.in/bitstream/handle/1944/1436/608-616.pdf?sequence=1

Marcum, J. W. (2003). Visions: The academic library in 2012. *D-Lib Magazine, 9*(5). doi:10.1045/may2003-marcum.

OCLC. (2012). *EZproxy.* Retrieved March 18, 2013, from http://www.oclc.org/ezproxy/

Profile, I. G. N. O. U. (2012). *Preamble.* Retrieved March 18, 2013, from http://www.ignou.ac.in/ignou/aboutignou/profile/2

Staff Reporter. (2011, July 4). Remote access to IGNOU e-resources inaugurated. *The Hindu.* Retrieved April 3, 2013, from http://www.thehindu.com/todays-paper/tp-national/article2157236.ece

Vollmer, T. (2010). *There's an app. for that! Libraries and mobile technology: An introduction to public policy considerations.* Washington, DC: American Library Association..

Compilation of References

360 *Resource Manager.* (n.d.). Retrieved May 09, 2013, from http://www.serialssolutions.com/en/services/360-resource-manager

Aabø, S. (2011). The value of public libraries: A socio-economic analysis. In M. Belloti (Ed.), *Verso un'economia della biblioteca: Finanziamenti, programmazione e valorizzazione in tempo di crisi* (pp. 169–176). Milano, Italy: Bibliografia..

ACRL. (2012). 2012 top ten trends in academic libraries: A review of the trends and issues affecting academic libraries in higher education. *College & Research Libraries, 73*(6), 311–320.

Adler, P. S., Aufderheide, P., Butler, B., & Jaszi, P. American University Washington College of Law, & Andrew W. Mellon Foundation. (2012). Code of best practices in fair use for academic and research libraries. Washington, DC: Association of Research Libraries..

African Journals OnLine. (2013). Retrieved May 25, 2013 from http://www.ajol.info/

Allword Dictionary. (2012). *Electronic resources.* Retrieved November 1, 2012 from www.allwords.com/word-electronic%2B

Almauk. (2012). *Economic impact toolkit.* Retrieved November 3, 2012, from http://almauk.org/working-together/our_activity/economic-impacts

American Library Association. (2012). Ebooks and copyright issues. In *The state of America's libraries: A report from the American Library Association.* Chicago, IL: American Library Association..

American Library Association. (n.d.). *What is fair use?* Retrieved February 27, 2013, from http://www.ala.org/Template.cfm?Section=copyrightarticle&Template=/ContentManagement/ContentDisplay.cfm&ContentID=26700

Ancient Writing Materials. (n.d.). Retrieved November 6, 2012 from http://www.skypoint.com/members/waltzmn/WritingMaterials.html

Anderson, K. J., Freeman, R. S., Hérubel, J., Mykytiuk, L. J., Nixon, J. M., & Ward, S. M. (2002). Buy, don't borrow: Bibliographers' analysis of academic library collection development through interlibrary loan requests. *Collection Management, 27*(3/4), 1–11. doi:10.1300/J105v27n03_01.

Appleton, B., Regan, S., England, L., & Fu, L. (2011). *Improving electronic resources management (ERM), critical work flow and operations solution.* Lafayette, IN: Purdue University..

Aramide, K. A., & Bolarinwa, O. M. (2010). *Availability and use of audiovisual and electronic resources by distance learning students in Nigerian universities: A case study of National Open University of Nigeria (NOUN), Ibadan study centre.* Retrieved November 15, 2012 from http://unllib.unl.edu/LPP/aramide-bolarinwa.htm

Arms, W. (2000). *Digital libraries.* Cambridge, MA: MIT Press..

Arnould, E. J., Price, L. L., & Zinkhan, G. (2004). *Consumers.* New York: McGraw-Hill..

Arnould, E. J., & Thompson, C. J. (2005). Consumer culture theory (CCT), twenty years of research. *The Journal of Consumer Research, 331*(4), 868–882. doi:10.1086/426626.

Association of Research Libraries. (2000). *Statistics and measurement program.* Retrieved February 29, 2000 from http://www.arl.org/stats/index.html

Ayrshire Post. (2010). *Council offers free ebook downloads.* Retrieved 2010 from http://www.ayrshirepost.net/ayrshire-news/scottish-news/2010/07/01/council-offers-free-ebook-downloads-102545-26766260/

Baker, G., & Read, E. J. (2008). Vendor supplied usage data for electronic resources: A survey of academic library. *Learned Publishing, 21*(1), 48–57. doi:10.1087/095315108X247276.

Bane, A. F. (1993). Business periodicals ondisc: How full-text availability affects the library. *Computers in Libraries, 15*(5), 54–56.

Barclay, T. (2011). *Records of the Ayrshire militia from 1802 to 1883.* Retrieved 2011 from http://south-ayrshire.lib.overdrive.com

Barnes, J. (1997). Electronic archives: An essential element in complete electronic journals solution. *Information Services & Use, 17*(1), 37–47.

Barnett, J. B. (n.d.). Marine science journal prices: A case study. *Journal of Educational Media & Library Sciences, 41*(3), 315 – 323.

Baron, S., & Warnaby, G. (2008). Individual customer's use and integration of resources: Empirical findings and organizational implications in the context of value co-creation. *Otago Forum, 2,* 62-79.

Beer, D., & Burrows, R. (2010). Comsumption, presumption and participatory web cultures. *Journal of Consumer Culture, 10*(1), 3–12. doi:10.1177/1469540509354009.

Berne Convention for the Protection of Literary and Artistic Works. (n.d.). Retrieved March 28, 2013, from http://www.wipo.int/treaties/en/ip/berne/trtdocs_wo001.html

Berners-Lee, T. (2013). *Linked data: Web science and the semantic web.* Retrieved April 10, 2013 from, http://www.edge.org/conversation/linked-data

Berners-Lee, T., & Shadbolt, N. (2011, December 31). There's gold to be mined from all our data. *The Times.* Retrieved 12 December, 2012 from, http://www.thetimes.co.uk/Ho/opinion/colunist/article3272618

Berners-Lee, T., De Roure, D., Harnad, S., & Shadbolt, N. (2005). *Journal publishing and author self-archiving: Peaceful co-existence and fruitful collaboration.* Retrieved March 20, 2013, from http://eprints.soton.ac.uk/261160/

BioMed Central. (2013). The open access publisher. *Springer Science+Business Media.* Retrieved March 5, 2013, from http://www.biomedcentral.com/about

Bittel, L. R. (Ed.). (1978). *Encyclopedia of professional management.* New York: McGraw Hill..

Black, I. R., & Cherrier, H. (2010, November-December). Anti-consumption sustainability: Sustainable consumption identity. *Journal of Consumer Behaviour,* 445–453.

Blogspot, I. G. N. O. U. (2011, November 23). IGNOU e-library services. *IGNOU 4 U Blog.* Retrieved April 12, 2013, from http://www.ignou4ublog.com/2011/11/ignou-has-introduced-suite-of-e-library.html

Blotner, L. S. (2007). Music libraries of tomorrow: Virtual or concrete, harmony or discord. In J. P. Cassaro (Ed.), Music libraries, and the academy (pp. 67-79). Middleton, WI: A-R Ed.s, Inc..

Bookseller Association. (2010). *Does anyone care about the impact of ebooks?* Retrieved July 2010 from http://bookseller-association.blogspot.com/2010/07/does-anyone-care-about-impact-of-ebooks.html

Borbely, M. (2011). Factors influencing self-assessment in a changing library environment. *Performance Measurement and Metrics, 12,* 7–22. doi:10.1108/14678041111124261.

Bouckaert, G. (2012, May). Managing performance: International and national trends. *Forum AP.* Retrieved September 27, 2012 from http://www.qualitapa.gov.it/fileadmin/mirror/i-valperf/materiali/2012-05-17_VdP_Slide_Bouckaert.pdf

Boyd, N. (1997). Towards access service: Supply times, quality control and performance related services. *Interlending and Document Supply, 25*(3), 118–123. doi:10.1108/02641619710170537.

Bradley, C. J. (1981). Oscar G.T. Sonneck: Architect of the national music collection. *Journal of Library History (Tallahassee, Fla.), 16*(2), 293–304.

Bradley, C. J. (1990). *American music librarianship: A biographical and historical study.* Westport, CT: Greenwood Press..

Braine, J. (n.d.). *A brief history of librarians and image.* Retrieved November 16, 2012 from http://home.earthlink.net/~cyberresearcher/History.htm

Brand, A. (1996). Standardisation of electronic document delivery: A practical example. *Interlending and Document Supply, 24*(2), 12–18.

Breeding, M. (2001). Offering remote access to restricted resources. *Information Today, 18*(4), 52–53.

Breeding, M. (2008). Helping you buy: Electronic resource management systems. *Computers in Libraries, 28*(7).

Breitbach, W., & Lambert, J. E. (2011, July-August). Patron-driven ebookacquisition. *Info Today,* 17-21.

Briglle, A., & Mitcham, C. (2009). From the philosophy of information to the philosophy of information culture(s). *The Information Society: An International Journal, 25*(3), 169–174. doi:10.1080/01972240902848765.

Broady-Preston, J., & Lobo, A. (2011). Measuring the quality, value and impact of academic libraries: The role of external standards. *Performance Measurement and Metrics, 12,* 122–135. doi:10.1108/14678041111149327.

Brody, T. (2006), *Evaluating research impact through open access to scholarly communication.* Retrieved March 20, 2013, from http://eprints.soton.ac.uk/263313/

Brody, T., Carr, L., Hey, J. M. N., Brown, A., & Hitchcock, S. (2007). PRONOM-ROAR: Adding format profiles to a repository registry to inform preservation services. *The International Journal of Digital Curation, 2*(2).

Brown, E. M. (2005). *History and definition of digital libraries.* Retrieved November 1, 2012 from http://www.southernct.Edu/~brownm/dl_history.html

Brown, D. J. (2003). *Electronic publishing and libraries: Planning for the impact and growth.* London: Bowker-Saur..

Browning, M. W., & Hass, L. M. (1991). Is business periodicals ondisc the greatest thing since sliced bread? A cost analysis of user survey. *CD-ROM Professional, 4*(1), 37–41.

Brown, S., Gummersson, E., Edvardsson, B., & Gustavsson, B. (1991). *Service quality.* New York: Lexington Books..

Buckland, M. (1997). *Redesigning library series: A manifesto.* Retrieved November 20, 2012 from http://sunsitebeakehay.edu/literature/library/redesigning/html

Budapest Open Access Initiative. (2001). Retrieved March 10, 2013 from http://www.opensocietyfoundations.org/openaccess

Budd, J., & Harloe. (1994). Collection development and scholarly communication in the era of electronic access. *Journal of Academic Information Management, 20*(5), 83–87.

Bunkell, J., & Dyas-Correia, S. (2009). E-books vs. print: Which is the better value? *The Serials Librarian, 56*(1-4), 215–219. doi:10.1080/03615260802698283.

Cabanes, A. (2010). *Copyright vs copyleft: Short introduction to these licenses.* Retrieved February 22, 2013, from http://aintzane.wordpress.com/2010/01/28/copyright-vs-copyleft-a-short-introduction-to-these-licenses

Calhoun, K., & Riemer, J. J. (Eds.). (2001). *New tools and possibilities for cooperative electronic resource description.* New York: Haworth..

Carpenter, T. (n.d.). *Standard columns – Electronic resource management standardization - Still a mixed bag.* Retrieved March 30, 2013, from http://www.niso.org/apps/group_public/download.php/5258/

Carpenter, T. A. (2013, March 6). Copyright transfer as a click-through – It's so easy to sign away your rights. *The Scholarly Kitchen.* Retrieved May 30, 2013 from http://bit.ly/WIOHIG

Carr, P. L. (2010). The commitment to securing perpetual journal access a survey of academic research libraries. *Library Resources & Technical Services, 55*(1), 4–16. doi:10.5860/lrts.55n1.4.

CEN. (2010). *Building the e-CF: A combination of sound methodology and expert contribution.* Retrieved November 11, 2012 from www.ecompetences.eu

Chadwick, A. (2011). *The hybrid media system: Politics and power.* New York: Oxford University Press..

Chandel, A. S., & Saikia, M. (2012). Challenges and opportunities of e-resources. *Annals of Library and Information Studies, 59,* 148–154.

Chan, G. R. Y. C. (2008). Aligning collections budget with program priorities: A modified zero-based approach. *Library Collections, Acquisitions & Technical Services, 32,* 46–52. doi:10.1016/j.lcats.2008.06.001.

Cherrier, H. (2010). Custodian behavior: A material expression of anti-consumerism. *Consumption. Markets and Culture, 8*(3), 259–289. doi:10.1080/10253861003786983.

Chesbrough, H., & Spohrer, J. (2006). A research manifesto for service science. *Communications of the ACM, 49*(7), 35–40. doi:10.1145/1139922.1139945.

Chew, K., Stemper, J., Lilyard, C., & Schoenborn, M. (2012). *User-defined valued metrics for electronic journa*ls. Paper presented at the Library Assessment Conference: Building Effective, Sustainable, Practical Assessment. Charlottesville, VA. Retrieved September 9, 2012 from http://libraryassessment.org/bm~doc/Chew_Katherine_2012.pdf

Chinese Open Access Portal. (2013). *The national science library (NSL) at the Chinese academy of sciences (CAS).* Retrieved May 25, 2013 from http://www.open-access.net.cn

CiteSeer. (2010). *The college of information sciences and technology, the Pennsylvania State University.* Retrieved March 5, 2013, from http://citeseerx.ist.psu.edu/index

Cleveland, G. (1998). *Digital libraries: Definitions, issues and challenges.* Retrieved November 6, 2012 from http://www.ifla.shodhganga.inflibnet.ac.in/dxml/bitstream/handle/1944/1395/28.pdf?sequence=1

CogPrints. (2013). Retrieved March 5, 2013, from http://cogprints.org/

Cohen, P. (2004, August 1). Spaces for social study. *New York Times,* p. 19.

Collins, M. (Ed.). (2008). Electronic resource management systems (ERMS) review. Elsevier, 267..

Collins, M., & Grogg, J. E. (2011). At ERMS length: Evaluating electronic resource management systems. *Library Journal, 136*(4), 22–28.

Commons, W. (2013). *Commons: International copyright quick reference guide.* Retrieved June 4, 2013 from http://bit.ly/13hhMAz

Connaway, L., Dickey, T., & Radford, M. (2011). If it is too inconvenient I'm not going after it: Convenience as a critical factor in information-seeking behaviors. *Library & Information Science Research, 33,* 179–190. doi:10.1016/j.lisr.2010.12.002.

Conway, P. (2010). *Measuring content quality in a preservation repository: HahtiTrust and large-scale book digitization.* Paper presented at the Seventh International Conference on Preservation of digital Objects. Vienna, Austria. Retrieved November 10, 2012 from http://hdl.handle.net/2027.42/85227

Cooke, L., Norris, M., Busby, N., Page, T., Franklin, G., Gadd, E., & Young, H. (2011). Evaluating the impact of academic liaison librarians on their user community: A review and case study. *New Review of Academic Librarianship, 17*(1), 5–30. doi:10.1080/13614533.2011.539096.

Copyright for Creativity – A Declaration for Europe. (2010). Retrieved from http://www.copyright4creativity.eu/Public/Declaration

CORAL. (n.d.). Retrieved May 06, 2013, from http://erm.library.nd.edu

CORE. (2013). *Connecting repositories, knowledge media institute.* Retrieved March 10, 2013, from http://core-project.kmi.open.ac.uk/

Corral, S. (2011). *Evaluating intellectual assets: New and Informal measures for the transcendent library.* Retrieved November 24, 2012 from http://www.york.ac.uk/media/abouttheuniversity/supportservices/informationdirectorate/documents/northumbriapresentations/Corrall-York%202011.pdf

Corral, S., & Roberts, A. (2012). *Information resource development and collection in the digital age: Conceptual frameworks and new definitions for the network world.* Paper presented at Libraries in the Digital Age (LIDA). Retrieved December 2, 2012 from http://ozk.unizd.hr/proceedings/index.php/lida2012/article/view/62/33

Cortez, E., & Colon-Aguirre, M. (2009). *What libraries and information professionals can learn from knowledge and project management.* Paper presented at the 17th Bobcatsss Symposium. Porto, Portugal. Retrieved January 31, 2012 from http://trace.tennessee.edu/cgi/viewcontent.cgi?article=1014&context=utk_infosciepubs&sei-redir=1&referer=http%3A%2F%2Fwww.google.com%2Furl%3Fsa%3Dt%26rct%3Dj%26q%3Dwhat%2520libraries%2520and%2520information%2520professionals%2520can%2520learn%2520from%2520knowledge%2520and%2520project%2520management%26source%3Dweb%26cd%3D1%26ved%3D0CDMQFjAA%26url%3Dhttp%253A%252F%252Ftrace.tennessee.edu%252Fcgi%252Fviewcontent.cgi%253Farticle%253D1014%2526context%253Dutk_infosciepubs%26ei%3D6XPXUOSDKtKThgf06YCwBg%26usg%3DAFQjCNFEYWAWmwRx9Bagcl9BkeyeB19Hbg#search=%22what%20libraries%20information%20professionals%20can%20learn%20from%20knowledge%20project%20management%22

Costa, A. F. (2012). Desigualdades sociais. *Sociologia. Problemas e Práticas, 68,* 9–32.

Cotter, G., Carroll, B., Hodge, G., & Japzon, A. (2005). Electronic collection management and electronic information services. *Information Services & Use, 25,* 23–34.

Courant, P. N., & Nielsen, M. B. (2010). On the cost of keeping a book. In *The Idea of Order: Transforming Research Collections for 21st Century Scholarship.* Washington, DC: CLIR Publication..

Cova, B., & Dalli, D. (2009). Working consumers: The next step in marketing theory? *Marketing Theory, 9*(3), 315–339. doi:10.1177/1470593109338144.

Creative Commons. (n.d.). Retrieved February 19, 2013, from http://creativecommons.org/icense/by/3.0

Crews, K. D. (2012). *Copyright law for librarians and educators: Creative strategies and practical solutions.* Chicago: American Library Association..

Crow, M. (2009, January 28). Message from President Michael Crow. *ASU News Online.* Retrieved December 15, 2012 from https://asunews.asu.edu/20090128_furloughprogram

CUFTS: Open Source Serial Management. (n.d.). Retrieved May 03, 2013, from http://researcher.sfu.ca/cufts

Cukadar, S., Tuglu, A., & Gurdal, G. (2012). Perspectives on new electronic resources management system for the ANKOS consortium. *Journal of Academic Librarianship.* doi:10.1016/j.acalib.2012.11.011.

Cullen, R. (2005). *Operationalising the focus/values/purpose matrix: A tool for libraries to measure their ability to deliver service quality.* Paper presented at the 6th Northumbria Performance Measurement Conference. Northumbria, UK. Retrieved November http://northumbria.ac.uk/sd/academic/ceis/re/isrc/conf/?view=standard

DAEDALUS. (2013). Retrieved March 5, 2013, from http://www.lib.gla.ac.uk/daedalus/

Dahlstrom, M., Hansson, J., & Kjellman, U. (2012). As we may digitize – Institutions and documents reconfigured. *The Library Quarterly, 21*(3/4), 455–474.

Dalkir, K. (2005). *Knowledge management in theory and practice.* Burlington, UK: Elsevier-Butterworth-Heinemann..

Daniels, K. (2010). Got value? Journal collection analysis is worth the effort. *Medical Reference Services Quarterly, 29*(3), 275–285. doi:10.1080/02763869.2010.494521 PMID:20677068.

DASH. (2013). *Digital access to scholarship at Harvard.* Retrieved March 15, 2013, from http://dash.harvard.edu/

Day, M. (2000). *Preservation of electronic information: A bibliography.* Retrieved November 20, 2012 from http://www.homes.ukolin.ac.UK/-lismd/preservation.html

Declaration, A. A. R. H. U. S. in Excellence. (2012). *Excellence revisited – The value of excellence.* Retrieved April 19, 2012 from http://www.excellence2012_dk/presentationspapers

Dekkers, M., Polman, F., te Velde, R., & de Vries, M. (2006). *MEPSIR: Measuring European public sector information resources: Final report of study on exploitation of public sector information – Benchmarking of EU framework conditions.* Retrieved December 18, 2012, from http://ec.europa.eu/information_society/policy/psi/docs/pdfs/mepsir/final_report.pdf

Denegri-Knott, J., & Molesworth, M. (2010). Concepts and practices of digital virtual consumption. *Consumption. Markets & Culture, 13*(2), 109–132. doi:10.1080/10253860903562130.

Despres, C., & Chauvel, D. (2000). *Knowledge horizons: The present and the promise of knowledge management. Woburn.* Butterworth-Heinemann..

Di Domenico, G. (2004). Self-assessment, skill, excellence: The EFQM model in the library. *Bollettino AIB, 44,* 429–444.

Digital Public Library of America. (2013). Retrieved March 20, 2013, from http://dp.la/

Dingley, B. (2003). U.S. periodical prices – 2003. *Library Resources & Technical Services, 47*(4), 363–371. doi:10.5860/lrts.47n4.192.

Directory of Open Access Journals (DOAJ). (2013). Retrieved March 10, 2013, from http://www.doaj.org/

Directory of Open Access Repositories (OpenDOAR). (2013). Retrieved March 10, 2013, from http://www.opendoar.org/

DOAJ. (2013). *The directory of open access journals.* Retrieved March 10, 2013, from http://www.doaj.org/

Dodson, A. (2003). *Citizenship and the environment.* Oxford, UK: Oxford University Press..

Duguid, B. (1995). *The unacceptable face of plagiarism? Pop parody panic.* Retrieved 23 March 2013 from http://downlode.org/Etext/plagiarism.html

Dusollier, S. (2012). DRM at the intersection of copyright law and technology: A case study for regulation. In E. Brousseau, & M. Merzouki (Eds.), *Governance, Regulations and Powers on the Internet* (pp. 297–317). Cambridge, UK: Cambridge University Press. doi:10.1017/CBO9781139004145.019.

EBSCONET: ERM Essentials. (n.d.). Retrieved May 02, 2013, from http://www2.ebsco.com/en-us/ProductsServices/ERM/Pages/index.aspx

EFQM. (2003). *Os conceitos fundamentais da Excelência.* Bruxelas: EFQM.

EFQM. (2012). *EFQM excellence model 2013.* Brussels: EFQM..

Eke, H. N. (2011). Digitizing resources for University of Nigeria repository: Process and challenges. *Webology, 8*(1).

Ekwelem, V. O., Okafor, V. N., & Ukwoma, S. C. (2009). Students' use of electronic information sources at the University of Nigeria, Nsukka. *African Journal of Library. Archives and Information Science, 19*(2), 89–97.

E-Resource Central: SirsiDynix. (n.d.). Retrieved May 04, 2013, from http://www.sirsidynix.com/eresourcecentral

E-Resource Taskforce Report. (2010). *Report of the Monash University Sunway Campus (MUSC) taskforce on contemporary collection development policy and procedure at musc for e-book resources.* (Unpublished / Restricted report).

Ess, C. (2009). Floridi's philosophy of information and information ethics: Current perspectives, future directions. *The Information Society, 25,* 159–168. doi:10.1080/01972240902848708.

European Commission. (2005). *The European charter for researchers.* Luxembourg: Office for Official Publications of the European Communities..

European Commission. (2007). *Key competences for lifelong learning – European reference framework.* Brussels: Commission of the European Communities..

European Commission. (2008). *The European qualifications framework for lifelong learning (EQF)*. Luxembourg: Office for Official Publications of the European Communities..

European Commission. (2012). *Communication from the commission to the European parliament, the council, the European parliament, the council, the European economic and social committee and the committee of the regions: A reinforced European research area partnership for excellence and growth*. Brussels: EC. Retrieved December 2, 2012, from http://ec.europa.eu/euraxess/pdf/research_policies/era-communication_en.pdf

European Commission. (2012). *Executive summary of impact assessment accompanying the document recommendation on access to and preservation of scientific information*. Brussels: EC. Retrieved December 2, 2012, from http://ec.europa.eu/research/science-society/document_library/pdf_06/impact-assessement-executive-summary_en.pdf

European Library. (2013). Retrieved March 20, 2013, from http://www.theeuropeanlibrary.org/tel4/

EUROPEANA. (2013). Retrieved March 20, 2013, from http://www.europeana.eu/

Fenner, A. (2004). *Selecting materials for library collections*. Haworth, UK: Information Press..

Ferguson, A., & Kehoe, K. (1993). Access vs ownership: What is most cost effective in the sciences. *Journal of Library Administration, 19*(2), 89–99. doi:10.1300/J111v19n02_07.

Filser, M. (2002). Le marketing de production d'expériences: Statut théorique et implications managériales. *Décisions Marketing, 28*(4), 13–22.

Florida, R. (2002). *The rise of the creative class. Nova Iorque*. Basic Books..

Floridi, L. (2010). *Information: A very short introduction*. Oxford, UK: Oxford University Press. doi:10.1093/actrade/9780199551378.001.0001.

Floridi, L. (2011). *The philosophy of information*. Oxford, UK: Oxford University Press. doi:10.1093/acprof:oso/9780199232383.001.0001.

Fons, T. A., & Jewell, T. D. (2007). Envisioning the future of ERM systems. *The Serials Librarian, 52*(1-2), 151–166. doi:10.1300/J123v52n01_13.

Franklin, B. (2005). Managing the electronic collection with cost per use data. *IFLA Journal, 31*(3), 241–248. doi:10.1177/0340035205058809.

Friend, F. J. (1996). Economic models for electronic libraries: Electronic documents and information: From preservation to access. In *Proceedings of 18th International Essen Symposium*. Essen: Essen University Library.

Gadd, E. (1998). Comparing paper and electronic short loan collections. *Library Management, 19*(5), 311–317. doi:10.1108/01435129810218492.

GALLICA. (2013). Retrieved March 20, 2013, from http://gallica.bnf.fr/

Gasser, U. (2006). *Legal frameworks and technological protection of digital content: Moving forward towards a best practice model*. Retrieved 3 April 2013 from, http://www.ftc.gov/bcp/workshops/techade/pdfs/Gasser1.pdf

Gessesse, K. (2008). Collection development and management in the 21st century with special reference to academic libraries: An overview. *Library Management, 21*(7), 365–372. doi:10.1108/01435120010372551.

Ginsparg, P. (2001). *Creating a global knowledge network*. Retrieved March 20, 2013, from http://people.ccmr.cornell.edu/~ginsparg/blurb/pg01unesco.html

Gizmodo. (2012). *What happens in 60 seconds on the internet*. Retrieved 25 May, 2013 from http://gizmodo.com/5813875/what-happens-in-60-seconds-on-the-internet

Global Libraries Initiatives. (2008). *IPA road map*. Seattle, WA: Bill & Melinda Gates Foundation..

Gold Rush. (n.d.). *Electronic resource management and discovery*. Retrieved May 09, 2013, from http://www.coalliance.org/grinfo/

Gonçalves, M. A., Moreira, B. L., Fox, E. A., & Watson, L. T. (2007). What is a good digital library? A quality model for digital libraries. *Information Processing & Management, 43*(5), 1416–1437. doi:10.1016/j.ipm.2006.11.010.

Google Books Project. (2013). Retrieved March 20, 2013, from http://www.google.com/googlebooks/library/index.html

Graveline, J. D. (2011). Launching a successful copyright education program. *College & Undergraduate Libraries*, *18*(1), 92–96. doi:10.1080/10691316.2011.550534.

Green, S. P. (2002). Plagiarism, norms, and the limits of theft law: Some observations on the use of criminal sanctions in enforcing intellectual property rights. *Hastings Law Journal, 54*(1). *iThenticate users guide.* (2012). Retrieved 20, 2013, from http://www.ithenticate.com/Portals/92785/media/iThenticate_qs_guide.pdf

Griffiths, J., & King, D. (1983). *Library cost benefit analysis: A SUNY/OCLC workshop manual.* Albany, NY: SUNY/OCLC Network Office of Library Services, State University of New York..

Gronroos, C., & Ravald, A. (2011). Service as business logic: Implications for value creation and marketing. *Journal of Service Management, 22*(1), 5–22. doi:10.1108/09564231111106893.

Gronross, C. (2011). Value co-creation in service logic: A critical analysis. *Marketing Theory, 11*(3), 279–301. doi:10.1177/1470593111408177.

Grover, D., & Fons, T. (2004). The innovative electronic resource management system: A development partnership. *Serials Review, 30*(2), 110–116. doi:10.1016/j.serrev.2004.03.003.

Gummesson, E. (2004). From one-to-one to many-to-many marketing. In *Service excellence in management: Interdisciplinarity, contribution: Proceedings from the QUIS 9 Symposium* (pp. 16-25). QUIS.

Gutenberg Project. (2013). Retrieved March 20, 2013, from http://www.gutenberg.org/

Guthrie, K. (2001). Archiving in the digital age. *EDUCASE Review, 36*(6).

Hahn, J. (2012). Mobile augmented reality applications for library services. *New Library World, 113*(9/10), 429–438. doi:10.1108/03074801211273902.

Halsey, R. S., et al. (2009). Library (institution). In *Microsoft Encarta 2009.* [DVD]. Redmond, WA: Microsoft Corporation.

Hansson, J. (2011). *Libraries and identity: The role of institutional self-image and identity in the emergence of new types of libraries.* London: Chandos..

Harnad, S. (2013). Paid gold OA versus free gold OA: Against color cacophony. Open Access Archivangelism. Retrieved March 20, 2013, from http://openaccess.eprints.org/index.php?/archives/1003-Paid-Gold-OA-Versus-Free-Gold-OA-Against-Color-Cacophony.html

Harnad, S., Brody, T., Vallieres, F., Carr, L., Hitchcock, S., & Gingras, Y. et al. (2004). The access/impact problem and the green and gold roads to open access. *Serials Review, 30*(4). doi:10.1016/j.serrev.2004.09.013.

Harrington, M., & Stovall, C. (2011). Contextualizing and interpreting cost per use for electronic journals. In *Proceedings of the Charleston Library Conference.* Retrieved December 13, 2001, from http://docs.lib.purdue.edu/cgi/viewcontent.cgi?article=1200&context=charleston

Harrison, R., Newholm, T., & Shaw, D. (Eds.). (2005). *The ethical consumer.* London: Sage..

Hartnett, E., & Price, A. (2011). iPotentila: Mobile electronic resource management an iPad. *Library Collections, Acquisitions & Technical Services, 35*(4), 118–128. doi:10.1016/j.lcats.2011.06.001.

Hathitrust Digital Library. (2013). Retrieved March 20, 2013, from http://www.hathitrust.org/

Hawbaker, A. C., & Wagner, C. K. (1996). Periodical ownership versus full-text online access: A cost benefit analysis. *Journal of Academic Librarianship, 2*(22), 105–109. doi:10.1016/S0099-1333(96)90176-7.

Herget, J., & Hierl, S. (2007). Excellence in libraries: A systematic and integrated approach. *New Library World, 108*(11/12), 526–544. doi:10.1108/03074800710838263.

HERMES: The Hopkins Electronic Resource Management System. (n.d.). Retrieved April 07, 2013, from http://www.ala.org/lita/ital/22/1/cyzyk

HERMIS. (n.d.). Retrieved May 06, 2013, from http://www.harrassowitz.de/subscription_services/hermis.html

Heting, C. (1999). *Electronic journals: Promises and challenges for academic libraries.*

Hiller, S. (2003). But what does it mean? Using statistical data for decision making in academic libraries. *Occasional Paper, 32*, 10-23.

History of Books. (2012). *Wikipedia.* Retrieved November 6, 2012 from http://en.wikipedia.org/wiki/History_of_books

Hobohm, H.-C. (2012). *Can digital libraries generate knowledge?* Retrieved December 1, 2012 from http://www.cceh.uni-koeln.de/files/Hobohm_final.pdf

Hodge, G. (2003). *Selected bibliography of digital archiving.* Retrieved November 20, 2012 from http://www.alpsp.org/biblio.pdi

Hodge, G. (2000). Best practices in digital archiving: An information life cycle approach. *D-Lib Magazine, 6*(1). doi:10.1045/january2000-hodge.

Hodges, D., Preston, C., & Hamilton, M. J. (2010). Patron-initiated collection development: Progress of a paradigm shift. *Collection Management, 35*(3-4), 208–221. doi:10.1080/01462679.2010.486968.

Howard Hughes Medical Institute. (2003). *The Bethesda statement on open access publishing.* Retrieved March 10, 2013 from http://legacy.earlham.edu/~peters/fos/bethesda.htm

Huijboom, N., & Van den Broek. (2011). Open data: An international comparison of strategies. *European Journal of E-Practice, 12.*

Hults, P. (2008). Electronic usage statistics. In H. Yu, & S. Breivold (Eds.), *Electronic Resource Management in Libraries: Research and Practice* (pp. 29–46). Academic Press. doi:10.4018/978-1-59904-891-8.ch003.

Ibrahim, A. E. (2004). Use and user perception of electronic resources in the United Arab Emirates University (UAEU). *Libri, 54*, 21–23. doi:10.1515/LIBR.2004.18.

ICAL. (2013). The second international conference on academic libraries on cloud computing for libraries. *ICAL 2013 Newsletter.* Retrieved April 11, 2013, from http://www.ipu.ac.in/ical2013/icalnews220213.zip

Idiegbeyan-Ose, J., & Ukpoghome, T. U. (2009). Distance learning in Nigeria and the role of the virtual library. *Gateway Library Journal, 12*(2), 75–85.

IGNOU Library. (2012). *Introduction.* Retrieved April 22, 2013, from http://www.ignou.ac.in/ignou/aboutignou/division/ldd/introduction

IGNOU NODLINET. (2012). *NODLINET.* Retrieved May 1, 2013, from http://www.ignou.ac.in/NODLINET/aboutnodlinet

Innovative. (n.d.). Retrieved May 06, 2013, from http://www.iii.com/products/electronic_resource.shtml

International Children's Digital Library. (2013). Retrieved March 20, 2013, from http://en.childrenslibrary.org/

International Records Management Trust. (2009). *Preserving electronic records: Training in electronic records management.* London: International Records Management Trust..

Italie, H. (2009). AP accuses Obama artist Shepard Fairey of copyright infringement. *The Huffington Post.* Retrieved from http://huff.to/LJU1

Jackson, M. M. (1998). *Maximizing access, minimizing cost.* The Association of Research Libraries North American Technology Programme/NAILDO Project.

James, B. (2004). A manifesto on WIPO and the future of intellectual property. *Duke Law & Technology Review.* Retrieved February 23, 2013, from http://scholarship.law.duke.edu/dltr/vol3/iss1/6/

Jenkins, F. W. (2012). Purposes and challenges of digitized collections for the humanities in academic libraries. *Library Student Journal, 7*(6), 1–19.

Jenkins, H. (2006). *Convergence culture: Where old and new media collide.* New York: New York University Press..

J-Gate. (2013). *The e-journal gateway.* Retrieved March 5, 2013, from - http://www.jgate.in/

Jing, G., & Jin, C. (2009). The innovative university library: Strategic choice, construction practices and development ideas. *Library Management, 30*(4/5), 295–308. doi:10.1108/01435120910957959.

JISC. (2009). *Libraries of the future.* Retrieved October 18, 2012, from http://www.jisc.ac.uk/publications/generalpublications/2009/librariesofthefuturebrochure.aspx

Johnson, S., et al. (2012). *Key-issues for e-resource collection development: A guide for libraries.* Retrieved 9 November 2012 from http://www.ifla.org/files/assets/acquisition-collection-development/publications/Key%20Issues%20for%20E-Resource%20Collection%20Development%20-%20AUG%2016%202012_5.pdf

Johnston, L. (2012). *Digital collections as big data.* Retrieved December 1, 2012 from http://www.digital-preservation.gov/meetings/ndiipp12.html

Jones, D. (2011). On-demand information delivery: Integration of patron-driven acquisition into a comprehensive information delivery system. *Journal of Library Administration, 51*(7-8), 764–776. doi:10.1080/01930826.2011.601275.

Jones, K., Kinnell, M., & Usherwood, B. (2000). The development of self-assessment toolkits for the library and information sector. *The Journal of Documentation, 56*, 119–135. doi:10.1108/EUM0000000007111.

JOSTOR. (n.d.). *The need.* Retrieved from http://www.jstor.org/about/need.html

Journal Finder. (n.d.). Retrieved May 09, 2013, from http://www.wtcox.com/journal-finder.cfm

Kapur, P. (2011). *Creative commons: Impact on Indian copyright law.* Retrieved February 19, 2013, from http://papers.ssrn.com/sol3/papers.cfm?abstract_id=2047662

Kasprowski, R. (2007). *Standards in electronic resource management.* Retrieved May 09, 2013 from http://www.asis.org/Bulletin/Aug-07/kasprowski.html

Keiskala, M., Hiekkanen, K., & Korhonen, J. J. (2011). *The impact of information technology enabled services on value co-creation.* Retrieved November 23, 2012 from http://www.requisiteremedy.com/docs/value-co-creation.pdf

Keller, M. (1992). *Foreign acquisitions in North American research libraries.*

Keller, M. (1992). Moving towards concrete solution base in fundamental values. *Journal of Academic Information Management, 18*(3), 8–15.

Kennedy, R. (2012, September 7). Shepard Fairey is fined and sentenced to probation in Hope poster case. *The New York Times.* Retrieved from http://nyti.ms/10OWoyX

Kent, A. (1979). *Use of library materials: The University of Pittsburgh study.* New York: M. Dekker..

Kidd, T. (1997). Electronic journals management: Some problems and solutions. *Managing Information, 4*(10), 25–26.

Kim, M. (2007). *The creative commons and copyright protection in digital era: Use of creative commons licenses.* Retrieved February 20, 2013, from http://jcmc.indiana.edu/vol13/issue1/kim.html

Kluft, D. (2012). *The devil's in the details: Dissecting the 350-page Georgia State University electronic reserves copyright ruling.* Retrieved June 2, 2013 from http://bit.ly/14q3tZT

Know Your Copy Rights. (n.d.). *Using works in your teaching.* Retrieved February 27, 2013, from http://www.knowyourcopyrights.org/bm~doc/kycrbrochurebw.pdf

Kozinets, R. V. (2002). Can consumers escape the market? Emancipatory illuminations from burning man. *The Journal of Consumer Research, 29*(1), 20–38. doi:10.1086/339919.

Kozinets, R. V., & Handelman, J. M. (2004). Adversaries of consumption: Consumer movements, activism and ideology. *The Journal of Consumer Research, 31*(3), 691–704. doi:10.1086/425104.

Kuny, T. (1998). The digital dark ages? Challenges in the preservation of electronic information. *International Preservation News, 17.*

Laitio, T., & Helsinki, D. (2012). *Counting what counts.* Retrieved November 11, 2012 from www.coe.int/t/dg4/.../HelsinkiReport_en.pdf

Langer, R. (2007). Marketing, presumption and innovation in the fetish community. In *Consumer tribes* (pp. 243–259). Oxford, UK: Buttherworth-Heinemman..

Lawrence, G., Jehoe, W., Rieger, O., Walters, W., & Kenny, A. (2000). *Risk management of digital information: A file format investigation council on library and information resources.* Retrieved November 20, 2012 from http:/www/clir.org/publib/reports/pub93/pub93.pdf

Le Deuff, O. (2009). *La culture de l'information en reformation.* Rennes, France: Université de Rennes..

Leadbeater, C. (2012). *Cloud culture: The future of global cultural relations*. London: British Council..

Lee, M. S. W., Fernandez, K. V., & Hyman, M. R. (2009). Anti-consumption: An overview and research agenda. *Journal of Business Research, 62*(2), 145–147. doi:10.1016/j.jbusres.2008.01.021.

Lehdonvirta, V. (2012). A history of the digitalization of consumer culture: From Amazon through Pirate Bay to Farm Ville. In *Digital Virtual Consumption*. New York: Routledge..

Lemke, F., Clark, M., & Wilson, H. (2011). Customer experience quality: An exploration in business and consumer contexts using repertory grid technique. *Journal of the Academy of Marketing Science, 39*, 846–869. doi:10.1007/s11747-010-0219-0.

Lessig, L. (2000). *Open code and open societies*. Paper presented at Free Software: A Model for Society? Tutzing, Germany.

Levine-Clark, M., Bosch, S., Anderson, K., & Nauman, M. (2009). Rethinking monographic acquisition: Developing a demand-driven purchase model. In *Proceedings of the Charleston Library Conference*, (pp. 549-557). Charleston Library.

Levine-Clark, M. (2007). Electronic books and the humanities: A survey at the University of Denver. *Collection Building, 26*(1), 7–14. doi:10.1108/01604950710721548.

Li, X., & Kopper, C. (2006). Cancellation of print journals in the electronic era: A case study. *Against the Grain, 17*(6), 1, 18, 20, 22.

Library of Congress. (2013). *Digital collections*. Retrieved March 20, 2013, from http://www.loc.gov/library/libarch-digital.html

Library. (2009). *Encyclopædia Britannica 2009 student and home ed*. Chicago: Encyclopedia Britannica.

Linn, M. Jr. (2009). Cost-benefit analysis: A disparagement of its misuse and misexplanation. *The Bottom Line: Managing Library Finances, 22*(3), 82–85. doi:10.1108/08880450910999640.

Lipinski, T. A. (2013). *The librarian's legal companion for licensing information resources and services*. Chicago: Neal-Schuman..

Littman, J., & Connaway, L. S. (2004). A circulation analysis of print books and e-books in an academic research library. *Library Resources & Technical Services, 48*(4), 256–262.

Lossau, N. (2012). An overview of research infrastructure in Europe – And recommendation to LIBER. *The Library Quarterly, 21*(3/4), 313–329.

Lund University Libraries. (2011, November 26). *Directory of open access journals: FAQs*. Retrieved November 10, 2012 from http://www.doaj.org/doaj?func=loadTempl&templ=about&uiLanguage=en

Mahajan, P. (2005). Academic libraries in India: A present-day scenario. *Library Philosophy & Practice, 8*(1), 1.

Majumdar, S., & Singh, R. (2007). *Information literacy and competency programme in academic libraries: a case study of DULS*. Paper presented at the 5th International CALIBER -2007. Chandigarh, India. Retrieved April 22, 2013, from http://ir.inflibnet.ac.in/bitstream/handle/1944/1436/608-616.pdf?sequence=1

Malnig, A. (2008). Libraries march toward a digital future. *Seybold Report: Analyzing Publishing Technologies, 8*(9), 8.

Mangrum, S., & Pozzebon, M. E. (2012). Use of collection development policies in electronic resource management. *Collection Building, 31*(3), 108–114. doi:10.1108/01604951211243506.

Maracke, C. (2010). *Creative commons international: The international license porting project*. Retrieved February 26, 2013, from http://www.jipitec.eu/issues/jipitec-1-1-2010/2417/dippadm1268743811.97.pdf

Marcum, J. W. (2003). Visions: The academic library in 2012. *D-Lib Magazine, 9*(5). doi:10.1045/may2003-marcum.

Markless, S., & Streatfield, D. (2006). *Evaluating the impact of your library*. London: Facet Publishing..

Max Planck Society. (2003). *Berlin declaration on open access to knowledge in the sciences and humanities*. Retrieved March 10, 2013 from http://oa.mpg.de/lang/en-uk/berlin-prozess/berliner-erklarung/

McCormack, A. (2010). *The e-skills manifesto: A call to arms*. Luxembourg: Digital Europe..

McCracken, E. (2007). Description of and access to electronic resources (ER): Transitioning into the digital age. *Collection Management, 32*(3-4), 259–275. doi:10.1300/J105v32n03_02.

McKenzie, J. (1998). The new plagiarism: Seven antidotes to prevent highway robbery in an electronic age. *From Now On: The Educational Technology Journal, 7*(8).

McMillan, G. (n.d.). *Management of serials in libraries.* Eaglewood, IL: Libraries Unlimited.

Metcalfe, J. (2012). *A pan-European professional development framework for researchers.* Strasbourg, Germany: European Science Foundation..

Meyer, R. W. (1992). Locally mounted databases: Making information as close to free as possible. *Online, 16*(1), 15–24.

Michalak, S. (1994). Planning academic library facilities: The library will have walls. *Journal of Library Administration, 20*(2), 91–113.

Mick, C. K. (1979). Cost analysis of information systems and services. *Annual Review of Information Science & Technology, 14*, 37–64.

moonlighter1965. (2013a, June 4). *Are European orphans about to be freed?* Retrieved June 4, 2013 from http://www.twitter.com/moonlighter1965

moonlighter1965. (2013b, June 4). *Five famous copyright infringement cases (what you can learn).* Retrieved June 4, 2013 from http://www.twitter.com/moonlighter1965

Mukherjee, B. (2012). *Information communication and society.* New Delhi, India: ESS ESS Publication..

Mullen, L. B. (2010). *Open access and its practical impact on the work of academic librarians: Collection development, public services and the library and information science literature.* Oxford, UK: Chandos Publishing. doi:10.1533/9781780630229.

Murdock, D. (2010). Relevance of electronic resource management systems to hiring practices for electronic resources personnel. *Library Collections, Acquisitions & Technical Services, 34*, 25–42. doi:10.1016/j.lcats.2009.11.001.

Mutula, S. M., & Ojedokun, A. A. (2008). Digital libraries. In *Information and knowledge management in the digital age: Concepts, technologies and African perspectives* (pp. 101–121). Ibadan, Nigeria: Third World Information Service..

Nabe, J., Imre, A. P., & Mann, S. R. (2011). Let the patron drive: Purchase on demand of e-books. *The Serials Librarian, 60*(1-4), 193–197. doi:10.1080/036152 6X.2011.556033.

Nas, T. F. (1996). *Cost-benefit analysis: Theory and application.* London: Sage..

News, B. B. C. (2010). *E books launch.* Retrieved July 2010 from http://news.bbc.co.uk/1/hi/scotland/10474210.stm

Ng, I. C. L., Vargo, S. L., & Smith, L. A. (2012). *Reconceptualising service through a service dominant logic.* Retrieved October 31, 2012 from http://www2.warwick.ac.uk/fac/sci/wmg/research

Nicholson, D. R. (2013). *Copyright and related issues.* University of the Witwatersrand. Retrieved June 5, 2013 from http://libguides.wits.ac.za/Copyright_and_Related_Issues

Niggeman, E. (2012). *The importance of open data to national libraries.* Retrieved March 1, 2012, from http://conference.ifla.org/past/ifla78/181-niggemann-en.pdf

Nisonger, T. E. (1996). Collection management issues for electronic journals. *IFLA Journal, 22*(3), 25–31. doi:10.1177/034003529602200311.

Nixon, J., Freeman, R., & Ward, S. (2010). Patron-driven acquisitions: An introduction and literature review. *Collection Management, 35*, 119–124. doi:10.1080/01462679.2010.486957.

Noh, Y. (2012). A study measuring the performance of electronic resources in academic libraries. *Aslib Proceedings, 64*(2), 134–153. doi:10.1108/00012531211215169.

O'Connor, S., & Jilovsky, C. (2009). Approaches to the storage of low use and last copy research materials. *Library Collections, Acquisitions & Technical Services, 32*, 121–126. doi:10.1016/j.lcats.2008.08.001.

OAIster. (2013). *OCLC.* Retrieved March 5, 2013, from http://www.oclc.org/oaister.en.html

Oakland, J. S. (2003). *Total quality management: Text with cases* (3rd ed.). Oxford, UK: Butterworth-Heinemann..

Oapen Library. (2013). *Publishing in European network.* Retrieved March 5, 2013, from http://www.oapen.org/home

Oapen Library. (2013). Retrieved March 10, 2013 from http://project.oapen.org/

Ochôa, P., & Pinto, L. G. (2006). *Quality – An on-going practice and reflection in a governmental library (1996–2006).* Retrieved March 1, 2012, from http://archive.ifla.org/IV/ifla72/papers/078-Ochoa_Pinto-en.pdf

Ochôa, P., & Pinto, L. G. (2012). Contextos emergentes da excelência. In *Actas.* Lisboa: B.A.D. Retrieved October 30, 2012, from http://www.bad.pt/publicacoes/index.php/congressosbad/article/view/299

Ochôa, P., & Pinto, L. G. (2007). Estratégias de gestão baseada em evidências: Investigação e prática em serviços de informação. In *Bibliotecas e arquivos: informação para a cidadania, o desenvolvimento e a inovação.* Lisboa: B.A.D.

OCLC WorldShare License Manager. (n.d.). Retrieved May 09, 2013, from https://www.oclc.org/license-manager.en.html

OCLC. (2012). *EZproxy.* Retrieved March 18, 2013, from http://www.oclc.org/ezproxy/

Odlyzko, A. M. (1995). On the road to electronic publishing. *European Bulletin, 2*(1), 49–60.

Odlyzko, A. M. (1999). Competition and cooperation: Libraries and publishers in the transition to competition electronic scholarly journals. *Journal of Electronic Publishing, 4*(4), 163–185. doi:10.3998/3336451.0004.411.

OECD. (2002). *Policies to promote sustainable consumption: An overview.* Paris: OECD..

Open Access Directory. (2013). Retrieved March 5, 2013, from http://oad.simmons.edu/oadwiki/Timeline

Open Access Infrastructure for Research in Europe. (2013). Retrieved March 10, 2013, from http://www.openaire.eu/index.php?lang=en

Open Access. (2013). *Infrastructure for research in Europe.* Retrieved March 10, 2013, from http://www.openaire.eu/index.php?lang=en

OpenDOAR. (2013). *Directory of open access repositories.* Retrieved March 10, 2013, from http://www.opendoar.org/

Ottman, J. A. (2003). *Green marketing: Challenges and opportunities for the new marketing age.* Lincolnwood, IL: NTC Business Books..

Pan, D., & Fong, Y. (2010). Return on investment for collaborative collection development. *Collaborative Librarianship, 2*(4), 183–192.

Pan, D., & Howard, Z. (2009). Reorganizing a technical services division using collaborative evidence based information practice at Auraria library. *Evidence Based Library And Information Practice, 4*(4), 88–94.

Payne, A., Storbacka, K., & Frow, P. (2008). Managing the co-creation of value. *Journal of the Academy of Marketing Science, 36*, 83–96. doi:10.1007/s11747-007-0070-0.

Perdue, J., & Van Fleet, J. (1999). Borrow or buy? Cost-effective delivery of monographs. *Journal of Interlibrary Loan, Document Delivery & Information Supply, 9*(4), 19–28. doi:10.1300/J110v09n04_04.

Peter Suber Website. (2013). Retrieved March 10, 2013, from http://legacy.earlham.edu/~peters/hometoc.htm

Petruska, K. (2012). *The GSU copyright case: Lessons learned part 1.* Retrieved January 30, 2013 from http://bit.ly/JwtpXg

Petruska, K. (2012). *The GSU copyright case: Lessons learned part 2.* Retrieved January 30, 2013 from http://bit.ly/KNGIE7

Pike, G. H. (2012, December 6). Window for terminating a copyright transfer agreement opens in 2013. *Information Today.*

Pinto, L. G., & Ochôa, P. (2012). Portuguese library assessment practices and transitions: A meta-evaluation model for the information and knowledge society. Paper presented in QQML. Limerick, Ireland..

Plum, T., Franklin, B. R., Kyrillidou, M., Roebuck, G., & Davis, M. (2010). Measuring the impact of networked electronic resources: Developing an assessment infrastructure for libraries, state, and other types of consortia. *Performance Measurement and Metrics, 11*(2), 184–198. doi:10.1108/14678041011064098.

Poll, R. (2007). Benchmarking with quality indicators: National projects. *Performance Measurement and Metrics, 8*(1), 41–53. doi:10.1108/14678040710748076.

Poll, R. (2012). Can we quantify the library's influence? Creating an ISO standard for impact assessment. *Performance Measurement and Metrics, 13*(2), 121–130. doi:10.1108/14678041211241332.

Poll, R., & Payne, P. (2006). Impact measures for libraries and information services. *Library Hi Tech, 24*(4), 547–562. doi:10.1108/07378830610715419.

Prabha, C. (2007). Shifting from print to electronic journals in ARL university libraries. *Serials Review, 33*(1), 4–13. doi:10.1016/j.serrev.2006.12.001.

Profile, I. G. N. O. U. (2012). *Preamble.* Retrieved March 18, 2013, from http://www.ignou.ac.in/ignou/aboutignou/profile/2

Prytherch, R. (Ed.). (2005). *Harrod's librarians' glossary and reference book* (10th ed.). London: Ashgate..

Public Library of Science (PLOS). (2013). Retrieved March 5, 2013, from http://www.plos.org/

PubMed Central. (2013). *The U.S. national institutes of health's national library of medicine (NIH/NLM).* Retrieved March 5, 2013, from http://www.ncbi.nlm.nih.gov/pmc/

Quandt, R. E. (2003). Scholarly material: Paper or digital? *Library Trends, 51*(3), 349–375.

Rankin, C. (2012). The potential of generic social outcomes in promoting the positive impact of the public library: Evidence from the national year of reading in Yorkshire. *Evidence Based Library & Information Practice, 7*(1), 7–21.

Reitz, J. M. (2004). *ODLIS: Online dictionary of library and information science.* Retrieved February 10, 2013 from http://lu.com/odlis/index.cfm

Reitz, J. M. (2005). *Dictionary of library and information science.* London: Libraries unlimited..

Renner, R. (2009). *E-books – Costs and benefits to academic and research libraries.* Retrieved October 18, 2010, from www.springer.com.cda/.../e-book+white+Paper.pdf

RePEc. (2013). *Research papers in economics.* Retrieved March 5, 2013, from http://repec.org/

Report of the CUNY Electronic Resource Management System Committee. (n.d.). Retrieved April 1, 2013, from https://www.google.co.in/url?sa=t&rct=j&q=&esrc=s&source=web&cd=1&cad=rja&sqi=2&ved=0CC8QFjAA&url=http%3A%2F%2F128.228.178.102%2Fexport_test5%2Fmain%2Fabout%2Fadministration%2Foffices%2FOLS%2FERMS012008.doc&ei=vOFWUf_bM4KrrAfhzoDoAw&usg=AFQjCNHLDK_vTVk6AOaufrUf449BjuazIg&sig2=zn8Km2M1r2HBvK1f1y4HlA&bvm=bv.44442042,d.bmk

ResearchMonitor: Priory Solutions. (n.d.). Retrieved May 09, 2013, from http://www.priorysolutions.com/ResearchMonitor

Reynolds, L. J., Pickett, C., van Duinkerken, W., Smith, J., Jeanne, H., & Tucker, S. (2010). User-driven acquisitions: Allowing patron requests to drive collection development in an academic library. *Collection Management, 35*(3-4), 244–254. doi:10.1080/01462679.2010.486992.

Ritzer, G., & Jungenson, N. (2010). Production, consumption, presumption: The nature of capitalism in the age of the digital 'prosumer'. *Journal of Consumer Culture, 10*(1), 13–36. doi:10.1177/1469540509354673.

ROAR. (2013). *Registry of open access repositories.* Retrieved March 10, 2013, from http://roar.eprints.org/

ROARMAP. (2013). *Registry of open access repositories mandatory archiving policies.* Retrieved March 10, 2013, from http://roarmap.eprints.org/

Robinson, O. F. (1995). *The criminal law of ancient Rome.* Academic Press..

Roncevic, M. (2004). Introduction. *Library Journal, 129*(5).

Ross, S., et al. (2011). *Digital library conformance checklist*. Retrieved November 10, 2012, from http://www.dlorg.eu/uploads/Booklets/booklet21x21_checklist_web.pdf

Royal Society. (2012). *Science as an open enterprise*. London: Royal Society. Retrieved September 20, 2012, from http://royalsociety.org/uploadedFiles/Royal_Society_Content/policy/projects/sape/2012-06-20-SAOE.pdf

Rupp-Serrano, K., Robbins, S., & Cain, D. (2002). Canceling print serials in favor of electronic: Criteria for decision making. *Library Collections, Acquisitions & Technical Services, 26*(4), 369–378. doi:10.1016/S1464-9055(02)00274-9.

Russell, C., Buttler, D. K., & American Library Association. (2004). *Complete copyright: An everyday guide for librarians*. Chicago: American Library Association.

Saarti, J., & Laitinen, M. (2012). Evaluating the effects of library e-resources and IL tuition on the research outcomes in Finnish top universities and the quality of the statistical data collected. Paper presented in QQML. Limerick, Ireland..

Saarti, J., & Juntunen, A. (2011). The benefits of a quality management system: The case of the merger of two universities and their libraries. *Library Management, 32*, 183–190. doi:10.1108/01435121111112899.

Saiaki, N. (2010). *The Bollywood amendment: Film, music and copyright (amendment) bill*. Retrieved February 19, 2013, from http://papers.ssrn.com/sol3/papers.cfm?abstract_id=1566350

Samper Tool: SMDB. (n.d.). Retrieved May 09, 2013, from http://www.sempertool.dk/?func=loadTemplate&template=smdbMore

Samuelson, P. (2004). *Tightening the copyright noose: Why you should be worried about the white paper on intellectual property rights and the national information infrastructure*, Retrieved February 26, 2013, from http://www.eff.org/IP/?f=tightening_copyright_noose.article.text

Sanville, T. (1999). Use levels and new models for consortial purchasing f electronic journals. *Library Consortium Management, 1*(3/4), 47–58. doi:10.1108/14662769910305740.

Schonfeld, R. C., King, D. W., Okerson, A., & Fenton, E. G. (2004). *The non-subscription side of periodicals: Changes in library operations and costs between print and electronic formats*. Washington, DC: Council on Library and Information Resources..

SciElo. (2013). Retrieved May 23, 2013 from http://www.scielo.org/php/index.php?lang=en

Scotsman. (2010). *Coming soon to your computer*. Retrieved 2010 from http://news.scotsman.com/news

Senge, P. (2006). *The fifth discipline: The art and practice of the learning organization*. London: Random House..

Sharifabadi, R. S. (2006). How digital libraries can support e-learning. *Iranian Journal of Information Science and Technology, 4*(1), 39–56.

Sharma, A. (2009). Indian perspective of fair dealing under copyright law: Lex Lata or Lex Feranda? *Journal of Intellectual Property Rights, 14*, 523–531.

Sharma, C. (2009). Use and impact of e-resources at Guru Gobind Singh Indraprastha University (India): A case study. *Electronic Journal of Academic and Special Librarianship, 10*(1), 3–8.

Shelburne, W. A. (2009). E-book usage in an academic library: Attitudes and behaviors. *Library Collections, Acquisitions & Technical Services, 33*, 59–72. doi:10.1016/j.lcats.2009.04.002.

Shen, L., Cassidy, E. D., Elmore, E., Griffin, G., Manolovitz, T., Martinez, M., & Turney, L. M. (2011). Head first into the patron-driven acquisition pool: A comparison of librarian selections versus patron purchases. *Journal of Electronic Resources Librarianship, 23*(3), 203–218. doi:10.1080/1941126X.2011.601224.

Shepperd, J., Grace, J., & Koch, E. (2008). Evaluating the electronic textbook: is it time to dispense with the paper text? *Teaching of Psychology, 35*, 2–5. doi:10.1080/00986280701818532.

Sherpa Plus. (2013). *Securing a hybrid environment for research preservation and access*. Retrieved March 5, 2013, from http://www.sherpa.ac.uk/projects/sherpaplus.html

Shim, J., & Siegel, J. (1989). *Encyclopedic dictionary of accounting and finance*. Englewood Cliffs, NJ: Prentice-Hall..

Silton, K., & Lemaistre, T. (2011). Innovative interfaces electronic resources management system: A survey on the state of implementation and usage. *Serials Review, 37*(2), 80–86. doi:10.1016/j.serrev.2011.01.002.

Smiers, J. (2012). *Digitisation and cultural democracy, an (as yet) unfulfilled promise.* Retrieved November 12, 2012 from http://www.coe.int/t/dg4/cultureheritage/cwe/CWE-TP-Smiers-en.pdf

South Ayrshire Council. (n.d.a). *eReads.* Retrieved from http://www.south-ayrshire.gov.uk/ereads

South Ayrshire Council. (n.d.b). Retrieved from http:www.south-ayrshire.gov.uk

South Ayrshire Libraries. (n.d.a). Retrieved from http://www.south-ayrshire.gov.uk/libraries

South Ayrshire Libraries. (n.d.b). *History blog.* Retrieved from http://sayrshirelib.wordpress.com

SPARC. (2012). *The scholarly publishing and academic resources coalition.* Retrieved March 5, 2013, from http://www.sparc.arl.org/

Sprague, N., & Hunter, B. (2009). Assessing e-books: Taking a closer look at e-book statistics. *Library Collections, Acquisitions & Technical Services, 32*, 150–157. doi:10.1016/j.lcats.2008.12.005.

Springer. (2009). *E-books – The end user perspective.* Retrieved October 21, 2012, from www.springer.com/…/e-books

Staes, P., & Thijs, N. (Eds.). (2010). *Growing towards excellence in the European public sector: A decade of European collaboration with CAF.* Maastricht, The Netherlands: EIPA..

Staff Reporter. (2011, July 4). Remote access to IGNOU e-resources inaugurated. *The Hindu.* Retrieved April 3, 2013, from http://www.thehindu.com/todays-paper/tp-national/article2157236.ece

Stamm, A. (2000). The end of an era builds new team spirit: Team playing at its best. In *Managing cataloguing and the organization of information: Philosophies, practices and challenges at the onset of the 21ˢᵗ century.* Binghamton, NY: Haworth. doi:10.1300/J104v30n02_13.

Stemper, J., & Barribeau, S. (2005). Perpetual access to electronic journals: A survey of one academic research library's licenses. *Library Resources & Technical Services, 50*(2), 91–109.

Stewart, C. (2011). Keeping track of it all: the challenge of measuring digital resource usage. *Journal of Academic Librarianship, 37*(2), 174–176. doi:10.1016/j.acalib.2011.01.002.

Steyaert, J. (2000). *Digitale vaardigheden: Geletterdheid in de informatiesamenleving.* The Hague, The Netherlands: Rathenau Institut..

Stone, G. (2012). *Techniques for electronic resource management.* Retrieved May 08, 2013, from http://eprints.hud.ac.uk/12972

Streatfield, D., & Markless, S. (2009). What is impact assessment and why is it important? *Performance Measurement and Metrics, 10*(2), 134–141. doi:10.1108/14678040911005473.

Suber, P. (2010). *Knowledge as a public good.* Retrieved April 10, 2013 from http://legacy.earlham.edu/~peters/fos/newsletter/11-02-09.htm

Suber, P. (2012). *Open access.* Cambridge, MA: MIT..

Swan, A. (2005). *Open access: Briefing paper.* Retrieved April 10, 2013 from http://eprints.soton.ac.uk/261005/

Swan, A. (2010). *Modeling scholarly communication options: costs and benefits for universities.* Retrieved April 10, 2013 from http://repository.jisc.ac.uk/442/2/Modelling_scholarly_communication_report_final1.pdf

Swan, A. (2011). *Open access map: Charting the growth and development of open access globally.* Retrieved April 10, 2013 from http://www.openaccessmap.org/about/

Swan, A. (2012). *Policy guidelines for the development and promotion of open access.* Retrieved March 20, 2013, from http://unesdoc.unesco.org/images/0021/002158/215863e.pdf

Swan, A. (2012). *Open access briefing paper from SCONUL.* Retrieved April 10, 2013 from http://blogs.warwick.ac.uk/libresearch/entry/open_access_briefing/

Swartz, A. (2008). *Guerilla open access manifesto.* Retrieved May 25, 2013 from http://archive.org/stream/GuerillaOpenAccessManifesto/Goamjuly2008_djvu.txt

Swords, D. A. (Ed.). (2011). *Patron-driven acquisitions: History and best practices.* Berlin: De Gruyter. doi:10.1515/9783110253030.

Tanner, S., & Deegan, M. (2012). *Inspiring research, inspiring scholarship.* London: JISC..

TDNet: E-Resource Management Solution Libraries. (n.d.). Retrieved May 09, 2013, from http://web.tdnet.com/

Teece, D. (2010). Business models, business strategy and innovation. *Long Range Planning, 43*, 172–194. doi:10.1016/j.lrp.2009.07.003.

Tenopir, C. (2012). Beyond usage: Measuring library outcomes and value. *Library Management, 33*(1/2), 5–13. doi:10.1108/01435121211203275.

Termens, M. (2008). Looking below the surface: The use of electronic journals by the members of a library consortium. *Library Collections, Acquisitions & Technical Services, 32*, 76–85. doi:10.1016/j.lcats.2008.05.004.

Toffler, A. (1980). *The third wave.* New York: William Morrow and Company..

Tomorrow's World Infographic from the BBC Lays the Odds on the Future. (2013). Retrieved May 27, 2013 from http://www.33rdsquare.com/2013/01/tomorrows-world-infographic-from-bbc.html

Tonta, Y. (2005). Internet and electronic information management. *Information Services & Use, 25*(1), 3–12.

Town, S. (2011). Value, impact and the transcendent library: Progress and pressures in performance measurement and evaluation. *The Library Quarterly, 81*(1), 11–125. doi:10.1086/657445.

Truccolo, I., et al. (2005). *EFQM (European foundation for quality management) and libraries: An organisational challenge for improving the provided services.* Retrieved March 1, 2012, from http://www.cro.sanita.fvg.it/reposcro/biblioteca/eahil_2005-truccolo-doc.pdf

Trueswell, R. (1969). Some behavioral patterns of library users: The 80/20 rule. *Wilson Library Bulletin, 43*(5), 458–461.

UKwired News. (2010). *South Ayrshire Council launches ebooks service.* Retrieved 2010 from http://www.ukwired-news.com/news.php/71630-South-Ayrshire-Council-launches-ebooks-service

UNESCO. (2011). *A basic guide to open educational resources.* Retrieved March 20, 2013 from http://unesdoc.unesco.org/images/0021/002158/215804e.pdf

UNESCO. (2011). *Guidelines for open education resources (OER) in higher education.* Retrieved March 20, 2013, from http://unesdoc.unesco.org/images/0021/002136/213605e.pdf

UNESCO. (2013). Retrieved March 15, 2013, from http://www.unesco.org/new/en/communication-and-information/access-to-knowledge/open-access-to-scientific-information/browse/1/

US Library of Congress. (1999). *Introducing to the programme for cooperative cataloguing BICO core record standard.* Washington, DC: US Library of Congress..

UWCLibrary. (2013a, January 29). *When including attachments in RefShare, please ensure that content sharing is not prohibited by copyright restrictions.* Retrieved from http://bit.ly/11JNZls

UWCLibrary. (2013b, May 24). *MT @waynestatelib copyright guidelines for posting online documents to blackboard & similar course management systems.* Retrieved from http://on.fb.me/19vEWX1

Van Dijk, J. A. G. M. (1999). *The network society, social aspects of new media.* London: Sage..

Van Dijk, J. A. G. M. (2008). One Europe, digitally divided. In *Routledge Handbook of Internet Politics* (pp. 288–304). London: Routledge..

Van Dijk, J. A. G. M. (2012). The evolution of the digital divide: The digital divide turns to inequality of skills and usage. In *Digital Enlightenment Yeabook 2012* (pp. 57–75). New York: IOS Press..

Vargo, S., & Lusch, F. (2008). Service-dominant logic: Continuing the evolution. *Journal of the Academy of Marketing Science, 36*(1), 1–10. doi:10.1007/s11747-007-0069-6.

VERA. (n.d.). *Jump start your library research: MIT libraries.* Retrieved May 09, 2013, from http://vera.mit.edu/

VERDE. (n.d.). *The library solution for efficient electronic resource management*. Retrieved May 09, 2013, from http://www.exlibrisgroup.com/category/VerdeOverview

Voima, P., Heinonen, K., & Strandvik, T. (2010*). Exploring customer value formation – A customer dominant logic perspective*. Helsinki: Hanken School of Economics. Retrieved September 2, 2012 from https://helda.helsinki.fi/bitstream/handle/10227/630/552-978-952-232-088-9.pdf?sequence=1

Vollmer, T. (2010). *There's an app. for that! Libraries and mobile technology: An introduction to public policy considerations*. Washington, DC: American Library Association..

Warnaby, G., Baron, S., & Konijer, P. (2009). *Toward an understanding of customer perspectives on organizational operant resources*. Paper presented at ANZMAC 2009. Retrieved January 31, 2012, from http://www.duplication.net.au/ANZMAC09/papers/ANZMAC2009-058.pdf

Watanabe, R. (1981). American music libraries and music librarianship: An overview in the eighties. *Notes, 38*(2), 239–256. doi:10.2307/939856.

Wei, D., & Sun, Y. (2010). The national digital library project. *D-Lib Magazine, 16*(5/6).

White, G. W., & Crawford, G. A. (1998). Cost-benefit analysis of electronic information: A case study. *College & Research Libraries, 59*(6), 502–509.

Williams, J. B. (2005). *Plagiarism, deterrence, detection and prevention*. Retrieved February 24, 2013, from http://www.economicsnetwork.ac.uk/handbook/printable/plagiarism.pdf

William, W. H. (2003). Criteria for replacing print journals with online journal resources: The importance of sustainable access. *Library Resources & Technical Services, 48*(4), 300–304.

Wilson, F., & Town, J. S. (2006). Benchmarking and library quality maturity. *Performance Measurement and Metrics, 7*(2), 75–82. doi:10.1108/14678040610679461.

Wind, Y., & Mahajan, V. (2002). Convergence marketing. *Journal of Interactive Marketing, 16*(2), 64–79. doi:10.1002/dir.10009.

Wolski, M., & Richardson, J. (2011). *A framework for university research data management*. Paper presented at CCA-Educause Australasia Conference. Sydney, Australia. Retrieved January 31, 2012, from http://www98.griffith.edu.au/dspace/bitstream/handle/10072/39672/69936_1.pdf?sequence=1

World Intellectual Property Organization. (n.d.). *What is intellectual property?* Retrieved February 20, 2013, from www.wipo.int/about-ip/en

World Digital Library. (2013). Retrieved March 20, 2013 from http://www.wdl.org/en/

Wright, H. S. (2000). Technology. In R. Griscom, & A. Maple (Eds.), *Music librarianship at the turn of the century* (pp. 29–35). Lanham, MD: Scarecrow Press..

Xie, C., Bagozzi, R. P., & Troye, S. V. (2008). Trying to presume: toward a theory of consumer as co-creators of value. *Journal of the Academy of Marketing Science, 36*, 109–122. doi:10.1007/s11747-007-0060-2.

Xihui, Z. (2010). Overview of digital library development in China. *D-Lib Magazine, 16*(5/6).

Zager, D. (2000). Collection development and management. *Notes, 56*, 567–573.

Zwass, V. (2010). Co-creation: Toward a taxonomy and an integrated research perspective. *International Journal of Electronic Commerce, 15*(1), 11–48. doi:10.2753/JEC1086-4415150101.

About the Contributors

Nihar K. Patra has more than 13 years of experience in the library profession, with substantial experience using latest IT infrastructure in the library including building up a digital library, Web-based information services, library portal development, and implementation of RFID. He has completed his MPhil in Library and Information Science and pursuing Ph.D. Mr. Patra is presently working with National Institute of Food Technology Entrepreneurship and Management (NIFTEM) Government of India as Deputy Librarian (In-charge of Knowledge Centre). He has 19 research publications in refereed national/international journals, conferences, and edited books. He is a Consultant for Digital Library, Library Portal Development and Library Automation. Mr. Patra has been honored with the Best DLISSUian award for the year 2010 bestowed by Alumni Association, Department of Library and Information Science, Sambalpur University, Odisha.

Bharat Kumar is presently Assistant Librarian at Management Development Institute, an AMBA accredited top ranked b-school of India. He holds Master of Philosophy (Library and Information Science) and Post Graduate Diploma in Computer Application. He has served in number of institutes/ universities in different capacities. He is reviewer of a learned journal of national repute and developed on-line course on Information Retrieval for SAARC Documentation Centre. He has attended number of training programs, conferences at national and international level. He has authored number of articles in journals, books and also presented papers in national and international conferences.

Ashis K. Pani, is Associate Dean of VIL Programmes and Chairperson the Center for e-Business. Presently working as Professor, Information Systems Area, XLRI, Jamshedpur, he has over 15 years of teaching, research, consulting, and administrative experience. He has received IBM best faculty award 2008. Also received best paper award in International Academy of E-Business in 2009. His research and teaching focus on how organizations can effectively use Information Technology (IT) in general and the Internet in particular. He is member of IEEE and life member Computer Society of India.

* * *

Praveen Babbar is Assistant Librarian in Library and Documentation Division at Indira Gandhi National Open University, India. Prior to this, he was associated with University of Delhi, India, and has more than ten years of experience. He holds PhD. from University of Rajasthan, M. Phil (Library and Information Science), Masters of Computer Application and Masters of Business Administration. He has taken many projects of Library Automation and Digitization like CALPI Library Setup for Swiss Agency. He has authored about 30 papers which have been published in national/international journals and presented in national/international conferences. He had been the speaker at various conferences including International M-Libraries Conference 2012 at The Open University, Milton Keynes, UK. He is a member of Special Libraries Association (SLA), USA, and is presently member of Career Guidance/Employment Committee of SLA Asian Chapter. He has also been the Webmaster in the Board of Asian Chapter, SLA. He has received many awards and scholarships including the 2013 Bonnie Hilditch International Librarian Award from SLA, Young Information Scientist Award 2012 by SIS, India, SLA Asian Librarian Award at the SLA 2010 Annual Conference in New Orleans, USA. He received the scholarship from Shastri Indo-Canadian Institute, 2009, and IFLA grant for the assignment in the year 2010. He is associated with several professional associations in various capacities in India and abroad including SLA, USA; Society for Library Professionals, India; Society for Information Science, India.

Sossamma K. T. George is presently Information Resources Librarian at Monash University Sunway Campus, Malaysia. She joined the Sunway Campus in November 2009 and heads the Information Resources Section, where her responsibilities include overseeing the library's acquisitions, metadata, and systems functions. With a background in economics, her interest in academic librarianship began when she took up a post with the University of Malaya in 1985 and pursued this interest professionally. Her career in the academic library field has spanned more than 28 years in both the public and private university sectors in Malaysia. Her interest in serving at academic libraries has allowed for a range of work experiences, which includes organizing and managing an economics and business library, serving as the quality manager and learning from the experience for 3 years and reference and information service provision. Her motivation to support and serve young enthusiastic minds pursue their dreams, knowledge and wisdom continues, particularly, by advancing professionalism, skills and service at Monash University Sunway Campus library and to help librarians keep pace with their changing profession.

Vesna Injac-Malbasa is Library Adviser at National Library of Serbia (NLS), professor of comparative literature; French government specializations in the field of cultural policy, cultural heritage, digital library and information sciences (1996, 1998, 1999, 2000, 2003, 2007), U.S. Government scholarship program for Information Management (2004), British scholarship program "The future education of Library and Information Science experts" (2003); president of Serbian Committee for UNESCO program Memory of the World; member of the National Commission for information and documentation at Institute for Standardization of Serbia; member of the international Contact group for the project the European Library since 2005; member of the coordination group of the World Digital Library since 2008; member of the Standing Committee of the Section on Statistics and Evaluation of IFLA since 2009; member of ASIST (American Society for Information Science and Technology) since 2002; coordinator in NLS of many European project of digitization; editor of many Serbian professional and research reviews and books; published dozen research monographs in the field of library and information science and over a hundred professional and research articles in domestic and foreign periodicals and proceedings of international conferences, often a speaker or lecturer by invitation.

Jean Inness is Head of South Ayrshire Libraries since 2007. She attended University of Edinburgh, where she gained an Honours degree in History. Jean spent a year working in the library of Queen Margaret University, Edinburgh, and then gained a Diploma in Librarianship from Strathclyde University, Glasgow. There has been a sustained development of bespoke online services, at the same time as meeting major efficiencies targets. The E book lending service, E book and E Audio book publications programme, South Ayrshire Libraries App, and South Ayrshire Libraries E Magazine lending service have all been introduced since 2008. In 2011, Jean was invited to speak on E-Services at: the CILIPS Spring Conference, the CILIPS Autumn Conference and the E Book Unbound Conference. Jean is the owner of the Linkedin Group "Scottish and Local History Enthusiasts." Her commitment to the study of Scottish history and genealogy is reflected in her on-going digital partnerships with Glasgow University (People of Medieval Scotland) and the National Library of Scotland (digitization of 19th and 20th century street directories).

Shiv S. Jha presently working as Assistant Librarian with National Institute of Food Technology, Entrepreneurship, and Management (NIFTEM), Government of India. He is masters in Library and Information Science from University of Delhi. His has more than 11 years of experience with substantial experience implementing latest IT in library including building up Digital Library, Web-based information services. He has privileged to be associated in libraries of some of the elite Institutes in India such as National Social Science Documentation Centre, Delhi; Nation Museum of Natural History, Delhi; National Institute of Fashion Technology, Delhi.

Smita Joshipura is serving as an Electronic Resources Management Coordinator at Arizona State University since 2007, where she is responsible for management of e-Resources from Acquisitions to Access. Prior to this, she was an Acquisitions Librarian at the same institution from 2000 onward. She has her Master's in Library and Information Science degree from India and University of Arizona, USA, and has rich experience for more than 20 years in Research, Academic, and Public Libraries in India and USA.

Christopher E. Mehrens is the Head of the Music Library at Arizona State University. He develops and manages the collections, services, and all aspects of operations of the Music Library; coordinates library services, collections, and programs with the ASU School of Music; and participates in the management and programs of the University Libraries. He also serves as the subject librarian for music on the Tempe campus. Dr. Mehrens holds a B.A. in music and B.M. in music history from the University of Washington (Seattle), an M.A. in music history and Ph.D. in musicology from the University of North Carolina at Chapel Hill, and an M.L.S. with specialization in music librarianship from Indiana University (Bloomington). His research interests focus American music and music criticism, interdisciplinary research methods, music collection development and management, leadership and library administration, and emerging trends in music librarianship.

Anne Moon is an Electronic Resources Librarian with almost 25 years of experience in academic libraries in South Africa. She has, since 2009, been employed at the University of the Western Cape, where she manages dozens of thousands of journals and books in electronic form, of which the majority are either subscription-based or once-off purchases. She previously held positions at Rhodes University (2004-2009) and the Cape Peninsula University of Technology (1989-2009). She holds an Honours degree in Librarianship and Information Science from the University of South Africa and a BA degree from Stellenbosch University with majors in German and Linguistics. Her areas of special interest include Electronic Resources Management (ERM) and Website administration (using commercial and open source content management systems). She was involved with the first South African implementation of the LibQUAL+™ survey instrument and also authored a published article, in terms hereof, in an Emerald journal in 2007.

Bhaskar Mukherjee is presently working as Associate Professor in the Department of Library and Information Science, Guru Ghasidas University, Bilaspur (CG), India. Previously, he has worked with Banaras Hindu University, Varanasi, India. Since last fifteen years, he is actively engaged in teaching and research. He has the exposure of various theoretical and technical aspects of library & information science teaching and as well as working experience with various types of libraries. Dr. Mukherjee's areas of specialization includes Open access, Webometrics, Knowledge organization and Information science and so far published 45 research articles in various journals of international and national repute like *JASIST, Library & Information Science Research, Scientometrics, Journal of Academic Librarianship, IFLA Journals* etc. He is the recipient of Raja Rammohun Roy Library Foundation award for contributing best article, Prabhakar Rao Gold Medal Award for positioning First Class First in B.Sc.(Geology) and UTD Gold Medal Award for positioning First Class First in Becholar of Library & Information Science and Master of Library and Information Science. He has written four books on *Information Communication and Society, Scholarly Communication in LIS, Number Building through DDC 22nd* and *Open Source Software for Libraries.*

Paula Ochôa graduated in History (University of Lisbon), a post-graduation diploma in Librarianship and Documental Sciences (University of Lisbon), a Master of Science in Information Management from the University of Sheffield (UK), and a PhD from the Universidad de Alcalá (Spain). Since 1991, she has been teaching in several Portuguese post-graduation and master courses in Information and Documentation Science. At present, she is an invited professor at the Universidade Nova de Lisboa (Nova University of Lisbon). She has authored several articles, papers, and book chapters on quality management, electronic resources management, organizational learning, and professional identity themes.

Leonor Gaspar Pinto graduated in History from NOVA University of Lisbon, a post-graduation diploma in Librarianship and Documental Sciences, a Master of Science in Information Management from the University of Sheffield, UK, and a PhD from the Universidad de Alcalá, Spain. She served Librarian at Lisbon Municipality from 1988 to 1999 and from 2003 to 2007; Head of Lisbon Municipal Libraries Network from 2008 to 2010; Head of the Documentation and Information Division of the Portuguese Commission for Citizenship and Gender Equality since 2013, and invited professor at the Nova University of Lisbon since 2010. She is the author of several articles, papers, and book chapters on performance evaluation, quality management, collections management, and knowledge management in information and knowledge services.

Hungwa Shidi holds a Master of Library Science (MLS) at University of Nigeria, Nsukka, graduated Library Science/Economics at Bayero University, Kano Nigerian Certificate in Education (NCE) at Kogi State College of Education, Ankpa, in 1994. He has worked as a Librarian with Champion Newspapers, Owerri, in 2003; Kings Comprehensive College, Mkar, Gboko; Benue State Library Board, Makurdi; and Benue State Ministry of Information and Orientation, Makurdi. He also teaches the Use of Library, Study Skills and Information, Communication Technology at the Benue State University, Makurdi and serves as the associate editor-in-chief of *Benue Journal of Library, Management, and Information Science*, Journal of Nigeria Library Association, Benue State Chapter. In the area of contribution to knowledge, he has published more than 10 articles in journals and book chapters in both national and international levels. Mr. Shidi is a certified Librarian of Nigeria and a member of Nigerian Library Association.

Solomon Uganneya is Deputy University Librarian and Associate Professor at the University of Agriculture, Makurdi, coordinating Use of Library and communication Skills programme and part-time Lecturer at the Department of Library and Information Science at the Benue State University, Makurdi, Benue State. He has Diploma in Librarianship from the University of Ibadan (UI), a Bachelors of Library and Information Science (BLIS) from Ahmadu Bello University (ABU), Zaria and a Master of Library and Information Science (MLS) as well as a PhD in Agricultural Librarianship from the University of Nigeria, Nsukka (UNN).

Priyanka Vishwakarma is a Research Scholar in the Department of Library and Information Science, Banaras Hindu University, Varanasi, India. She is UGC-NET qualified meritorious student of the Department, stood first class first among female in her postgraduate degree and awarded Gold Medal. Her present research interest is on Bibliometrics, Evaluation of Scientific and Technical Journals, Webometrics, etc., and so far contributed few papers in journals. She has worked with project on developing Website on Pt. Madan Mohan Malaviya of Banaras Hindu University, Varanasi, India.

Jennifer Wright currently works at Western Kentucky University, in Bowling Green, Kentucky, where she recently accepted a position as the Owensboro Campus Librarian. She received her MLS from Indiana University – Bloomington in 2010, and her MA in Sociology from WKU in 2011. Her research interests include collection development, information literacy, and the integration of technology into libraries and library practices.

Index

A

Aggregator 30, 41, 46, 53, 64, 90, 158, 174, 214
Author Rights 147

B

Blackboard Online Course Management System 115
Blog 112, 181-182, 190, 210, 212-213, 215, 219-220, 233, 235

C

Cloud Computing 12, 221, 228, 230, 235
Collection Development 5, 7, 12, 14-15, 17-19, 24-26, 28-30, 33, 36, 48, 60-61, 69-71, 77, 80, 83-85, 95, 102, 131-132, 196, 208, 231
Consortia 9-10, 17, 21, 26, 62, 83, 90, 95, 97, 99, 131, 133, 172, 188, 231
Consortium 9, 21, 26, 28, 30, 44, 91, 95, 111, 122, 145, 176, 179, 183, 223-224
Consumer Culture 31-32, 37, 47, 50, 52, 56-57, 61-62, 64-65, 68
Copyleft 155, 164
Copyright 5-6, 8-9, 13-14, 35, 56, 58, 91, 106, 108-117, 147-158, 160, 164-165, 167-168, 170-171, 180, 186-188, 216, 221, 227-228, 230
Cost Benefit Analysis 17, 23, 26-27, 29-30, 86, 92-95, 102-103
Cost-Effectiveness 86, 94, 96
Creative Commons 42-43, 110, 115-116, 147, 151, 156-158, 164-165, 170, 182

D

Derivative Work 116, 156, 228
Desiderata 69, 78, 85
Digital Agenda 31-32, 37-39, 41, 47, 65

Digital

Digital Collection 1, 7, 9, 144
Digital Era 147, 164, 224
Digital Rights Management (DRM) 81, 110, 114, 116, 163
Digital Surrogate 69, 85

E

E-Acquisitions Processes 195
E-Books 1, 4-5, 18, 28, 66, 69-71, 73-77, 80-82, 84, 87, 108, 110-112, 116, 119, 135, 141, 186-187, 195-198, 203, 205-210, 212-220, 227-230
E-Journals 1-2, 4-5, 7, 16, 23, 28, 58, 66, 86-87, 89-90, 95-102, 105, 108-109, 116, 119, 131, 135, 137, 140-141, 144, 171-172, 174, 182, 192, 196, 206, 227-229, 231
Electronic Reserves (E-Reserves) 106, 116
Electronic Resource Management (ERM) 5, 17-19, 22, 25-30, 32-33, 36-37, 44, 46-48, 53-57, 68, 99, 104, 118-123, 130-133, 135, 137-141, 144-146, 166, 210
Electronic Resource Management Systems (ERMS) 5, 18, 21, 28, 119-124, 133, 135, 138, 144-146
Electronic Resources Access 195
Electronic Resources (ER) 1-4, 6, 11-12, 14-37, 46-48, 50, 54, 56, 62-63, 65-67, 69, 76, 79, 84, 86-87, 90-91, 96, 99, 101, 104-105, 111, 116, 118-123, 131, 134-141, 144-146, 166, 191, 195-197, 203, 205, 208, 210, 221, 223-228, 230, 234-235
Electronic Resources Strategies 195
Embedded Librarianship 106, 109

F

Fair Use 6-9, 14, 91, 106, 108, 110-114, 116-117, 147, 151-154, 164
Fee Based Access 1, 5

CPSIA information can be obtained at www.ICGtesting.com
Printed in the USA
BVOW05*1545221013

334131BV00009B/107/P